THE GALLERY OF MEMORY

Literary and Iconographic Models in the Age of the Printing Press

Lina Bolzoni's impressive study of the memory culture of sixteenth-century Italy appears here for the first time in English translation. Since its original publication as *La stanza della memoria: Modelli letterari e iconografici nell'età della stampa*, published by Einaudi of Torino in 1995, Bolzoni's study has been praised by critics and ranked with the classic texts in the field – those by Paolo Rossi, Frances Yates, and Mary Carruthers.

The book takes as its starting point a striking paradox: that the antique tradition of the art of memory – created by an oral culture – reached its moment of greatest diffusion during an age that saw the birth of the printed book. Bolzoni's examination of this phenomenon, in which archaic and modern elements came together in a precarious equilibrium, reveals the profound ties that existed at the time between memory and creativity, and between words and images.

Drawing on the multiplicity of practices that relied on techniques of memory, Bolzoni presents diagrams, cipher alphabets, rebuses, and emblem-like pictures characteristic of the late-medieval and early-modern periods, indicating their use for literary games and preaching. In doing so, she skilfully reconstructs a particular mentality, a way of apprehending words and images that was of central importance for a long period of time but that has since been forgotten.

(Toronto Italian Studies)

LINA BOLZONI is Professor of Italian Literature, Scuola Normale Superiore, Pisa.

The Gallery of Memory

Literary and Iconographic Models in the Age of the Printing Press

LINA BOLZONI

Translated by Jeremy Parzen

UNIVERSITY OF TORONTO PRESS
Toronto Buffalo London

© University of Toronto Press 2001
Toronto Buffalo London
utorontopress.com
Printed in the U.S.A.

Reprinted in paperback 2019

ISBN 978-0-8020-4330-6 (cloth)   ISBN 978-1-4875-2495-1 (paper)

∞ Printed on acid-free paper.

Toronto Italian Studies

Library and Archives Canada Cataloguing in Publication

Title: The gallery of memory : literary and iconographic models in the age
   of the printing press / Lina Bolzoni ; translated by Jeremy Parzen.

Other titles: Stanza della memoria. English

Names: Bolzoni, Lina, author.

Series: Toronto Italian studies.

Description: Series statement: Toronto Italian studies | Translation of:
   La stanza della memoria.

Identifiers: Canadiana 20190187972 | ISBN 9781487524951 (softcover)

Subjects: LCSH: Printing – Italy – Venice – History – 16th century. | LCSH:
   Venice (Italy) – Intellectual life – 16th century. | LCSH: Italian literature –
   Italy – Venice – History and criticism. | LCSH: Italian literature – 16th century
   – History and criticism. | LCSH: Books – Italy – History – 1450-1600. | LCSH:
   Oral tradition – Italy – History – 16th century. | LCSH: Illustration of books –
   Italy – 16th century. | LCSH: Memory.

Classification: LCC Z155 .B6413 2019 | DDC 686.20945/09031–dc23

University of Toronto Press acknowledges the financial assistance to its
publishing program of the Canada Council for the Arts and the Ontario Arts
Council, an agency of the Government of Ontario.

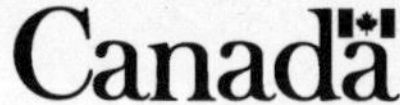

Contents

Contents vii

Illustrations

Colour Plates   following page 134

Preface

Two refined gentlemen were having a lively conversation as they travelled on horseback towards Vigevano on a hazy day in October 1543.

If we lived at the end of the nineteenth century and this book were a novel, it could begin like this.

Since this is a book about memory, and memory has always played with the different aspects of time, we would like to start off in just this way – with this scene as described in a letter from the sixteenth century.[1] The first gentleman is the marquis of Vasto, Alfonso d'Avalos (1502–1546), the Spanish governor of Milan, and the patron and prince celebrated by Ariosto in *Orlando furioso* and immortalized in a splendid portrait by Titian (plate II); the second is Girolamo Muzio (1496–1576), one of the numerous literati who gravitated towards d'Avalos. In order to relieve the tedium of their journey each of them tries to outdo the other in poetry. Muzio begins one of his sonnets with the following couplet: 'Aura che movi le veloci penne / verso colei che muove le mie pene' [Breeze, you who move your swift wings / towards her, who moves my sorrows].[2] The quality of the poetry certainly leaves something to be desired, and d'Avalos, in fact does object to it, but for a reason that would never occur to us. 'He said to me,' writes Muzio, '"You give wings to the wind, but painters will paint them thus ..." and he filled his cheeks with air.' The problem is thus the manner of depicting the winds: the image suggested by the words does not correspond to that which one generally sees in paintings, and which d'Avalos is trying to act out by filling his cheeks with air. In his defence Muzio recites lines from many different poems, in both Latin and Italian, where the wind has wings. The marquis is amazed by this performance: 'you must have done a lot of reading,' he tells Muzio. 'Certainly,' retorts Muzio, 'but not as much as Giulio Camillo.'

Thus, at this point another character enters the scene: Giulio Camillo, man of letters and philosopher, Friulian and cosmopolitan, a master rhetorician, a fat man who knows how to enchant his interlocutors despite his stuttering, a man who is known above all for his plans to construct a large theatre of memory, a device that will be able to furnish its users with the words and images necessary to give form to all knowledge. After being evoked in this scene, Camillo does not leave; following the conversation on horseback described above, Camillo and d'Avalos will meet and speak together for three mornings. The result is a sort of infatuation: 'Be it true or not that this man possesses the *secret* of memory, I want him,' announces the marquis, saying that he is ready to pay four hundred *scudi*. What a pity (or perhaps it is providential) that Camillo, overly dedicated to the pleasures of love, was to die the following year.[3]

This whole story must seem rather strange to today's reader: these characters operate within the confines of a cultural code far removed from our own, a code in which the words of poets are translated into visible images, compared with paintings, and enacted through the language of the body. The code is founded upon a science of images, which is formed through extensive reading, which travels across and unites different forms of expression, which relies upon memory. Indeed, it culminates in the art of memory.

This book attempts to meet the challenge of such cultural strangeness and distance. The goal is to reconstruct the space that memory created for itself in sixteenth-century culture and the figures upon which it relied. By doing so we can rediscover a mode of perceiving words and images, a mode of receiving (and creating) them, that long enjoyed central importance but that has been discarded and forgotten because of its differences from our own. At the same time, along our path we will find themes and opinions that in many ways are not so far from our own, since they are also part of our contemporary reflection and experience: the dialogic and intertextual nature of literature; the relationship between writing, literary tradition, and reception; the status of images, the strategies of and the reasons behind their charm and power; the play of relationships that they create between the human body and the psyche.

But let us clarify the boundaries of the question. This will allow us to see how the concept of memory assumes particular richness in the cinquecento: a period of emerging modernity, though knowledge and experience have not yet become specialized or fragmented. First of all, the importance of memory is bound into a cultural code based on a precise hierarchy of values. Memory is, in other words, an essential component of the classicizing canon, which clearly establishes itself in the sixteenth century, thus affecting Italian literature for centuries. It is during this century that literary models are set forth and fixed: in 1525 Pietro Bembo's *Prose della volgar lingua* [Discussions of the vernacular language] sanctions the rigorous division of written and spoken language, and in this work he proposes Petrarch's lyric poems as the ideal model of language and grammar; from the 1540s on, the debate over Aristotle's *Poetics* provides an opportunity to outline a system of literary genres. At the end of the century the work culminating in the Accademia della Crusca's dictionary of the Italian language marks the final outcome of a process of establishing fixed cultural norms. This process is closely interconnected with the vicissitudes of the literati (both as individuals and as a group), with a fertile period of literary production in Italian vernacular literature, and with the development and diffusion of printing.

Many scholarly works have shed light on the different phases of this process.[4] One feature, however, has remained obscure: the role of memory and the close connection between words and images that memory helps to create. The literary and iconographic canons are established and defined together. Repertories of mythography are published. In the *Hieroglyphica* of the mythical Egyptian priest Horapollo, with a commentary by Pierio Valeriano (1567), hieroglyphic images are transformed into icons of moral and metaphysical ideas. The *Iconologia* of Cesare Ripa (1593) teaches how 'to represent all that can occur to human thought with the proper symbols.' At the same time collections of emblems and devices demonstrate different possible ways of combining textual and pictorial fragments.[5]

In a world so obsessed with giving itself norms and establishing models, memory plays an essential role. If, in fact, imitation of the old is a stage in the production of something new, and if a writer's individuality cannot be expressed without appropriating 'other' texts, then writing means above all remembering.[6] The whole game depends on the relationship between imitation and variation. It is essential, therefore, for an author – and his ideal reader as well – to recall easily the text used as a model. But what to remember? First and foremost, language, metaphors, formal artifice, but also images – that great iconographic baggage that ancient literature and art have handed down, now made available for hermeneutic play. Thanks to allegorical interpretation, for example, a text can suggest numerous meanings; its images are diffracted, as if reflected in different mirrors. As Terence Cave writes (with an image happily chosen from Rabelais), the texts used as models become cornucopian texts: the play of interpretation and imitation/emulation transforms them into fountains of infinite wealth.

In light of this it is easier to understand why Camillo, the master of memory whom we have just met, was such a celebrity in his time. Ariosto and Tasso, for example, praise him because he has found a quick and easy way to teach the secrets of fine writing.[7] His method consists in providing logical schemes by which the figures that adorn classical texts can be dismantled, then reproduced and varied. Especially in his *Topica*, Camillo teaches how to apply to literature that technique (the use of topical places) that ancient rhetoricians used to find arguments supporting their own theses.[8] As we will see, we are dealing with an important and widespread tradition: it is a tradition that teaches methods and techniques for learning and remembering the secrets of rhetorical figures, thus bringing to light the logic hidden in literary 'artifice.'

The other reason for Camillo's fame is his theatre of memory.[9] Inside its complex structure the memory of human scientific knowledge (and of literature) is entrusted to a system of images – painted by great artists like Titian and Francesco Salviati – images that have unfortunately been lost. Camillo's theatre is the incarnation of the myths of the century: it unites repertories of words and images; it utilizes both the mechanism of the logical and rhetorical diagram and the magical fascination of the icon; all of this, in turn, is entrusted to memory and its capacity to give new forms to the things that it preserves. This book will show how such a complex edifice is taken apart throughout the course of the century, and, at the same time, how its different components continue to live together and to blend, as they influence each other and also interact with the new situation created, in part, by the printing press.

A rich tradition of scholarship – from Paolo Rossi to Frances Yates and Mary Carruthers – has rediscovered and brought to light the role played by the art of memory in Europe's cultural panorama over the centuries.[10] Its long history is a fascinating mixture of continuity, variation, and diversity. The orators' techniques of memory reinforcement were handed down by the classical world to the Middle Ages. These techniques, based on observation of the mind's natural functions, use three essential components: places (*loci*), order, and images (*imagines agentes*).

The idea is to establish an ordered route of places in the mind. To each is assigned through an interplay of associations an image related to the thing to be remembered. Whenever necessary, a practitioner of this art retraces the places of his memory and finds the images that will reactivate the interplay of associations. The recollections linked to those associations are thus brought forth. There is memory of things and concepts (*memoria rerum*) as well as memory of words (*memoria verborum*). The technique has been called the art of memory, artificial memory, or *local* memory (in reference to the *loci*).

The basic techniques have been around for a long time. The Christian world inherited them from the pagans and changed them according to its own needs, giving them an aura of morality and piety. In the sixteenth century the art of memory sees the moment of its greatest splendour as it becomes a part of the complex quest to revive the ideal of an encyclopedia of learning and to master a universal key for access to knowledge.

The goal of this book is to redirect the traditional subject matter of scholarly analysis: it deals with the practices related to memory, rather than with the treatises on the art of memory. It is an attempt to reconstruct an *average* set of convictions and techniques shared by the wider culture, and its focus is not on the great theoreticians of memory who revived and creatively renewed the tradition, like Giulio Camillo and Giordano Bruno. Nevertheless, on the one hand I take as my point of departure Camillo's theatre, and on the other I focus on the practices, experiences, and uses of memory that form the basis for Bruno's daring studies.

My analysis is based on two convictions. The first is that the treatises on the art of memory are only the tip of the iceberg and that their rules – often dry and repetitive – are just the backdrop of a cultural drama that developed on many levels. I have used the treatises only as an incentive to remap the territory in which the techniques of memory interact with different experiences: with literature, for example, with the translation of words into images and images into words, and with experiments with the imagination (plate V).

My second conviction has to do with the transformations accompanying the development of the printed word.[11] It is thanks to the circulation of books that we can speak of an *average* or *middle* culture and the creation of a widespread set of ideas and practices in which different medical and philosophical theories about memory, for example, live side by side, and in which, more importantly, they are put to use.

Printing – and, even earlier, writing itself, as Marshall McLuhan and

Walter Ong have taught us – is not purely a tool. It has a feedback effect upon the subject using it, and it contributes to changes in the perception of the self and in the perception of the world. This insight proves to be very suggestive when applied to problems of memory. It helps us to understand some of the essential moments of that continuous, yet varied, series of events that typifies the presence of the art of memory in European culture. In ancient Greece memory is a goddess, Mnemosyne, mother of the Muses. This myth is a faithful expression of the vital role that memory plays in a society where writing has not yet been introduced. With the introduction of writing memory comes down from Olympus and enters the world of the city and its human professions: it becomes an art, something that can be taught and practised.[12] Writing, moreover, removes words from the unrepeatable temporal flux of oral communication and transforms them into objects positioned in space, into things that can be seen and analysed. Writing influences even the way in which the mind is perceived: thought takes on a spatial dimension, and thus intellectual processes are described in terms of movement. We can see how this is also essential for memory. It appears as a space divided into *places*, in which are deposited perceptible images that may be preserved or vanish away. The moment that memory becomes an art, writing remodels it in its own image and likeness. The comparison between the techniques of memory and those of writing becomes itself a topos: the lines that a scribe marks on a tablet are like the *loci* that the master of memory affixes on the tablet of the mind. The letters that permit us to read words with the distance of time are akin to the *imagines agentes*, repositories of the chain of associations that regenerates memories.

The perception of words and mental faculties in terms of space and visualization is enormously expanded by the phenomenon of the printing press. This book analyses a paradoxical situation: a long phase of rich, but precarious, equilibrium. Techniques of memory reach their greatest development in a world in which their meaning and importance are gradually being stripped away from them by the development of technology, especially by the printing press. At the same time, we will see how techniques of memory interact, often productively, with the new possibilities created by the printed word. Among other things, the printing press helps to expand that sense of the mirroring relationship between the mind and writing to which I have alluded, between mental places and textual places, between inner experience and the external world. Through a sometimes dizzying and illusionistic play of relationships, poems can be transformed into galleries, texts into palaces, collections into encyclopedias and castles inside the mind, and vice versa.

But now let us see how our route through the territory of sixteenth-century memory unfolds in the different chapters of this book.

There is a long and persistent tradition that holds images and diagrams in low esteem. A rich heritage of tables and diagrams has consequently been removed both from our critical panorama and, physically, from the pages of books. Modern editions of sixteenth-century poetic and rhetorical texts generally reproduce only the words. The first two chapters of this book discuss this visual heritage, and show how the diagrams that these texts used are not merely curious accessories but an integral part of the text itself, inasmuch as they give expression to a precise cultural project and a way of perceiving and communicating knowledge.

In the mid-1500s method becomes one of the new aspects of the art of memory. Great faith is placed in the possibility of formulating a method that will rigorously regulate both knowledge and the ways of communicating and recalling it. The diagrams, the tables, and the large schemes in the form of *trees* visualize the logical path to be taken, and hence all of the material is presented to the eye reordered and reorganized in a clear, effective fashion that is easy to remember. The new directions of logic and dialectics interact productively with the new possibilities created by the book and by the ordered and reproducible space of the printed page.

The first two chapters of this book show how visual techniques play an important role in those decades of the century that saw the greatest expansion of printed vernacular texts and the formation and consolidation of a classicizing Italian canon. 'Making knowledge visible,' for example, is an essential component in the modern, yet utopian project of the Accademia Veneziana (chapter 1), which sees its maturation in the Venice of Aretino, Titian, and the printer Aldo Manuzio. Although it relies on the patrimony and political prestige of a great Venetian family, the Accademia Veneziana's cultural program is addressed to the world: in the name of good letters and beautiful books it dreams of ending the lacerating political and religious divisions of the cinquecento.

The use of visual schemata (diagrams, trees), however, extends far beyond the Accademia Veneziana and its projects. The second chapter follows these schemata through university courses, scholastic books, and the rhetorics and poetics of Aristotelians and Platonists, laymen and ecclesiastics. It is thanks to texts like these that models of fine vernacular writing and the literary canon, developed in debates over language and genre, become a shared cultural heritage. At the same time, the medium transforms the message, and the forms of communication remodel the contents. In the sixteenth century visual charts not only place before the eyes of all, in a rapid and effective way, the path to follow in order to write well, but tend to reduce the procedures of literary composition to a combinatorial mechanism. Diagrams subject the great works of literature to anatomical dissection according to one widely known metaphor, and according to another commonly held conviction they also create the conditions in which one can recompose the parts and give life to a new body (or text). The visual schemata thus tend to become actual machines for producing texts: situated midway between the library and the writing desk, they act as an *interface* between the reading of texts and the creation of new ones. Rhetorical machines, in fact, regulate and structure memory, and therefore they provide material ready to use for invention. They offer words and images already predisposed for reorganization in the *places* of the text.

The literary classicism of the early cinquecento can be perceived as an automatic, reproducible mechanism, almost a game. This is the idea of one of the the main protagonists of the second chapter, Orazio Toscanella, schoolmaster and collaborator of the major Venetian editors. Forgotten today, in his time he enjoyed a certain fame in Italy and Europe (it is highly probable, for example, that it is his book that Federico Borromeo was consulting and annotating on 1 January 1595). The third chapter starts with this provocative idea of a game – which has affinities to the modern school of thought, from Johan Huizinga to Gregory Bateson, that has emphasized the analogy between literature and play.[13] Going backward in time, to the incunabula of cinquecento classicism, we bring to light the ludic dimension that is present in Bembo's *Asolani* and deeply embedded in the basic mechanisms of the literary practice of the period. The imitation of literary models becomes a competition, a virtuoso's game of variation based on the words and images handed down from the past and chosen from a codified literary canon. The game needs, in fact, a closed and artificial space, and it requires (and mobilizes) the memory of all those who participate, both the writer and his audience: the game does not work if the writer cannot find an interlocutor capable of remembering, and hence recognizing, the text that is the object of imitation or emulation.

Within the literary code the ultimate objective of the writer's game appears to be that of giving form to the sayable: in the three books (and three dialogues) of the *Asolani*, for example, literature puts itself on stage, and makes visible its universal, yet paradoxical dimension, which consists in this case of saying everything about Love: everything in favour, everything against it, and other things besides. So we understand how an unsuspected link associates the great dialogues of the early cinquecento (*Gli Asolani*, but also Castiglione's *Il Cortegiano* [The book of the courtier], which originated in the choosing of a game) with the strange and fascinating game-books that would appear in the course of the century, like the *Triompho di fortuna* [Triumph of fortune] by Sigismondo Fanti or the *Sorti* [Chance] by Francesco Marcolini. Through play, in fact, these books guide the reader along a path – or better yet, along different paths – of words and images. Starting with a question, the reader/player finds all possible answers, as well as the opposites of those answers. Cultural memory is broken into fragments of stanzas, condensed into images that can be recombined throughout the course of the game. In this way each player can see/remember his own future, and everyone can remember/write his own text. Thus, literary classicism interacts both with the literature of paradox and with the age-old tradition of didactic/mnemonic games that, already in use in the universities in the age of humanism, would become the fad of eighteenth-century Europe.

The perspective of memory, moreover, makes it possible to link the classic texts of the early cinquecento with those collections of games produced at the end of the century that mobilize an entire heritage of cultural, literary, and, above all, iconographic memory, transforming it into an occasion for play. If imitation is, in certain respects, a form of play, and the dialogue is an enactment of the nature and rules of literature, we can understand how there are games that draw upon the memory of literary texts and, vice versa, may culminate in the production of a text. Innocenzo Ringhieri's *Cento giochi liberali e d'ingegno* [One hundred free games of wit] is an example of the reciprocal translatability of literature and games. His one hundred games further suggest to the educated and alert reader the hidden meanings, the cultural and religious disquiet, that play can simultaneously express and mask.

But it is not only this central category of literary classicism, that is, imitation, that reveals new perspectives when shown through the double lens of play and memory. The entire fabric of writing is involved. The central part of the third chapter analyses those areas of cinquecento experience in which metaphorical and combinatorial play have an effect on the written word, on its decomposition into visualizable parts, on the single letters of the alphabet. We meet rebus/sonnets, cryptic codes, machines for memory, and alchemical works that exalt the new magic of the printing press. We can thus see how memory techniques combine with something that has fascinated European thought in both the sixteenth and succeeding centuries, that is, the analysis of the nature of the sign, experimentation with mixed languages, the search – between play and metaphysics – for a language that unites the letter and the spirit, word and image.

In a certain sense the fourth chapter undertakes a journey in the opposite direction: it passes from memory techniques and the texts in which they are operative to the human subjects who produce them. We examine the nature of the images used by the art of memory, and we delineate the interior space in which they take *place*. These spaces are situated in an intermediate zone, between body and soul, between sensation and rationality, between desire and logic. The images of memory appear, in their turn, to be endowed with disquieting autonomy, with a vitality that can become difficult to control and limit. In many respects they are similar to the phantoms of Eros.

At this point, as we follow the image of the window onto the heart, we encounter different sciences (physiognomy, the art of gestures, the art of memory) that promise to construct an observatory into human interiority, to create an opening through which one can see the gallery of *phantasmata* that inhabits the internal space between the mind and the heart. A long tradition taught how to give shape to these phantoms: repertories and treatises provide the sixteenth century with a grid through which one can observe the inner self, using as signs the physiognomy, the gestures, and the movements of the body. The same grid allows for the reverse procedure. It teaches the painter and the writer how to give shape, through the language of the body, to the passions, the moral dispositions, the *motions* of the soul. Knowledge of this art is the common heritage of the orator, the actor, the cultured reader, and the artist. The art of memory easily recycles these diverse experiences and, in turn, incorporates and augments them: in order to animate the images of its internal theatre, it arranges them precisely in ways that make the language of the body the sign and expression of the language of the soul.

If the first three chapters, then, deal with the mechanical and, in some ways, abstract dimensions of the art of memory, here we focus on its strong ties to the imaginary and the body. In the process we see that even the diagrammed trees of rhetorical figures and the surface of the literary text reveal an emotive and corporeal depth. As we retrace the intertextual relationships – citation, reappropriation, and plagiarism – that link treatises on memory to treatises on rhetoric and the figurative arts, we rediscover a feature of rhetorical figures that a long season of formalism has hidden from our critical horizon: the ability of the rhetorical figure to depict on the face of the text (as Quintilian puts it) those same passions that gestures depict in our body. This is what allows the art of memory to translate the text into an internal theatre: precisely because memory techniques reproduce internally that theatre of passions which rhetorical figures create on the surface of the text.

The last two chapters show other ways in which the art of memory constructs the map that links interiority with external experience, the visible with the invisible. The fifth chapter deals with the ways by which the tradition of mnemonics teaches how to translate words into images and images into words. These treatises, besides bequeathing a true and proper iconological repertory to their readers, accustom them to projecting narration in a cycle of images, to seeing the literary text in the form of a building, and to perceiving poems as palaces or galleries. Such intellectual habits provide a precise setting for the well-known passage in which Galileo compares the *Orlando furioso* to a splendid picture gallery and the *Gerusalemme liberata* [Jerusalem delivered] to a Mannerist *cabinet*, in which the objects in the collection are piled up in a chaotic and ostentatious way.

In a century in which the panegyric triumphs in literature and the arts, the art of memory teaches how to see biography and portraiture from a single perspective: portraits, in fact, become a synthetic expression or memory-image of a biography. We thus understand how the biographical portraits of Paolo Giovio's *Vite* [Lives] correspond to and ideally superimpose themselves on the famous gallery of portraits in his villa at Como: the paintings in the gallery are the visualized and synthesized version of the biographies. For analogous reasons, in his *Discorso sopra le imagini sacre e profane* [Essay on religious and lay images] Gabriele Paleotti, bishop of Bologna, places Vasari's biographies of the artists and the accompanying portraits of the 1568 edition on the same level. He thus inaugurates a book model destined for enduring success.

Not only is the function played by the art of memory in securing the translatability of words and images evidenced by treatises on mnemonics: it also finds valuable confirmation from those occupied first-hand with projects for pictorial works (like Pirro Ligorio at the Villa d'Este in Tivoli) or from those analysing the work of an artist on the heels of its creation, like Francesco Sansovino when he became an interpreter of the Loggetta in Piazza San Marco, a structure which his father had only recently brought to completion.

While the image of the collection already appears in the fifth chapter, the sixth chapter reconstructs the methods, the metaphors, the ideas through which collecting and the art of memory cross paths and interact. If for many centuries memory has been understood and described as a place containing treasures, the extraordinary reality of the great collections of the sixteenth century greatly expand the potential of the metaphor and cause it to be taken literally: memory, aided and empowerd by art, *becomes* the actual chamber of the treasure, the place where a unique collection has been deposited. And thus Saint Teresa of Avila, wishing to find an image that will enable her to remember and articulate, albeit in an inadequate way, the condition of her soul in the moment of mystical union with God, will compare it to the small chamber where the duchess d'Alba kept her treasures. The techniques of memory thus move with ease among words, images, and objects, interested as they are in guaranteeing maximum translatability among diverse planes of reality and in activating – and controlling – a protean game of metamorphosis.

This book is in part an elaboration of earlier essays that are occasionally cited.

Having reached the end of a project that took many long years to complete, I would like to remember and thank at least some of those persons who have been close to me throughout. It was Paola Barocchi who years ago started me off by allowing me to construct an archive of texts on the art of memory, published and unpublished, in the Library of the Scuola Normale in Pisa. I would also like to recall the adventurous experience of the exhibition *La fabbrica del pensiero: dall'arte della memoria alle neuroscienze* and its catalogue (translated into English as *The Enchanted Loom: Chapters in the History of Neuroscience* [New York: Oxford University Press 1991]), and also of the conference *La cultura della memoria* [The culture of memory], and, most of all, the friends with whom I shared it, particularly Massimiliano Rossi.

As my research progressed, I had the pleasure of discussing the different themes and viewpoints that presented themselves to me with

Nicola Badaloni, Eugenio Garin, and Ezio Raimondi. I owe much to their generous help.

During my research and sojourns as a visiting professor in the United States (at Harvard and the University of California, Los Angeles), I have found patient listeners as well as affectionate and stimulating interlocutors. I would like to remember the long and wonderful conversations with Elizabeth Cropper, Charles Dempsey, and David Quint, between Baltimore and New Haven. A special thanks to Grazia Stussi: it is difficult to express how important her curiosity and her intelligent and warm solidarity have been for me. Sandra Pesante made her expertise in the field of old printed books available to me, and Amneris Rosselli and Ivan Garofalo have attempted to initiate me into the mysteries of Greek medicine.

A final thanks to Carlo and Luisa who helped me to give an ending to this book on the shores and above the waters of the Pacific Ocean.

I would like to thank Massimo Ciavolella and Ron Schoeffel, who made it possible for this book be translated into English, the intelligent and scrupulous copyeditor Joan Bulger, and my friend Lisa Chien for helping me with the revision of the final draft.

The English version of *La stanza della memoria* is dedicated to David Quint, who read and revised the text with infinite patience and imagination. I cannot sufficiently express my gratitude for his generosity and friendship.

The Gallery of Memory

CHAPTER ONE

Making Knowledge Visible: The Accademia Veneziana

1 Federico Badoer and the Founding of the Accademia Veneziana

In just a few short years at the heart of the cinquecento the splendid yet ephemeral story of the Accademia Veneziana was played out. Also known as the Accademia della Fama (after the name of its device, a winged woman whose feet rest on a globe, with a horn in one hand and a scroll in the other that reads, 'I fly to heaven that I may rest with God'; figure 1), the Academy was founded in 1557 and continued to grow until 1561, when it abruptly collapsed.[1] Old and new, realism and utopia, all existed side by side in this short-lived yet highly significant venture. Hermetic and cabbalist leanings were blended with the use of the most modern editorial technology, and the myth of Venice lived side by side with a cosmopolitan perspective.

The Academy was born out of the initiative of Federico Badoer (1519–1593), a member of a patrician family that had traditionally played an important role in the political life and history of Venice.[2] Badoer began his successful political career very young. From adolescence on, however, his love of letters had an importance for him well beyond that which was generally required of a promising young patrician. This passion led to friendships with other young nobles who shared his interests, like Daniele Barbaro and, most importantly, Domenico Venier. It also led, however, to a deep conflict between the obligations that arose from his family's role in public affairs and his love of learning and desire to devote himself exclusively to his studies. The establishment of the Academy became a way to resolve this conflict.

His love of letters won for the young Badoer the praise of famous literati like Claudio Tolomei and Pietro Bembo, as well as Pietro Aretino,

1 Device of the Accademia della Fama

who was probably an intermediary in his contacts with Titian.[3] At the centre of a dense network of relationships, Badoer also represented great hope for those seeking protection and patronage. Many of the restless characters who frequented the printers and publishers of Venice – Niccolò Franco and Anton Francesco Doni, for example – looked to him with great interest.[4]

In 1543 young Francesco Sansovino, son of the famous architect Iacopo Sansovino, dedicated to Badoer one of his *Lettere sopra le dieci giornate del Decameron* [Letters on the ten days of the decameron]. With a tone somewhere between the serious and the mischievous, Sansovino stated that women, according to the laws of nature, ought to be common property and that monogamy was the fruit of the same corruption that had altered the customs of earlier times. A woman's infidelity, therefore, was a proper return to ancient, natural customs.[5] In these pages Badoer was a part of the playful 'carnivalesque' reversal of common morality that was enunciated in the name of nature-inspired reform. In 1548, however, his name also appeared as the addressee of a work devoted to the subject of matrimony: *De re uxoria* by Francesco

Barbaro, translated into Italian from the Latin by Alberto Lollio for one of the prestigious Giolito editions.

Some years before, Badoer had appeared as one of the interlocutors – together with Luigi Alamanni and Domenico Venier – in the *Dialoghi della naturale philosophia humana* [Dialogues on natural human philosophy] by Antonio Brucioli. Brucioli, a Florentine republican living in exile in Venice, played a very important role in Italian evangelism with his biblical translations and commentaries until 1548 when he was tried and imprisoned by the Inquisition. In a discussion of the relationship between the interior and exterior man in the 1544 edition of the *Dialoghi*, Brucioli has Badoer maintain that human intellect can be raised to a point at which it becomes the equal of angelic intellect and the two can join together.[6] In contrast with traditional orthodox views, the distance between the angelic and the human worlds thus tends to disappear.

Badoer was also one of the addressees of the letters of Andrea Calmo. A curious work in Venetian dialect, this text was intended for the most part as a repertory for actors' improvisation.[7]

Thus, young Federico was clearly active on the cultural scene of Venice. The portrait of him handed down by these texts, however, is highly varied: a mixture of libertine game playing, patronage, a taste for literature, and philosophical and religious commitment on the margins of orthodoxy.

When he founded the Academy in 1557, Badoer was already the veteran of a prestigious diplomatic mission to the imperial court. According to Girolamo Tiraboschi, the great literary historian of the eighteenth century, the birth of the Academy was closely related to the group of poets and literati that gathered in the home of Domenico Venier, who had been immobilized by an illness in his youth.[8] Badoer's brotherly friendship with Venier is evidenced by the letters of Bembo, Aretino, and Lodovico Dolce, as well as by the fact that in 1542 Paolo Manuzio, a future member of the Academy, dedicated his collection of letters in Italian to both Badoer and Venier. In a number of instances the two young men were also associated with the older and more noted Girolamo Molin: in Aretino's celebrated letter of 1537, for example, where he describes, in a burlesque and celebratory hodgepodge, a 'voyage to Parnassus'; and also in Doni's *Marmi* [The marble steps]; and in Girolamo Parabosco's *Diporti* [Games].[9] Although Venier and Molin were not among the signatories of the Academy's *Capitoli* [Agreements], they certainly gave direct help and added the weight of their prestige to the undertaking.[10]

While this group was the original nucleus of the Academy, Badoer's participation undoubtedly made it into something fundamentally different. From its beginnings as a group of friends and literati, the Academy developed into an institution characterized by a complex internal structure, by strong extension into the outside world, and by the intention to play a prestigious role in the life of the Republic. In official documents, for example, Badoer wrote that the Academy was born through divine inspiration, which he closely connnected with its political activity and public service; he extolled the 'utility, delight, and great ornament' produced by the Academy.[11]

The external activity of the Academy developed on two levels: public lectures and editorial activity. Internal activities included debates on certain *questions*, readings of ancient and modern texts, and discussions on what works ought to be printed. Great care was given to the public image of the Academy. The letters of Bernardo Tasso, who in 1559 accepted the position of chancellor of the Academy on the basis of rather favourable financial considerations, provide an example of the careful orchestration of public readings and the particular attention given to the quality and quantity of the audience.[12] Consensus was a vital condition for such an ambitious project, which had been 'upset' by the 'difficulties' and 'malice' and 'envy of men' since its beginnings, as Tasso reported.[13] In the early years, however, the Academy was in a phase of full expansion. Badoer's *Instrumento* (an act registered with a rotary), although limited solely to the 'regents' and 'secretaries' of the various parts of the Academy, listed one hundred members at the end of 1560. In 1558 the library had been inaugurated and would later be opened to the public, wrote Carlo Sigonio, who held the office of regent of the Humanists.[14] With its public lectures on 'matters of states, provinces, and kingdoms,' the Academy directed itself to a specific group of consumer: young Venetian patricians.[15] To them, the future leaders and administrators of the Republic, it intended to introduce the most modern techniques in the fields of logic, linguistics, and rhetoric.[16] The Academy offered the Republic the fruits of a sophisticated culture, independent, even with regard to the places and modalities of the transmission of knowledge, from the world of the university.[17]

Editorial production, the other component of the Academy's public life, was entrusted to a printer with a prestigious name: the director of the printing press was none other than Paolo Manuzio [Paulus Manutius]. The excellent quality of the books published by the Academy, that is, the beauty of the type and the paper, played an important role. Molin reminded Tasso of its excellence in this area when it was trying to convince him to give his *Amadigi* to the Academy for publication, and the Council of Ten cited it in its deliberations in May 1560, when it decided to grant the Academy the rights to publish all official acts of the Republic.[18] The high standards of printing marked an element of continuity with the Aldine tradition. Even the structure of the Academy, that is, the union of literati and printers, was modelled after the Academy of Aldo Manuzio [Aldus]. There was a strong connection, as we will see, even in the editorial program.[19] One element of divergence and a substantial peculiarity with respect to the Venetian tradition, however, was the direct involvement of a patrician in the editorial enterprise.

2 The Editorial Program: The New Vernacular Literature and 'Ancient Knowledge'

The Academy's *Somma*, or compendium, published in 1558 and followed the next year by a Latin version, was a faithful portrait of a most ambitious editorial project. It was in its way a manifesto, a calling card, that the Academy put into circulation throughout Europe and Italy. The encyclopedic dimension of the *Somma* made it into a sort of universal catalogue, even though its contents wre in sharp contrast with the works that had actually been printed: these were meagre in number, and the criteria according to which they had been chosen were rather unclear. This gives rise to the suspicion that the publicity for the *Somma* and the calculated dosage of dedications – aimed at eliciting the approval and protection of clergymen, merchant noblemen, and political exponents from different fields – were more important than anything else in the early phase of the Academy's life. It is for this reason that the *Somma* offers us such useful data for the reconstruction of the cultural model to which the Academy aspired.

The correspondence between the structure of the *Somma* and that of the Academy, for example, is an interesting first indication of this model. The division into disciplines in which the different works of the *Somma* are catalogued was exactly the same as the division of the *Consiglio delle scienze* [Council of the sciences], which determined the subdivisions among the members of the Academy. The same encyclopedic model thus inspired the internal organization of the Academy as well as its editorial program.

The *Somma* bears witness to a continuity with the Venetian Renaissance and humanist philological tradition (as exemplified by the work

of Aldo Manuzio), which was characterized by a strong relationship
between the printing industry and the new wave of interest in vernacular language and literature. The members of the Academy intend, writes
Molin to Tasso, to publish ancient books in every discipline, and

> not only to purge those books of their infinite errors and inaccuracies,
> which they in truth carry with them to the great detriment of scholars, but
> to bring them out into the light, together with many useful annotations,
> disquisitions, glosses, and translations in different languages ... Besides
> this, they intend to produce new works, and works never printed, of their
> own as well as others.[20]

The number and quality of the translations into the vernacular projected by the Academy are truly remarkable. There are works on mathematics, some of the most obscure Platonic texts, and also a
contemporary text, *De harmonia mundi* [On the harmony of the world]
by Francesco Giorgio Veneto, a work that already smacked of heresy.[21]
The Academy thus became a protagonist in a process that found its
fulfilment in Venice between 1550 and 1560: the vernacular was acquir-
ing a strong self-awareness, a sense of its own dignity and autonomy,
in the field of poetry (both in theoretical reflection as well as in experimentation in the highest of genres) and generally in the field of printing. The great number of classical texts translated into the vernacular
responded, as Amedeo Quondam wrote, 'to both the supply and the
demand of mainstream literature.' It was both the result and also the
cause of an extension of literacy that gave access to reading to a much
wider audience.[22]

The case of *De harmonia mundi* is indicative of the Academy's strong
interest in the hermetic and Neoplatonic tradition, as well as the pre-
Socratic philosophers and Pythagorean thought. The Academy thus
embodies a continuation of Marsilio Ficino's work in rescuing, translating, and elaborating the Platonic and hermetic traditions.[23] This is
evident even in its concept of poetry: poetry is seen as a repository of
hidden knowledge and understanding that simultaneously reveals and
hides itself, thus reserving access to its treasures for a select few. The
Somma promises, in fact, a discourse 'on poetic theology, divided into
four books, in which one can clearly see how the greatest mysteries of
philosophy are hidden under the skin of the ancients' fables as well as
some of the modern poets.' Also promised are works on Homer, Virgil,
and Ovid that will both provide the key to the secrets of knowledge

hidden in their texts and allow one to recognize the structure of each work and its rhetorical figures.[24]

The concept of poetry as a repository of hidden knowledge gives a particular connotation to the Bembist classicism still vigorous in the environment of the Academy. The stylistic models codified in Bembo's *Prose della volgar lingua* [Discussions of the vernacular language], characterized by the predominance of Petrarch's lyric poerty, are clearly present, although not exclusive. One projected work is an edition of Petrarch that is to be accompanied by autograph fragments of Petrarch's *Rerum vulgarium fragmenta* taken from a codex that had belonged to Bembo.[25] Also promised is an edition of 'Dante, clarified by a new and most learned commentary that will reveal his deepest meanings perhaps better than any other before it.'[26] A full recognition of the value of Ariosto's poetry will inform a treatise, still to be published, on the wisdom of the *Orlando furioso*, a work 'on the beauties of Ariosto,' that is, 'the moral and natural allegories of the poet, comparing him with Homer and Virgil in the offices of poetry.'[27]

This approach to poetry is typified by an unpublished text that Giacomo Tiepolo dedicated to Badoer and his Academy, *Il primo discorso sopra il Dante poeta* [The first essay on Dante the poet]. In this case the initial verses of the *Divina Commedia* become the pretext for the construction of a sort of patchwork of Neoplatonic, hermetic, and cabbalist themes. Dante's *selva oscura* [dark wood], for example, is interpreted as chaos (or first matter). The trees of the Earthly Paradise, however, are 'the fruit-bearing trees of illustrious and everlasting ideas.' Their true meaning is revealed to man only at the culmination of a process of moral elevation by which he realizes that he has 'within himself the Earthly Paradise unknown to many because they dwell in vain on the rind of the holy writings.'[28] The poetic text thus offers a way to penetrate into a world of eternal truths that man can find in the depths of his own interior self. This commentary on Dante's poetry gives Tiepolo the opportunity to expose ideas that had thrived for some time in the works of Giorgio Veneto and Camillo. They are ideas that must have been both familiar and dear to Badoer and his friends.[29]

The conceptions that inspired these editorial programs perfectly matched the poetic practices and theoretical reflections of the leading poets of Badoer's brotherhood. It is highly probable, for example, that it was expressly for the Academy that Celio Magno wrote his *Prefatione sopra il Petrarca* [Introduction to Petrarch], a text which proclaims the primary religious character of poetry. The result is the reversal of the classical hierarchy of genres: the first position goes to the lyric, thus permitting a marriage of the ancient poetry of the psalms with the modern experience of vernacular poetry.[30]

Another text on poetics, *Ragionamento della poesia* [Discourse on poetry] by Bernardo Tasso, was read aloud in the Academy. In accordance with the humanist model, this work exalts poetry inasmuch as it 'embraces and encloses in its bosom all the arts and sciences.' The rediscovery of Aristotle's *Poetics* and the work of his translators and commentators are seen in a quasi-providential light: 'now, in the fortunate and happy circumstance of this century,' Tasso writes, learning the art of poetry

> is not so difficult as in past centuries when men strained, often in vain, merely to read and observe the great poets through prolonged study and vigils. Now the *Poetics* of the famous philosopher, certain and reliable guide, leads us along the difficult roads of poetry and teaches us with such order and detail this art that has been buried for so long in the murky darkness of the world's ignorance.[31]

In keeping with the climate of the Academy, Tasso's *Ragionamento* appears to have been born out of the effort to reassemble the literary experience of different epochs within a unified framework and to hide (almost as if to exorcise) the conflicts that had already appeared in contemporary poetics behind a screen of syncretic unity.

3 The Structure of the Visual Encyclopedia

Both the *Somma* and the *Instrumento* of 1560 contain elements that help to explain the nature of the encyclopedism that inspired the outline of the *Somma* and the structure of the Academy. In the *Instrumento* Badoer dictated some instructions before leaving for an official mission (he left the Academy in the hands of three nephews and Abbot Morlupino):

> In order that it [the Academy] may be understood and consequently better supported by them and by others, I wish to represent my concept and the form I have given it. I founded this Academy in the likeness of the human body, which, having been made in the likeness of God, I believe could not be of greater perfection.

In the place of the head, therefore, I made the Oratory, where all of the noble and illustrious doctors of the Academy may observe the sacraments and the divine office. For the chest, the Council of all the Sciences, Arts, Faculties, and all the provinces and states of the world.
For the right arm, the Economic Council.
For the left, the Political Council.
For the right thigh, the Treasury.
For the left, the Chancellery.
For the right leg, the Gallery.
For the left, the Secretariat.
For the right foot, the Printing Press.
For the left, the Library.[32]

Thus, in the *Instrumento* of 1560 encyclopedism is presented through the commonplace figure of the human body as microcosm. Badoer uses it here as a global metaphor, capable of providing him with all the necessary subdivisions and relationships: the *loci* of the human body also function as the *loci* of the Academy. In other words, they give spatial and logical positions to the internal divisions of the academic system (or, in this case, organism). We can visualize Badoer's *concept* and *form* through this Arcimboldesque imagery, similar to that which would inspire books like the Arcimboldo of the professions (Paris: rue Saint-Jacques, à la 'Pomme d'Or') by Nicolas Larmessin, published at the end of the seventeenth century.

The ideas and images used by Badoer were common, not only in the environs of the Academy, but also in some of the movements that were taking hold throughout Europe. For example, in his *Discorso intorno alle cinque parti de l'oratore* [Essay on the five parts of oration] (published in 1560, together with his *Lettere volgari*), Paolo Manuzio stresses the importance of *dispositio,* or the ordering of material in oration. He notes that the love of classification is the fruit of the imprint left by God on man and the order of the universe.[33]

The concept of the musical, mathematical model of divine order impressed on the microcosm and macrocosm has great repercussions in the human arts. It becomes, for example, an easily reproducible source of delight, not only in the universe of words, but also, as Vitruvius had already taught, in architecture. In 1535 similar criteria had been invoked by Giorgio Veneto (a figure greatly admired by the Venetian Academicians) to guide the restoration of the Church of San Francesco della Vigna.[34]

Analogous notions are present in the works of Francesco Patrizi, to whom the library of the Academy had been entrusted. In 1560 he published an essay on the lyric poetry of Luca Contile (the Academy's regent of the Council of Sciences) in which he specifies two conditions necessary for the construction of a new rhetoric: the first is that it has to be based on the correspondence between the mode in which human discourse is generated and developed and the mode in which divine ideas develop and give life to things; the second condition is the use of a renewed and broadened range of topics, along the lines of that which has been achieved by Themistius, Rudolf Agricola, and Camillo (three authors who greatly influenced the editorial programs of the Academy).[35]

The year 1560 also saw Badoer's name appear prominently in a small encyclopedic work published in Padua: the *Fabrica intellectualis* [Intellectual edifice] by Marcantonio Luigini, member of a noble family of Udine, who, besides showing strong interest in the works of Erasmus, had attested relations with Camillo.[36] With youthful audacity the author of twenty-seven years recreates the world in this undertaking. The six divisions of the short work refer, in fact, to the six days of creation, and the style in which each part begins is obviously modelled after the Book of Genesis. The biblical model is then blended with chivalry: each of the parts is presented as a 'duel' in which the author claims to have participated at the court of Maximilian II. The 'godfather,' or sponsor, of the 'sermonic' duel, that is, the first one, dedicated to the sciences of language, is Badoer, to whom, Luigini claims he has dedicated a large collection of rhetorical and linguistic writings. Another member of the Academy is the godfather of the fourth duel, which is devoted to alchemy, physiognomy, chiromancy, and the art of memory. This part of the work is dedicated, in fact, to Agostino Valier, lecturer in philosophy at the School of Rialto and future cardinal. Thus, the founder of the Academy and one of its illustrious representatives both appeared in 1560 in the work of an author who was interested in encyclopedism and the art of memory and who would later produce prophetic commentaries on the Books of Esdras as well as on Revelation.

The passage from the *Instrumento* cited above illustrates that Badoer's encyclopedism, rife with metaphysical notions, is clearly related to the new research in logic, rhetoric, and the art of memory that was developing in the Veneto. All of this reflected what was happening throughout Europe. During the sixteenth and seventeenth centuries European encyclopedism fed upon a unique blend of combinatorial theory and

Lullian metaphysics, Neoplatonic and hermetic influences, and the new dialectics and rhetoric.[37]

The Academy's *Somma* of works intended for publication helps us to understand what all of this actually means. Each work is carefully classified in an encyclopedic framework that orders the various disciplines. Within each discipline the theme of completeness and thoroughness returns incessantly, promoted evidently by the need to advertise (for example, there is promised a treatise on 'the duties commonly held by secretaries in *all* the courts of Christianity,' and one on '*all* the useful techniques necessary for proofs in *any* subject').[38] The theme of exhaustiveness is commonly associated with innovation and, above all, with classification. In the case of the latter, this may simply mean putting a repertory into order, but in most cases the connotation is much more complicated. The term *idea* denotes the exemplary character of the classification, its capacity to guarantee the comprehensive classification of the whole and its parts. The didactic dimension of this perspective becomes clear in the description of a promised edition of Aristotle's '*Economics, digested into an idea in order that with greater facility one may come to understand all the teachings on how to govern the family distributed in this brief, yet highly useful book.*'[39] It is indeed this all-encompassing classification and its capacity to reproduce the *idea* that guarantee mastery of the whole (that is, that which has been dispersed), as well as facility and rapidity of learning. Tasso's praise of Aristotle's *Poetics*, cited above, is certainly not very different when he points out that the reason for the book's singular usefulness is that it 'taught the art of making poetry with some such classification and detail.'[40]

Further information on the type of encyclopedism pursued by the Academy comes to us from two books, both of which are entitled *Etica* [Ethics]. The first has the rubric: 'the universal tree of all the moral virtues of Aristotle's *Ethics*, in which one can see, in beautiful classification, not only the means, excesses, and shortcomings of these virtues, but all of their detailed divisions.' The second promises 'the moral virtues of Aristotle's *Ethics* meticulously digested into trees, separated from each other, with all of their parts minutely divided into their branches; they will demonstrate the beautiful form of this body, the high virtue of the philosopher, and will make visible the knowledge of this science.'[41] With its repertories and its universal and particularized *trees*, this visualized encyclopedism is capable of achieving an easy yet complete form of teaching, making knowledge of the different arts and sciences visible. Undoubtedly this type of book is intended to appeal to students: the attention given to the scholastic market is made clear in a letter 'to the scholars of fine arts' accompanying the list of works sent by the Academy to the book fair in Frankfurt in 1559.[42]

The blend of didactic objectives and new ways of ordering and visualizing knowledge linked the Academy's projects to the logical-pedagogic reform that found its true voice in the late-fifteenth century and the first half of the sixteenth century in the works of Rudolf Agricola and Peter Ramus. The Academy's *Somma* thus provides early evidence of the diffusion of Ramism in Italy.[43] There is no question that great attention was given to the work of Agricola. Together with other Academy projects, in fact, a translation of Agricola's *De inventione dialectica* [On dialectical invention] was subsequently completed by Orazio Toscanella, a schoolmaster and major publisher of didactic texts.[44] Thanks to Toscanella's works and the iconographic apparatuses that accompany them, we can form an idea of the trees and the classification system mentioned in the Academy's programs. The method is one of visualization: through the use of diagrams, words are organized on the page in such a way that they reproduce the processes of the mind in the subdivisions of a given problem, from the general to the particular (see figure 2). Following the path outlined in the text (and faithfully reproduced by the positioning of the *loci* on the page), one learns and one remembers the logical path followed by the author, and thus the classification of the material is impressed on the mind. Had Walter Ong known of the Academy's programs, he could have added a valuable chapter to his book on the relationship between Ramism and the development of the printed word.[45] The Accademia Veneziana offers highly suggestive confirmation of Ong's hypothesis: it was a modern editorial institution that devoted a great deal of its program to the effective visual representation of content through the utilization of new directions in dialectics.

4 The Places of Knowledge: The Library and the Palazzo

There are other elements that offer evidence of the profound relationship between the book and the Academy's cultural model. Earlier we mentioned the encyclopedic nature of the *Somma*, or compendium, of books that the Academy intended to publish. The *Somma*, therefore, is also a catalogue of an ideal library, a catalogue of an encyclopedia. This

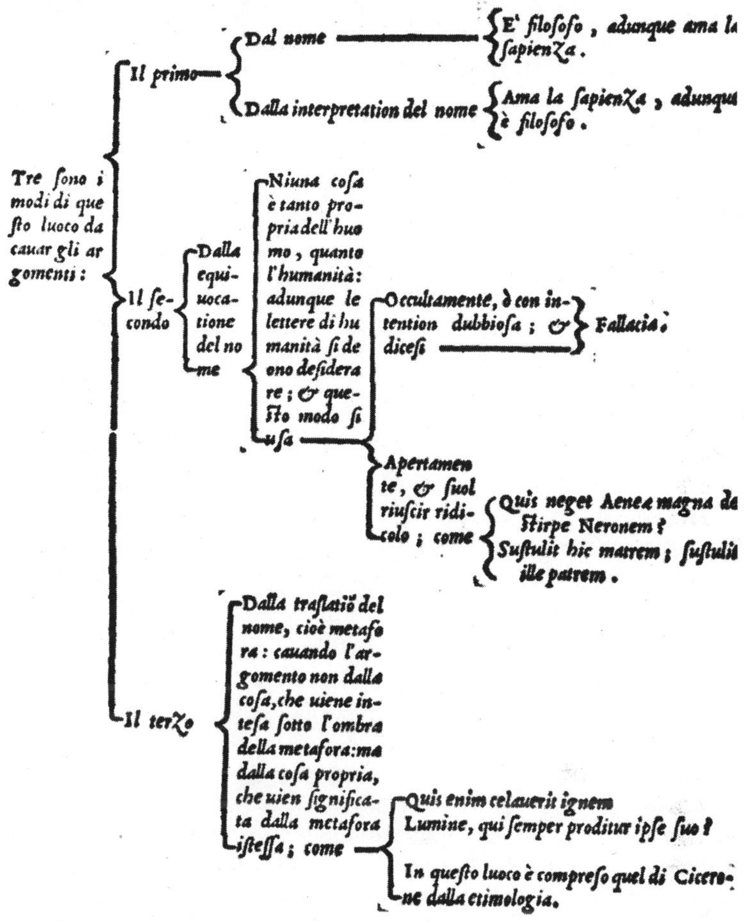

2 An example of a *tree* from Rudolf Agricola, *Della inventione dialettica* (Venice: Giovanni Bariletto 1567), p. 75

perspective sheds an interesting light on the offer made by the Academy to the procurators of San Marco on 12 July 1560, regarding the public library. The Academicians, it says, are willing to lend their help in both the conservation of books and new acquisitions:

nor will we fail to apply our efforts to the organization of those books, as it becomes necessary, so that those things contained solely in the intellect can be visually understood: and for this reason all of the sciences and arts will be placed together in one section, according to their true classifica-

tion, using labels, and languages will be in the other section, and there will
be distinctions according to which one may discover both the things
worthy of praise and the things that, for some defect, are in need of
betterment.[46]

We find here the same key terms that are used in the *Somma* for
editorial projects that seek to make knowledge visible. It is a matter of
creating spatial organization in the library. The positions or *loci* of this
dispositio will correspond to a logical and real classification, (that is,
'according to their true classification'). Moving through the shelves, the
library user will execute an operation analogous to that of the reader of
one of the books planned by the Academy, whose eyes will follow the
paths outlined by the diagrams and trees of the sciences and the arts.
But the operations – that is, the physical pathways of the library and the
path of the eye running across the printed diagram – are not actually
mirror-images of each other, and hence a gap is created. Book production is not yet developed enough to rise to the occasion. There are still
pigeon-holes to be filled in the topics outlined by the encyclopedic tree:
'there will be distinctions,' the *Somma* notes, 'according to which one
may discover both the things worthy of praise and the things that, for
some defect, are in need of betterment.'

The Academy thus began to play a significant role in the events that
would lead to the birth of modern bibliography, which at the end of the
1540s had already reached an important stage with Konrad Gesner's
landmark *Bibliotheca universalis* [Universal Library].[47] The Academicians intended the library to mirror and complement the project set
forth by the *Somma*: it would mark the material realization of encyclopedic classification that could be seen and directly perceived by the
intellect. Palazzo Badoer itself, seat of the Academy, was used in the
meantime to fulfil this task. The *classes* into which the Academy was
divided were called *chambers* because they were located in different
rooms. The places of the palazzo physically corresponded to the different branches of knowledge and the different activities of the Academy.

The *Instrumento* expressly called for the interdependence of the cultural program and the economic and financial activities of the Academy (this would ultimately contribute to the Academy's downfall). Not
only did the Academy include a printing house, and hence an editorial
enterprise, but a part of Badoer's estate was also assigned to each of the
scientific *councils*. The make-up of the council of the Treasurer – especially the terminology used to define it – shows us how the same

encyclopedic cultural model used in the editorial projects structured the economic department of the Academy:

> there are in the council of the Treasurer, in addition to the head post itself, twelve posts below that of the councillor, who are the heads listed below; namely:

the useful	the harmful
the necessary	the superfluous
the honourable	the dishonourable
the possible	the impossible
the easy, and	the difficult, and
the pleasant	the unpleasant[48]

Thorough classification within a single division of the Academy thus relies on antithetical *topics*.[49] The polysemy of recurrent terminology like *places* and *heads* in the *Instrumento* derives from the will to classify and organize, and from its materialization in the chambers and furnishings of the palazzo: these terms indicate the divisions of the disciplines and activities, as well as the physical place, that is, the part of the palazzo to which a given division corresponds.

The interdependence of the Academy and the Badoer family was to be rendered visible by the iconography of the façade of the palazzo. There was a plan, in fact, to place, next to the 'Saint Mark with the Badoer arms,' 'the device of the Academy, with the inscription, Accademia Veneziana.'[50] The palazzo would thus be transformed into a universal *theatre* of knowledge.

5 The Academy's Political Aspirations

What was the impact on the outside world of such an ambitious project? There was certainly no lack of editorial shrewdenss in the Academy's catalogue: others would ultimately complete some of its projects, like the anthologies of poetry and the collections of letters and orations, with a fair amount of success. The encyclopedic nature of the project, however, made its realization problematic. What was the reason, then, for this *excessive* dimension in the Academy? A simple lack of realism? Late-humanist Utopianism? Or was its program just a front for rather dubious and certainly unsuccessful mercantile and financial dealings, as some critics have claimed? There is surely more to the story than this. Giusto Fontanini has noted that the Academy was founded 'with the great spirit of a prince rather than that of a private citizen.' Zeno has written that 'the idea behind this academy was noble and pertaining to a sovereign,' while Marco Foscarini wrote that 'it was more akin to a public university than a private assembly.'[51]

The scope of the Academy's program went well beyond the prestigious designs of Federico Badoer, private citizen; his megalomania also reflected his hopoe that the work of the Academy would attract the interest and patronage of the Venetian state. This was the meaning behind the offers made to the Procurators of San Marco and the Signory. The Academy sought to establish a close link with the state, and thus to become a vehicle for the expression of its cultural politics. A clear indication of this was its very name: 'the Venetian Academy, *par excellence*, like the Florentine Academy,' wrote Fontanini. In other words, Badoer's Academy aspired to be, not one of many, but *the* Academy of Venice, like the prominent Florentine Academy, which had already become the official organ of the Medici state.[52] Badoer recognized that the Venetian Republic needed to have its own cultural institution, as did Tuscany and other European states. The Accademia Veneziana became a candidate to fill this role. But this brought about an element of ambiguity. It is difficult to imagine that the government of the Republic would sanction an undertaking so closely tied to a single patrician family.

Some steps, nonetheless, were taken in this direction. On 31 May 1560 the Council of Ten decreed that the Academy was to print all official documents of the Republic, and on 12 July of the same year the procurators of San Marco accepted Badoer's *Supplica* [Supplication] and granted him the use of a public space, the Vestibolo della Libreria [Library Vestibule], for Academy gatherings. This location and its surroundings were highly significant. The Library had been constructed by Sansovino in 1536 to house Cardinal Bessarion's manuscripts. Its completion, as Tafuri has noted, was a vital part of the urban renewal promoted by Doge Andrea Gritti.[53] The Library was situated next to the ancient Basilica of San Marco and the Ducal Palace: culture, in other words, now celebrated its own rites in conjunction with the religious and political life of the city (with a new style imported by Sansovino and his collaborators). In 1560, the same year that use of the Library was granted to the Academy, Titian portrayed Wisdom (plate I) on the ceiling of the Vestibule: she would oversee and ideally symbolize the meetings of Badoer's brotherhood.

During this period there was a strong relationship between the cultural climate of the Academy and the iconography of the paintings commissioned by the Republic for its public buildings.[54] Of great interest, in this light, is a passage in Badoer's *Supplica* to the procurators of San Marco:

> [The Procurators] must similarly know that, since the Most Illustrious Signory, in accordance with the will of the Most Serene Doge, has made to this Academy a determination in writing about the building of the [Ducal] Palace, that the Academy should make a plan of those pictorial inventions that are to be placed in front of the doors of the illustrious College and Senate, the Council of Ten, and the Chancellery, and has given it similarly the task of choosing the painter, the Academy has produced in writing the most beautiful invention, and the greatest adornment to this Most Serene Republic, that has ever been made, not only in this city, but in any other city in the world, considering the matter appropriate to represent the task of governing a state in a Christian and virtuous manner, with security and splendour.[55]

Thus, in an official capacity the Academy prepared an *invention* for one of the chambers of the Ducal Palace. The thematic nucleus (that is, the perfect state) coincided perfectly both with the idealized self-image promoted by the Republic through its buildings in Piazza San Marco and with the cultural and political model that the Academy sought to realize. The Academy's competence in the field of visualized messages was thus sanctioned by the state.

6 The Collapse of the Academy

That same year, 1560, also saw the beginning of the Academy's financial troubles. The collapse of the Academy reflected the difficulties faced by sixteenth-century literati who sought to find a professional position outside the university and separate from the court or the church. In 1560 Francesco Patrizi and Luca Contile left Venice and the Academy. Paolo Manuzio left for Rome, where he would offer his services to the Holy See for the implementation of its editorial policies following the Council of Trent.[56] Recent studies have shown the fundamental frailty of sixteenth-century publishing, its high costs, and the weakness of the hypothesis upon which it relied, that is, the strong growth of an audience of readers, in particular those capable of reading the vernacular.[57] Many of the literati who had worked in printing enterprises left Venice in the 1560s and 1570s. Badoer's economic troubles must be considered in this context in order to be fully understood.

In the past the specific reasons behind the rapid and dramatic demise of the Academy and its founder have been the subject of the most disparate hypotheses. The proceedings brought against Badoer for financial reasons (considerable debts assumed in the name of the Academy) probably had political implications. On the occasion of his arrest in 1568, the Council of Ten claimed to have knowledge of 'the plots of Badoer and his German collaborators, for which he was condemned by our judges who had been deputized for this purpose.'[58] The Academy's international relations had fostered suspicions in at least some of the Venetian governors.

There is no doubt that the religious question played an important, albeit unclear, role in the life of the Academy. Earlier we mentioned the plan to translate Giorgio Veneto's *De harmonia mundi* and the fact that young Badoer appeared in one of Brucioli's dialogues. Paolo Manuzio was linked not only to supporters of Catholic reform, like Luigi Contarini, Ludouico Beccadelli, Givanni Morone, and Reginald Pole, but also to Pietro Carnesecchi, follower of Juan Valdés, who was decapitated and burned in 1566.[59] In the collection of *Lettere volgari di diversi nobilissimi uomini* [Vernacular letters of various noblemen] published by Manuzio in 1542, with a dedication to Venier and Badoer, there is a substantial presence of individuals who were destined to exile or execution because of their participation in the religious debate. Republished in 1545 with the addition of a second volume, this collection was destined to have great success, and it sparked the professional interest of the censors: in the copy conserved in the Biblioteca Universitaria di Pisa (H.b.10.14), for example, some of Bonfadio's letters and an entire letter by Aretino to Sperone Speroni of 10 November 1542 were carefully cancelled in black ink (figure 3). The letter sent by Aonio Paleario to Benedetto Ramberti was completely cut out of the volume; Paleario, who had been accused of Protestantism on more than one occasion starting in 1542, would be hanged in Rome in 1570.

The great care devoted by the censor to this collection of vernacular letters edited by Paolo Manuzio – official printer of the Holy See from 1560 on, and respected representative of Venetian Ciceronianism – is an indication of the new severity of the situation. The opinions of historians vary widely on the actual enforcement of the *Index of Prohibited Books* printed in Venice in 1549. It is clear, however, that the monitoring and repression of books became harsher and more widespread towards

Di Venetia, il X di
Nouembre. M. D. X L I I.

A' M. PAOLO MANVTIO.

Honoratissimo M. Paolo. Aspettando di giorno in gior
no nuoua d'hauer fermo lo stato mio, & desideran=
do che la fusse la prima ch'io ui dessi di me, dopo
questa mia fastidiosa infermità non ui ho scritto co
m'era mio debito. hora che le uostre lettere ui potran=
no arrecar contento, per intender come'l corpo (à
Dio gratia) sta bene dalla passata infermità, & l'a
nimo riposatissimo & quieto sotto l'ombra del mio
nuouo patrone il signor Duca d'Vrbino, non ho
uoluto defraudare di questo piacere, ma dirui, che
sua eccellentia che l'anno passato, come uoi doueui sa

3 The end of a letter from Pietro Aretino to Sperone Speroni and the beginning of a letter to Paolo Manuzio. The letter to Speroni, dated 10 November 1542, has been censored. In Paolo Manuzio, *Lettere volgari di diversi
nobilissimi uomini* (Venice: Manuzio 1560). Pisa, Biblioteca Universitaria,
H.b.10.14

the end of the 1550s.[60] In July 1559, despite the resistance of Venetian
publishers, even the Republic accepted the Roman *Index*. The huge
bonfire of prohibited books in March of that year cast a sinister light on
the climate that was developing in Venice.

And yet it was in the the late 1550s that the Academy began to
develop its editorial politics. In the dedications of printed works we do
find tones of the Counter-Reformation, often linked to the addressee,
but we also find cultural ecumenism, which, in its relations with the
Germanic world, acted to repress religious conflicts. The Academy,
fully aware of the importance of the German book market, presented

itself as a prestigious channel of cultural exchange between Italy – Venice in particular – and the German-speaking world. Great hopes and plans matured, especially in the year 1559: the Academicians prepared a list of books that they intended to send to the book fair in Frankfurt and attached a letter, addressed to 'the scholars of good arts,' that was inspired by humanist and Erasmian themes of the cult of good letters, which would induce men to better themselves, cultivate their virtue, and put an end to the decadence of the times.[61] The answer to the letter was probably written by Pier Paolo Vergerio, a great friend of Paolo Manuzio, who had opted by then for reform and, consequently, for exile.[62] His answer shows in exemplary fashion how certain possibilities had by then disappeared, and how neither the Catholic nor Protestant world had space for the Academy's projects. He asked the Academicians, in fact, not to send any theological books to Germany since two equally unacceptable paths lay before them: a paganizing humanism that denatured Christianity or the bloody violence of the Inquisition. Vergerio's letter mercilessly shed light on contradictions between the real world and the Academy's cultural program, with its now illusory cosmopolitanism and a syncretism that was now seen as ambiguous and unacceptable.

Some of the new cultural elements promoted by the Academy would nonetheless remain intact throughout the century. Patrizi's work, for example, could serve as a litmus test.[63] The framework of his youthful *Città felice* [The perfect city] and the Academy's marriage of politics and culture overlapped considerably. Much more realistic was the sceptical vision that inspired his dialogues of 1560 and 1562, *Della historia* [On history] and *Della retorica* [On rhetoric]. It is not so farfetched to think that Badoer's failure must have weighed heavily on this evolution. At the same time, many notions associated with the Academy remained in Patrizi's work. 'The most ancient wisdom,' for example, is at the heart of his *Nova de universis philosophia* [New philosophy on general principles of reality]. In 1591, when he dedicated this work to Pope Gregory XIV, Patrizi indicated the need to follow a rational path to religious conversion, as opposed to war and violence. It was in analogous terms that, the 'scholars of letters in Germany' had written to the Academy; they recognized that this was the only correct path, even if by now an impractical one, to take in facing the current religious crisis in Europe.

Towards the end of the century, moreover, there would be those in Basel who looked to the Academy's publishing program with great interest: further evidence that, despite defeat and condemnation, something of the Academy lived on.[64]

CHAPTER TWO

Trees of Knowledge and Rhetorical Machines

1 The Easy Road to Knowledge or the Joy of Method

Francesco Robortello

On 31 October 1549 Francesco Robortello (1516–1567), a young man of letters from Udine, gave the inaugural oration of his course on rhetoric in Venice.[1] After teaching at Lucca and the University of Pisa, he had obtained this new, prestigious commission from the Venetian Senate. The preceding year, in Florence, he had published the first commentary on Aristotle's *Poetics*, thus beating out his colleague and rival, Vincenzo Maggi.

In Venice, and then at the Universities of Bologna and Padua, where he became professor of oratory in 1561, Robortello's popularity among the students was impressive. Just as impressive – and much more dangerous – was the envy of his colleagues. A rumor was spread about that Robortello had poisoned a doctor in Lucca who had been his adversary in a literary dispute. In Venice it appears that his predecessor, Battista Egnazio, attacked him with a knife in retaliation for an insult. In Padua classes were suspended after Robortello and Sigonio quarrelled over the best classrooms; despite Cardinal Seripando's fervent efforts, the possibility of their reconciliation had become extremely unlikely.

A large printed folio – a true manifesto – in the Museo Correr in Venice (Fondo Donà della Rose, 447/29) shows us that, beyond the rather sordid academic conflicts, something important was at stake, namely the problem of method. Through a large, detailed diagram and tree, this manifesto visualizes the entire course on rhetoric given by Robortello in 1549 (figure 4).

4 Detail of a *tree* visualizing the course in rhetoric given by Francesco
Robortello in 1549. Venice, Museo Correr, Fondo Donà delle Rose, 447/29

The Latin inscription in the bottom-left corner explains how the
diagram works:

In hope of a successful result, Francesco Robortello from Udine – who, by
order of the scholastic authorities, will teach a course on rhetoric in Venice
this year based on the ancient rhetoricians – offers this table to his listeners
for their perusal: all things that have to do with the art of speech – from
Cicero to Quintilian, Hermogenes, or Aristotle – have been positioned in

the places of the table. Anyone can consult it, and thus can know the origin of every question and the heading to which one must refer. In this way, every time a controversy arises in interpretation, all that can be disputed about it will be readily identifiable in its place.[2]

At any given moment the students – and everyone else who attends the lessons – will have the *place* at which the lecturer has arrived before their eyes; they can consider the specific articulations of a given argument, and at the same time they can see the network of relationships and derivations that unite that *place* with the rest of the material. The instructor's voice is thus precisely reflected in the layout of the table. Sight has come to support, control, and direct listening. The procedure by which the table is constructed imposes an ordered classification on all subjects relating to rhetoric. The division of the branches of the tree move from the general to the particular. Viewers are able to review the author's procedure in ordering his subject with their eyes and their minds. As the accompanying inscription points out, the table can perform various functions: it is an ordered receptacle of the knowledge passed down by the ancients, but it also guarantees knowledge and functionality for the viewer. Knowledge of rhetoric is put forward in such a way that it is ready for reuse: at the same time, the *places* of the tree contain the tradition and *places* of rhetorical invention. In other words, the table condenses and classifies techniques and knowledge in such way that they can be reactivated according to a given need.

The key to Robortello's method was thus the use of topics and a visualization of the procedures used in classification. Like the members of the Accademia Veneziana, Robortello was clearly influenced by the dialectical reform that began with Rudolf Agricola and was then developed and refined by Peter Ramus in the 1540s and 1550s.[3] Walter Ong has noted that the protagonists of the new dialectics – especially Ramus – tended not to give credit to the Italian humanists who had inaugurated this innovative process. However, except in rare instances, the Italians acted in much the same way. When he presented his manifesto in 1549, Robortello, for example, cited classical authors, but he cut out, so to speak, more recent works. One might call this the 'politics of citation': it was characterized by choices that reflected the climate of religious and cultural divisions in the cinquecento. When Robortello began his course in Venice, Agricola's teachings were well known in Europe and had borne fruit in the works of Philipp Melanchthon and Johannes Sturm, for example. Giulio Camillo had been dead for only five years, and his work in rhetoric had been based mainly on a renewal of the functions and number of topical places; at this time his work was for the most part still unpublished, but his fame was great, especially in the circles frequented by Robortello (whose father-in-law, Antonio Bellone, had been, among other things, a fervent participant in the human and intellectual adventure of Camillo).[4]

Robortello's Venetian manifesto created a direct link to the ancient world: Aristotle and Hermogenes, Cicero and Quintilian seemed to be his only true interlocutors. More recent notions and experiences were expunged from sight in his printed text. The panorama becomes more complex when we examine the manuscripts. An unknown student of Robortello, for example, left us his notes from a course devoted to Cicero's *Topica*, held at the University of Bologna in 1557.[5] In this case, Agricola is mentioned expressly as Robortello's most important interlocutor – and adversary. Although Agricola had introduced, said Robortello, 'some type of innovation' [nescio quid novi] into a prestigious and fundamentally exhaustive tradition that spanned the centuries from Aristotle to Cicero, Quintilian, and Boethius, the results were disappointing. According to Robortello, 'there is nothing new here' [nihil novi attulit].[6]

The attack on Agricola returns in the manuscript of a short work entitled *Discorso in materia delli luoghi topici* [Essay on the subject of topical places]. Agricola's criticism of Aristotle's method, according to Robortello, is the result of his participation in the faulty intellectual practices of the times: 'for some reason people do not read books from cover to cover anymore. Instead, most skip through them to get quickly to the main point. This means the end of the sciences and the written arts of antiquity.'[7] Hurriedness, carelessness, anxiety to produce, haste to earn: these, says Robortello, are the true reason behind the distaste for the ancients and the false proclamations of new results. Robortello's faith in Aristotle slows his acceptance of the new methods, and allows him to see their nature and limits with great lucidity.

Despite this resistance, Robortello is far from being insensitive to the new climate. He is engrossed in a search for a new, clear, easy, and

Sexta refutatio criminis.
Plancius est asperius aliquando locutus.
Idem affectus.   Locus proprius ex materie amoris nu. 16.
                  καὶ μὴ φιλόγενσι, μηδὲ δυσιειδὴς.
Asperius inquit.

F. S.	L. T.	F. V.	F. STR.	N.
Subiectio. Vide Quintil. et dialogismus Rufin. nu. 21. et acerrima epiplexis per uerbum. Ergo prolata. in qua indigna-tio inest.	à diuersa causa. Locus refell. ca lum. 24. τὸ ferre. ἀττικαταΝ.ἀτ πάθαι ἔ ἔνευσ. Asperè locutus est, ergo puniendus. Liberè locutus est, ergo laudandus.	προηγμὶτον. Ferendi.		

Non hæc protulit, ut asperè loqueretur, et aliquem læderet.
sed ut more maiorum in rep. liberè loqueretur.

Idem affectus.   Locus proprius ex materie amoris 36.
                  καὶ τῆς μὴ φιλατρομίνου.
Vbi nam ille mos.

F. S.	L. T.	F. V.	F. STR.	N.
epiplexis et pysma.	à causa. à libertate et ab æquitate iuris talis sermo prouenit, non ab asperitate. Locus eal. refel. ut ante.	μεταφορὰ et ινϑ́γεια conueniens Irato.		v - - v

H 2   Idem

5 Geometric grid, from Francesco Robortello, *De artificio dicendi* (Bologna: Alessandro Benazio 1567)

efficient method to understand and imitate the rhetorical artifice used by the great writers of antiquity in prose and in poetry. Here, too, as in his relationship with Agricola, there is a difference in the two media – the manuscript and the printed book – through which his work has reached us. A rectangular grid, based mostly on Hermogenes, is proposed, for example, as a diagram to display the figures used by poets. An analysis of some odes by Horace shows how to use it. The printed version, *De artificio dicendi* [On rhetorical artifice] (Bologna: Alessandro Benazio 1557), has a geometric depiction of the grid (figure 5), while the visualization of the diagram in the manuscript is much more animated and imaginative (*Methodus perquirendi artificii in scriptis poetarum antiquorum* [Method of the required artifice in the writing of the ancient

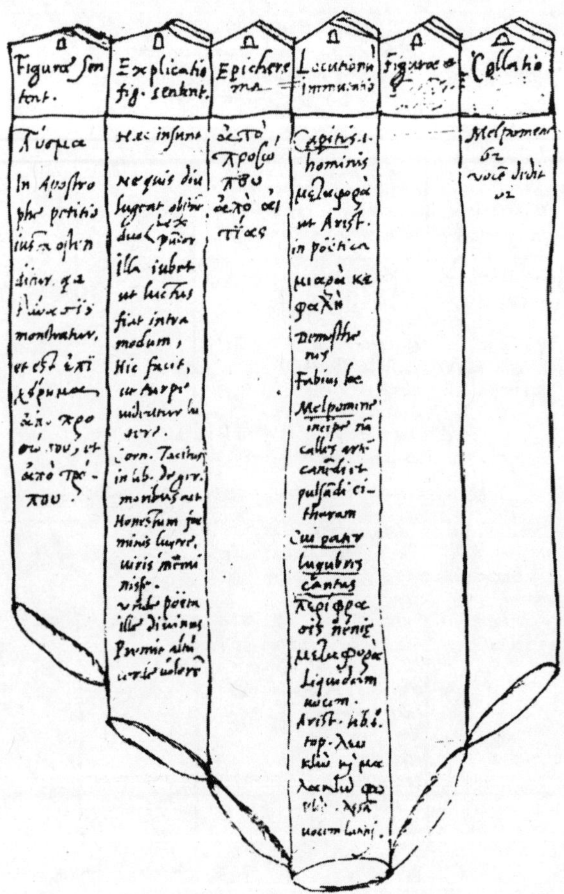

6 Diagram in the form of a *zampogna* (a musical instrument), from Francesco Robortello, *Methodus perquirendi artificii in scriptis poetarum antiquorum*. Paris, Bibliothèque nationale, cod. Lat. 8764

poets], Paris, Bibliothèque nationale, Lat. 8764, folios 25–41). Here the simple figure of the tree reproduces the first two parts (that is, the *argumentum* [subject] and the *caput* [heading], with the poem's subject reduced to a single proposition and then to a *quaestio* [question]). The other six parts rarely rely on geometric visualization, that is, through parallel vertical lines. For the most part the lines tend to be embellished with detailed decorations that change them into tree trunks, or pillars, or the pipes of a rustic bagpipe (figure 6). They are also accompanied by astrological symbols that reconnect the vertical columns with the plan-ets and constellations. A taste for ornamental variation and a fascination with associations are therefore evident in the manuscript. The geometric model thus tends to take the form of a system of images of memory.

The case of Robortello shows us once again how the medium – that is, the manuscript or the printed book – acts in a complex yet subtle way with regard to the text. It conditions the content and the mode of presentation. Naturally the problem is broader in character. It would be interesting to see how the use of visual aids (that is, trees, tables, and diagrams) in Italy from the 1540s on, augmented by the new dialectics, interacted with the debate on literary language, rhetoric, and poetics, and how all of these related to the book industry and the new formats, ever richer and more elaborate, in which the texts were presented.[8] The Accademia Veneziana has already given us a most interesting example. We will now look at some others. They constitute very different episodes and refer to different philosophical horizons, but their very diversity is significant – a sign of how effective the new techniques of visualizing method were, so much so that they could cross not only diverse fields of study but also diverse cultural choices. It should be noted, however, that, despite the multiplicity of these cases, they appear to share a common thread. One of the most mysterious, yet most active, characters of the cinquecento literary debates, Triphon Gabriele, the 'new Socrates' whose fame was based on his personal example and oral teachings, will appear with impressive frequency behind the texts and the characters that we will encounter.[9]

Bernardino Partenio

In the 1560s Giulio Camillo's fame was still alive and thriving. Besides his theatre of memory, his *Topica* was celebrated as a work that promised to provide an easy, brief, and complete method for the imitation of exemplary texts. The *Dialoghi della imitatione poetica* [Dialogues on poetic imitation] by Bernardino Partenio (ca 1500–1589), published in 1560, is a good example of how Camillo's work was being received.[10] Partenio was a character of some interest. Between 1538 and 1544, in his native Spilimbergo (near Udine), he founded an academy which would realize an Erasmian project: Hebrew was taught there as well as Latin and Greek. Partenio's *Pro lingua latina oratio* [Oration in favour of the Latin language] culminates in a celebration of Camillo's theatre, the 'wonderful apparatus' 'that he called a theatre because it made available before the eyes of everyone, as in a play, the riches of not just one, but all the authors of the Golden Age.'[11] The definition of the theatre as an apparatus is noteworthy: as we will see in the case of Toscanella, the apparatus represents an essential moment in this environment, an indispensable step on the path to literary formation. It is the ordered selection and collection of material taken from texts to be imitated. Camillo's theatre found its *raison d'être* and received its name, writes Partenio, because it made the apparatus visible and available to everyone. Like Viglius Zuichemus, a friend of Erasmus who visited the theatre, Partenio is impressed by the enormous number of materials amassed by Camillo, but the two have extremely different points of view and reactions: while Viglius scornfully compares Camillo's work to that of Nosoponus, the character consumed with impossible Ciceronian ideals in Erasmus' *Ciceronianus, or A Dialogue on the Best Style of Speaking*, Partenio is overwhelmed by admiration.[12] Camillo, he says, presented his material

> with such clarity ... in places marked in such a way that human intelligence could not devise anything simpler or more grandiose. In sum, I remember having seen in Venice, when he himself showed it to me, such a multitude and variety of words gathered and positioned in his great tomes that I was amazed that one man alone could adorn his work with such riches and decoration (even though I had first thought of it myself without, however, ever having personally experimented with it).[13]

Thus, the book has decisively and thoroughly established itself in the foreground: the wooden amphitheatre, of which Viglius had spoken, has disappeared (perhaps because Camillo did not show it to Partenio, thus limiting his initiation to a single component of the theatre). The entire space is occupied by the book, actually by large volumes that contain the riches and virtues – well classified and conveniently positioned in their *places* – of Cicero's texts.

Originally written in Italian and only later translated into Latin, Partenio's *Dialoghi della imitazione poetica* [Dialogues on poetic imitation] mark a phase in which he finally accepts the new literary trend of writing in the vernacular. Not unimportant, in this light, is the fact that in 1555 Partenio was probably teaching at the Accademia Olimpica in Vicenza, which had been founded by Gian Giorgio Trissino (1478–1550), a literary theorist, philologist, dramatist, and poet. For this occasion Paolo Manuzio wrote to Partenio: 'Join this heroic undertaking, illustrious friend, share with others the treasures of true learning through your voice and pen.'[14]

Partenio's admiration for Camillo, which he had fostered since his youth, remains unchanged. He remembered hearing Camillo talk of epideictic rhetoric when he was just a boy, in Venice, at the home of Sebastiano Serlio (1475–1554). In the *Pro lingua latina oratio*, Partenio writes: 'I believed that certainly no man, not even a god, could speak and know as much as he.'[15]

In the *Dialoghi della imitazione poetica* literati of different generations are united in weaving a robe of praise for Camillo. Partenio portrays himself as being in the company of Paolo Manuzio and Francesco Luigini on their way to Murano to pay homage to two of the great figures of the previous generation, Triphon Gabriele and Gian Giorgio Trissino. The first to celebrate Camillo is Triphon himself: he promises to explain to Manuzio 'what these poets' fantastic ways consist of and where they come from.'

Do you know, he asks him, the sources from which the proofs and the arguments are drawn?

The places that they call topics, answered Manuzio confidently.

Of course, replied Trifon, the wonderment of all these poetic figures are seen to be drawn from these very same sources. Giulio Camillo alone knew this, and no other before him, save those who, by chance, had learned from him. So great was this discovery that he who understands it can by himself formulate other highly laudable and divine figures of speech, as did the ancient Greeks and Latins.

Later it is Trissino who sings the praises of Camillo. He remembers Camillo's extraordinary ability to 'understand profoundly' the poets, to penetrate 'their marrow' and reveal their 'slightest secrets':

I begin to laugh, he says, every time I see some of his followers who steal from those of his writings that have somehow fallen into their hands, as they boldly strive to pass themselves off as Giulio Camillo, shamelessly pretending to be the authors of that which is not theirs, disdaining to acknowledge anything whatever of his. They boldly speak and brag, and possessing Master Giulio's alchemy, they even show off mounds of gold they have transformed. But we can see how gold and silver turn to iron and lead in their hands. They spew out figures, ideas, forms, quotations, concepts, harmonies, the models of eloquence of Hermogenes, when they understand nothing of him but his name.[16]

In the pages of Partenio we find some of the themes that pervade the prefaces of sixteenth-century editions of Camillo's work: praise for Camillo's methods and their extraordinary utility is almost always accompanied by the concern that his unpublished works may become the object of plagiarism. But in the words that Partenio puts into the mouth of Trissino there is something more: the allusion to alchemy is a precise reference to the occult, *transformational* dimension that Camillo attributes to his work on words and the subject matter of eloquence. It is for just this reason that the actions of the plagiarists, who have robbed and bastardized Camillo's discoveries, are represented as an alchemical procedure in reverse. From gold and silver they extract iron and lead, just as fertile depositories of topics can be transformed into banal repertories: 'they spew out figures, ideas, forms, quotations ...'

Giovan Mario Verdizzotti

In 1560 a part of Camillo's *Topica delle figurate locutioni* [*Topica* of figurative locutions] was published by Giovan Mario Verdizzotti (ca 1537–ca 1640) with the usual praise. Verdizzotti writes that:

> [from] this sweet, most fragrant source ... derive all the beauty and goodness of ornate eloquence; this short work is such that any noble intelligence can easily use it to show quickly the fruits of his labours, as much as few are barely able to show in their writing despite long hours of imitation and observation of many authors.[17]

Verdizzotti was a young man of letters, an artist and engraver, a friend of and secretary to Titian, and in addition a friend and adviser of a young and rather unheedful Torquato Tasso (who had followed his father, enlisted by the Accademia Veneziana, to Venice).[18] Camillo's work is followed by a brief piece by Verdizzotti himself, *Del quadripartito uso de' luoghi topici* [On the fourfold use of topics]. Faithful to the principle that everyone must 'yield, however he can, some utility to the world,' he notes that 'it does not seem inappropriate to use this opportunity to inform young scholars of the wonderful use of topics.' He writes that he hopes to inspire others to 'seek out and find anew in similar studies things beneficial to others and glorious for themselves.'[19] His pedagogic stance, his association of utility with glory, his trust in an easy and productive method, and his belief in topics as the central unifying element in rhetorical procedure are indicative of the way Verdizzotti embraces and develops Camillo's teachings.

These are themes very similar to those that inspired the programs of the Accademia Veneziana. It is thus noteworthy that at the end of his edition of Camillo's *Topica* Verdizzotti prints a sonnet addressed to the 'most noble and excellent Accademia Veneziana':

> Glorious, magnificent, and virtuous souls,
> famous progeny of Jupiter, worthy of the saints;
> proud emblems of the Lady of the Sea,
> your remarkable, unique deeds sustain her;
>   now that the Sun of justice severs and
>   stifles the wrath and rage of the wicked
>   Hydras, follow the sublime desire which leads
>   to Him, even in spite of unworthy peoples;
> may hate and envy return in derision along
> the darkest of paths to their nest and quit
> the clear shores of the blissful Adriatic;
>   and with noble care and her golden fame
>   in a cry of joy, may Innocence, true and chaste,
>   now unfold her victorious wings towards Heaven.[20]

This edition of *Topica delle figurate locutioni* thus becomes a sort of cultural manifesto. The act of republishing and celebrating Camillo's writings – exalted for their pedagogical as well as their rhetorical efficacy – is closely linked to support for a cultural institution, the Accademia Veneziana, even though, at the time, the Academy was undergoing a serious crisis, and it would be forced to close, as we have seen, the following year, in 1561.

After Girolamo Molin died in 1569, his friends – Domenico Venier in particular – were busy promoting an edition of his lyric poems. While the book has a dedication from Celio Magno to Giulio Contarini, the task of writing the author's biography fell upon Verdizzotti's shoulders. He seized the opportunity to give the book a particular flavour. He extols the collaboration among great scholars of different generations. He fondly remembers the young Molin's friendship with the old masters, like Bembo, Triphon Gabriele, and Trissino, as well as his relations with illustrious figures with whom the generation gap is not so wide: Domenico Venier, Andrea Navagero, Daniele Barbaro, Bernardo Cappello, Luigi Cornaro, Sperone Speroni, Bernardo Tasso, and, of course, Giulio Camillo. Verdizzotti also recalls Molin's love for vernacular poetry, which lived side by side with his interests in painting, sculpture, music, as well as his knowledge of Hebrew, Greek, and Latin. Interesting, too, is the moral portrait that Verdizzotti draws of Molin. Although Molin was hardly indifferent to the charms of beautiful women, he never married for fear that such a union might interfere with the *otium*, or leisure, required for his literary studies. He rarely accepted public duties, but he was indignant at those who abused their political office; he was angered, writes Verdizzotti, by those who were 'laden with riches and decorated with great authority yet did not perform deeds worthy of their station, as he most certainly would have done.'[21]

Verdizzotti's biography of Molin thus turns into a celebration of a literary environment, an impassioned evocation of a magical moment in the cultural history of Venice. The search for an easy and enjoyable path to master knowledge and literary authorship is one of the components of that moment and the cultural climate in which it thrived.

2 The Tables of Sacred and Profane Rhetoric

Giason Denores

Giason Denores (ca 1530–1590), a man of letters of strong Aristotelian convictions, generally makes a brief appearance in manuals of Italian literary history because of his condemnation of Giovanni Battista Guarini's *Il pastor fido* [The faithful shepherd]. Guarini, he believed, was guilty of mixing tragedy and comedy and thus infringing the canon of literary genres. The circles that Denores frequented were common to many among our cast of characters: he was a friend of Paolo Manuzio, and he never missed an opportunity to proclaim himself a student and friend of Triphon Gabriele. In 1574 he published his *Breve trattato dell'oratore* [A brief treatise for the orator], which has a clear practical aim: it is addressed to the young heirs of noble Venetian families, that is, to those who will later practise the art of eloquence in politics and judicial administration. In order to enhance the efficacy of the work, he published with it an 'essay ... on the distinctions, definitions, and divisions of rhetoric articulated *in multiple tables* for easy classification.'[22]

Such a procedure would become a constant in Denores' work. In 1578 he reduces into tables not only the treatise on *Rhetoric* but 'all of the human philosophy' of Aristotle: he believes that this is the way to bring to light the secret of Aristotle's greatness and to visualize the hidden structure that makes his thinking great. From the tables, he writes, 'one will easily understand the wondrous artifice used by him in writing and classifying this work, and how we have tried diligently to follow him for the common benefit and utility and greater facility of such precious knowledge.'[23] It is this map and classification of Aristotelian procedures that guarantee both comprehension and memorization of the philosopher's teachings. Denores finds it misleading to stop at knowledge of the precepts without penetrating the methodology that has shaped and positioned them. In that way, he writes in the introduction, 'the more precepts that we commit to memory, the more we will find ourselves entangled and confused by their great number.' Method, therefore, is identified as the new key to the art of memory.

In the three books of Denores' *Della rhetorica* [On rhetoric], published in 1584, there is a description of how to construct true and proper rhetorical machines. As we shall observe below, they are curiously similar to those produced by an author never cited by Denores: Orazio Toscanella. An initial and rather short treatise devoted to the traditional precepts of the art of rhetoric is followed by twenty orations by great authors. The exemplary character of each oration is illustrated by an analysis of the artifices with which it has been constructed. The work ends with 'tables and wheels in which one can easily view the employment and the execution of all the devices of oratory.' The *wheels* (folios 260v, 264v–265v; figure 7) mark the achievement of a method that is highly self-confident and eager to pass from analysis to application.[24] Although their form seems to be reminiscent of the Lullian model, their scant framework seems rather to hearken back to archaic medieval models. The three wheels correspond to the three genres of rhetoric. They are formed by concentric circles divided into different parts. The text written on each part refers to internal divisions of each genre. The 'quadrant of the proofs' can be applied to each of the circles and thus used to arrive at the *inventio* of the arguments. Denores guarantees that whoever uses his wheels 'will not only find arguments in every matter that he may propose in this genre, but will also easily

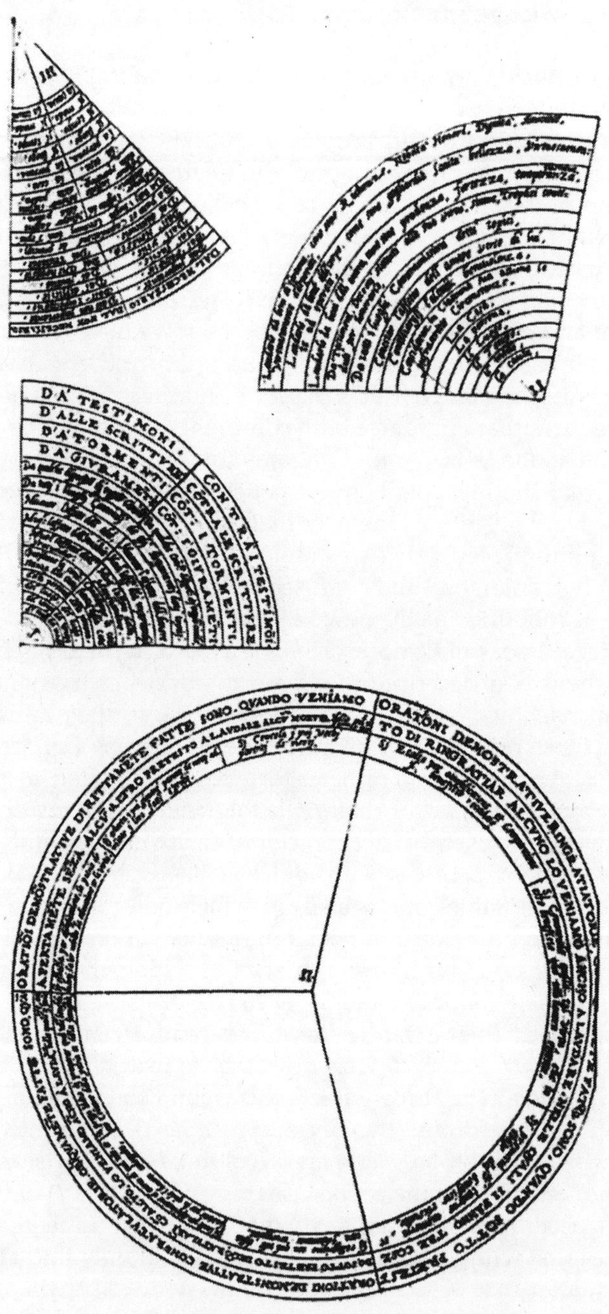

7 Wheels, from Giason Denores, *Della rhetorica* (Venice: Paolo Megietto 1584)

understand and observe the devices in the orations of ancient and modern writers.' The wheels, therefore, open the doors to the treasures of eloquence: they guide the critic's eye and the writer's hand.

Although the wheels have been derived from an ancient and prestigious textual tradition, in the end they render that tradition useless – thanks to the principle of economy, at the level of space and time, which has inspired them. At least, this is what Denores suggests when he guarantees that by using the wheel of the judiciary genre we will be able to find 'in the blink of an eye' everything we need to produce 'not only the invention of arguments and rhetorical proofs, but also in large part their arrangement, and we will reduce our thought to a relatively few main points without having to reread the books of [Aristotle's] *Rhetoric* every time we want to compose an oration.'[25]

Agostino Valier

Denores advertised his *Rhetorica* as a work 'extremely useful for preachers, judges, and lawyers,' that is, for religious and secular oratory. The impact of these new techniques was real indeed in the field of religious rhetoric. A case in point is the work of Agostino Valier (1530–1606).[26] A member of an illustrious Venetian family and a nephew of the famous scholar Andrea Navagero, Valier (see p. 12) had been a member of the Accademia Veneziana in the capacity of philosopher; in 1558 he became a lecturer in philosophy at the School of Rialto. Subsequently he embraced a career in the church: in 1562 he became bishop of Verona, and in 1583 cardinal.

One of his first biographers, Giovanni Ventura, after describing the studies in logic and philosophy of the young Valier, emphasizes his skills in memory and improvisation, that is, his great mental speed and agility:

> he knew how to understand everything, even occult and abstruse things, and in his mind he perfectly remembered the places of Aristotle, one by one. Sometimes for practice, as he himself used to say, he would challenge the masters to dispute about any place in Aristotle, and at times he seemed to surpass them with the readiness of his memory.[27]

The attention to method and its connection to memory turn out to be a constant throughout Valier's life. In a text written in his youth, *Qua ratione versandum sit in Aristotele* [The method for studying Aristotle], composed around 1555, the praise he gives to Aristotle is accompanied by quotations from the 'divine Plato.' The primary aim, he says, is to focus on 'the method and classifications with which Aristotle discovered and taught all of the arts' [qua ratione sive ordine Aristoteles omnes fere artes invenerit et docuerit] since 'classification is almost the soul of things' [ordo est quasi anima ipsarum rerum], and it is essential if one wishes to 'commit to memory' [ad commendandum memoriae] the fruits of one's study.[28]

In 1560 Valier was in Rome, where he participated in the 'Noctes Vaticanae,' an academy founded by the young Carlo Borromeo (cardinal and archbishop, one of the most important figures of the Counter-Reformation in Italy, canonized as Saint Charles Borromeo in 1610). The members of this brotherhood – Sperone Speroni and many future cardinals were among them – were all required to practise the arts of eloquence and memory.

In a short work published in 1574, *Memoriale a Luigi Contarini cavaliere sopra gli studii ad un senatore convenienti* [Memorandum to Luigi Contarini, Knight, on the studies useful to a Venetian senator], Valier writes:

> The method of articulating the arts and sciences, which is commonly called *method,* is more appropriately called *synopsis* because it places the sum of things before your very eyes. It was endorsed by the ancient philosophers and praised highly by Plato: I, as you well know, have always delighted in it.[29]

The old interests, therefore, had endured, and they actually found new motivation, even after Valier began his career in the church. He played an important role, in fact, in the revival of preaching and theoretical reflection upon it led by Borromeo. Valier's *Rhetorica ecclesiastica* [Ecclesiastic rhetoric] was destined to enjoy extraordinary success both in Italy and abroad. In 1575 a new edition of the work was published in Paris, along with a large table entitled 'Rhetoricae ecclesiasticae synopsis' [Synopsis of ecclesiastic rhetoric] (figure 8). The work is dedicated to Cardinal Carlo Borromeo. It was Borromeo, the dedication states, who asked his friend Valier to produce this visualized version of his manual for the use of those who do not have time to read the entire book. The judicious use of space in the diagram, therefore, permits a better use of time. But this – the dedication guarantees – is not the only advantage. The trees help to eliminate confusion by placing before the eyes 'even the most minute differences among things' [vel minimas

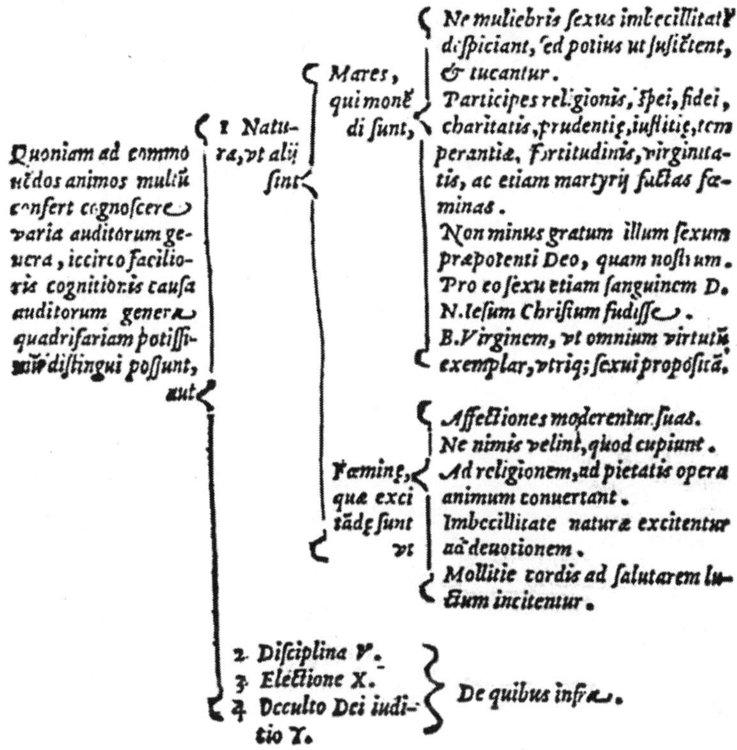

8 A table, from Agostino Valier, *Libri tres de rhetorica ecclesiastica. Synopsis eiusdem rhetoricae* (Paris: Thomas Brumennius 1575)

rerum differentias] and imprinting them in the memory, 'custodian of all the sciences and arts' [quae est custos omnium scientiarum atque artium]. They do this so effectively that only those who use this method will appear to be the true masters of knowledge and of the capacity to transmit it. The result, writes Valier, is an extraordinary intellectual pleasure:

this most noble method (as you well know, since you have passionately cultivated this type of division of the arts and various disciplines) brings about an extraordinary sort of pleasure whereby the soul seems not to learn things but rather to see them as if they were painted from life. In this way we can express, inasmuch as our human frailties permit, the divine similitude that is in ourselves. In fact, just as God knows all with just one look, we too can see each of the arts and sciences with just a glance.[30]

Valier thus places the entire package of new techniques and methods that has been developed in profane rhetoric at the service of the Counter-Reformation church to enable it to fulfil its new persuasive role. It is interesting to note that he defends the method of distinction and division in the name of Plato (who is cited more than once as its best teacher and practitioner); it would have been highly embarrassing for it to be associated with the teachers of logic and rhetoric who found their audience primarily in the Protestant world. There are also echoes of the Accademia Veneziana, albeit here in a different context, in the enthusiasm for the new method, the celebration of the immediate perception of knowledge that the new method permits, and the connection between the method and the mark of divinity that lies within us. The diagrams, it is asserted, bring to light and make practicable the human capacity to imitate God by perceiving together, in a single glance, the whole and its parts. Moreover, because of its ability to produce a comprehensive picture of the classification of things (and thoughts), the new method makes it possible to breach the barrier between teacher and student. The teachers who use his table, writes Valier in the dedication, 'imprint onto the minds of others all that which they have conceived in their own minds' [quidquid mente conceperint, in aliorum animis imprimunt].

Carlo Borromeo

Carlo Borromeo (1538–1584) is represented by Valier not only as having sponsored his synoptic table, but also as himself an expert and participant in what we – prompted by Valier's expression – may call the 'pleasure of method': 'this most noble method (as you well know, since you have passionately cultivated this type of division of the arts and various disciplines) brings about an extraordinary sort of pleasure.' Valier's testimony indeed express the truth. In fact, Federico Borromeo (1564–1631), Carlo's younger cousin, dedicates the third and central book of his *De sacris nostrorum temporum oratoribus libri quinque* [The sacred orators of our time, in five books] to Carlo's talents as a preacher. Federico remembers that, 'when he [Carlo Borromeo] prepared a sermon, he used an art whereby the subjects and places were arranged on the branches of a drawing of a tree. I believe that he did so because his memory received no small help from this method. I have collected these trees in eight volumes.'[31] He adds that he has deposited the eight volumes in the Ambrosian Library in Milan, although he fears that they will be lost.

His worries would prove to be unfounded: eight codices in the Ambrosian Library (F 189 inf.–F 197 inf.) still preserve the extensive material to which Carlo Borromeo attributed such great importance in his last will and testament.[32] These eight volumes bear witness to a constant and singular faith in a rhetorical and mnemonic method that was used effectively on a double frontier: between the Protestant and Catholic worlds, and between secular and religious culture.

Federico Borromeo was also susceptible to the lure of tables, of visualization, and of the automation, if you will, of rhetorical invention. In fact, we shall shortly encounter him again.

3 The Map of Possible Texts

Ludovico Castelvetro

Aristotelianism and an interest in the new methods of visualization thus thrive side by side in the texts on poetics and rhetoric of the high cinquecento. We have already discussed the case of Denores, but the richest and most interesting example of this potential coexistence is found in the work of Ludovico Castelvetro (1505–1571). Castelvetro was an Aristotelian dissatisfied with Aristotle, an intransigent rationalist, an erudite reader of Dante and commentator on Petrarch, a man of letters impassioned by questions of philology and theology, whom the Inquisition would burn in effigy in Rome and force into an exile that would end with his death.[33]

Castelvetro's use of diagrams and his predisposition for a method close to Ramism have already been emphasized by Ezio Raimondi in an essay dedicated to his *Sposizione a XXIX canti dell'Inferno dantesco* [Commentary on XXIX cantos of Dante's *Inferno*].[34] Delving into a field rather unfamiliar to literary critics, Raimondi not only identifies the logical and philosophical nature of the method used by Castelvetro but also shows how critically fertile it is, permitting Castelveltro to adopt a new perspective on Dante's text and to map and reorganize spatially the logic behind its choices and *dispositio*.

The model preferred by Castelvetro is the tree. It can be found, for example, in the *Sposizione a XXIX Canti*, where it is used to visualize how the damned of Malebolge are positioned and arranged. There are

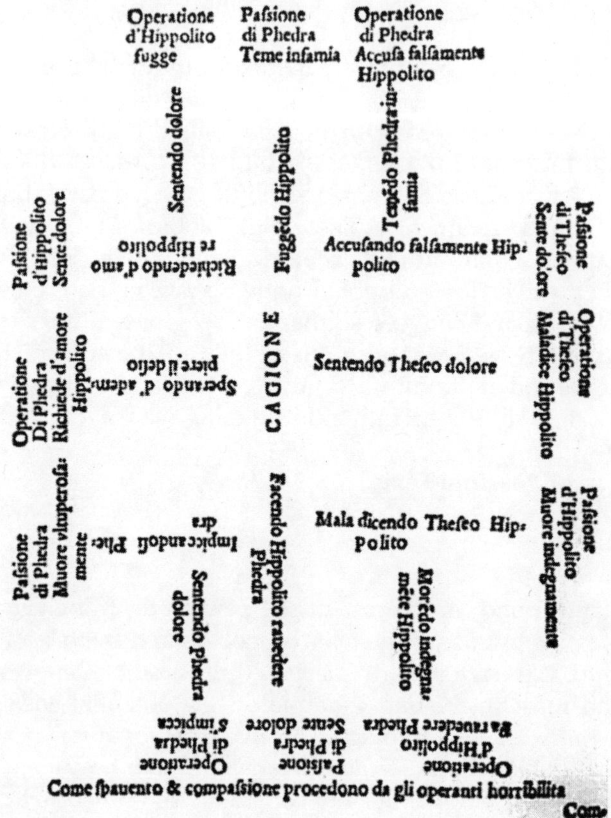

9 The wheel of Phaedra, from Ludovico Castelvetro, *La Poetica d'Aristotele vulgarizzata et sposta* (Vienna: Gaspar Stainhofer 1570)

even more examples in the *Esaminatione sopra la Ritorica a Caio Herennio* [Commentary on *Rhetorica ad Herennium*], written around 1563,[35] and the *Poetica d'Aristotele vulgarizzata et sposta* [Commentary and translation of Aristotle's *Poetics*], which Castelvetro finished in 1567 and published in 1570 in Vienna and again in 1576 in Basel.

Castelvetro's use of geometric and other models is much more limited. A wheel is used in the *Poetics*, however, to show how 'reason, operation, and passion generate and are generated by each other.'[36] The examples are taken from Seneca's *Phaedra* (figure 9). The spokes of the wheel are used to visualize the connection between the passions of the two protagonists and their consequent actions. The succession of actions is recomposed in an order of oppositions: the passion of one of

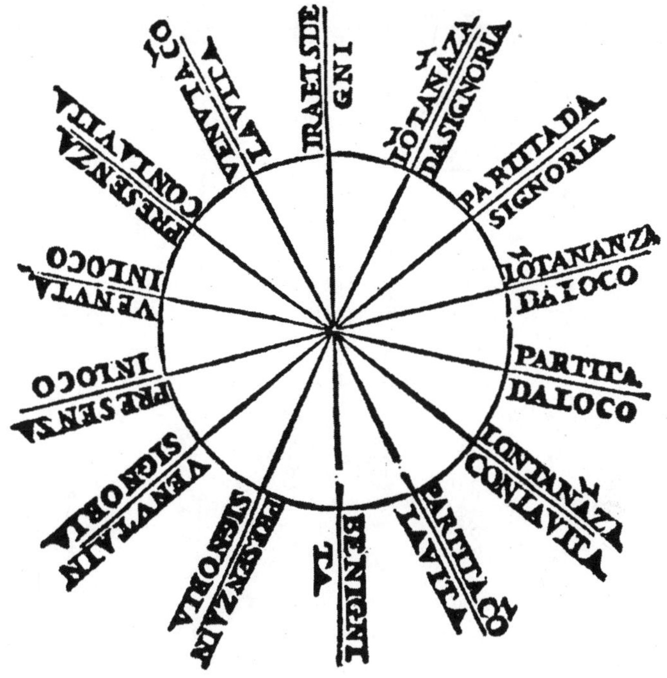

10 The artificial wheel, from Giulio Camillo, *Trattato delle materie*, in *Opere* (Venice: Domenico Farri 1579)

the characters is inevitably followed by his actions, which in turn generate the action and passion of the other character.

What comes to mind – along with Lullian wheels and the medieval tradition of rhetorical wheels – is the more recent example of the *artificiosa rota* [artificial wheel], created by Camillo in the *Trattato delle materie* [Treatise on subject matters] (figure 10); it visualizes the method used to find the *materia* [subject matter] necessary to compose a sonnet to celebrate Ercole d'Este, when he became duke of Ferrara. The generative nucleus, the so-called *gorgo dell'artificio* [whirlpool of artifice], forms the centre of the wheel, while the opposing places are arranged along the spokes (arrival in the signory, departure from the signory, etc.).[37] In effect, Castelvetro's work follows in Camillo's footsteps – albeit with a note of critical diffidence.[38] Castelvetro owned copies of Camillo's works, both published and unpublished, and he cites Camillo as his predecessor in a passage of his commentary on the *Rhetorica ad Herennium* where he claims that he himself is the first to have discovered and defined the rhetorical figure of *parole partimentevoli*,

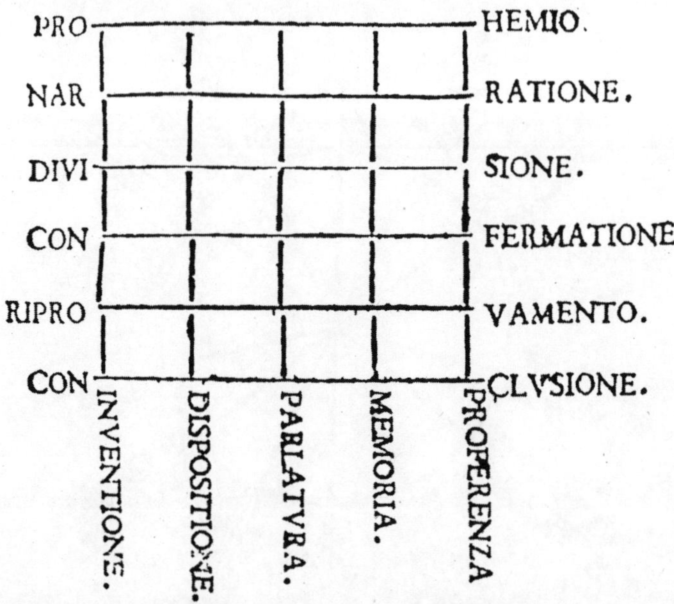

11 A grid, from Ludovico Castelvetro, *Esaminatione sopra la ritorica a Caio Herennio* (Modena: Andrea e Girolamo, eredi del Cassini 1653)

[compartmental words], in which the designation of the part evokes the whole (p. 134, folios 127–128).

The taxing reflections on rhetoric contained in Castelvetro's commentary on the *Rhetorica ad Herennium* are closely linked with his reflections on poetics. His commentary on Aristotle's *Poetics* is, in fact, announced right after the citation of Camillo (*Esaminatione sopra la Ritorica* ... [Examination of the *Rhetoric* ...], pp. 134–135, folio 128). Moreover, one of the geometric models used for visualization – the so-called *grata* [grid], a rectangular diagram (figure 11) – originates in the interaction of rhetoric and poetics. On the grid constructed by Castelvetro the five *qualitative parts* of discourse (that is, *inventio, dispositio, elocutio, actio,* and memory) lie along the horizontal axis, while the six *quantitative parts*, according to the Aristotelian definitions from which they are taken (that is, proem, narration, division, confirmation, *riprovamento* [recapitulation], and conclusion lie along the vertical axis (*Esaminatione sopra la Ritorica* ..., p. 16, folio 10).

In the *Poetics* Castelvetro recycles the same model: the *qualitative parts* of tragedy ('favola, costume, sentenzia, melodia e vista' [story, costume, judgment, melody, and scene]) have the same functions, he writes, as the traditional elements of rhetoric) (*inventio, dispositio*, etc. have in 'diceria' [discourse or prose] (I, 340). In the same fashion the *quantitative parts* of tragedy (proem, chorus entrance, exordium, etc.) correspond to the *quantitative parts* of an oration. 'Using the proper proportions,' he continues, 'we can liken every oratorical discourse and every tragedy to a grid that has the qualitative parts lengthwise, running all the way across like rods, and crosswise it has the quantitative parts that occupy only a prescribed space in the form of other rods' (I, 341). In an analogous fashion the lines composing the grid in the commentary on *Rhetorica ad Herennium* are called *doghe* and *stanghe*, that is, staffs and bars (p. 16, folio 20).

The model is in essence a geometric figure: the internal partitions of the rectangle allow the user to visualize the play created between the parts of the text and the modalities with which they have been arranged by the author. The *places* of the grid reconstruct the logic with which the *places* of the text have been structured:

> because each quantitative part of the discourse is not stretched out for the whole discourse, it does not occupy the whole thing but is content to have a small part; nor does it go beyond the confines of that part, since, in the same manner, none of the quantitative parts of tragedy occupy all of the tragedy; but since each one is in its assigned place, it does not run outside the confines of its place, and for this reason, using the proper proportions, we can liken every discourse and every tragedy to a grid.   (*Poetica*, I, 341)

At the same time, however, the geometric model seems to acquire material depth and palpable consistency. The lines of the geometric model are rods, staffs, and bars. They, in turn, form a grid. In other words, they give shape to a type of window or, better yet, an observatory that gives a new perspective on the text. Their organizational mechanisms allow the text to be taken apart and recomposed.

This oscillation between fascination with geometry and reference to the bodily image and figure brings to mind the case of Robortello (who was also a friend of Castelvetro) discussed above (p. 27); here, once again, the models used for visualization in the manuscript take different shapes than those used in the printed book. This oscillation, however, is the result of an ancient tradition: it is commonly known, for example, that the tree, one of the images most used in the Middle Ages for classification, mnemonics, and mysticism, is merely a tangible, decorative version of the diagram.[39]

A certain flavour of the allegorical and mnemonic procedures so dear to the medieval mind can also be observed in some of the pages of Castelvetro's *Poetica*. We see, for example, the passage in which he explains the model of the *six carts* that he uses to visualize the types of change in fortune that can take place in the characters of tragedy. He has used, he assures us, a division much more wide-ranging (and therefore more useful and exhaustive) than that used by Aristotle. His six carts have the task of making us understand both the entire network of relations that can be created in tragedy among the different moral types of characters that undergo a change and also their subsequent reactions and passions.

> Now, to thoroughly understand this subject which was proposed and imperfectly described by Aristotle, let us imagine that there are six carts; the pole of three of the carts is Nτὸ φιλάνθρωπον or 'human pleasure'; the tail of these carts is τὴν εὐαριστιάν or 'thanking God'; the pole of the other three is τὸ μισάνθρωπον or 'human displeasure,' while the tail is *dirae*, or 'curses.' The bed of the first cart of the first three will be a saintly person passing from a state of misery to that of happiness; and its right wheel will be hope and its left wheel felicitation. The bed of the second cart will be an evil person passing from happiness to misery ... (*Poetica*, I, 367–368)

There is no need to continue: one can clearly see from the model in the passage cited here that everything rests – like the wheel of the *Phaedra* – on the logic of opposites. But the model, which is geometric by nature, remains in the background, while the corporeal image of the six carts comes to the foreground as if it were a parade that visualizes and celebrates the structure of tragedy.[40]

Again the process used here by Castelvetro has a medieval flavour. The pole of his carts is pleasure, the wheel is hope, etc. The carts recall a particular type of medieval image in which writing is used to label (and allegorize) the different parts. We can see, for example, a knight from the thirteenth century (plate IV) who combats the vices with hope as his helmet, perseverance as his lance, good will as his horse, and so on.[41] As in Castelvetro's carts, allegory, classification, and memory techniques are closely related; they come together to build this sort of puzzle, which in turn becomes the image.

Among the more interesting passages are those in which Castelvetro introduces visual models in the text. Here he expresses a highly lucid, yet complex, awareness of the meaning, function, and origin of his methodology. Side by side with the themes commonly stressed by other authors (some of whom we have already encountered, as well as some whom we will meet later on), we find in these passages a rather personal tone. Castelvetro believes visual instrumentation to be part of a systematic search intended to bring to light the *art* of the word. In other words, it is an attempt to achieve clear control over the mechanisms of rhetoric and poetics: this art does not limit itself to merely describing the text but becomes, as he writes in his commentary on *Rhetorica ad Herennium*, the 'science of the reason why' (p. 28; folio 11).

From Castelvetro's perspective, diagrams and other techniques for visualization mean giving the reader a handy and efficient tool for comprehension of the text. They highlight connections and distinctions and thus allow for an understanding of the text that is at once unified and detailed. This is possible, on the one hand, because the model comes about through a rigorous process of definition and articulation of the material, and, on the other hand, because the model photographs that process and is based on an ordered organization of the results. 'Thus, all together, there are ninety-five of them,' writes Castelvetro on the 'types of resemblance,' or the different ways in which poetry achieves mimesis; 'but in order that it may be understood, *fully* and *distinctly*, I will arrange them *in order, separately as well as grouped together*' (*Poetica*, I, 66).

The strength of the diagram lies in its capacity to reproduce the structure of the cognitive process as well as the structure of the object itself; we have seen how the image of the grid is used, and how it is unfolded in great detail 'using the proper proportions' (*Poetica*, I, 341). It is for precisely this reason that the diagram becomes the ideal instrument of communication between sensible reality and intellectual reality. It satisfies the needs of the body's eye as well as the mind's eye. For example, the tree used to visualize the different causes of the suffering which afflicts characters of tragedy is introduced in the following manner: 'but in order for that which has been said to be better *understood*, and virtually *subjected to the sense of sight*, it will be represented in the figure below' (*Poetica*, I, 376). And Castelvetro says of the tree illustrating the different *figurae verborum* in the same text: 'Now, as you can see with your own eyes, there are many places that our author has not yet filled with his examples since they were unknown to him' (I, 122).

Here another characteristic of the diagram becomes clear: not only does it serve as an interface – to use a computer metaphor – between body and mind but, by reproducing the totalizing scheme of possible definitions and divisions, it also highlights the shortcomings of the text in question. It thus shows the gap between the true science of rhetoric and the practical application of its teachings. For the very reason that it visualizes the deep structure of the text and draws a map of its possibilities, the diagram thus allows the reader to see even that which is still missing in the rhetorical and poetical elaboration of the text. It spotlights even the places that have remained empty. The same thing was supposed to happen in the Biblioteca Marciana once the books had been reorganized and rearranged by the Accademia Veneziana (see ch. 1, p. 16).

All of its characteristics make the diagram a highly efficient instrument of memory; 'but in order to secure each thing in memory ... one ought to make a grid ... in which all of the things contained can be seen, together and by themselves,' writes Castelvetro in the presentation of the grid which we have already examined from his commentary on *Rhetorica ad Herennium* (p. 16, folio 10). 'Now, in order that the things stated above can be better understood and deposited in the memory, we will gather them together in just a few words and we will present them as in a figure' – this is how the tree of the different ways in which characters are denominated in the various literary genres is introduced in his *Poetica* (I, 271).

In effect, Castelvetro believes that the use of diagrams and the other tools of visualization is the essence of the art of memory, and here he is in full agreement with the tradition of European thinkers who hold the questions of memory and methodology to be closely related. At the same time, the section of his commentary on the *Rhetorica ad Herennium* dedicated to natural and artificial memory gives us a picture that is in certain aspects more restless and complicated than we may have expected. As is common in his writings, Castelvetro takes a strong, polemical position from the outset. Contrary to an age-old tradition, he denies that artificial memory can aid natural memory, and he gives it a purely subordinate function. Natural memory, 'encumbered by many acquired things,' can entrust some of them to 'artificial memory by which natural memory is virtually recreated and will be able to learn and store many other things. But this is not an aid to natural memory; it is, rather, a way of avoiding that it is overladen and giving it space to renew itself' (p. 94, folio 65). If this hierarchy is not maintained, the very nature of memory will be weakened. It is like someone accustomed to riding a horse, writes Castelvetro, who is unable to face travel on foot.

Castelvetro holds that artificial memory uses the same tools as natural memory. For the two most important ones (that is, reduction of the things to be remembered to a limited number and order), logic and dialectics play an essential role: 'the art of reducing many things to a small number has been taught above ... and those who have knowledge of predicates are capable of doing so. There are many who discuss order, and especially Rudolf Agricola in the third book of his *Inventione*' (p. 97, folio 67). The explicit allusion to Agricola's *De inventione dialectica* is very important, and, as we will see below, it helps us to place Castelvetro's position beside Orazio Toscanella's.

Castelveltro becomes more obscure when he discusses the possibility of using a different manner of retracing recollections in artificial memory – a different manner than that used in natural memory. It 'can have many guises, as many as the number of representational arts (of which Aristotle makes some mention in the *Poetics*); and there are many more, if we consider them merely in their parts, because many things can resemble a part that are not able to resemble the whole,' he writes. 'Many songs and sonnets have been woven by Petrarch in this way, and it is a lovely and wondrous thing. But because the authors who have spoken on this art have limited themselves to one manner alone, that is to say, the use of places and images,' I too, Castelvetro concludes, will do the same (p. 98, folio 67). There follow some remarks on the greater utility of images of memory that are actually visible – like paintings positioned in different places – and on the utility of allegorical images that are capable of giving bodily shape to abstract concepts, or of condensing a multiplicity of meanings, and, consequently, parts of a discourse.

Although the art of memory is only briefly discussed in his text, Castelvetro's concept of it is much broader than that traditionally found in the treatises. His is an art of memory that knows how to exploit all the resources offered by the 'representational arts' (those in which vision, bodily movement, and harmony come into play, as he says in his *Poetica*, I, 26; II, 352); and also an art of memory that can control that play of similarities of which Petrarch's *Canzoniere* provides such a rich collection.

Alongside the diagram and an art of memory based on an organized, rational map of knowledge, there appears the notion of another kind of art of memory, one capable of influencing the senses and exploiting all the visual possibilities related to representation. The first example of resemblance that comes to Castelvetro's mind is, tellingly, that of things that 'can resemble a part,' while 'they are not able to resemble the whole.' As is apparent in the section of his commentary on the *Rhetorica ad Herennium* dedicated to the *figurae verborum*, Castelvetro is fascinated by the capacity of certain rhetorical figures to play off the relationship of the part to the whole, to evoke, as if in an illusionistic game, the whole by putting a detail in the forefront, or to break down and split it up, as in a game of diffraction. But we can discern how Castelvetro unites his predilection for diagrams with his interest (much less clearly articulated) in a completely artificial art of memory that relies entirely upon similarity and illusionistic effects. At the centre of his thought there remains, however, the problem of *sight* and the way in which perception, representation, and the creation of images are developed between body and psyche.

Francesco Patrizi

We have already mentioned in chapter 1 (p. 22) some of Francesco Patrizi's restless intellectual vicissitudes. Now we will see how the lure of the new dialectics and the tools of visualization by which it is characterized are present on various levels in his undertakings. In 1573 Patrizi worked for a short time as a publisher and produced, among other books, a work by Silvio Belli, mathematician, architect, one of the founding members of the Accademia Olimpica in Vicenza, and a collaborator of Palladio. Belli's book, entitled *Della proportione et proportionalità communi passioni del quanto* [On proportion and proportionality, common passions of the quantum], promises 'true and easy intelligence of arithmetic, geometry, and all the sciences and arts.' The promise is guaranteed, it is claimed, by the discovery of a plain and easy method based on natural order. All of this is actualized in a large diagrammatic table. As Luciano Artese has shown, this complex tree was probably influenced by Ramist logic.[42]

Patrizi himself was deeply interested in the new directions of dialectics. This can be seen clearly in the various and troubled stages of his long reflection on the problems of language, rhetoric, and poetics. His dialogues of 1560 and 1562, *Della historia* [On history] and *Della retorica* [On rhetoric], offer a systematic demolition of many of the myths held dear in the humanist tradition. At the same time Patrizi tries to outline the possible bases of a 'heavenly rhetoric,' a 'mathematical science' of language.[43] It would have to be based on the divine imprint that has been left in man, and it would have to construct a universal model capable of reflecting the structure of things, their organization and proportions. Analogous themes – as we have already seen (p. 12) – are stressed in the *Discorso*, or preface, of Luca Contile's *Rime* [Lyric poems], published in 1560. The structures of human discourse, it states, imitate the structures of the cosmos, and consequently the creative development of divine ideas. The problem is then to elaborate a method that will allow us to capture and imitate these structures. The road to follow, according to Patrizi, is to construct a new rhetoric that utilizes the new *Topica* elaborated by Rudolf Agricola and Giulio Camillo, but at the same time extends and multiplies the components.

We must remember that Patrizi is the enthusiastic publisher of Camillo's *Topica*, and that he has extolled Camillo as the man who breached the ancient boundaries of rhetoric and gave it a new, universal dimension: 'he expanded it in such a way that it has been extended throughout all the places of the theatre of the world.'[44]

It is indicative that Patrizi's research – even his work in poetics – is followed with such interest and sympathy by a personage like Theodor Zwinger of Basel, a doctor and philosopher trained in Ramist logic.[45] Patrizi's vast work in poetics – which he left incomplete and, in large part, unpublished – results from an attempt to use topical places and visualization systematically in order to construct a model representing all the possible forms of poetry. Patrizi holds that poetics is merely one part of the science of language. It thus has a universal dimension and cannot be encompassed by the limits of any system of literary genres, nor can it be delimited by criteria of content. Its essential characteristic is fiction making, that is, the capacity to reshape the subject matter and produce new forms. The ways in which imagination acts, Patrizi believes, can be described, quantified, and represented visually. The task of the poet is to produce wonderment. His playing field lies somewhere between two opposite orders, the believable and the unbelievable. The poetic universe can thus be represented as the outcome of a combinatorial game of elements derived from these two topical sources. Patrizi actually arrives at a calculation of 33,600 possible combinations, but he immediately points out that this number could grow infinitely if other topical places are allowed in the game: the places, used previously only for dialectic argumentation, that 'Giulio Camillo, with uncommon insight, has accommodated to figurative oratorial and poetical locutions, and we ... now use ... as the source of poetic marvel and poetic wonder.'[46]

The central parts of Patrizi's poetics are accompanied by trees, tables, and diagrams. These are intended to give visible form to a logical model of all possible poems. This model can be infinitely extended – in part, because it has secretly been cross-referenced to the deep structure of the cosmos. Patrizi writes:

> It can truthfully be said that all of the principal headings and all of their subordinates are present in each other, and each one in all the others, and all of them in each one, and the ancient dogma is renewed in them: that all things are in all others, and here is the place of that wondrous mixture taught to us by Plato in *Philebus*. (*Deca dogmatica universale* [Dogmatic decade of the universe], III, 222)

Because of its universal scope, this model indicates not only the places that are filled (that is, the possibilities that have been fulfilled) but also the empty places and the poems that have not yet been written. And here, beyond the use of diagrams, lies an important point of contact between Patrizi and the man who had been the principal object of criticism and polemic in his *Poetica*: Ludovico Castelvetro. Regardless of their constrasting positions, they share this common ground. It is interesting to remember here that, as Aldo Stella has shown, the Venetian tribunal of the Inquisition was concerned by the friendship between Patrizi and a certain Castelvetro, heretic and exile.[47]

4 Orazio Toscanella: The Intellectual as Teacher and Publisher

One of the characters whom we have already encountered, Orazio Toscanella (ca 1520–1579), allows us to observe in detail the context in which the techniques of visualization belonged: to see, that is, the questions from which they originated, how they functioned, and the myths that they called into play and helped to cultivate.[48] For this reason, we shall dwell at some length on Toscanella and his numerous books, copies of which can still be found in rare-book collections throughout the world.

During the course of his life Toscanella followed two professions that greatly influenced each other and often overlapped: he was a preceptor, that is, a schoolteacher who prepared young students for the university, but he was also a strong collaborator of the principal Venetian publishers. His editorial production was directly related to his professional life. Many of his works were actual scholastic manuals, which took advantage of his didactic experience, and which he then put to the test in the classroom. Toscanella achieved a certain fame: he published books abroad and became a member of the Accademia della Fratta, collaborating on some important collections of lyric poems. All of this, however, was not enough to guarantee him sufficient economic security to protect him from the accidents of fate. The dedications of his books and his letters make constant reference to his personal misfortunes and to the aid that he has received or been denied. Living on the earnings from teaching and publishing thus appears to have been a risky business – a treacherous and tortuous road, rather than a reliable situation. So it is easy to understand why Toscanella sought help at court in the 1570s: although his appeals to the Gonzagas went unheard, his links with the Medicis proved to be more fruitful, first with Duke Cosimo, and then, and most importantly, with Francesco I.

In each of Toscanella's scholastic manuals there is a section reserved for his dreams and frustrations as a schoolteacher: this is the part dedicated to the students' exercises. His *Institutioni grammaticali volgari et latine* [Vernacular and Latin grammatical constructs] (Venice: Giolito 1567), is a true treasure in this sense. A passage intended for translation from Italian into Latin, for example, is dedicated to a proposal for a sort of scholastic field trip to Paolo Giovio's Museum, which evidently was already in rather precarious conditions. We have to hurry, writes Toscanella, 'because few will experience the dignity of such a machine. Those who come to read these memoirs will not see [it] with their own eyes' (p. 299). There are also complaints about the students' behaviour: disruptive, distracted, lazy, more interested in women and entertainment than in their studies. The students believe that 'study causes a man to rot, while having fun helps to prolong life' (p. 298). Toscanella's celebration of the nobility of letters is closely related to his self-promotion and his financial aspirations. He tends to dwell on the time and energy he has dedicated to his studies and on the importance of a strong humanist preparation, even for a young member of a good family. At the same time he complains of the fact that his salary does not grow in proportion to the services rendered: 'precepts, every day I cause you to increase your knowledge, but you never increase your reward to me' (p. 207). He makes it clear that any kind of compensation will not go unappreciated: 'the students brought me two lambs; maybe I will also get a suit of double silk' (p. 355). He also hopes for legal action against those who have inflated the price of books:

> those who appraise these books at no less than twenty ducats appraise
> them for more than their worth. They are worth no more than fifteen

ducats. It is true that those who want to save money buy books from the booksellers and not at resale, because at resale the books are always sold at a price higher than that originally paid. If the law fined those who resell books, they might not sell them so dearly.   (P. 205)

His dream of social elevation and public appreciation of the value of the literary profession is even expressed in a story: the pitiful case of the young and beautiful Elena, who has married Antonio, 'an educated but poor young man. For this reason, she has been beaten by her brother, and the doctor fears she will lose her life' (p. 229). The conclusion of the tale – a text intended for translation into Latin – is that justice will be served when the brother has been punished and exiled.

The humanist theme of the nobility of letters has thus found a new formulation. The study of literature offers the poor man of the chance to rise socially ('and it is no less clear that many poor men have begun to work in letters and the world remains full of amazement,' writes Toscanella in the dedication of his *Discorsi cinque* [Five discourses], published in 1575);[49] while to the rich man the study of literature offers another card to play in terms of his career and public image. At the same time Toscanella's twofold professional experience brings the scholar's quantitative condition, so to speak, to the forefront: the themes of the time spent over the books, the paper used, the energy needed to study, to write, to teach, to extract the secrets of the books, and to reformulate them, in lectures and in writing, in an easy and effective manner.

The theme of hard work sometimes inspires heroic tones, as in the dedication of his commentary on Cicero's *Pro Milone* (*Oratio Ciceronis pro T. Annio Milone examinata* [Venice: Pietro Franceschi 1576]). Toscanella writes that he has always tried to make himself useful to scholars, 'and the toll of this labour has caused me to fall victim to an incurable disease. And, in any case, no rest has followed this labour. I have decided indeed to exhale my last breath before interrupting the labour of writing.'[50] His self-portrait in other works is a bit more realistic, as in his *Dittionario volgare et latino* [Italian and Latin dictionary] (Venice: Comin da Trino 1568). Under the entry 'Agricoltura' [Agriculture] Toscanella promises an Italian translation of the ancients' reflections on the subject, 'provided that the greed of the booksellers does not stop me ... May God help me, because I write what I write to earn my living, not for the glory' (folio 29v).

Beginning in 1574, the incurable disease mentioned in the dedication to the *Oratio Ciceronis pro Milone* becomes much more real in his letters to the grand duke of Tuscany. Here Toscanella gives on account of the various stages of his sickness and his fear that he will end up in a public hospital, as well as a description – perhaps the most unsettling element for us – of the doctors' treatments: according to a letter of 25 April 1578, they had lanced 'four hundred blisters full of burning liquid.'[51]

In Toscanella's writings the traditional themes of honour and glory thus give way here and there to another dimension of his life: the voice of his body, his illness, his fatigue, and fear. In the face of these hardships, the question of his finances takes centre stage as a response and exorcism of his fears. The examples used to fill the divisions of the different rhetorical trees become accordingly much more interesting. Among the 'trees of virtue' contained in the *Armonia di tutti i principali retori* [Harmony of all the principal masters of rhetoric] (Venice: Giovanni Varisco 1569), he uses the following example to illustrate the tree of magnificence (figure 12): 'Libraries, lecture halls, and colleges built at great cost. And also great spending for printing and typesetting, etc.' (folio 35v). Under the heading of 'magnificence' Toscanella gives an ideal collocation to his main pursuits in life: teaching and publishing.

Toscanella was an industrious collaborator of the most important Venetian printers. It is easy to understand why he found Gabriele Giolito to be his most intelligent interlocutor, the most interested in his work and most professionally honest. Toscanella's praise of Giolito fills his dedication to Giolito's son, Giovanni, in the *Institutioni grammaticali*: the father is presented as the embodiment of an ideal coexistence of honesty and utility, the perfect balance between the cult of letters and financial compensation. Gabriele Giolito, writes Toscanella, 'has always loved scholars in a singular fashion, and he has always valued the study of letters. Not only has he always hosted erudite men in his home and paid tribute to the most famous of them in Italy. He has also spent an almost infinite amount of money in printing many fine, learned works with a refined, graceful typeface,' works that are as unique as the phoenix in Giolito's device. Giolito has also solicited and promoted new works. It was he, writes Toscanella, who urged him to write the *Institutioni grammaticali*: 'I was happy to oblige, not only because he had courteously paid me, but, moreover, because I could see him burn with the desire to let scholars of this profession benefit through this work.'

The happy balance reached in the relationship between Giolito and Toscanella would not last for long. A long period of great difficulties is

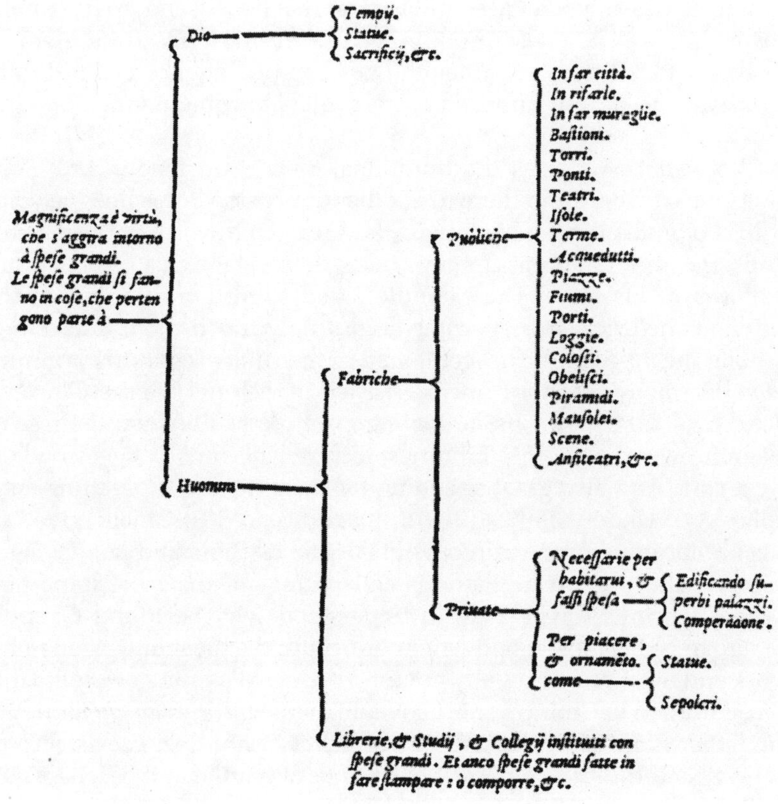

12 The tree of Magnificence, from Orazio Toscanella, *Armonia di tutti i principali retori* (Venice: Giovanni Varisco 1569)

reported in Toscanella's will, written in January 1579. For example, in order to publish the *Essercitii di Aftonio Sofista* [Exercises from Aphthonius the Sophist], an author popular in the schools of the time, in 1578, Toscanella borrowed money from one of his chambermaids. His will orders the executors to return the money to the woman, and he also urges them to publish his *Storia universale* [Universal history]. But his plans proved to be overly ambitious: after Toscanella's death his son-in-law wrote that his inheritance was not sufficient even to pay off Toscanella's debts.

5 Against Pedants and in Support of the Vernacular and Useful, Helpful Books

The theme of utility played a fundamental role in the making of Toscanella's books. He was keenly interested in producing works that offered the general public a quick and simple path to literary writing and knowledge in general, a path easy to verify and reuse. His interest in the usefulness of his books was accompanied by a heated polemic against the pedants. In the introduction to Agricola's *De inventione dialettica* [On dialectic invention] (Venice: Giovanni Bariletti 1561), Toscanella writes:

> Do not let yourselves be deprived of this book by those who say that we must go back to the most ancient of sources. They do so because they have travelled those long roads, and they would like to be the ones to lead us down them. We need authors who teach us and not authors who, in order to show off their science (which is actually very profound), entangle our brains in such a way that we are forced to go back to the oracle of Apollo in order to free them. What does it matter that there are authors more learned that Rudolph if they yet teach us less? Why should we go back to the most ancient of sources if only to come back all muddied?   (Rudolf Agricola, *Della inventione dialettica tradotto da Oratio Toscanella ... et tirato in tavole dal medesimo di capo in capo con alcune annotationi utilissime e affronti importantissimi* [On dialectic invention, translated by Orazio Toscanella ... and illustrated by him in tables, from chapter to chapter, with some highly useful annotations and important comparisons])

What gives a particular flavour to Toscanella's polemic against the pedants is his faith in the new tools that help to breach the arrogance of his more conservative colleagues. Those new instruments are the use of the vernacular (that is, Italian), modern typographic technology, and the new directions in the fields of logic and rhetoric.

His works written in the early 1560s best illustrate how Toscanella sees himself as part of a movement to establish and expand the use of vernacular. To those who continue to favour the exclusive use of Latin (at least in some fields of writing), Toscanella responds not by citing historical or theoretical arguments but by pointing to a widely recognized fact: there already exists a vast number of books written in Italian, both new works and translations of earlier texts. Toscanella himself has contributed to the growing use of the vernacular in the fields of science and philosophy by translating works of mathematics and astronomy.[52]

Toscanella's preference for Italian over Latin is closely related to his techniques for presenting texts. Whether it is a rhetorical treatise or a literary text, he applies the same process of reducing the material to trees that we have seen in publications from the Accademia Veneziana as well as in other authors' works on rhetoric. It is as a result of these procedures that Toscanella is able to cover new ground in the dissemination of knowledge; while the use of the vernacular makes the texts accessible to a new and expanded audience, the instrumentation offers the public even more possibilities. All of these reasons are listed, for example, in Toscanella's introduction to *Retorica di M. Tullio Cicerone Gaio Herennio ridotta in alberi con tanto ordine e con essempi così chari et ben collocati, che ciascuno potrà da sé con mirabile facilità apprenderla* [Rhetorica a C. Herennium by M. Tullius Cicero, reduced into trees, with such organization and with examples so clear and well-positioned that it can be studied with amazing facility] (Venice: Lodovico Avanzo 1561). The reduction into trees, the organization, and the examples – 'so clear and well-positioned' (that is, positioned in the correct *places*) – allow the reader to view the components of the text with pertinent, and up-to-date, instructions for use: examples taken from poetry and from contemporary events – from Ariosto's *Orlando furioso* or from the accounts of the conflict between Venice and the Turks – indicate a modern use for the treatise on rhetoric that had been attributed to Cicero. 'It can be studied with amazing facility,' promises the title. By analogy, it could be thought of as something like a computer program with the user's instructions incorporated into the system itself.

To have the components of the text laid out before one, conveniently organized for recomposition – Toscanella believes that this is the road to follow. This is the tool that allows the user to expand his capacity for memory efficiently. Toscanella guarantees that the method works, even in its simplest form, that is, when it does not resort to diagrams but limits itself to an alphabetical organization of the important segments of the text. Take, for example, *Modo di studiare le pistole famigliari di M. Tullio Cicerone dove s'insegna la copia, il numero, l'elocutione, la materia et la varietà con molte altre cose necessarie all'eloquenza, con regola et con facilità maravigliosa per ordine d'alfabeto* [How to study Cicero's *Epistulae ad Familiares*, in which the copiousness, the rhythm, the expression, the subjects, variations, and many other things necessary to eloquence are taught with classifications and amazing facility in alphabetical order] (Venice: Giolito

1560). Toscanella writes that he has constantly used this method:

> because by listing all the words under the principal chapters, it was possible to break down the epistle and make it easier to consider the connections and references separately. A man forgets many things, or at least some things, when forced to read continuously, but this way, by *seeing the anatomy of every word*, he can discern every last detail without any trouble and thus he can study it diligently.   (P. 31)

That which is under and inside the human body is rendered visible in a theatre of anatomy; similarly – this analogy was also dear to Giulio Camillo – it is possible to dissect texts and penetrate their compactness. The mechanisms of their structures can be forced out and made visible. Doing this – with the help of the manuscript page, or the printed page, which enormously increases the scale – allows one to extract the text from the blurry, unitary flow of reading. Just as writing has extracted the word from the *continuum* of oral communication, made it visible, and made it possible to dissect and analyse it, Toscanella wants his instruments to reproduce the logic of that process by disproportionately multiplying the possibilities of the reader's reception. In the dedication to *Concetti et forme di Cicerone, di Boccaccio, del Bembo, delle lettere di diversi et d'altri ... raccolti a beneficio di color che si dilettano di scrivere lettere dotte e leggiadre, tutti posti sotto i suoi proprii generi in ordine di alfabeto* [Concepts and forms in Cicero, Boccaccio, Bembo, and the letters of other different authors ... collected for the benefit of those who enjoy writing erudite and beautiful letters, all placed under the appropriate genres in alphabetical order] (Venice: Lodovico Avanzo 1560), Toscanella writes that this work is 'worthy of the eyes and ears of the learned,' besides being 'highly useful to all scholars of our most exquisite language [that is, Italian].'

To break down the text, to lay bare its structure, to make visible the instruments he himself has used – this is the great advance made by Toscanella with respect both to earlier translators from Latin into Italian and to those who have limited themselves to descriptive analyses of the exemplary texts.

Toscanella believes that topics and their visualization make it possible to penetrate the text at a more abstract and universal level while at the same time bringing it closer to the senses: making it almost tactile but most importantly making it visible. In his *Oratio Ciceronis pro Milone* he writes that Robortello's *De artificio dicendi* (discussed above, p. 27), 'as if using its finger, has pointed to the best and surest way of all.' At the same time, Toscanella uses the anatomical analogy again to associate the theme of deeper analytical penetration with that of vision: 'the more minutely they dissect the human body, the deeper their knowledge; similarly, those who dissect orations piece by piece will know them better' (p. 5).[53] Besides the trees found here and there throughout the text, Toscanella loves to use a single, large tree – unitary, analytical, logical, and even palpable – for the visualization of his teachings. *Armonia di tutti i principali retori*, published in 1569, for example, is accompanied by a large 'table in which scholars can see all of the elements of rhetoric at a glance.'

The use of the human body as a model, evoked by the reference to anatomy, is an expression of yet another essential component of Toscanella's way of thinking and the processes he follows: he perceives the literary tradition as a single, large organism. He believes texts in Latin and texts in Italian belong to the same whole: they are part of a treasury, a sort of depository of material and recyclable solutions. A good example is found in a work that we have already mentioned, *Concetti et forme di Cicerone, di Boccaccio, del Bembo, delle lettere di diversi et d'altri* ... Under the various rubrics that group the material in alphabetical order (for example, 'accusar' [to accuse], 'allegrarsi' [to be happy], 'consolare' [to comfort], and so on), Toscanella accumulates textual fragments taken from the most reliable of sources. Like the editions of the canonical authors (both Italian and Latin), the anthologies of new literary works have become one of the most successful editorial products of the day. In order to enrich the survey, Toscanella adds examples that he has penned himself. He thus outlines a repertory filtered through other repertories such as Geronimo Garimberto's *Concetti* [Concepts] and Aldo Manuzio Jr's *Eleganze* [Elegance].[54]

The literary tradition – Latin and Italian – is thus unified by a practice of imitative reappropriation of the text that varies and *perfects* it in an increasingly artifical direction. In the spaces between the texts, however, there are some reflections of a more general nature that tend to place the unity of the literary tradition into a cycle of human vicissitudes, thus enclosing the treasury of words in a circle of things. In the *Discorso del tradurre* [Essay on translation] (Venice: Pietro Franceschi 1575), for example, Toscanella maintains that it is possible to translate Latin texts into Italian word for word, with absolute fidelity to all of the author's stylistic choices. In a polemic against those who have denied such possibilities he writes:

I do not know how they have the courage to say these things because the world ought to be renewed, and all things that the ancients embraced with words ought to be extinct; and in their place there ought to be other things, of a different genre and type, and consequently it would then be necessary to find new words to express them.   (P. 30)

There are also some interesting references in *Gioie historiche aggiunte alla prima parte delle Vite di Plutarco* [Historical joys added to the first part of Plutarch's *Lives*] (Venice: Giolito 1567). In one of the rubrics of the second part (dedicated to chronology) there is a list of historical figures who 'garnered celebrated fame for themselves in 1514' (folio 119r). Together with Camillo, we find here Peter Ramus, Erasmus, Thomas More, and Guillaume Postel. This is a rather unorthodox list for the end of the 1560s, and highly significant: reformers and utopianists are grouped together with those who have committed themselves to the renewal of logic and rhetoric and the study of new ways to master thought and words.

A little later in the text, after his discussion of the various opinions on the chronology of the world, Toscanella writes: 'I am of the opinion (provided that my opinion is not in contradiction with the Holy Roman Church and its censors, to whom I have always submitted all of my writings) ... that the world will last until Saturn has completely finished its course' (folio 121r). Through the manuals and the erudite repertories the view has opened onto the stars, and the astrological theme of the cycles of the world can be seen from below. In the end it is the identity of the cosmic cycle that guarantees the unity of the literary tradition and the possibility to know it and reappropriate it through the tools of rhetoric and dialectics, which are capable of crossing through the diversity of language and the barriers of time unscathed.

6 The Labyrinth of Words and the Order of the Library

The smell of the library permeates the corpus of Toscanella's work; each of his books is the result of his effort to master the heritage contained in books and to make it available in order to write yet more books. The index, the repertory, and the apparatus have a dual function for Toscanella: they serve as a model in which elements of 'anatomy' can be ordered, and at the same time they are the key to the penetration of books, a map that guides the user through the forest of words handed down by others. Italy and Europe were plagued by the need for efficient cataloguing tools; Toscanella enjoyed a certain amount of fame abroad, and he utilized and cited Italian as well as foreign dictionaries and repertories by scholars like Ambrogio Calepino (1435–1511), Mario Nizolio (1498–1566), and Joannes Ravisius Textor [Jean Texier] (ca 1480–1524). The criteria for the selection of material, of course, are not always clear and reliable. One of the more important examples is the *Dittionario volgare et latino* [Latin and Italian dictionary] (Venice: Comin da Trino 1568). Toscanella says that it embraces 'the best of the handbooks in a concise fashion,' but, besides its gross oversights and lopsidedness, it betrays a basic uncertainty in the classification of material and the character and dimensions of the standards of measurement with which the anatomy of the text is to be captured. The various entries thus create a network of information that could be extended at will. For example, each letter of the alphabet is followed by its meaning and abbreviation in Roman epigraphs and the form by which it is portrayed in the figurative alphabets of Johannes Romberch's art of memory (figure 13):[55] 'A: those who belong to the profession of artificial memory customarily use the following images instead of the A – a compass and a three-legged ladder' (folio 1r); names of plants and animals evoke the devices and the hieroglyphics in which the corresponding images appear; the nouns and verbs that refer to literary *topoi* become containers for the corresponding poetic 'splendours,' either through quotations or through references to other repertories. The entry 'aggiorna' [(to) dawn], for example, makes the following reference: 'If you want to see the various ways in which Virgil described the dawn, read that short work entitled *Solis ortus* that is usually included in the Virgils *in folio* together with the *Aeneid*, and you will see a great abundance [of examples] that has something of the divine' (folio 27r). If you want to see, it goes on, the figures of other poets (Ovid, Lucan, Statius, etc.), you have to consult Textor's *Officina*, and in case you do not have a copy, 'look at the table *Aurorae descriptio* or *ortus diei descriptio*, and you will find miraculous descriptions full of sweetness' (folio 27v).

Not only is the book placed – theoretically and physically – in the library (in the sense that it is born there, from the dismantling of the books to which it continuously refers), but the book itself tends to become the *whole* library: it is an open container, generally ready to absorb all other books. The dictionary, as we have seen, is expanding in the direction of the encyclopedia and the iconological repertory. It also becomes a pretext for publicizing friends, booksellers, or printers, for promoting works by the author himself – those in print or forthcom-

13 The first part of a mnemonic alphabet, from Iohannes Romberch,
Congestorium artificiosae memoriae (Venice: Melchiorre Sessa 1553)

ing – or even for praising the beautiful women of Venice. But the same
can be said generally of all of Toscanella's works. He has spent his
whole life writing the same book without ever leaving, as Anton
Francesco Doni would have said, the wheel of the alphabet (or the
wheel of books that Agostino Ramelli invented for his *Diverse et artificiose
machine* [Different rhetoric machines]; figure 14) and without ever mastering all of its possible combinations.[56]

In Toscanella's relentless dedication to illustrative texts and an *anatomy*
destined never to be completed there is a sort of melancholy obsession,
like that of Erasmus' Nosoponus, or that which impels the alchemist to
burn the midnight oil. 'Those who practise the art of metals, who
change the substance of one metal into another' – this is Toscanella's
definition of the alchemist in his *Dittionario volgare et latino*, and he then
adds: 'I have many ancient, woundrous manuscripts of this profession'
(folio 33v).

The theme of hard work, however, is generally associated with praise
of the multiple resources that have been made available by Toscanella's
techniques. In *Modo di studiare le pistole di Cicerone* he writes:

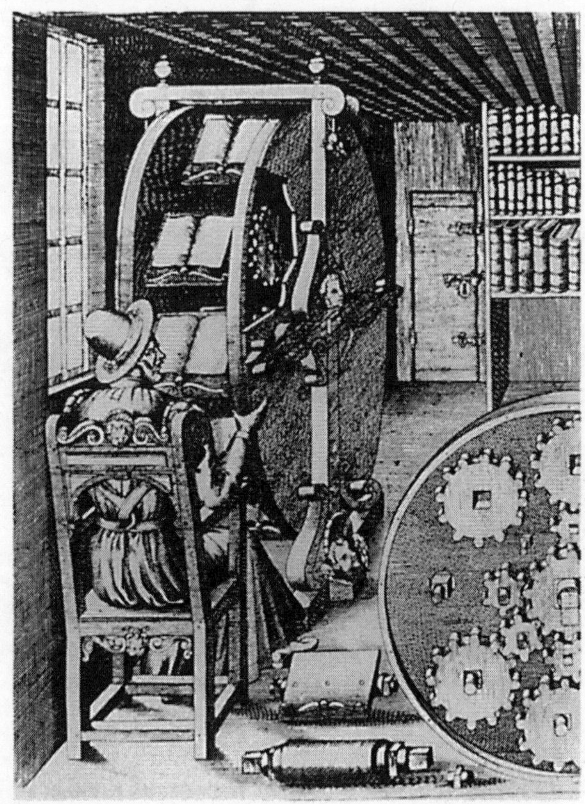

14 The wheel of books, from Agostino Ramelli, *Diverse et artificiose macchine* (Paris: in casa dell'autore 1588)

> When I was learning to write variations, I used these rules and recommendations, given here on the subject of variation, to write Ciceronian epistles in Latin and Italian, from top to bottom, each different in more than a hundred ways, and each greatly different and diverse from each other. (P. 186)

From Latin to Italian, and vice versa – Toscanella performs in direct competition with Cicero himself and shows the Latin orator the other ways in which he could have written his works.

The section in *Discorso del tradurre* dedicated to Boccaccio is also very important. The elegance of the prose of his tales, writes Toscanella, is so great that he must have 'first written them in Latin, and then translated them into Italian, by making the translation of each word correspond to the nature and place where it had been positioned in Latin' (in *Discorsi cinque*, folio 34r). He claims that Domenico Venier has shown him some of Boccaccio's autographs that would furnish proof of this rather bold hypothesis. In any case, even if it were not so, concludes Toscanella, no one can deny that Bembo made his letters great by imitating the *numerus*, or rhythm, that Cicero had used in his epistles.

Even if Boccaccio did not translate himself from Latin into Italian in the *Decameron*, it *could* have been true: besides the example of Bembo, this is proved by the fact that Toscanella has translated and rewritten the texts of Cicero in Italian and Latin. The models used in rhetorical and scholastic exercises thus tend entirely to encompass and project themselves in the modes of literary creation.[57]

7 Rhetoric Machines

This tendency can be seen clearly in the many passages of Toscanella's works in which he celebrates the apparatus as a simple collection of words, syntactic connections, and rhetorical figures.

As we have seen, Toscanella teaches that the easiest and surest way to master the treasures of eloquence is to dissect the text and then organize it alphabetically using rubrics or places. A good part of Toscanella's work is the fruit of this meticulous labour. The scope and the utility of the procedure tend, however, to expand: from an efficient instrument for reading and reappropriating an author, it becomes a component of the way in which an author's own work is conceived. The projection of method onto the generative processes of the texts studied is fairly frequent in *Bellezze del Furioso di M. Lodovico Ariosto* [The beauty of Ludovico Ariosto's *Furioso*] (Venice: Pietro Franceschi 1574). In his commentary on Ariosto's poem, Toscanella tries his hand at a close analysis of the orations pronounced by the various characters, and the result is not completely devoid of insight. The knowledge of rhetoric displayed by Ariosto on different occasions has only one explanation according to Toscanella: Ariosto needed to devise a strong apparatus for the orations, a preset apparatus that he could exploit to its utmost. This idea quickly takes on greater significance: 'it can be seen, by those who observe carefully,' writes Toscanella, 'that [Ariosto] had created an alphabetical apparatus of descriptions of beauty, laments, narration, various events, and similar things by imitating most of the better poets; and he did not leave out any poet that he had read, and, thus, depending on the occasion, he used and honoured each one'

(p. 278). The knowledge displayed in the description of a naval battle (canto 39, stanza 80), for example, is a result of the fact that Ariosto 'had placed in his apparatus every type of boat, instrument, and term related to the above-mentioned art, under the chapter on Navy' (p. 282). All that a master of rhetoric like Toscanella has to do is carry out the inverse process and extract the words listed in the specific chapter of the apparatus. He does this 'so that they can be seen without the accompaniment of the other words and so that my students, when they see all of this, will burn with the desire to make their own alphabetical apparatus' (p. 283). From the model text, therefore, to the apparatus, to the new text, and back again to the apparatus: the resulting circular movement can be closed into itself in a mirror-like repetition, or it can be expanded in the shape of a spiral, thus generating other texts.

This critical depiction of Ariosto as listing his models and then recycling them at the right moment seems somewhat farfetched. Some problems are posed, moreover, by the passage in which Toscanella affirms that his fellow poets – such as Domenico Venier, Giorgio and Pietro Gradenigo, and Celio Magno – have been greatly aided by 'judicious and thorough surveys of Petrarch's concepts and forms, which they compiled' (p. 209). Magno was a close friend of Toscanella's from the 1560s until the time of his death. We know, moreover, that they collaborated on a 'reduction into trees' of Agricola's *De inventione dialectica*. Perhaps Toscanella's portrayal of Magno, and of other poets close to him, is not totally unreliable when he depicts them as poets who have no qualms about reinforcing their literary memory with the proper instrumentation.

But how does one use an apparatus to arrive at a new text? How can the elements derived from the anatomy of the literary tradition be revitalized simply by inserting them in a new organism? Toscanella faces this problem by constructing actual rhetoric machines for his readers. There is a complex cultural tradition behind this activity: besides renewed interest in Lullism and the influence of Camillo, rhetoric machines were part of an intellectual heritage that ranged – as Luciano Artese has shown – from Agricola to Sturm, Ramus, and, in particular, Cornelius Auwater, a famous scholar from the Collegium trilingue of Louvain, and a student of both Agricola and Sturm.[58] The result has a unique flavour; it is shaped by the fact that Toscanella practises and experiments with the same techniques that he teaches, and that he is fascinated by the possibilities offered by paper and the ordered

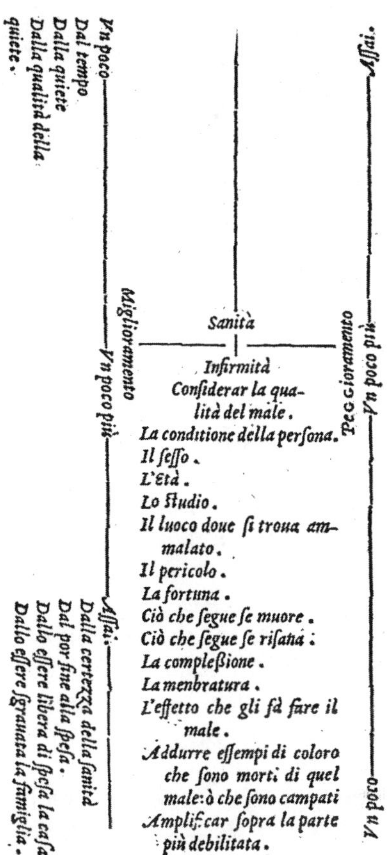

15 Rhetorical machine with *Sanità* [Health] and *Infirmità* [Infirmity] at its centre, from Orazio Toscanella, *Modo di studiare le pistole di Cicerone* (Venice: Gabriele Giolito 1560)

space permitted and guaranteed by the page – both handwritten and printed.

Take, for example, the mechanism that Toscanella constructs in *Modo di studiare le pistole di Cicerone*. He puts two opposite terms in the centre of a page (for example, *sanità* [health] and *infirmità* [infirmity], as in figure 15), and around them he arranges (again in a pattern of opposites) the possible consequences of the two terms: improvement/aggravation, much/little, etc. Within this basic structure of opposites, there is an ample series of places from which one can extract material (the quality of the illness, the person's condition, gender, age, etc.) and end up with 'examples of those who died of that illness or those who

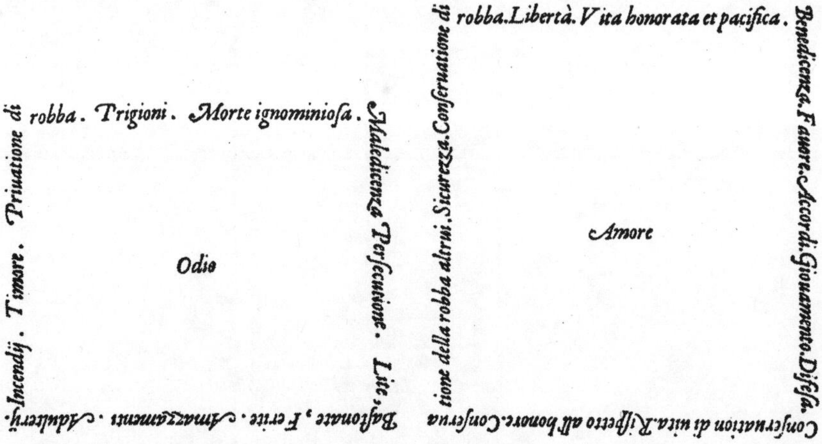

16 Rhetorical machine with *Odio* [Hate] and *Amor* [Love] at its centre, from
Orazio Toscanella, *Modo di studiare le pistole di Cicerone* (Venice: Gabriele
Giolito 1560)

survived it' (p. 52). At this point those who follow Toscanella's instructions can then use a repertory that we have already mentioned, Textor's *Officina*; the part entitled 'De homine' [On man] lists the cases of men who died of fever, apoplexy, worms, gout, drowning, etc.[59]

It is not very difficult for Toscanella to construct his rhetoric machine: a simple piece of paper divided accordingly and organized. It is not surprising, however, that Toscanella, with his large family to support, chooses to depict the theme of sickness and the related financial worries. The *places* that furnish the material under 'health improvement' are called 'ending the expenses,' 'the family relieved,' etc.

Later Toscanella recommends an analogous procedure: 'The material can also be obtained in the following manner: by always putting the principal subject in the middle of the piece of paper and then putting around him all of the principal things that this man can imagine doing to this end; and by using the things that would be most like his thought' (*Modo di studiare le pistole di Cicerone*, p. 54). He gives two examples that centre on 'love' and 'hate' (figure 16), and then makes the following observation: 'with this organization, you can proceed to an almost infinite degree because with each word around *love* you could similarly make a circle by considering the things that fall upon that word, things that have been added to it or in some other way have participated with it ... And this great recollection is highly useful in increasing the amount of material' (p. 56).

The procedure used to construct the rhetoric machine lies halfway between the use of topical places and the use of free associations: it is based upon the dismantling of the real as well as the automation of imagination. All that is needed to build the machine is a simple piece of paper, but at the same time it is a machine that can be infinitely expanded. The model is a circle in which every point on the circumference can in turn become the centre of another circumference. Inside this 'material-grabbing' machine, which helps one to move creatively through the forest of words, is the notion (held so dear by Giordano Bruno) of a universe of infinite worlds where the centre is everywhere and the circumference nowhere. But the theme of the 'infinite infinites' has also appeared in the editorial program of the Accademia Veneziana: in the section of the *Somma* dedicated to the books on mathematics that the Academy intended to publish, there is a promise of a 'Discourse on infinity, in which it is clearly proven that there can be an infinity of infinites and every body can have an infinite number of movements at its centre.'[60]

Toscanella's machines in the *Armonia di tutti i principali retori* are much more complex. The basis of the procedure there is a method that was prescribed by Agricola, as well as others: the discourse is reduced to a single proposition; the principal terms of the discourse (subject and predicate) are then reported in places so that they can be used to generate lavish descriptions. The comparison between the two types of material creates the direction for development of the discourse. The example given by Agricola is 'if the philosopher should take a wife'; the two principal terms are thus *philosophy* and *wife*. The idea is to make their characteristic elements interact.[61]

The first step, explains Toscanella, is to identify the subject and predicate of the sentence intended as the nucleus of the text under construction. Then the subject and predicate have to be introduced into the four principal figures of the work. There are thus four wheels based on the Lullian model (figure 17). The nine first principles of Lullism (God, angels, heaven, man, etc.) provide a grid for all that can be expressed. They are arranged in the first wheel, which contains the subjects (S); the second wheel contains the absolute predicates (A); the third contains the 'respective predicates' and their relationships, denoted by triangles (T); the fourth contains the questions (*if, who, of what, why*, etc.). The wheels become the principal tools of an ambitious operation that seeks to reconcile the ancient with the modern masters of rhetoric. A large table is used to visualize the questions under consid-

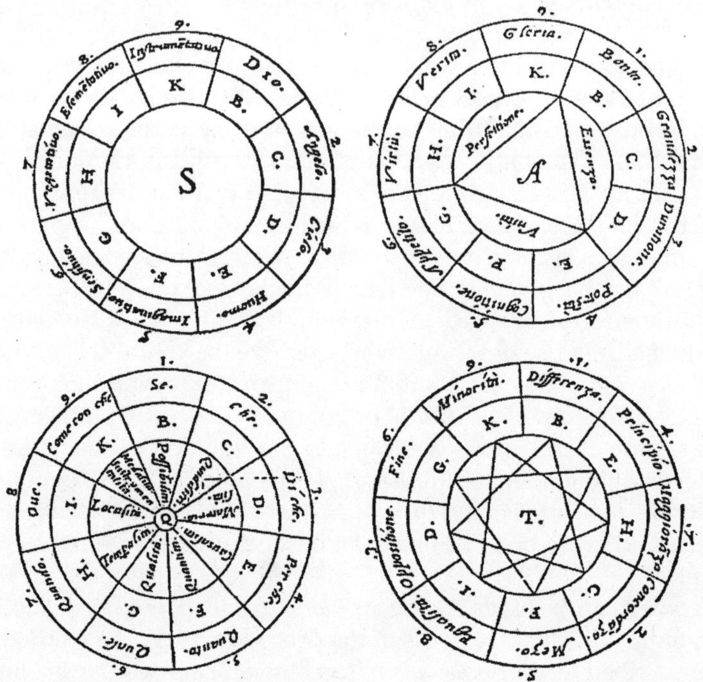

17 The four wheels, from Orazio Toscanella, *Armonia di tutti i principali retori* (Venice: Giovanni Varisco 1569)

eration (for example, the components of the single genres). Not only does every page refer back to the general table, but the internal references, from tree to tree, are seemingly continuous. A single *place* of a tree, in fact, can be the synthetic representation of something that has been analysed and developed in a complex diagram on another page. The effect is similar to that which we have seen in the circular machines mentioned above: every point on the circumference can become the centre of another circumference; here the network of trees grows and multiplies upon itself, thus allowing a glimpse of an infinite table and endless diagrams. The pages of the book thus send the user to a multidimensional space.

But, more than anything else, Toscanella directs the reader's attention to the four wheels. He guarantees that 'as long as he becomes familiar with [the wheels] and practises using them, a man can easily find the means to try anything he wants and to increase the number of terms and questions' (*Armonia di tutti i principali retori*, folio 20r).

According to Toscanella, these are universal models capable of providing the necessary discourse for any occasion. The metaphors he uses to describe how they work refer to spatial models of thought that have been influenced and expanded by the printing press and the new logic. To prove that God is eternal, Toscanella writes, *'I go* to the figure that contains universal subjects, with the letter S in the centre, and in *chamber* B I find God.' Since the predicate is *eternal*, 'I go back to the figure that contains absolute predicates, with A in the centre, and there I look for the predicate that goes with "eternal," and *I find* "duration" in *chamber* D of the above-mentioned figure of absolute predicates; then I get the means in figure A in *chamber* C for size, and I form the discourse in the following manner: The thing that has infinite size has eternal duration. But God is infinite, and therefore God is eternal' (folio 24r).

Toscanella is trying to demonstrate the automatic quality of the procedure. The figures, when used correctly, work just like machines for thinking and writing, and from them one can obtain all necessary material. And like the Lullian wheels, they can be turned. The third figure, for example, is used in oratorical syllogisms. If you cannot find what you are looking for, writes Toscanella, turn the wheel 'one letter after another.' The machine model thus interacts with the spatial model. The original physical sense of *places* is reinforced and expanded by applying it to the different divisions of the wheels: they become *chambers*, similar to the rooms of a building containing a treasure-house of eloquence. In relation to this, the procedure is presented as physical movement: 'I go to the figure ... in the chamber ... I find ...' The user passes through the rooms of the places where the necessary items are given. If I need to prove that man is the master of all the animals on earth, writes Toscanella, *'I go into* in the figure of absolute predicates, in *chamber* E, and I find *power*; with this predicate I then *enter* the figure of the corresponding predicates and, *passing through the chambers, I arrive at chamber* H, where I find a corresponding predicate that suits my purpose' (folio 24v).

For Toscanella, mastering the secrets of rhetoric thus means following a road through a splendid palace where a great treasure has been amassed. Thanks to machines built just for this purpose, it is possible to master the treasure and use it.

It is interesting to note that analogous images of restless, whirling motion are present even in Castelvetro's writings, and they too are used to describe processes of logic and rhetoric. We have already mentioned that Castelvetro claims to have discovered 'compartmental words' in his commentary on *Rhetorica ad Herennium*. He is trying to show that many of the figures of the text can be listed in this category. 'Most of the examples listed under the figures can be seen by *running after them*. Now as an example of *pronominationis* [periphrasis], some call the Gracchi the "grandsons of Africanus." But if you *revolve* the Gracchi through the ten predicamental faces, ... you will arrive at a face that the Greeks call πρός τι and you will see that they are related to Africanus, as his grandsons.' The same holds true, adds Castelvetro, when you call the cold 'lazy': 'if you revolve "cold" using the predicamental wheel, you will find how it can affect laziness in others under [the figure of] AFFECT.'[62]

A mental process is thus described in terms of motion. It is a matter of 'running after' the individual figures in the disordered space of the work (disordered because, as we have seen, Castelvetro does not believe the rhetorical grid to be entirely reliable). The figures used to represent procedures of logic and rhetoric are closely related to this revolving mechanism ('If you *revolve* the Gracchi through the ten predicamental faces'; 'if you revolve "cold" using the predicamental wheel').

There is already a tradition of a physical, spatial dimension in topics. 'Utility was greatly served by those who found certain SEATS for subject matter, which they called PLACES; and from these discoveries, as through certain signs, we were permitted to go about those seats carrying the mind around them and to know what was possible in each of them,' writes Toscanella in his Italian translation of *De inventione dialectica*.[63] The image of *places* is accompanied by the image of 'carrying the mind around,' or, in other words, the image of intellectual labour brought about by movement through space.

It is primarily the book that has fuelled this set of images. The treasure-house of eloquence, the encyclopedia, and the concept of library all overlap, and the printed page itself becomes a rhetoric machine and a depository of places that can be physically entered. In one of the *Discorsi cinque*, entitled 'Modo di trovar materia da discorrere in ogni occorrente concetto, o pensiero che si voglia chiamare' [Method for finding subject matter on any necessary concept or thought desired] (1575), Toscanella, as usual, refers to topical places. Once the chapters are identified, he writes, 'with each one of the chapters, one by one, *I will be able to enter* the indexes and tables in Celio Rodigino's *Antiche lettioni* [Ancient lessons] and Pietro Vittorio's *Varie lettioni* [Various lessons]' (p. 50). We can find identical images in the earlier text, *Modo di studiare le pistole di Cicerone* (1560): 'I have not changed the Italian words in this concept because, as the scholar uses the same order to *enter* into the *Fabrica del mondo* [Workshop of the world] and Alunno's *Ricchezze volgari* [Vernacular riches], ... he himself can change it into Italian the way I did it in Latin' (p. 180). One year before his death, in the *Essercitii di Aftonio Sofista* (Venice: Domenico and Giovan Battista Guerra 1578), Toscanella praises the use of examples taken from the animal world, and he recommends using Pliny 'by finding the necessary names in the table and by *entering*, using the direction of the table' (p. 29).

This is a constant in Toscanella's way of thinking and expressing himself: just as one enters the *chambers* of the Lullian wheels, one also *enters* books, indexes, repertories, dictionaries, and all the tools that sixteenth-century publishing was using more and more. Even the books and libraries were becoming part of a much bigger mechanism as they became the gears in the great machine used for building texts.

8 The Art of Memory: Access to Rhetoric Machines

What function does the art of memory have in this mechanism? Toscanella's position is indicative of the multiform nature of the art of memory during this period. He knows and teaches the art of memory in its traditional form, that is, using the *imagines agentes*. In *La Retorica a Herennio ridotta in alberi*, for example, he explains that to remember a line by Domenico Venier – 'Fredda è madonna, e tal che'l ghiaccio stesso' [Cold is my lady, just like ice itself] – one can construct an image of a 'nude woman blowing on her hands, with ice laid on her talon, that is to say, her heel' (folio 134v). As often happens in *memoria verborum*, the game of associations generates an erotic fantasy, in this case spiked with a touch of sadism. The examples that follow – of amazing performances of mnemonic skills in Venice – are also part of this tradition (folio 137r).

The most famous example of a modern system of memory, Camillo's theatre, was well known to Toscanella, and he cites and uses it, especially in his commentary on *Orlando furioso*. As we will see in chapter 5, the images of the theatre are interpreted as allegories and iconographic *inventions*, and even their mnemonic function is seen from this perspective.

Toscanella does not embrace the trend in the art of memory that promises rapid access to universal knowledge. In the anthology *I motti, le facetie, argutie e altre piacevolezze* [Mottos, witticisms, humour, and other pleasures] (Venice: Bernardino Fasani 1561), there are two anecdotes based on the same pattern. Two professors (Carlo Sigonio and Bernardino Tomitano) have made a rather astonishing promise to their students (that they will teach them a 'secret of memory' that 'allows one to learn with amazing facility). At the moment when they seem about to concede to the students' clamouring, each makes a revelation that negates the secret: 'voluntary and continous study' is Sigonio's recipe; while Tomitano makes his students write: 'if someone sees Venus rise every day, he will have a powerful memory' (folio 64r).[64]

Like other authors we have encountered in this chapter, Toscanella is most interested in another type of art of memory; while he gives little importance to images, he concentrates his attention on topical places. They are intended to be containers of material and generative models. The premise for this mnemonic model comes from Agricola's work on dialectics, which Toscanella had translated. For someone who has practised dialectics to be able to obtain subject matter from places, he writes, he must know the number and nature of the places.

> I will not let myself believe that committing the places to memory is enough. I want them to be ready, practised, and held before the eyes unhindered. No one can read something quickly without tripping along the path of the words: he has to stop and think about this letter and that; nor is he able to find quickly the places he needs. It is easier to look for the places first.

To Agricola, holding the places in the memory means modelling the mind and making it into an able gymnast of invention. Once again the model provided by writing is dominant. The map of places needs to be fixed, clear, ordered, and distinct, just like a written text. The letters of the alphabet are not compared to the images of the art of memory, as they had been traditionally, but to its topical places: they are the new alphabet of the mind, and they provide access to an endless game of invention and combination.

We will have great speed and rhetorical prowess and an extraordinary capacity for improvisation, Agricola maintains, 'if we first commit to memory all the places and all the precepts in such a way that with just a glance, unrestrained, we can see what we like ... The astonishing strength of the human mind is enormous, and in the end nothing is difficult, except that which is not desired.'[65]

Toscanella echoes this, especially in *Armonia di tutti i principali retori*, the work in which he shows his strongest ability for synthesis, syncretism, and visualization. Among the more interesting examples is the inscription that accompanies the table of *terms* relating to the *faculties* of philosophy, medicine and morality. Familiarity with these terms, Toscanella writes, 'is of great help in speaking and writing well, and in organization'; with their help 'a man is capable of comfortably discussing the faculties to which these terms belong, and they function *as local memory* for those fully instructed in these faculties' (folio 31v).

The wheels, diagrams, and tables that function 'as local memory' are thus the protagonists of a new art of memory: they make up the map that allows us to find our bearings in the vast seas of logic and encylopedism, and together they provide access to the rhetoric machines that Toscanella has devised.

Throughout his life Toscanella produced repertories, divulged *secrets*, and contructed machines that promised to go back to the origins of eloquence in a given text and reconstruct it. All of this was part of the cultural climate of the times, and it responded to the expectations of his contemporaries. It therefore allowed Toscanella to make a living, albeit a precarious one. We might ask ourselves to what extent he believed in the efficacy of his tools. A letter sent in 1577 to Belisario Vinta, secretary to Francesco de' Medici, offers insight into this question. Toscanella was working to incorporate news about the Medici in his *Storia universale* (in his will he instructed that this text be published; see p. 56 above), but his delay with the details of the ceremonies had not pleased his patrons. He assured them that he had followed all of the dictates of the art, but, as Cicero used to say, it is necessary to be concise and efficient: 'I mean to say that I am like those who grow old using play swords in fencing school. They know how to strike and parry, but they have never seen a rapier, or rather, they have never practised with a proper weapon.'[66]

At the end of his life Toscanella scrutinized himself with unforgiving lucidity. He seems always to have kept himself on this side of the line that divides games from reality, wooden swords from deadly ones, and rhetorical exercises from true literary creation. His rhetoric machines are fascinating in the way games are: they are fun, they are clever, and they have endless possibilities. Sometimes it is better when one does not try to put them to work.

9 Machines Used to Construct Sermons

Francesco Panigarola

> Father Panigarola left yesterday. He and others engaged in various dis-
> cussions in the presence of these princes. Friday evening he and I dis-
> cussed local memory. I hold that it is extremely difficult, if not impossible,
> adducing that it was impossible to commit the one hundred and ten
> thousand places to memory, as one authority on local memory claims. He
> conceded that such a number was extremely difficult, if not impossible,
> but the same could be accomplished with just a few places, and it could
> help in three things especially: first, to remember those things that have no
> natural order; second, to forget those things once used that one then
> wanted to forget; third, to repeat, from the middle to the end, the things
> said at the beginning.[67]

The details of this conversation, which took place in November 1577 at
the court of the Estensi in Ferrara, are taken from a letter that Francesco
Patrizi sent to Tarquinia Molza, the inspirational muse of his *Amorosa
filosofia* [Philosophy of love] and his brilliant student of Greek language, literature, and philosophy.[68]

The individual defending the art of memory in the face of Patrizi's
scepticism (and exaggerations regarding some of its practioners) was
Francesco Panigarola (1548–1594), a Franciscan friar famous for his
amazing memory, and author of a treatise on local memory (*Trattato
della memoria locale*) that was published together with his work on
preaching.

Panigarola was destined for a successful career in the church (he later
became bishop of Asti), and he would become most famous as the best
preacher of his times, at least according to an opinion that reached
Emanuele Tesauro (1592–1675), one of the great Italian literary theorists
of the seventeenth century, author of *Il cannocchiale aristotelico* [The
Aristotelian telescope]. Panigarola had close ties with Carlo Borromeo,
and, like Valier, he played an important role in the attempt to give holy
oratory all of the rich instrumentation typical of lay prose and poetry.[69]
Besides Panigarola's sermons, an extraordinary testimonial of this tradition comes to us via a work of his published in 1609, *Il predicatore,
overo Demetrio Falereo dell'elocuzione, con le parafrasi, e commenti, e discorsi
ecclesiastici ... ove vengono i precetti, e gli essempi del dire, che già furono dati
a' Greci, ridotti chiaramente alla pratica del ben parlare in prose italiane e la*

vana elocutione de gli autori profani accomodata alla sacra eloquenza de' nostri dicitori e scrittori ecclesiastici [The Preacher, or rather, Demetrius Phalereus, *On Style*, with paraphrases, and commentary, and ecclesiastic discourse ... in which the precepts and examples of oration, once given to the Greeks, have been clearly reduced for the practice of writing well in Italian prose, and in which the style of our lay authors has been corrected for the holy eloquence of our ecclesiastic orators and writers]. This text gives a detailed analysis of Demetrius of Phaleron's precepts on *elocutio*, or style, and it provides a schematization for Italian literature. Boccaccio, on the one hand, and Tasso, on the other, offer reference points for a formal renewal of ecclesiastic discourse that would act as a model for innovations in seventeenth-century literary prose. 'Lord and bestower of the infinite riches of eloquence' – this is how Tasso describes his friend the preacher, who in turn writes of the poet that he is 'always astonishing.'[70]

The truly lavish size of *Il predicatore* is in itself an indication of the infinite resources of *elocutio* that it teaches. It is evidently geared towards the most erudite and influential priests. For the young seminarian, there is *Panigarola*'s rather slim treatise *Modo di comporre una predica* [How to write a sermon] (Venice: Giacomo Vincenti 1603), which is dedicated to *inventio*. Written in 1581, this remarkably popular text would be published again and again, in Italian as well as Latin and French. It provides us with some interesting information for our study. While the interest of Borromeo and his group in a method based on dialectics and topical orders is illustrated by the large synoptic table accompanying Valier's *Rhetorica ecclesiastica*, Panigarola's short treatise allows us to see the method put into action, or, rather, a method that has been reduced to a pure combinatorial mechanism.

The treatise begins by proposing a grid of twelve genres. The grid is the product of a combination of the three traditional genres and the various types of sermons. The twelve boxes contain, the user is assured, 'all the sermons to be found in the world' (*Modo di comporre una predica*, folio 3r). It then teaches how to obtain everything that is needed for one's purpose. The starting point of the process is the traditional one: the subject is reduced to a proposition (for example, *fasting is necessary*), which is then broken down into the subject (*fasting*) and predicate (or related *passion*, that is, *is necessary*). Armed with these two keys, the preacher enters the 'forest' of all that has already been said (and, consequently, that can be said) in order to collect the necessary material. The treatise indicates different possibilities that are simpler and more functional as they go along. We can begin in the library: 'We must enter our library, and there, using all the books we have, we procure, obtain, and put aside almost a forest of all the concepts that can serve us in the given subject matter' (folio 62r). The first phase of the procedure (that is, the collection of material) is marked by multiplicity and confusion: Panigarola speaks of a 'forest' because 'as we obtain [material], we also lay out a confused sort of forest or wood on just a bit of paper; in the end we arrange it, so to speak, we divide it and make it into a garden' (folio 10v). The piece of paper, the division, and the arrangement serve to mediate between order and disorder, or, in other words, between the forest and the garden; or, to use another image taken from Panigarola, between the heap of bricks taken from the furnace and the text/building.

There is, however, a short cut and a way to reduce the risks and the travail of a journey through the forest/library: the use of repertories and concordances. Volumes that offer good graphic instrumentation, writes Panigarola, are particularly efficient, and also notes and apparatus that facilitate usage and at the same time multiply the possiblities of citations and correspondence. The optimum in this sense, according to Panigarola, is the *catena aurea* of the Bible that was 'printed in Paris by the Supreme [Pontiff].' It has 'not only the names annotated in the margins, but also the most minute places of the authors. This way one can study the Scriptures and the Fathers together, and since the annotations are scrupulously faithful, you can attach more than a thousand of them to the pulpit, all thanks to a single book' (folio 11v).

Thus, the repertory, when used correctly, is projected onto the pulpit and an effect of proliferated illusion is created: a self-contained multiplicity of references and allusions to other books. The repertory has become the ideal book inasmuch as it is capable of condensing the anatomized library and preparing it to be recycled. The index and the table have become its most important parts: they provide the map with which the two 'keys' of the sermon – the subject and the predicate (or *passion*) – can be efficiently arranged. By entering the index, as Toscanella would have said, we can access the material that we need. 'There are so many authorities,' writes Panigarola, 'who awaken the intellect and produce concepts for our purposes that there should be enough for every line of reasoning, however many and however long they may be' (folio 13r). It is clear, therefore, that the places of the texts – the places of the repertories primarily – serve as topical places. These deposits of material show the way ('awakening the intellect') for its reappropriation and its possible combinations.

At this point, according to Panigarola, all we have to do is introduce the prepared material into a grid created with the *dispositio* in mind. He recommends that each one of the discovered *concepts* be indicated with a number and then re-grouped under the three *chapters*, or principal subjects, to be developed in the sermon. Some of the collected material that has no place here can be recycled in the introduction. A suitable *selvetta* [small forest] (folio 25r) provides all that is needed for the pauses and the entertaining moments required by the sermon. Panigarola's predilection for diminutive suffixes and nicknames (for example, *selvetta, epiloghetto* [little epilogue], *introduzioncella* [short introduction], *prologhino* [short prologue], etc.) is indicative of his pyschological outlook. The diminutives display his confidence and his total control of the secrets contained within the mechanism he describes. This mechanism simultaneously produces the text of the sermon and guarantees rational and emotional control of the audience. It is simple and easy, the text intimates, for anyone who, like the author, knows how to use it: it is like playing with words and people's souls. For example, in the *prologhino*, Panigarola writes, 'we could create some *scherzos* made of opposition or similarity, or something else' (folio 46r). They are like the musical *ricercata* [*ricercare*] (a polyphonic prelude to a piece of music): it is not part of the madrigal, but 'it allows the listeners to determine what they can hope for in the talents of the player' (folio 42r). In the same fashion the *prologhino* acts as a guide for the listener's mind, and it thus creates a sort of musical harmony with the preacher's words. Panigarola asserts that the *prologhino* can take a wide of variety of forms. Even here he gives us a clear indication of the self-confidence of the method: the treatise intimates that the rhetorical mechanism it proposes works well and functions far beyond the limitations and needs of the single user.

Federico Borromeo

Federico Borromeo (1564–1631) (a younger cousin of Carlo Borromeo), who became a cardinal in 1587, and bishop of Milan in 1595, was also enticed by the prospects of a sermon-writing technique that could satisfy both rhetorical and religious needs.[71]

As we leaf through Borromeo's private papers (written between 1594 and 1595), we discover the abbreviation A.R.L. written here and there throughout the manuscripts. It stands for *ars rhetorica logica*, that is, the art of rhetoric and logic, with which we are already familiar. It can be used 'only with places, with or without a table, by means of figures'

(*Miscellanea adnotationum variarum* [Miscellany of various notations], in *I Quaderni di Palazzo Sormani* 9 [Milan 1985]: 9).[72] It provides diagrams for the reading of others' texts ('It returns to their chapters things that would otherwise be difficult to put back in order. It facilitates the reading of many books,' p. 10).[73] It is useful in orations, when one needs to interpret a text or participate in a public debate. It provides tools with which one can remedy lapses of memory and improvise a discourse ('si aliquid ex memoria exciderit, si ex tempo[re] dicendum sit' [when something is lost from memory, or when one must improvise]). It can help one to formulate simple, everyday orations as well as those addressed to God ('familiaribus sermonibus, divinis praecationibus' [for personal sermons or divine prayers]: and it plays an important, albeit hidden, role in the way to 'pursue the study of the Holy Scriptures,' interpret them, and use them in sermons. It is helpful, writes Borromeo, to use the 'A.R.L. to the greatest degree you believe possible, but hidden and mixed with other things' (p. 69).

This art also becomes a tool for mental discipline and for the creation of internal order. Its connection with memory becomes clear in a list entitled 'De vario usu A.R.L.' [On the various uses of the art of rhetoric and logic]. It is claimed that this art is used 'to act wisely in human vicissitudes; to make conjectures on the future, guided by wisdom; to discover secrets; to augment capabilities of invention' (p. 9).[74] The classical and medieval notions that memory is part of *prudentia* (the virtue that allows one to control the three faces of time) here co-exists with the modern idea of memory as a method for invention and as part of a procedure for building a text.

Borromeo has great curiosity about mnemonic tools. In his miscellany he recalls the performances of Iacopo Mazzoni (1548–1598), who used mnemonic verses to remember the chronologies of emperors and popes, or maps. But Borromeo also makes use of classical techniques (that is, *loci* and *imagines*), as recommended in *Rhetorica ad Herennium* (p. 78). He even cites a method for reading used by Cardinal Guglielmo Sirleto (1514–1585): 'it is no mystery that he would almost sing as he was reading because then things stay more securely in the memory' (p. 113).

As a young man Federico's interest in memory was related to his curiosity about the occult: 'I burned with desire for the strangest of sciences,' he writes in *De suis studiis commentariis* [Commentaries on his own studies] as he recalls his sojourn in Bologna (April 1579–October 1590), 'and great was my effort to master the artifice of memory and other similar things that young men admire through their natural curiosity.'[75] Interesting evidence is also provided in a letter sent to Carlo Borromeo on 16 March 1580 from Federico's preceptor, Galeazzo Capra: 'I give you the usual dispatch, actually better than usual since [Federico] proposed twenty subjects at the penultimate academy. He possesses great knowledge, and he used it in this exercise in local memory, but not in other things.'[76]

What does 'but not in other things' mean? The preceptor probably wants to assure Carlo of the purely technical, as opposed to magical, nature of the art of memory practised by his young cousin.

In *De cabbalisticis inventis* [On cabbalistic invention], Federico speaks of Giulio Camillo's *Idea del theatro* [Idea of the theatre] in the same way. He labels this work, although with some hesitation, as an interaction between the cabbalist and Lullian traditions. 'We believe that even Giulio Camillo, a man of rare ingenuity, wanted to base his ideas and his theatre on the Hebrew Cabbala and the art of Raymond [Lull]. We do not know if he was successful or if he merely tried in vain to do so.'[77] Evidently Federico is made uneasy by this connection to the Cabbala and the wide range of relationships that it brings into play. The system of relationships associated with the *sephiroth* (that is, divine names) that was used by many cabbalist authors is entirely unacceptable, he writes: 'Giulio Camillo made similar observations in his *Theatre*, and it seems that he first adhered to the ideas of the cabbalists, but then he understood that they were fruitless and that they served no other purpose than slightly to embellish and vary the discourse.'[78] On the one hand, Federico is fascinated by those experiments in which Lullism, the Cabbala, and the art of memory have been brought together; on the other hand, he feels compelled to reassess the meaning and importance of such experimentation. Even Camillo's theatre needs to be brought down to a purely technical and rhetorical level.

As we have seen in the notebooks mentioned above, Federico's attitude towards the art of memory is similar to that of the other protagonists of this chapter. The true art of memory – or, at least, its most useful and important version – is the dialectic technique. This art allows the user to recycle directly the heritage of literary memory; it teaches combinatorial techniques, and consequently helps the user to present himself well even when the initial material is of poor quality. Borromeo notes that, 'when you readily know a hundred things and have them at your fingertips, it is incredible how useful they are on endless occasions. Cardinal Ascanio [Colonna] knew no less than two hundred places from Sallustius, Cornelius, and Marcus Tullius. He told me so himself' (*Miscellanea adnotationum variarum*, 80).

But Borromeo's references to the tools of this art are much more interesting. There is a note dedicated to the operation of a table and four figures, each marked with letters of the alphabet. Three of them stand for the subject, the predicate, and the middle term. The latter is obtained from the various *chambers* of the figures ('dat medium dum variatur in cameris' [it gives the middle through variations in the chambers]), and herein lies the creative nucleus of the entire construction. 'Siste hic mente et omnia intellige' [Reflect carefully on this and you will understand all] – the cardinal, writing on 1 January 1595, uses this self-exhortation to inaugurate the new year.

Thanks to these accurate notes we can imagine ourselves spying on Federico in his study, trying to see which books he has left open on his desk. We will probably find there a book that we already know, Orazio Toscanella's *Armonia di tutti i principali retori*. This work culminates in a large table and four wheels. We might imagine that we are watching Federico as he attempts to follow the instructions that will allow him – as Toscanella guarantees – to produce every type of subject matter and text.

But Borromeo does not cite his sources, and we can only hypothesize that he used Toscanella's work. It is certain, however, that among his many and varied interests, he was undoubtedly attracted to this art of logic and rhetoric that promised to control and empower the mechanisms of memory and literary creation.

CHAPTER THREE

Memory Games

1 The Game of Imitation

> I am like those who grow old using play swords in fencing school. They
> know how to strike and parry, but they have never seen a rapier, or rather,
> they have never practised with a proper weapon.[1]

As we have seen in chapter 2 (p. 75), this was how Orazio Toscanella
responded to Francesco de' Medici's secretary when he criticized the
style of Toscanella's *Storia universale*. Towards the end of his life
Toscanella looked back on the long hours he had spent constructing
repertories, trees, tables, and text-producing machines, and with unforgiving clarity he compared his toil to a game that imitates reality but
has no effect upon it. The swords he has handled and constructed
cannot hurt anyone. They just look like real swords. As Toscanella
reflects on his lifelong search for a method that will generate a new text
from the reading of another, he cannot but think of it as if it were a
game.

This is by no means a foreign image that has come to Toscanella in a
moment of personal crisis. Despite its rather dark outlook, the analogy
is intended to express a feeling common (albeit often in an underground form) to the literary experience of the sixteenth century.[2]

> Semper mihi placet antiquis alludere dictis
> atque aliud longe verbis proferre sub iisdem
>
> [I often enjoy alluding to/playing with phrases from the ancients and,
> while using the same words, expressing another meaning.]

These are the words of Marco Girolamo Vida (ca 1485–1566) in the section of his *De arte poetica* (ca 1517) dedicated to *elocutio*.[3] The term *alludere* means both *to allude to* and *to play with*. An intertextual relationship is based on the play of continuity and difference. On the one hand, this play depends on the memory of an erudite reader who is capable of recognizing the allusion and perceiving the texts which the author is imitating. On the other hand, it aims for an effect of estrangement, created by violating the reader's expectations, as the familiar words are used to express very different concepts.[4] The world of play fascinated Vida, and he even dedicated an elegant poem in Latin, *Scacchia ludus* (1527), to the game of chess.

In a much richer fashion an analogous idea pervades *Gli Asolani* by Pietro Bembo (1470–1547).[5] This work, which Bembo began at the end of the fifteenth century, was first published in 1505, and then in a new version in 1530. It is a complex synthesis of philosophical and literary experiences, old and new alike. The dialogues – which are set in the villa of a Venetian noblewoman, Caterina Cornaro, in Asolo (hence, the title) – speak of love in Italian, and thus offer a new linguistic model for Italian literature as well as a manual for social etiquette. The work would ultimately establish itself as a canonical text. The 1530 edition of *Gli Asolani*, together with Castiglione's *Il Cortegiano* [The book of the courtier], published two years earlier, marks a watershed in the copious production of texts dedicated to love and women in the sixteenth century.

In the first book of *Gli Asolani* the character Perottino builds up a negative representation of love that ends in his weeping (and the women listening to him cry too). In the second book, however, another character, Gismondo, launches a counter-attack by calling in the bet, and he shows that his friend's construction is entirely founded on a bluff. Perottino has placed before the eyes of his interlocutors poetic metaphors and mythical characters, pretending that they are real. In fact, however, he is merely drawing upon a repertory of images and literary and iconological topoi that he can vary at will. Gismondo insists that it is poets who give shape to what can be spoken, and consequently they fill up all the places in the grid, or game board, of topics. They describe themselves, for example, as overwhelmed by the rain of tears and the wind of sighs, even if they are happily in love; 'but they do this in order to give various subjects to the ink of their pens, so that by varying their inventions with these colours, the picture of love is all the more graceful in the eye of the beholder.'[6]

The interlocutors of *Gli Asolani* say everything there is to be said for and against love, as well as many other things. For this reason the dialogues become a way of visualizing and enacting literature and the pleasure that it produces. Literature plays with words and images, recombines them in a new way, and even turns the various *cards* of the tradition upside down. To speak joyfully of your lady's absence using the topoi of her striking appearance and the loss of your heart is like placing a bet, a test of one's abilities in a game of technical skill. Gismondo introduces a poem in the following manner:

> you may often have heard lovers feign having lost their hearts and carry on with tears, laments, and the pangs of suffering. Not for this reason, however, I, too, in one of my [poems], have feigned having lost my heart and did so *as a wonderful game for delightful amusement*. And lest I speak to no purpose, listen to some of my miracles.[7]

The stanzas of the song introduced by Gismondo in this passage are separated by commentary that underlines the crescendo of 'miracles,' which are precisely its virtuoso use of images. Gismondo the poet – as Emanuele Tesauro might have said – shows off his talents as a juggler.[8] It is as if he were saying to his audience, 'look, it keeps getting harder and harder.'

This, however, creates a risk: if it is all only a game of variations, the dimensions of things, and of truth, become inaccessible or non-existent. The third book of *Gli Asolani* attempts to respond to such a danger when its hermit-interlocutor exalts a Neoplatonic ascent to the cosmic and divine experience of love. The third book thus presents itself as an instance of revealed truth. The prologue is in fact dedicated to showing that truth exists and that it can be attained and spoken about despite all of the difficulties and uncertainties. Among the dangers to be avoided, the prologue states, is trust in others' opinions. In the long list of reasons given against an unfounded trust, however, there is a parenthesis: 'it often happens, although I do not know how, that as we speak or write of a certain thing, belief in the very thing that we are discussing gradually creeps into our minds.'[9] This parenthetical statement, which interrupts the discussion of truth, is very revealing because it invokes the autonomy of words and their capacity to enchant. The game of rhetoric and literature risks getting the better of the players: its phantoms can take on the form and trustworthiness of true things.

The sixteenth-century notion of play is closely interwoven with literary production, even where we would least expect it – well within the parameters of the developing canon of vernacular classics. Here we can see the deep connection between the game and memory. Both games and the imitation of the classics can function only in a closed world made up of clearcut rules known to all and easily remembered. Classical texts require an erudite reader who possesses a good literary memory and who is capable of making that memory interact with the text: when Gismondo in *Gli Asolani* shows how he has varied and exhausted the image of the lost heart, he is also making clear the rules of the game: he makes his interlocutors participants in the memory that lies at the basis of his poem (in this case a Petrarchan theme that has frequently been exploited in fifteenth-century poetry). Sharing memory, therefore, is an essential component of playing together. Otherwise the text cannot be adequately received, and the author/player will have no fellow-players and be left alone at the games table.

As we have noted in chapter 2, the tools of memory became more and more sophisticated throughout the course of the sixteenth century. Readers no longer relied on memory produced only by the consumption and analysis of literature. A good example is the collection of topical places compiled by Bembo, which Vittorio Cian interprets as merely an example of an encylopedic fad.[10] The unidentified calligrapher of this late sixteenth-century manuscript writes more precisely that '[Bembo] used these places – which are called "common" places, although they ought to be called the "places" of things he had read in the best books – as support for his memory.' He adds that Bembo 'excercised his memory using these places since nature had not given him a particulary strong memory.'[11] We have seen, in fact, how the art of memory, especially in the geometric, mechanical version promoted by the new directions in rhetoric and dialectics, plays an important role in this intellectual environment. It structures the literary memory of those who write and those who read: in both cases, it facilitates access to the necessary topical matter. We can now add that the dimension of play can be detected in the hidden folds of the texts where nature and mechanisms of imitation are analysed, and put on display. If, however, we look for the point where literary writing, play, and the art of memory come together, we will find that imitation is just one aspect of the question; rebuses, ciphers, and alchemy are also all part of the scene. This blend creates the possibility for exchange and reciprocal translatability between games and texts.

2 The Metamorphosis of Writing: Calligraphy, Ciphers, and the Rebus

Let us begin with a *sonetto figurato* [shaped sonnet], a kind of rebus used by Giovanni Battista Palatino in a treatise entitled *Libro nuovo d'imparare a scrivere tutte sorte lettere antiche et moderne di tutte nationi, con nuove regole misure et essempi. Con un breve et utile trattato de le cifre* [New book for learning to write all sorts of ancient, and modern letters of all nations, with new rules, measures, and examples. With a short, useful treatise on ciphers] (Rome: Baldassare di Francesco Cartolari 1540). Emanuele Casamassima's studies have clearly shown that the writing treatise of the sixteenth century has become a genre unto itself. Writing books from this period are extremely valuable to palaeographers because they provide a portrait of 'the history of the last creative period in Latin calligraphy to which we owe all the graphic forms of western civilization.' Palatino's treatise is among the most important in the genre: his collection of writing models, writes Casamassima, became 'the best known and most reissued of all time.'[12]

In 1540 Palatino was a young man, about thirty years old. Originally from Calabria, he had become a Roman citizen only two years earlier, and he was extremely proud of his status as *civis Romanus*.[13] He was a professional calligrapher, and the secretary of the Accademia dello Sdegno [Academy of the Disdainful], to whom he dedicated his *Libro nuovo*. The interests and humours of Pope Paul III's Rome were well represented in the life of the Academy: the love of letters was joined to a taste for practical jokes and extravagance, and a lively carnival spirit.[14] Protected by the young Cardinal Alessandro Farnese, the Academy could count many illustrious individuals among its members, like Claudio Tolomei (1492–1577) and Francesco Maria Molza (1489–1544); there were as well minor literary figures, like Gerolamo Ruscelli (died 1566) and Dionigi Atanagi (ca 1510–1570), who would later have an important role in the Venetian printing industry, especially in the packaging of popular anthologies of new Italian literature.[15] Even a famous artist, Giulio Clovio (1498–1578), miniaturist of the splendid *Farnese Hours*, was a member of the Academy.[16] The interest in the visual arts was very much alive: the Accademia della Virtú, formed

a b c d e f g h i k l m n o p q r s t u x y

[Utopian alphabet symbols]

TETRASTICHON VERNACVLA VTO
PIENSIVM LINGVA.

Vtopos ha Boccas peula chama.

[Utopian script]

polta chamaan

[Utopian script]

Bargol he maglomi baccan

[Utopian script]

soma gymnosophaon

[Utopian script]

Agrama gymnosophon labarem

[Utopian script]

bacha bodamilomin

[Utopian script]

Voluala barchin heman la

[Utopian script]

lauoluola dramme pagloni.

[Utopian script]

18 The alphabet of the Utopians, from Thomas More, *De optimo reipublicae statu deque nova insula Utopia libellus* (Basel: Froben 1518)

just before the Accademia dello Sdegno and closely related to it, met twice a week to read and analyse Vitruvius. The rediscovery of Vitruvius was of great importance for the construction of graphic models: from Luca Pacioli and Sigismondo Fanti on, there were numerous attempts to apply Vitruvius' geometric proportions to constructing the forms of letters.

From its very title it is clear that Palatino's book associates calligraphy with ciphers.[17] This association had already become a tradition, and it was indicative of the variety of the ideas that were coalescing around the letters of the alphabet. The writing models intended to be used for the different scripts were intertwined with ancient models (or, in some cases, pseudo-antique ones) and with exotic, imaginary alphabets. The expansion of the known world and new antiquarian studies stimulated not only better documentation of the various types of alphabets but also wonderful games of variation and invention. In 1518, for example, an imaginary alphabet attributed to the inhabitants of Utopia (figure 18) accompanied a new edition of Thomas More's work, and it became a component of the 'utopia game' that drew in some of More's illustrious friends, like Erasmus and Pieter Gillis.[18]

It was only natural, then, for a calligrapher like Palatino to be fascinated by ciphers, and more generally by the metamorphosis of the alphabet. He named Ruscelli, Atanagi, and Trifone Benci (died 1572), all members of the Academy, as his teachers in matters of 'ciphers.' Ciphers were clearly a shared interest, but the concerns of each give us an idea of the different forms that the blend of script and ciphers could take. Ruscelli was especially interested in the technical, experimental aspect of the art of writing, that is, the preparation of the ink and paper and the various techniques for sharpening the pen, all the necessary tools for writing as described in the manuals. He was above all a true master of the 'secrets,' that is, those practices very near to magic which taught how to make things appear and disappear. Palatino writes, in fact, that he has learned from Ruscelli 'some wonderful, useful secrets for invisible writing on glass.'[19]

Trifone Benci, however, was a diplomat.[20] Under Cardinal Pole he would later serve as copyist and reviser of the proceedings at the Council of Trent, and in the 1550s he would be assigned to work on encoded messages for the Vatican. An ugly yet gracious man of letters, as his friend Marcantonio Flaminio described him, he was called *Trifone delle cifre* [Trifone of the ciphers] or *Chimerae filius* [Son of the chimera], the man who put the secrets of ciphered language at the service of the Vatican. Yet he too must have been appreciative of the fascination of game playing, of witty paradox, of the erudite *divertissement*. In *Il convito overo del peso della moglie* [The banquet, or on the wife's weight], a dialogue published in Rome in 1554 by a Calabrese doctor, Giovan Battista Modio, it is Trifone Benci himself who proposes the subject of cuckoldry as a topic of conversation for the select group of guests invited to lunch by the bishop of Piacenza.[21] The proposal is warmly received, and the guests proceed to discuss the origin, the nature, and the effects of horns with a slew of strange quotations, far-fetched allegories, and unlikely etymologies.

The *sonetto figurato* [shaped sonnet] with which we began appears in the section of Palatino's book dedicated to ciphers.[22] It is coupled with *cifre quadrate* [squared ciphers] (figure 19), in which the letters of an entire word (all capitals) are condensed into one square. Palatino writes that they are made 'only for pleasure and beauty' (folio 24v). Thus, the textual space in which the *sonetto figurato* appears is devoted to a form

19 Squared ciphers, from Giovan Battista Palatino, *Libro nel quale s'insegna a scrivere ogni sorte lettera* (Rome: Valerio Dorico 1561)

of communication that simultaneously reveals and conceals, the product of virtuoso skill and play. Let us see how the author introduces the *sonetto figurato* (figure 20):

Regarding the figures [ciphers], there is no other fixed rule except that their forms must clearly and distinctly be suited to the subjects, with as few letters as possible. Nor should they require much orthography or ornate Tuscan language; nor does it matter if the same figure is used for the middle or end of one word and the beginning of another since it is

20 The sonnet/rebus, from Giovan Battista Palatino, *Libro nel quale s'insegna a scrivere ogni sorte lettera* (Rome: Valerio Dorico 1561)

impossible to make all subjects and figures suited to the words, and the fewer letters the ciphers have the better they are.   (Folio 45r)

Within these rules the *sonetto figurato* becomes a kind of example or object for imitation. It is significant that Palatino turns to the sonnet, which had already been used for enigmas and riddles in the early sixteenth century. At the same time the traditional components of *elocutio* or style (orthography and ornate Tuscan language) take a back seat. Here the painted figure takes priority over linguistic expression so that the focus becomes the meeting/collision created by the presence of two differently encoded forms of expression – the word and the image. In this kind of product *beauty* is that which pleases the eye, first and foremost. It is the harmonious, varied arrangement of different components on the page. In this sense the *sonetto figurato* accentuates and complicates, as a literary *divertissement*, the attention given to the overall beauty of the page and the elegance in the arrangement of letters, typical concerns of earlier writing books. Beauty is also found in the play between the visible and the legible.[23] Thus, the *sonetto figurato* is similar to other mixed-media works like the impresa and the emblem that were so popular in the sixteenth century. The fact that Paolo Giovio (1483–1552) criticizes recourse to the rebus in his *Dialogo dell'imprese militari e amorose* [Dialogue on military and amorous devices] (1551), the most authoritative work on the genre of iconographic devices, shows just how fragile the borders between this and other genres have become.[24] Pietro Aretino gives us a rather unconventional version of the device in the prologue to one of his comedies, *Il marescalco* [The Marescalco]. Here the playwright puts different types of characters on stage, including the *innamorato* [lover], who wears a device/ rebus described by the actor as 'uno *amo*, un *delfino* e un *core* che *disciferato* vuol dire: *amo del fino core*' [a *lure*, a *dolphin*, and a *heart*; when *deciphered* this means: I love with a pure heart].[25]

But what are the specific rules of the game? The most important thing, writes Palatino, is to find visual images that are 'suited to the subjects.' Once this has been achieved, there are no restrictions on how these can be arranged: 'nor does it matter if the same figure is used for the middle or end of one word and the beginning of another.' The freedom of movement of the visual image on the chessboard of the text is the result of the type of relationship it has with the signifier. What exactly does Palatino mean when he writes that the form needs to 'be suited' to the subject? He means that it has to make the signifier visible, or, where that is not possible, to make at least part of the signifier visible.

This play of estrangement and contamination among different types of codes of signification works not only in the latter case (where the contamination of the signifiers is supported by the metonymic logic of fragmentation) but also in the former. Returning to the *sonetto figurato* reproduced in figure 20, let us take, for example, the *viole* [violets] used at the end of the first line of the first tercet, visualized not with the flowers (one of the traditional figures of feminine beauty) but with two violas.[26] In this case the visual image plays with the double meaning of the word, and thus produces something other than what the reader would expect, given the context, with regard to the relationship between the signifier and the signified. The image becomes part of the space opened up by reducing the text to its writing and by the central (and autonomous) position taken by the letter and its different combinations. When written, and especially when printed, words in a certain sense become things: we see here how all of this is taken literally, and how it thus becomes an opportunity for creativity and play.

In some ways the image brings about an understanding, although a rather rough one, of what modern critical theory has called the 'autonomy of the signifier.' The ABBA rhyme scheme of the quatrains, for example, strikes the eye (literally). Also, as Giancarlo Innocenti has acutely observed, the recurring presence of body parts used to visualize parts of words (the chest, the eyes, the feet, etc.) seems to suggest fetishism. Indeed, the body parts evoke a floating, dismembered image of woman, thus providing confirmation of Jean-François Lyotard's idea that, by subverting the space of the text, the rebus makes the traces of desire, the figure hidden within the language, come to the surface.[27]

Palatino's *sonetto figurato* is thus based on the mixing of two expressive codes, the linguistic and the iconic. It plays on the disassembling/visualizing/reassembling of the signifiers, or rather of the words as they appear when written down. Closely tied as it is to the centrality of the written word, it requires a spatial element in order to bring together its letters and visual images within a series of *loci* that, in turn, are arranged in an ordered succession: a characteristic necessary to follow their successive migrations.

Many decades later, in 1602, our sonnet reappears in a treatise on the art of memory, the *Ars reminiscendi* of Giovan Battista della Porta (ca 1535–1615), a famous Neapolitan magician, naturalist, and man of letters.[28] The plagiarism is not very surprising because it was a rather common practice at the time; what is striking, however, is that here plagiarism has crossed the boundaries of texts belonging to different genres.

Della Porta's work dedicated to ciphers, *De furtivis literarum notis vulgo de ziferis* [On secret writing, commonly called ciphers], Naples: Giovanni Maria Scoto 1563), helps us to understand how this is possible. Since Della Porta is anxious to remove from himself any suspicion of magical or diabolical practices, he limits this work to the purely technical aspects of cryptography: ciphers are one of the types of possible languages. On the one hand, they belong to one of the high cultural codes of the sixteenth century, that is, *sapienza riposta* [secret knowledge]: mythology, hieroglyphics, ancient poetry, and the works of the alchemists are all secret codes that make truth accessible to the elite while concealing it from the common man. On the other hand, by the same power ciphers become an emblematic expression of all those types of communication in which something is simultaneously expressed and hidden. They bring into play that shadowy space that opens up between the manner in which a message is presented and its actual meaning. Ciphers cross all social boundaries; there is an exchange of techniques, notes Della Porta, between cabbalists and knights on one side, and ladies, lovers, boys, and tavern patrons on the other.

The field of ciphers extends far beyond linguistic symbols; great attention is paid to gestures, to the expressive capacity of the eyes, the face, and even other parts of the body. 'Manus etiam vix dici potest quot motus habeant' [It is scarcely possible to describe the variety of the motions of the hand], writes Della Porta (p. 24). We may imagine that he has in mind the Neapolitans and their intense gesticulations. The truth is that he is copying, word for word, from Quintilian: 'Manus vero, sine quibus trunca esset actio et debilis, vix dici potest quot motus habeant' [As for the hands, without which all action would be crippled and enfeebled, it is scarcely possible to describe the variety of their motions], writes Quintilian on the subject of *actio*, the orator's body language or delivery, in *Institutio oratoria* (11.3.85).[29] These sections of Della Porta's treatise are closely related to the rhetorical tradition, and also to the art of memory. Cosma Rosselli, for example, in *Thesaurus artificiosae memoriae* [Treasure-room of artificial memory] (Venice: Antonio Padovano, 1579), pp. 103–105, recommends that we have recourse to the silent alphabet of sign language (figure 21). However, they also owe a great deal to comedy and to the manuals on love that teach the art of seduction, dissimulation, and secret communication.[30] The use of writing and painting together, writes Della Porta, can act as a cipher, and he gives the example of the rebus (p. 19).

With Della Porta ciphers become an expression of all the possible forms of artifice, of all the ways to create ambiguity. For this reason, when ciphers rely only on words they also have recourse to rhetorical figures. The fifth chapter of Della Porta's first book is dedicated to the ways of formulating metaphor, metonym, and allegory, and it is marked by a natural predilection for amphiboly and enigma. Even shaped poems are seen as a type of cipher and consequently treated as an erudite *divertissement*. The only rule, Della Porta says, is to place the important letters in different positions: 'semper tamen unico servato ordine ex arbitrio contineant' [they can be arranged however you like, as long as a single order is maintained] (p. 60).

It is thus a matter of creating a particular arbitrary order. The freedom to associate ideas must develop within a freely chosen order, but an order that is established once and for all: this is a common principle in the art of memory. Even here – as in Palatino's *sonetto figurato* – everything is based on the projection of the text onto a predetermined

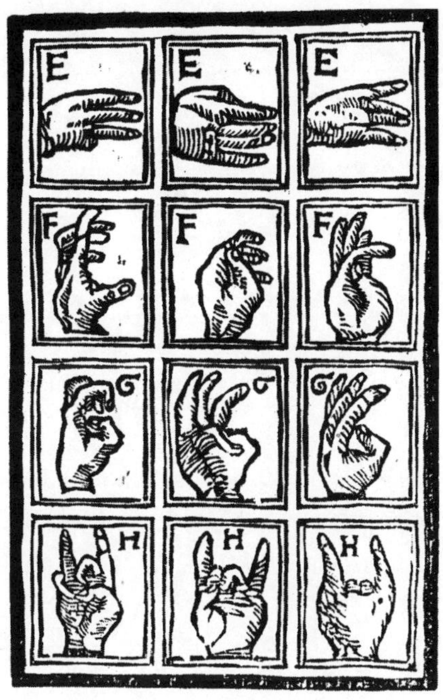

21 The silent alphabet of sign language, from Cosma Rosselli, *Thesaurus artificiosae memoriae* (Venice: Antonio Padovano 1579)

grid that becomes a chessboard of *loci*. In effect, whether in texts devoted to ciphers or in manuals of mnemonics, we find such grids (sometimes actual chessboards are used, as in the work of Iacobo Publicio and in Thomas Murner's *Logica memorativa* [Logic of memory] (figure 22), and also round grids formed by concentric circles).[31] In the manuals of cryptography (as in Della Porta's, p. 73; figure 23) these grids are actually placed beside the ciphered text and used to indicate the *loci* in which the letters of the message have been placed. At the same time the order in which they are to be put back together is made visible. In manuals dedicated to memory they make visible the system of *loci*.

While Della Porta's work on ciphers is a large-scale exercise in language and its various forms and combinations, it also overlaps with some areas of the art of memory. We will now examine the context in which Della Porta recycles Palatino's *sonetto figurato* in his *Ars reminiscendi* (Naples: Giovan Battista Sottile 1602), pp. 17–20. He uses it

22 Image with a chessboard, from Thomas Murner, *Logica memorativa* (Strasbourg: Iohannes Gruninger 1507). This is one of the fifty-one cards of a mnemonic game that Murner used to help students remember the *Summulae logicales* of Petrus Hispanus.

in the part dedicated to the *memoria verborum* [memory of words], actually the most difficult case of *memoria verborum*, where the words to be remembered cannot be translated into images. One can resort to a visual pun, writes Della Porta, or one can create an image that refers to the word to be rememberd through a resemblance to its meaning or to the written word itself: 'one type [of resemblance] is derived from the meaning of the word, another from its written form, from the way in which the letters are arranged. Let us begin with the latter, which is the most reliable' (p. 22).[32] This indicates a clear preference for what we may call spatial games:[33] the word can be manipulated, in effect, by dividing it, adding to it, or taking away from it, or by transposing different syllables or single letters.[33]

23 A schema made up of concentric circles for cipher messages, from
Giovan Battista Della Porta, *De furtivis literarum notis vulgo de ziferis*
(Naples: Giovanni Maria Scoto 1563)

If, for example, you cannot remember the word *num* [if], writes Della
Porta, all you have to do is add the letter *a* to the beginning to make it
into *anum* [old woman] (p. 26). Now the word corresponds to the image
of a little old woman who has come to inhabit your little theatre of
memory.

But how can you remember this procedure when you need to? How
will you be able to retrace your mental steps to the word that you
originally needed to remember? The problem is the same in the case of
ciphers: you need both to mask, or cipher, the word and then to equip
yourself with instruments that allow you to uncover the technique and
decipher the message. Della Porta recommends the traditional technique: the image in one's memory needs to be labelled with attributes

that refer back to the type of operation that has been accomplished. When something is added to the beginning of a word, the label is placed at the head of the image; when something is added at the end of the word, the object/label is placed at the foot of the image, and so on. Della Porta promises, for example, that all you need to do is to give your little old lady a hat to remember *num* instead of *anum*. The image in memory thus becomes a rebus in which the solution is obtained by subtraction (of the letter *a*, in this case). Procedures like these help us to understand the strength of the spatial perception of the word. The word is reduced to its written shape, a set of forms arranged on the page. The whole game is based on a correspondence between the *loci* of the body and the *loci* of the word. Body and text overlap. One can mentally write on both of them (this theme will be discussed in chapter 4 below).

Another way to associate a word with an image is to break it down into visible parts, using the procedure that we have seen in Palatino's *sonetto figurato*. Indeed, it is at this point in the treatise that Della Porta copies out the sonnet and offers it as a useful exercise for beginners: 'To help beginners in this exercise, we have included some poetry in Italian, with its images, so that it can be used as an example in other cases' (*Ars reminiscendi*, pp. 16–17).[34] The sonnet/rebus is thus used as an exercise for beginners: its ingredients are produced by the manipulation of its literal meaning and thus facilitate its own memorization; it accustoms the reader to the mental gymnastics needed to break any connection between signifier and signified imposed by the context. The word is isolated in space and broken down in such a way that its iconic capabilities can be developed. This is precisely an introduction to the art of memory.

In the last section of his treatise Della Porta uses an analogous procedure for shaped alphabets and numbers (figures 24–26). Here again he uses mostly material that he had recycled.[35] The process used to break down the signifier can arrive at a single letter: through the principle of *resemblance* every letter develops its visual, imagistic potential within the confines of a relatively homogeneous semantic field (the human body or work tools). The examples shown here have been around for centuries, and they will flourish in many different forms for centuries to come. What is interesting is that throughout the course of the sixteenth century these alphabets are used in writing books, in manuals on ciphers, as well as in texts devoted to the art of memory. Perhaps the idea originally comes from the sheets of vellum used by itinerant in-

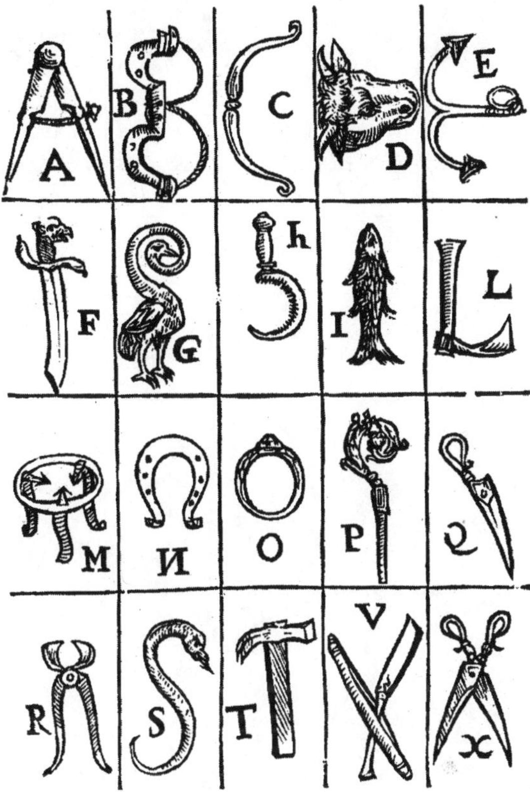

24 A shaped alphabet composed of animals and tools, from Giovan Battista Della Porta, *Ars reminiscendi* (Naples: Giovan Battista Sottile 1602)

structors to teach the alphabet during the late Gothic era.[36] Teaching, in effect, has always meant the cultivation of memory. The visual association at the heart of memory techniques certainly has a role in the teaching of the alphabet, and it is probably the precursor of the refined ornamental initials used in sixteenth-century prints: true *lettere parlanti* [talking letters], as Franca Petrucci Nardelli has called them.[37] Used to decorate the page, they remind the informed reader of a constellation of stories and characters through the simple coincidence of the initial letter.

We have seen how figurative alphabets and the sonnet/rebus both play on a twofold register of letter and image, circulating between texts and genres with the greatest ease; only to us, centuries later, do these genres appear isolated and distant from each other.

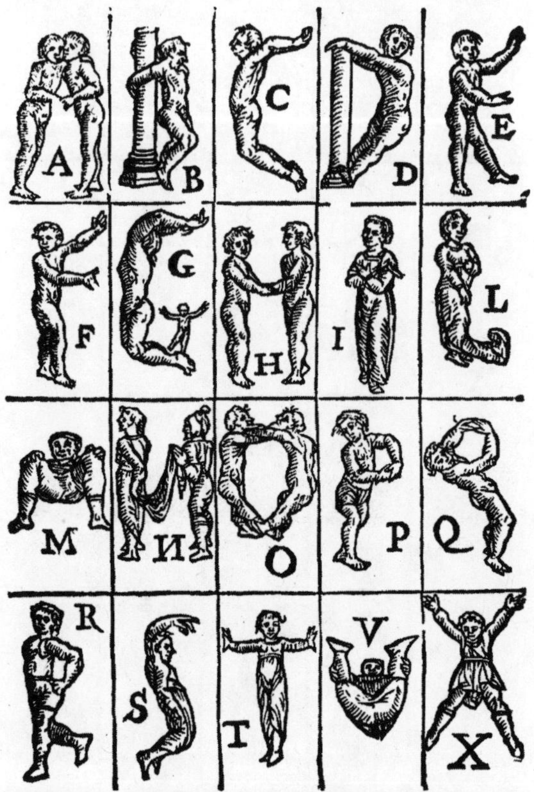

25 A shaped alphabet based on the human body, from Giovan Battista Della Porta, *Ars reminiscendi* (Naples: Giovan Battista Sottile 1602)

3 Ciphered Codes and Images of Memory: The Model of the Machine and the Fascination with Secrets

The close connection between the rebus, ciphers, and the art of memory has thus brought us back, by a peripheral path, to a fundamental area of concern that produced a rich tradition of literary and philosophical experimentation in the sixteenth century: the nature of language and the possibilities of expanding its boundaries by mixing expressive codes; and the nature of the sign, its relation to truth, and its operational effectiveness. This subject took different forms: for example, the search for an original and universal language, capable of stitching words and

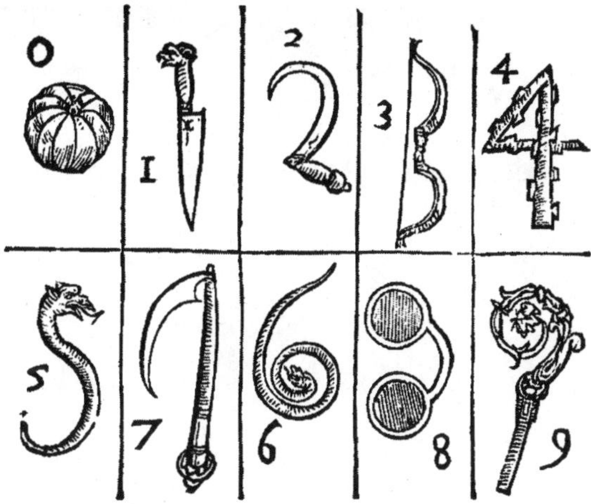

26 Shaped numbers, from Giovan Battista Della Porta, *Ars reminiscendi* (Naples: Giovan Battista Sottile 1602)

things back together;[38] shaped poems and words *messi a tavola* [placed on the table];[39] and even the myth of frozen words, that is, words that become solid under certain conditions and can thus be seen. This last topos spanned the centuries, from Plutarch to Baron Münchausen, and, as Carlo Ossola has written, it found its 'exemplary "topos" and manifestation during the Renaissance, in a gathering of literary types, from Calcagnini's apology to Castiglione's facetious parable, to Rabelais's actual hermeneutical myth.'[40] We might add that Anton Francesco Doni gives a satirical version of this topos that is, as usual, sharp and perceptive: 'Oh, you're really laying it on thick up here in the clouds,' says Doni's Momus to the academician Peregrino, in *I mondi* [Worlds]. 'If the words could be seen, you wouldn't say them.'[41]

This need to manipulate and give bodily shape to language oscillates between metaphysical anxiety (the desire to obtain the secret language of the universe) and technical virtuosity (the challenge of mechanically controlling or altering the different combinations of language). These opposing forces are clearly present in two authors for whom the art of memory is closely related to ciphers: Giovanni Fontana and Jacques Gohory. Around 1430 Giovanni Fontana (died ca 1455) used ciphers to write his treatise on mnemonics, *Secretum de thesauro experimentorum ymaginationis hominum* [Secret of the treasure-room of experiments in

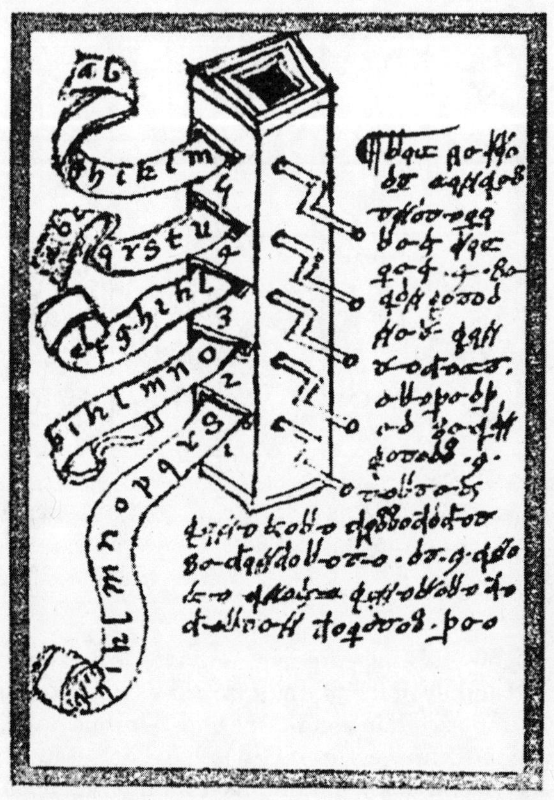

27 A memory machine, from Giovanni Fontana, *Secretum de thesauro experimentorum ymaginationis hominum*, reproduced in E. Battisti and G. Saccaro Battisti, *Le macchine cifrate di G. Fontana* (Milan: Arcadia 1984)

man's imagination].[42] Ciphers are not simply a tool for keeping a secret, but a means of saving content and remembering it. Traditionally both internal and external tools have been used for memory; Fontana, however, depends entirely on the latter. His external tools are actual machines (figure 27) with rollers that turn and allow for different combinations of letters. Similar to the combination lock, but with a code made of letters instead of numbers, these memory machines can also be used to construct encrypted messages. For Fontana it is not just a matter of applying the canonical rules of the art of memory; he writes that the places and mental images discussed in the tradition are respectively the material and form of the procedure. The same model can be applied to his machines: 'my machine, made of iron and other materials, can be considered as matter. The shape and arrangement of the letters can be considered as form' (p. 147).[43] His machines are the extension of a mental mechanism, but their relationship can also be reversed: 'for this and other reasons, it appears that clocks have been invented to preserve for us the memory of time and past motion. I have also constructed many clocks that worked with wheels and smoke. They called me to work even when I had neglected it, as if they themselves had actual memory' (p. 147).[44] The machines can thus take the memory of their creator and make it their own as if they were its animators and custodians.

A doctor, an engineer, an expert builder of automata and wonderful, awe-inspiring optical effects, Fontana also proves his expertise in illusionistic techniques, in the scenographic skills needed to arrange images in the theatre of the mind. For someone like Fontana, who boasts of having taught perspective to Jacopo Bellini, the problem of arranging images in interior mental space is an optical, perspectival problem. In calculating the light necessary to illuminate the *loci* of memory, for example, one can use the same rules as those used to trick the physical eye and control it artificially.

For Fontana, therefore, ciphers are an effective tool for the art of memory, and they inhabit a territory in which the fascination with machines comes together with refined techniques of perspective and wonderful illusionistic effects. In a culture so heavily influenced by Neoplatonism and the Cabbala the construction and use of ciphers mean handling something that touches on the deepest and most secret levels of reality. This is evident in the case of Jacques Gohory (1520–1576), a French man of letters imbued with Italian culture, translator of Machiavelli, friend of the poets of the Pléiade, follower of Paracelsus, founder of a splendid garden and an academy where botany, music, and alchemy were studied.[45] He also sees ciphers as a tool of artificial memory. Divine secrets, moreover, are hidden behind their rather simple appearance: 'They are like the Silenus of Alcibiades, a sort of ridiculous blanket placed over something marvellous, or like a scanty dress that covers a beautiful girl. But enter, for herein are the gods, as Heraclitus used to say.'[46]

Throughout the course of the sixteenth century the image of the Silenus invites the intellectual to follow a road towards the interior, to pass through the bark to the core, to confront the scandal of appearances, the paradox of lowliness and ugliness.[47] Seen in this light, ciphers for Gohory are a way of giving form to Pythagorean numbers, to the cabbalist names for God, to the first principles of Lullism. They are the signs of the secret alphabet of reality, the letters with which the book of the cosmos was written. Ciphers are thus the hidden face of writing. They open a door both to arcane wisdom and to the secrets of beauty. Plato's *Cratylus*, writes Gohory, has revealed the hidden but actual bond between words and things. It thus becomes possible, indeed essential, to study the expressive characteristics of the single letter:

> he who gives names to things, if wise, must study them most diligently. I ask myself: how much care does the art of eloquence – which claims to be supreme among all the others – devote to the matching of letters so that the combination of the vowels and the consonants does not result in asperity, unpleasant and disconnected? and how much care does it devote to the computation and rhythm of the syllables?   (Folio 14v)[48]

The cipher has therefore become a tool for rethinking the ways in which knowledge and beauty are related and the ways in which they generate each other. It is in this context that Gohory honours the studies of the alphabet undertaken by Albrecht Dürer (1471–1528) and places them on the same level as those of Camillo: 'the letter "I," according to Dürer, was the basis for the composition of all ciphers and all letters, inasmuch as it was a straight line' (Folio B3v).[49] Camillo, writes Gohory, has succeeded in wedding the combinatorial art of Lullism with the splendour of eloquence: in his theatre, 'with amazing order, he accumulated, as in a cornucopia, everything necessary to deal with any subject matter whatsoever in an elegant and copious way' (folio C3v).[50] The Lullian art would have been perfect 'si subtilitatis laudem eloquentiae splendore adaequasset' [if it had united the splendour of eloquence with the value of subtlety] (folio C3v). This position is very close to that of Ruscelli, Palatino's teacher in matters of cryptography (see p. 89).[51]

Ciphers, therefore, are tools of an art of memory that is also an *ars combinatoria*, that is, a method for knowing and representing the hidden structure of reality. In *Della tramutatione metallica sogni tre* [Three dreams concerning the transmutation of metals] (Brescia: Marchetti 1572), a work devoted to alchemy, Giovan Battista Nazari (1533–ca 1599) gives

28 A three-headed dragon, from Giovan Battista Nazari, *Della tramutazione metallica sogni tre* (Brescia: Pietro Maria Marchetti 1559)

this interrelationship a narrative form and pictorial expression.[52] In the guise of a vision, this book recounts a journey through the three kingdoms of alchemy: the sophist kingdom, based on false principles and inspired by greed; the real kingdom, functioning in nature; and the philosophical kingdom, which produces true metamorphosis, the transformation of the human into the divine. The primary model for this work is an alchemical reinterpretation of the *Hypnerotomachia Poliphili* (1499). The pilgrim-hero of Nazari's story passes through forests, villages, lakes, tombs, gardens, labyrinths, arches, pyramids, places generally characterized by elaborate architectural constructions and decorated with statues and enigmatic inscriptions.[53] He stops to look at the 'odd inventions,' and then 'considers them and goes over them in his memory.'[54] The reader is invited, even required, to do the same, as she/he turns the pages of the book and finds bizarre, hideous, and startling illustrations, such as a dragon with three heads (p. 146; figure 28), or an emasculated Mercury with no hands or feet (p. 11; figure 29), or a donkey playing a pipe surrounded by dancing monkeys (p. 16;

29 Mercury emasculated, with his hands and feet amputated, from Giovan
Battista Nazari, *Della tramutazione metallica sogni tre* (Brescia: Pietro Maria
Marchetti 1559)

figure 30). The various steps of alchemical transformation are represented in a theatrical, dramatic manner; the characters of myth are
subjected to cruel torture. 'Then, from a distance, I could see a large
village adorned with many towers,' we read, for example, in the second
dream. 'When I came closer, I began to hear screams, as if therein lay
the infernal Styx' (p. 73). Driven by his desire for knowledge, the
pilgrim then overcomes his hesitation and moves towards a large
flaming stove, in which

I compassionately watched the weeping and afflicted as he [the father of
Tantalus] embraced the melancholy son of Earth. Their cries filled my ears
with compassion, and they caused Echo to resound throughout the caverns nearby, all the more when they were bathed with the supple white
flesh of the cruel and fragile father of Chiron. Alas, whoever should see

30 A donkey playing a fife, from Giovan Battista Nazari, *Della tramutazione metallica sogni tre* (Brescia: Pietro Maria Marchetti 1559)

their mangled limbs, their destroyed delicate bodies, will no longer need to learn what pain is.   (P. 74)

This is not the first time that mythology has been subjected to alchemical reinterpretation. At the same time, however, one cannot help but be struck by the way Nazari treats the mythological characters: there is a definite insistence on the physical description of the torment, and a strong emotional appeal in the direction of horror and pity. Clearly these images are effective *imagines agentes* of the art of memory, arranged in the *loci* – memorable in their own right – of the architecture and the natural sites evoked by the text. If the illustrations and the words used to describe them are striking for their unusual character, the emotional charge in the scenes of torture is destined to be imprinted in the reader's mind. The reader is thus called upon (required, as we were saying earlier) to retrace internally the path described by the author.

In a different way the use of ciphers plays the same role. The enigmatic nature of the message forces one to hesitate, to devote the time and concentration that are necessary to understand, to know, and to remember. In addition to the strange statue of Mercury, the pilgrim finds an inscription of *zifferati versi* [ciphered verses], an octave of ciphers. Only after accepting their challenge, and 'after long consideration,' does the pilgrim come to understand that these rhymes are intended to put him on his guard against false alchemy. They also provide a key to understanding the meaning of the statue of Mercury, that 'astute figurative invention' that will remain obscure to those who 'rashly' move forward, fooling themselves that they will reach their destination sooner.

While the ciphered message accompanying the statue of Mercury is made up of common letters of the alphabet that have merely been switched in their order, much stranger letters are used in the engraving on the large plaque hanging above the entrance to the village in chapter 20 of the second dream (pp. 70–71). Forty-five forms of the letter A are used (figure 31) in a virtuoso attempt to give shape to the beginning of all alphabets, real or not. Of course, we are in the middle of a journey of initiation, and the letter/cipher, with its different forms and combinations, is called forth to symbolize the creative process. The same thing happens, although in a more systematic fashion, in chapter 8 of book 3, where the letters of the alphabet are arranged along the branches of a tree and a large table is used to visualize the system of correspondences between each letter and the different stages of the alchemical process. Even here the letters, which are organized on the *loci* of the tree, act as both ciphers and images of memory.

The most singular aspect of this fiction, however, is that the village, with the plaque with its forty-five forms of the letter A hanging over its main entrance, is a celebration of Gutenberg and the invention of movable type. The typesetting workshop is described as an alchemic transmutation accompanied by blood, death, and suffering. The result is a dark mass covered with 'a white veil ... obscured by straight lines, in such a way that through it you could see the Trojan siege, the wars of the Romans and the Carthaginians, and all that man wishes to know' (p. 72). The printing press had made knowledge visible: the letter – in its dimension as a symbol, but also in its material consistency, in its new 'technical reproducibility' – is impregnated by human experience and transmits it to future generations, giving shape, memory, and

31 The forty-five forms of the letter A, from Giovan Battista Nazari, *Della tramutazione metallica sogni tre* (Brescia: Pietro Maria Marchetti 1559)

visualization to the chaos of history.[55] Nazari's work is indicative of the complex combination of myths, expectations, and meanings that coalesce around writing in the sixteenth century, a mixture of thought consolidated and reinvigorated by the printing press.

It is not surprising, then, that in 1466–1467 (and thus with exceptional anticipation) Leon Battista Alberti (1404–1472) expresses his interest in the new German techniques of printing, and does so in a text dedicated to cryptography.[56] Geofroy Tory (ca 1480–ca 1533) is directly involved with the printing press when he weaves an extraordinary network of associations, images, and meanings around the letters of the alphabet (figure 32) in his *Champ fleury* (1529).[57]

32 A letter of the alphabet, from Geofroy Tory, *Champ fleury* (Paris: sold by
Geofroy Tory and Giles Gourmont 1529)

4 Games That Generate Texts

Sigismondo Fanti's 'Triompho di fortuna'

Sigismondo Fanti, a contemporary of Ariosto, and also from Ferrara,
was an astrologist, a mathematician, an expert in military architecture,
and a disenchanted observer of a world where only the poor died by
hanging.[58] His works allow us to reweave, so to speak, the scattered
threads of our discourse.

Fanti is the calligrapher and author of *Theorica et pratica ... de modo
scribendi fabricandique omnes litterarum species* [Theory and practice of
script and the production of every type of writing] (Venice: Giovanni
Rossi 1514), a work which looks to Vitruvius for the construction of
letters in geometric proportion (figure 33; see also p. 88 above). This text
has a practical aim: to help the calligrapher and anyone who needs to
engrave on marble. But another dimension of meaning is apparent

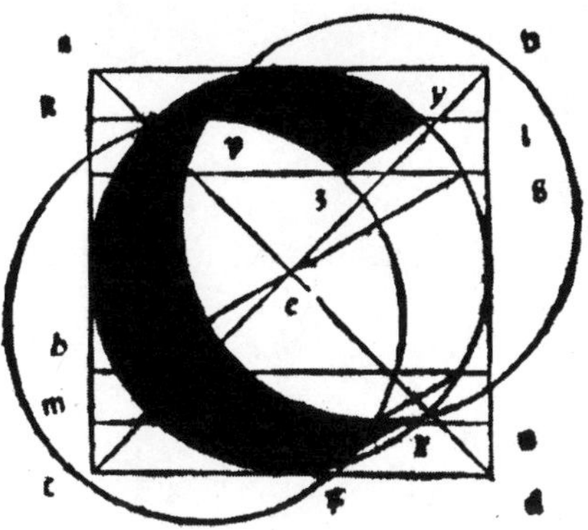

33 An example of a letter drawn using geometric proportions, from
   Sigismondo Fanti, *Theorica et pratica de modo scribendi fabricandique omnes
   literarum species* (Venice: Giovanni Rossi 1514)

between the lines, among the brief comments and in the splendid
illustrations. The vicissitudes of the shapes of the letters, for example,
prompt Fanti to reflect on the cycles of the cosmos. In three thousand
years, he writes

> letters and language will change, and maybe men will be almost like those
> at the beginning. And giants will be born anew, and do not believe that
> Sunday, the day of the Lord, will actually be the natural day, and the same
> holds for the other days of the week. But the day we eat meat will perhaps
> be Friday, or perhaps Saturday. And the same holds for the offices of the
> church: with the mutation they will no longer be correctly officiated at the
> right time.   (Folio 20v)

As a remedy for this tottering world, Fanti promises – for the appropriate compensation – to reform the calendar so that customs and rituals
can once again reflect the order of the cosmos.[59]

More than anything else, Fanti is proud of his method: 'geometric
reason' allows him, he claims, to understand and reproduce the letters
of the ancients. But his method has an even deeper purpose: it can
make the 'true and proper ... proportion' of nature visible at the level of
writing. Herein lie the seeds of Geofroy Tory's fascination with Fanti.

As an expert in the hidden meanings of writing, it is only natural that
Fanti would work in cryptography. A seventeenth-century biographer
called him 'a great master of writing in ciphers.'[60] He is also the author

(or builder, we might say) of a book/game entitled *Triompho di fortuna* [Triumph of fortune], published in Venice in January 1527. The splendid frontispiece (sometimes attributed to Dosso Dossi, and sometimes to Baldassare Peruzzi) presents us with an image of the pope, seated in precarious balance atop the world (figure 34). One of the cranks of the sphere is in the hands of an angel of good fortune while the other is in the hands of a demon of evil fortune: an extraordinarily powerful image, as Robert Eisler has noted, considering that a few months later the cranks would be decisively turned downward after the Sack of Rome.[61]

In *Triompho di fortuna* the entire cosmos and all knowledge are dismantled and put back together in the course of a game. They are first put into ciphers, so to speak, and then revealed. The intentions of the author and the game are expressed and interpreted by a mysterious character named Mercurio Vannullo of Rome. Although the structure obliges the reader to follow its linear path, the book, with its splendid illustrations, really ought to be dismantled and used like a combination of a deck of cards and a road-game.[62] You play by following a route along which you stop according to the question you have chosen (one of seventy-two possible questions) and the roll of the dice. The *places* of the route are represented by a copious iconographic apparatus which is encyclopedic in scope. You begin with fortune (actually with the twelve iconographic figures of fortune) and then move on to the twelve noble houses of Italy until you get to the seventy-two wheels and thirty-six spheres (figure 35) in which sky and earth, great figures of antiquity and modernity, princes, warriors, philosophers, poets, and artists have all been assigned their places. You finally arrive at the answers, which have been reorganized around images of sibyls and the most famous of astrologers.

This work belongs to the tradition of the *libro delle sorti* or [book of lots].[63] At the end of the game you have, of course, an answer, a prophecy that responds to your initial question. But the complexity and the encyclopedic nature of Fanti's *Triompho* make it into something quite extraordinary. Marco Guazzo's sonnet to the reader promises:

> Herein one will learn much
> of that which noble nature retains in itself
> and at the same time enjoy a magnificent game   (Folio 6r)

The prophecy, the *gioco delle sorti* [game of lots], is just one component

34 Frontispiece in Sigismondo Fanti, *Triompho di fortuna* (Venice: Agostino Portese 1527)

of a design to transmit encyclopedic knowledge through play. Another model operates in the text: that of didactic/mnemonic games. In the eighteenth century they would become a fad, but they are already well-established by the beginning of the sixteenth century. In the seventeenth century – and this, too, is highly significant for our study – they also interact with the genre of literary paradox.[64]

One indication of the relationship of Fanti's text to this tradition is the way in which it describes the workings of the game. Once the query has been chosen, for example, '*you will enter* the table of the Triumph of Fortune' (folio 3r); with regard to answers relating to salvation or condemnation, 'Reader, *you will make ... various entrances* in the present triumph ... and without a doubt, you will find such praiseworthy, perfect and full maxims that in the end you will be thoroughly satis-

35 The wheel of lasciviousness, from Sigismondo Fanti, *Triompho di fortuna* (Venice: Agostino Portese 1527)

fied' (folio 15v). The squares of the game are thus places into which you actually *enter* (physically and mentally). We have already seen the same device in Toscanella's rhetoric machines and Castelvetro's diagrams.

The entrance into and visits to the various places in the game act as a springboard for the scientific and moral teachings that the author has deposited in them. The following are some of the recurring formulas: 'in this place we show that ...'; '*in this place* Fanti *exhorts* people to let time take care of vendettas' (folio 13r); '*under the shadow* of the present question, the author teaches and gives the fundamental points to be fought over on one side and the other' (folio 7v). Thus, all of knowledge is present in this work. It is all conveniently subdivided in the various places, and it can easily be given to the user.

Of course, in order for this to be possible, the organization of the places is fundamental, and thus the disposition that characterizes the text. The prefatory note to the section entitled 'Della significatione delle figure' [On the meaning of the illustrations] claims that, 'however playful, amusing, and erudite this work may appear at first glance, it is nonetheless organized with amazing artifice, and many different savours can be extracted from it' (folio 15v). Each one of the initial seventy-two questions is marked by three small figures. One of these reappears at the end of the game, in the centre of the square that contains an astrological chart. The astrological response is expressed and interpreted in a quatrain (figure 36). The text specifies that every detail of the image has a meaning, and it gives some general suggestions on how to decipher it. The system of signification, it appears, is based in part on a type of hieroglyphic dictionary. The dove, for example, indicates happiness and purity; the snake indicates wisdom; a palm held by a woman and a man is a prophecy of a happy union. However, the system is also based on card games: there is a suit that indicates each type of event (nocturnal birds and swords, for example, indicate danger). The number of objects represented introduces further specifics: for example, three swords mean that three wounds will be inflicted, or that a person is in danger of being wounded three times. The prophetic and mnemonic function of these images is clear; while there is a recurring invitation to memorize the verse and teachings given by the text, the images, conveniently positioned in the various places, will help the reader to do so. In other words, the game constructs a path along which there are continuous cross-references between the words and images. Taken as a whole, it acts to imprint on the mind the memory of knowledge and one's own destiny.

As we mentioned earlier, in the final responses each astrological chart is marked by both a mnemonic image and four lines of verse. Taken together, the verses form what is almost a long didactic poem of more than six thousand lines (obviously not of the best craftsmanship). Aware of its shortcomings, Fanti apologizes, citing as precedents Cecco d'Ascoli and Cino da Pistoia, not to mention Dante himself (folio 2v). This encyclopedic repertory in verse, however, is interesting for a variety of reasons. On many subjects Fanti defends every position and its opposite. The answers relating to the nature of women are particularly significant: whether or not they are the equals of men; whether it is bad not to be a virgin at marriage; whether women can dedicate themselves to study and to war; and so on (folio LIXv, 20; folio LXIr, 3; etc.). A

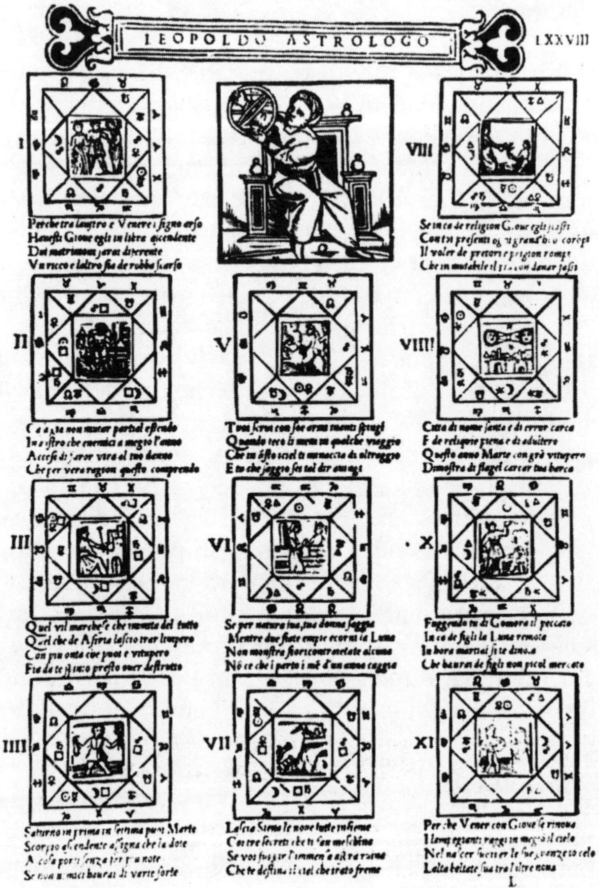

36 A table of answers, from Sigismondo Fanti, *Triompho di fortuna* (Venice: Agostino Portese 1527)

series of undeniably feminist answers are promptly negated by contrary answers. This reminds us that in the seventeenth century mnemonic/didactic games are considered to be a component of literary paradox: not only do they unite opposites according to the model of *serio ludere* [serious play], but they can transmit openly ambiguous and contradictory messages. In any event, in sixteenth-century culture the paradox seems to be an obligatory medium for the discussion of women: it is this compromise formation that allows one to confront (and exorcise) the problems posed by the feminine universe.[65]

The long didactic poem at the end of *Triompho di fortuna*, which can be variously disassembled and put back together, is most interesting when considered from the point of view adopted in this chapter. As we have seen, in some ways literature is a game, and the terms of the discourse can easily be reversed; thus, a game can be used to produce a text. Each of us can do this by submitting more questions to the *Triompho di fortuna* and by letting ourselves be guided through the wheels and spheres until we reach a final response: a poem ready and waiting, made just for us. Fanti's game is the place of all possible destinies and stories. If we were to play with time ourselves, we might imagine that Fanti and Italo Calvino meet: the place would naturally be a castle (or a tavern), of crossed destinies.[66]

Francesco Marcolini's 'Sorti'

But we should invite at least one other character to take part in this meeting: Francesco Marcolini (ca 1500–ca 1560). Originally from Forlì in Romagna, Marcolini was an editor in Venice; working closely with Pietro Aretino, and later Anton Francesco Doni, he actively promoted the publication of new works in the vernacular. An erudite and refined man who contributed to the renewal of typography, Marcolini was also a lover of music and the arts.[67] In 1540 (and then again in 1550) he published *Le sorti intitulate giardino di pensieri* [A book of divinations entitled the garden of thoughts], a work similar in scope to Fanti's *Triompho di fortuna*.[68] Here again we are faced with the book/game. Its use calls for a combination of choice (you choose one of the prescribed questions, of which there are thirteen for men and thirteen for women, and twenty-four for either sex) and chance (drawn from a deck of cards). Each player is guided along a path of words and images that leads to a final answer in the form of a tercet, part of a complex network of conceptual and iconographic associations. Here again the game produces a text, or rather a textual fragment that can be combined with other fragments in various ways. This book/game, as we have been saying, is also the place of all possible stories. Once again we find paradoxical topics, the presence of contrary theses, even though the anti-feminist stance seems to prevail: if a man, for example, asks if he is loved, he is sent to the image of fame; if it is woman who asks this question, she is sent to vanity. Marcolini's work makes evident the circular relationship – and recycling – that establishes itself between play and literature: the questions regarding love and women are, on the one hand, related to the ancient tradition of questions [*dubbi*] and to other games of the courts of love; on the other hand, they are the very same questions that will fuel a genre of literature destined for great editorial success in the 1540s and 1550s.

Marcolini's *Sorti* offer us an extraordinary gallery of images: an iconological dictionary that preceded Cesare Ripa's by decades. But Marcolini's images are not simply inserted into a fixed yet arbitrary order (such as an alphabetical order, for example); rather, they are inserted into a network of relationships that makes them ready for combinatorial games. Matrimony, for example, is portrayed by a masculine figure with his feet chained to a yoke, and it is associated with necessity, pleasure, experience, and regret (p 12). The images of philosophers accompany images of abstract concepts that correspond to various events and situations in life (truth is followed by Polemon, matrimony by Pherecydes, victory by Bias, and so on). This treatise is a type of theatre of memory, and its structure deserves further study.[69] Certainly Camillo's influence is still very much alive in Marcolini's circle and among his closest collaborators, who include Aretino and Doni, of course, but also Sebastiano Serlio (1475–1554), whose *Regole generali di architettura* [General rules of architecture] was published by Marcolini in a splendid edition in 1537.

In the *places* of its pages Marcolini's book/game arranges words and images that both remember and prophesy, that distil knowledge of the past in order to indicate our fortune. The subtitle, 'Garden of thoughts,' is indicative: the thoughts to which the words and images refer are arranged and combined like the flowers in a garden. The work is based on the old model of the anthology, or *florilegium*, which assumed new meaning and complexity in the sixteenth century, an age when the refined art of gardens and *ars combinatoria* were both widely cultivated. As Amedeo Quondam has shown, in Pietro Aretino's *Ragionamento delle corti* [The dialogues on the court], published two years earlier (1538), 'Marcolini's garden' has become the emblematic place for literature freed from the court and the church.[70]

Marcolini is apparently aware of the dimension of hidden meanings and the combinatory logic on which the game relies. The reader is, in fact, called upon to become similarly aware, and to play along, from the begininng of the text (and the game). Marcolini writes that his book had been devised with such ingenuity,

that you will discover different things for the same point (but all of them

as anwers for that point) that you may wish to know, and words will also
be found for the various points. And no one ought to be amazed by this
because, since I had to demonstrate the artifice of chance and since celestial influence produces differing effects within each small period of time, I
have decided in my work that, in interposing a delay before seeing the
fortune of this and that person in this work of mine, even though they ask
the same question, the lines of poetry come out varied, and when they ask
different questions, they will encounter the same tercets in response to
them.   (P 4)

The book/game, therefore, is intended to reproduce the game of
unity and variety that characterizes the way fortune works. Its pages
suggests routes that cross even though they start at different places or
routes that do not cross even though they start at the same place.
Decades later, Emanuele Tesauro writes that the game of tarot cards
represents the different conditions and desires of men, 'as if a player
holding a deck of cards has the world in his hand and, metaphorically,
playing is nothing else than making confusion in the universe.'[71]
Marcolini, as well, has associated games with the possibility, or illusion, of having the 'world in his hands,' but his true dream has been to
construct an amusing, ingenious duplicate of the world. He uses it as a
way of confronting chance through the combinatorial art of words and
images, through the enchantment of poetry and painting.

5 Texts That Produce Games

Works like those of Fanti and Marcolini can be considered a refined
elaboration of a genre – the so-called *libri de la sorte* and *libri de la
ventura*, or books of fortune – that was very popular in the fifteenth and
sixteenth centuries. At any rate, the game of sortilege was played both
in and out of princely courts. It was common to play it during celebra-
tions of the Epiphany: A line of poetry is read (or a book is opened at
random and read), and then the passage is assigned to one of those
present whose name has been arbitrarily chosen. There is evidence that
such amusements took place at the court of the Este in Ferrara. Isabella
d'Este, for example, drew a verse from Petrarch in a game of lots: 'Fior
di virtù, fontana di beltade' [Flower of virtue, fountain of beauty]. It is
easy to imagine that such a lot was a rather fortunate one, not only for
the woman, but also for the courtier who had the task of glossing and
interpreting this match.[72]

More significant, although more unsettling, was the lot – a line from Ariosto's *Orlando furioso* referring to the Saracen character Rodomonte – drawn by Giordano Bruno while he was playing this game with his fellow novitiates in Naples sometime in 1565–1566: 'd'ogni legge nimico e d'ogni fede' [enemy to every law and every faith] (28.99.8). Bruno would later tell his fellow-prisoners in Venice that he had embraced this lot as his own, as a sign of his character and his destiny: 'he was extremely proud of this, and he said that he had drawn a line of poetry that reflected his nature.'[73] At the summit of Mount Ventoux Petrarch had drawn his lot from Saint Augustine's *Confessions*.[74] It was common in the sixteenth century to consult the great works of Italian literature for this purpose; Petrarch's *Canzoniere* and Ariosto's *Orlando furioso* were used for amusement, games, erotic and courtly homage, as well as for the restless search for prophecy, for a true sign of one's destiny. In any case the many varied examples indicate a widespread practice by which literary texts were chopped up, minced, abbreviated, reduced to words/objects that could be reshuffled, drawn in a game of lots, and associated with people and situations.

This widespread practice was also the seed of Fanti's and Marcolini's splendid book/games. Now we will see how an analogous mechanism functioned in other sixteenth-century texts in accordance with much more complex modalities. While the games of Fanti and Marcolini produce mere fragments of text (in addition to images of one's destiny), the books we are about to examine play on literary and cultural memory and actually produce games from texts. But, as in the case of Marcolini, these devices of memory show that the relationship can be reversed. It is still a matter of maintaining an open relationship between memory and invention, inasmuch as the latter is understood to be the capacity to produce both words and actions in conformity with the rules of the game.

The ten books of Innocenzo Ringhieri's *Cento giochi liberali e d'ingegno* [*One hundred witty games*] (Bologna: Anselmo Giaccarelli 1551) are dedicated to Catherine de' Medici, queen of France.[75] But the book is also dedicated to women in general, and every one of its games is an occasion to praise them. We will limit our discussion of this rich and interesting book to showing how the mechanisms of memory come, literally, into play.

Ringhieri's work requires (while simultaneously providing and mobilizing) an enormous heritage of cultural memory. In the first place, it has strong ties both in its structure and in its language to the canonical texts of literary culture, such as the *Canzoniere*, the *Decameron*, *Il cortegiano*, and *Orlando furioso*. Ringieri's book establishes an intertextual connection with works considered to be easily recognizable in the reader's memory. These texts furnish the material for the game and the occasion for play. The true and proper game, moreover, appears little more than a pretext: each of the one hundred games is a mosaic of the common cultural memory of the sixteenth century that will be sliced up and subdivided into parts that are assigned to each player.

Each participant in the game, therefore, is identified with that part of knowledge, that fragment of the encyclopedia, that is assigned to and is to be enacted by him/her. The different types of participation range from the reading of a verse to gestures, to presentations that lie between dance and the theatre. Not only is one of the games a comedy (in which each type of character is associated with a line of the play), but the theatrical model is expressly indicated as being analogous to the game, or, better, to the 'free game of wit,' proposed by Ringhieri. In fact, when faced with having to exorcise the fears brought about by the Game of Death, Ringhieri reminds the players that in the theatre painful events are mixed with pleasurable ones in order to make the various events of life visible and recognizable. His games do the same thing by 'creating a likeness to such theatrical games' (folio 64v). We have already encountered this structure: Ringhieri proposes a didactic/mnemonic game in which memory is reactivated through theatrical presentation. In any case, the material to be remembered is 'treated' and then put back into the text, so to speak, in such a way that it is geared both for memory and for the game. Now we can look at how this result is obtained.

As we have noted, at the basis of Ringhieri's games is the middle-to-high cultural knowledge typical of the sixteenth century. In order to play you have to know the classics of Italian literature, but most importantly you have to be able to handle a cultural code in which words and images interact. You must be familiar, for example, with the science of the *impresa*: in the Game of the Knight you have to determine 'the device, motto, and colours of [the knight's] clothes and costume' (folio 1 r–v) before he enters a joust. It is also necessary to be an expert in mythography and iconography: in the Game of Fortune, for example, each player is assigned wings, an anchor, or sails (in other words, one of the attributes of fortune). But in the Game of the Three Fates, if you have to forfeit, then you must respond to questions [*dubbi*] regarding the characteristics of traditional imagery: you have to say, for example, why the figure in the middle is painted 'larger than the first and the last' (folio 11r). You also have to know the language of ciphers, disputations of the figurative arts, treatises on love, the canon of feminine beauty, and so on.

But now let us see how this knowledge is fragmented and then set into motion according to the logic of the game. In the second book many of the games are naturalistic. They have to do with the sea, the mountains, lakes, and so forth, all filtered through literature: their different names are associated with the topical conventions with which they appear in literary texts. The name of a spring or river, for example, is accompanied by a verse that describes its effects and characteristics. Here you have, writes Ringhieri, a 'nice array of rivers and selected verse aptly dispensed' (folio 22v). This poetic cento, or anthology of poetic fragments, gives shape to the list of names by constructing it around a network of associations that help you to remember it: it is thus ready for use either in the game or in literary composition. Ringhieri's *Cento giochi* is fundamentally similar to Ravisius Textor's *Officina*, a repertory of literary topoi that we have mentioned in relation to Toscanella in chapter 2. In the introduction to the Game of Lakes, Ringhieri himself gives an example of how memory and invention can spring forth from the material furnished by the text: 'My merciful, gracious ladies, never do nature's serene, resplendent, docile lakes *return to my memory* without *reminding me similarly* of the tranquillity and quiet of your hearts' (folio 23r).

The Game of Madness orders its material according to conventions already familiar to us. After listing a series of qualities and their opposites, it directs the players to draw a tree of folly and then asks in which place of the tree (roots, trunk, etc.) each quality should be situated. Here folly has been 'drawn out into a tree,' as Toscanella would say, and this is what facilitates the game. 'Now you understand,' notes Ringhieri, 'the *figure* and the law of the Game of Madness' (folio 15r).

Together with this mnemonic cento and the ordered space of the tree, another ingredient of the art of memory enters the game – the image, described in detail and contrived so as to activate a chain of meanings. There are games, in fact, that use images in a manner akin to Doni's *Pitture* [Paintings] and Camillo's theatre. Thus, the Game of Envy begins with a long description of its devastating effects and its habitat. 'This is the *portrait and the painting*, my dear ladies, that I have chosen to give you of wicked, insatiable envy,' writes the author (folio 116v). The image's function as a mnemonic *summa* becomes more evident as the game develops. Indeed the game is based on a series of questions regarding the subject matter: what is envy? where is it? what does it live on? etc. After describing the fates in the game we mentioned above, Ringhieri notes: '*in the figure* here below, one can better *learn and see* (folio 10v).

The mechanisms used by the text also become clear in the Game of Proteus: the fable of Aristaeus and Proteus (taken from Virgil's *Georgics*, 4.387ff.) is broken up in such a way that it is transformed into a game of witty remarks and rejoinders. For example, the first player may say, 'what does ...,' and the next player continues by saying 'Aristaeus the shepherd do?' The next player says, 'he,' and the next, 'falls asleep in the cave,' and so on until the end is reached. In this '*place*, once the circle has been completed, the first [player] does not wait for the others to prompt him to answer with his bits, but recites the entire speech or oration' (folio 91v). The dismantling of the text makes the myth easy to remember and represent. The physical *place* in which each player is positioned will correspond exactly to the *place* of his or her bit of text (and therefore to its *place* in the memorization of the whole).

Many of the *questions* to which a player must respond after being forced to forfeit a game deal with the hidden meanings of the myth, and they indicate the path of its possible reuse in another context (for example, to speak on the subject of the metamorphoses produced by love). When dismantled in this fashion, the myth becomes a topos for literary invention. One of the so-called questions asks whether Proteus signifies first matter, 'as the virtuous gentleman Bocchi demonstrates in one of his learned symbols' (folio 92r). This is an important citation, because it alludes to a work by Achille Bocchi, the *Symbolicae quaestiones* [symbolical questions], that would not be published until several years later, in 1555. Ringhieri thus boasts of his intimacy with one of the central figures of culture in Bologna.[76]

A lecturer in Greek, 'rhetoric and poetry,' and 'humanities' at the university, Achille Bocchi (1488–1562) had an extended network of cultural relations. He knew Hebrew, was an impassioned scholar of the Cabbala and hermetism, and was a friend of Erasmus. In 1540 he spoke before the Inquistion on behalf of Lisia Fileno (Camillo Renato), who was ultimately condemned as a heretic. In 1546 Bocchi built the splendid palazzo that would become the home of the Accademia Bocchiana: the first printed work published by this Academy was his *Symbolicae quaestiones*. For a number of reasons this work, entitled in full *Symbolicarum quaestionum de universo genere quas serio ludebat libri quinque*

[Five books of questions in symbol forms concerning universal creation, the subject of serious play] (Bologna: Nuova Accademia Bocchiana 1555), is a worthy backdrop for Ringhieri's book. The *Symbolicae quaestiones* focuses on the close-knit relationship between linguistic and pictorial codes. The reader traverses a gallery of splendid, mysterious images engraved by Giulio Bonasone, each of which is marked by a motto and interpreted in a Latin poem. Together, the word and the image guide the reader towards the truth and beauty of hermetic wisdom. The work contains hints of religious reform which the complexity of its codes of expression and its playful form allow it simultaneously to express and to hide.

It is significant for our purposes that one of Bocchi's symbols (pp. 180–181) is dedicated to Giulio Camillo: it depicts a nightingale competing with itself, fooled by its own shadow and its reflection in the water. The symbol for Camillo celebrates both the charm of song and the complex relationship between shadows and ideas.[77] The Bocchi symbol cited by Ringhieri concerning the arcane meaning of Proteus (pp. 124–125; figure 37) is dedicated to Renée of France (duchess of Ferrara), who supported Protestantism, and her father, King Louis XII. The citation thus becomes an underground form of homage to France in line with the Francophile nature of the whole work. At the same time, only those familiar with the symbol know to whom it is dedicated. Renée's religious choices, clearly favourable to reform, make us suspect that even here the game of hidden meanings is at work, that network of allusions accessible only to the chosen few. Ringhieri's work seems to have used those same techniques of communication that, as Delio Cantimori has shown, were familiar to the Italian Nicodemists (who masked their true religious beliefs behind an outward appearance of Catholic orthodoxy).

Other passages from *One Hundred Witty Games* give us an idea of the authors who are important to Ringhieri and of his literary and artistic sympathies. He names Claudio Tolomei (p. 67) as one of his friends. The Game of Poets also provides useful information. Among the Italian poets, Ringhieri lists Bembo and Ariosto, while other writers are divided according to the parts of classical rhetoric: under *inventio* he cites Marcantonio Flaminio, Giulio Camillo, and Francesco Berni, while Bocchi, Aretino, Triphon Gabriele, and Castelvetro appear under *dispositio*. Bernardo Tasso, Annibale Caro, and Sperone Speroni are found under *elocutio* (p. 138). This is a significant review, national in scope, though clearly dominated by the Veneto.

37 *Proteus*, dedicated to Renée of France, from Achille Bocchi, *Symbolicarum quaestionum de universo genere quas serio ludebat* (Bologna: Nuova Accademia Bocchiana 1555)

While Camillo's theatre is important as a model for Ringhieri's construction of the images used in some of his games, he himself appears here as poet. There is another section of the text, however, where Camillo's presence, although not mentioned, is felt in a stronger and more significant way: this is the part dedicated to the Game of Paintings. Twenty-one names of 'excellent painters,' ancient and modern, are grouped in three lists of seven names each. This classification is an indication of a rich and thriving artistic sensibility. Among the modern painters Ringhieri lists Michelangelo and Mantegna, Rosso Fiorentino, Perin del Vaga, Giulio Romano, Francesco Salviati, and 'Don Giulio the miniaturist,' the same Giulio Clovio who, together with Palatino, was a member of the Accademia dello Sdegno. Each player in the game is given the name of a painter. Her/his task is to identify one of the things necessary for the complete mastery of painting: 'if for no other reason,' writes Ringhieri, 'than because, *by playing, one can know all the perfection of painting,* and the way to achieve excellence in it, *as can be seen here in the figure*' (p. 145). There follows a list of the seven types of knowledge necessary to be a painter.

This passage faithfully reproduces, almost to the letter, a passage from Camillo's *Trattato dell'imitazione* [Treatise on imitation] devoted to the seven steps by which the perfect art of painting can be measured.[78] Camillo is not credited for this passage, but his influence here is as strong as ever. It helps us to understand the meaning of the expressions that we have stressed in the passage from Ringhieri cited above ('*by playing ... as can be seen here in the figure*'). For Camillo the possibility of reducing to seven steps the perfect art of painting (and also the art of eloquence, and all the arts for that matter) is closely related to his theatre. His *Trattato dell'imitazione*, printed in 1544, is actually one of seven orations that he wrote in defence of his project. Camillo believes that these seven steps serve to make visible the idea, that is, the perfect model of each art. The seven steps thus allow one to know the model, to remember it, and to bring it to life in one's own work. Ringhieri gives a simplified, playful version of all of this, but he proves to have a sophisticated grasp of the meaning and structure of Camillo's project.

Thus the most recent experiments in the art of memory have made a decisive reappearance in Ringhieri's system. One can play with texts because they can be manipulated and visualized so as to make them, at the same time, easy to memorize and reuse. The declared didactic purposes of Ringhieri's *One Hundred Witty Games* let us see its continuity with that method of reading texts which we have analysed in chapter 2, a way of reading that is geared towards reappropriation. The method breaks the text down and seeks to reorganize it according to patterns and imagery that are easy to remember, and with the same ease these fragments provide the tools for the writing of new texts. Just as the character Gismondo in Bembo's *Gli Asolani* shows us that classical imitation can also be a game, so Ringhieri's book demonstrates that the same procedures used in imitation can also be used to play with the literary tradition.

A work much more famous than Ringhieri's, the *Dialogo de' giuochi che nelle vegghie sanesi si usano di fare* [Dialogue on games commonly played at evening parties in Siena] by Girolamo Bargagli (1537–1586), which was written in 1563–1564 and published in 1572, presents an extremely different formal character, but for our purposes it reveals basic mechanims that are very similar.[79] Here we are far from the abstract, encyclopedic nature of Ringhieri's work; although he is never mentioned, it appears that Ringhieri was Bargagli's polemical target:

> there have been those who have tried to put [some of these games] down on paper in order to teach them to others. They have dreamt up these whimsical games themselves, without thinking whether or not they are for pleasure; and by putting them into practice, they can create difficulties, or even impossible outcomes, because they do not realize that the theory of games must be in agreement with their practice.   (P. 124)

Bargagli refers to a precise moment, historical and cultural, in which these games were played – Siena and the Accademia degli Intronati [Academy of the Thunderstruck] in its most splendid moment, before the wars had swept it away. Through retrospective play the frame of Bargagli's dialogue creates an exponential effect of distance: to recall these games means remembering a lost moment in the life of Siena, in the history of the Academy, and in the author's own history (he had indeed abandoned his studies to become a solicitor).

The games are recalled and proposed as an example, according to a strongly normative scheme, which inscribes them within rhetorical and moral canons of decorum. While on the one hand the dialogue has a pervasive and explicit erotic ambience, on the other it is transformed into a manual of manners for men, and especially for women, who are an essential part of the games: rules of discretion and decorum in conformity, therefore, with the moral climate of the late cinquecento. Yet ancient myths and associations continue to prevail. Take, for example, the way in which the character Attonito [Dumbfounded] (Lelio Maretti) asks Sodo [Solid] (Marcantonio Piccolomini) to begin his discourse: because of the wars, he says, games have not been played for many years and, consequently, 'like the men who came after the Flood, we find ourselves entirely ignorant of those arts that were once practised with great refinement, and, for this reason, you, almost like a new Deucalion, must show us the true way to play games that had reached such perfection before the deluge of the wars' (pp 54–55). There is thus a strong relationship between games and civility, and the Academy is the utopia, the secluded place, where this relationship finds expression and is celebrated. The revival and discussion of the games is like the creation of a new life, a new birth, a new beginning to the life cycle.

The basic mechanism of the games is similar to that which we have seen in Ringhieri. Here, once again, an entire cultural tradition is brought into play. The games derive their matter and their methods from the texts and diverse cultural practices of the sixteenth century. This dialogue by Bargagli could easily be used to reconstruct an archive, to describe the median cultural memory of this period. As in Ringhieri, textual memory is fragmented and then brought to life again through theatrical techniques. As one might expect, however, in Bargagli's work the dramatic aspect is richer and more complex; the Accademia degli Intronati had had direct experience with the theatre, and Bargagli himself was the author of a comedy entitled *La Pellegrina* [The pilgrim]. When you play a game, writes Bargagli, you have to know how to choose the right part for each player, 'like shrewd actors who do not try to take the best role when they put on a play, but the role they think they can best portray and the role best suited to their voice and person' (p. 142). As in Ringhieri's book, there is a Game of Comedy among the games proposed by Bargagli. This is an indication that even Ringhieri's abstract, didactic encyclopedia has borrowed something from actual and widely played games.

While the two texts have the same basic method – utilizing cultural memory through games and theatre – Bargagli's use of literary memory is livelier. He has a strong predilection for the multiple and paradoxical reappropriation of literary memory: the texts, chosen so as to avoid any religious problems, are, in Riccardo Bruscagli's words, 'cut up, scissored, pulverized' in such a way that they make up 'an archive of memory from which you could borrow the wit and acumen necessary for the brilliant performance of games.' By playing on the diverse textual competence of the participants in the game, 'quotations are comically twisted and misunderstood in a running fire of interpretative paradoxes.'[80]

It is significant that in the context of this mannerist dissolution of an entire tradition Bargagli understands the canonical texts as so many types of games: 'And therefore I believe,' says the academician Frastagliato [the Notched] (the future heretic Fausto Sozzini), 'that each day of the *Decameron* can be called a game because all the characters tell a story on the same subject, each different from the other' (p. 71). In the same manner the interpretation of the poetry of Petrarch becomes a sort of game in the Academy, a game in which everyone can participate and debate. The same is true of *Il Cortegiano* (p. 71) and *Gli Asolani*, each singled out as a useful reference for the Game of the Figure of Love (pp. 160–161) in which the players have to speak for and against love. Viewed in light of these academic games and of the new cultural climate in which they thrive, the interpretation of the literary tradition as a source of play is at once unfaithful to it and pitilessly revealing: it brings out and foregrounds what in the early sixteenth century was hidden in the folds of the text.

CHAPTER FOUR

Body and Soul: The Nature of Images

1 The Map of the Soul and Medicine for Memory

In the previous chapters we have discussed the construction and use of images of memory. It would be misleading, however, to think of these images as mere tools of memory, for they are, in fact, something more and different. As they begin to inhabit the spaces of the mind – beyond those of writing – the images of memory take on a life of their own. In a rather obscure but highly interesting passage Aristotle had already compared the images of memory to dreams:

> In sleep we sometimes have other thoughts besides the mental pictures. This will become obvious to anyone if he concentrates and tries to remember his dream immediately upon rising. Indeed some men have seen such dreams, e.g., those who think that they are arranging suggested subjects according to some principle of memorizing; for they often find themselves envisaging some other imaginary concept, apart from the dream, into position. (*On Dreams* 1.458b.20–25)[1]

We have talked about mental images and operations being carried out in the spaces of the mind, using this terminology for the sake of simplicity and convenience, but we must not forget that *mind* meant something profoundly different in the sixteenth century from what it generally means today. The art of memory, indeed, thrives in a borderland somewhere between physical and intellectual perception: it is intended to create bridges, modes of communication, and reciprocal translatability between body and psyche. There are other factors, however, that converge in the same direction. On the one hand, there is a rich tradition of classical philosophy and medicine that conceives of images through which we know and remember as *phantasmata*, as something that acts internally but also retains a sensory status. On the other hand, it is easy to imagine how centuries of experience in memory techniques have given scholars some idea of the complex nature of mental images and their capacity to *inhabit* their creators, to come alive and escape their control. To use modern terms, we could say that memory techniques seek to move between the brain and the mind; they try out *remedies* inspired by theories of localization (that is, the idea that memory originates in a particular area of the brain) as well as hypotheses that oppose localization, or, at least, hold this problem to be a secondary one.[2] To be sure, different philosophical and medical concepts regarding the mechanisms of knowledge and memory persist and make themselves felt. But with the advent of the printed word a sort of consensus begins to take shape in which the various traditions flowed together. In this chapter we will examine various aspects of this consensus about memory in the hope of shedding light on something that until now has remained obscure: the relationship of the art of memory to the body, and the ways in which it has tried to discover and influence the intermediate zone between *res cogitans* and *res extensa*, an area which a long post-Cartesian tradition has habituated us to regard as empty and impracticable.

Like a seal that leaves its imprint in wax, our perceptions leave an imprint of motion that generates 'a sort of picture, the having of which we say is memory,' writes Aristotle in *On Memory* (1.450a.30). His theories hold perception and memory to be closely related, and they place the *phantasma* – the trace that the external world leaves inside us – at the heart of both. 'Memory,' according to Aristotle, 'even the memory of objects of thought, is not without an image. So memory will belong to thought in virtue of an incidental association, but in its own right to the primary perceptive part ... It is apparent, then, to which part of the soul memory belongs, namely the same part as that to which imagination belongs' (1.450a.10–22).[3]

But it is not just natural memory that belongs to our imagination: Aristotle's reference to the art of memory is intended precisely to clarify the status of imagination. The latter does not exist, he writes in *On the Soul*, without perception, but it must not be confused with perception, 'for it is possible to produce something before our eyes, as those do who set things out in mnemonic systems and form images of them' (3. 3.427b.18–22).[4] Mnemonics must have been a component of common experience. We have already seen how Aristotle brings it into play in order to clarify the elusive mechanism of dreams; here it is used to shed light on imagination, on its ambiguous state of dependency and autonomy with regard to the perceptible world.

Thus, imagination and the art of memory live side by side; the latter tries to control and amplify the action of the former by shaping it for its use and consumption. The *virtus imaginativa*, writes Saint Thomas Aquinas, operates through images, through the perceptible forms received and preserved through sensation, and it does so by manipulating and transforming them: 'it puts together and separates the forms present in imagination' [componit et dividit formas imaginatas] (*Summa theologica* 1, 78, art. 4). *Virtus imaginativa*, states Avicenna, 'is wont to manipulate the two treasure-houses constituted by perceptible forms and by forms present in memory, and it always represents forms: it begins with perceptible forms or forms in memory and from there proceeds towards an opposite or similar form or towards something related to it.'[5] According to Avicenna, imagination functions through similarity, opposition, or contiguity. These are the three 'laws of association' enunciated by Aristotle in *On Memory* (2.451b.15–20), when he describes the ways in which we can track down a recollection that has escaped us by starting with something that is still present in our memory. They are the three laws by which imagination manipulates forms and by which one recollection is to be associated with another, thus bringing it back to life in our conscious minds. They are also the three laws, we may observe, by which metaphor and metonym are created, giving life and form to language.[6]

From the earliest books on this theme and the endless variations on them produced in the Middle Ages and the Renaissance, memory, imagination, and the knowing and artificial manipulation of images are closely related. They live side by side in a delicate and vital borderland whose location and internal map are constantly redrawn. There are actually two distinct traditions that often interact and influence each other.[7] The first holds the brain to be at the centre of perception and the cognitive process, whereas the second identifies the heart as the centre of life and the different faculties of the soul (this is the position of Aristotle and the Stoics). The first tradition goes back to the Hippocratic position. It is renewed and elaborated on by Plato, to whom we also owe the tripartite division of the soul: reason is assigned to the brain, while the heart is the seat of the passions and the liver is the place of the faculties in control of nourishment (*Timaeus* 69e–73a). The tripartite model ultimately influences even those who, faithful to Aristotelian teachings, localize the soul and its principal functions in the heart. Take, for example, the adjustment proposed by Avicenna: what puts the soul and the body in communication is the *spiritus*, a subtle substance generated in the heart; it spreads throughout the body, and, once purified, it arrives in the brain where it can give life to the faculties of common sense. Thus, the heart is the centre of everything, but the mental faculties have their seat in the brain:

> in the brain the spirit reaches its summit; it is able to transport the faculties, perceptions, and motions to the different parts of the body so that they are able to execute their own functions ... The heart can be the source of the power of nourishment, which is enacted in the liver, as well as the faculties of imagination, memory, and form, which are enacted in the brain.[8]

Through this type of adjustment the medical and philosophical thought of Aristotelian derivation is combined with the brain-centred Platonic tradition, which has found a new elaboration and renewed fortune in Galenic doctrine. It is clear how, beyond the disagreements of different medical and philosophical traditions, a sort of consensus has come into being. It holds that the higher functions of the soul originate in the different ventricles (or hollows) of the brain. Avicenna's map is highly sophisticated; the 'inward senses' are divided into five powers or faculties corresponding to fantasy, the imagination, the *vis imaginativa* (imaginative power, which operates through the forms assembled in the imagination), the *vis aestimativa* (conjecturing or surmising power), and the *vis memorativa*. Each is assigned a space that corresponds to its function and its relationship to the others. *Virtus formalis* [perception] and *sensus communis*, Avicenna writes,

> have their place in the first part of the brain thanks to the spirit that fills that ventricle. The reason for this is that they must supervise the other senses, which, for the most part, originate in the first part of the brain. Thought and memory have their places in the other two ventricles, but memory takes the rear so that the spirit of thought is in the middle, that is, so that it is between the treasure-house of perceptible forms and the

treasure-house of abstract concepts. The space between each of them is the same so that both, together with judgment, rule in all of the brain.[9]

As we have seen, the frontiers of the map, the internal divisions, are subject to various changes and simplifications; Avicenna's five faculties, for example, tend to be reduced to three.

It is interesting to note the persistence of a scheme that localizes the different faculties of the mind in the brain and holds memory to be closely related to imagination and fancy. There is iconographic evidence of the close ties that for centuries united the art of memory and the notions examined here. The images used to illustrate the map of the brain's ventricles and their corresponding faculties appear in medical texts (figure 38) as well as in manuals of mnemonics (figure 39). Evidently they are a common reference point. As we will see, literature and the practice of memory reflect the ambiguities and tensions of the tradition, whether it is the ambiguous relationships that imagination and perception entertain between body and soul, or the coexistence, never fully reconciled, of the two poles represented by the heart and the brain.

In a tradition ranging from Aristotle to the seventeenth century, imagination is held to be the mediator between soul and body, between perception and intellect: 'the image,' writes Robert Klein, 'is the subtle body of thought, just as imagination is the subtle body of the soul.'[10] The fantasy, the imagination, also becomes a point of contact between man and the world, between the particular and the universal. Indeed, with a formula destined for great success, Marsilio Ficino takes up again and carefully reworks a syncretistic process that has distant origins: the Aristotelian tradition of the imagination converges with the Neoplatonic and hermetic tradition of the *pneuma*, the *spiritus phantasticus*. The stuff of dreams, prophecies, enchantment, and love, that which makes the creation of images, of *phantasmata*, possible in man, is the same principle that animates the cosmos, that mediates between the soul of the world and matter. In the same way it puts man's soul in communication with his body, reason with sensation.

From these rather summary observations we can form an idea of how practising the art of memory in the sixteenth century calls into play body and soul (and earth and sky, in cases where the influence of Neoplatonism is particularly strong); building the places and images of

I Titian, *Wisdom*. Venice, Vestibule of the Library of Iacopo Sansovino

II Titian, *Portrait of Alfonso d'Avalos*. Paris, private collection, on loan to the Musée du Louvre

III Physiognomies of various personages. Varallo Sesia, Sacro Monte

IV *A knight battling against the vices*. London, British Library, cod. Harl. 3244

V Mnemonic images from a fifteenth-century treatise by Bartolomeo of Mantua, *Liber memoriae artificialis*. Paris, Bibliothèque nationale, cod. lat. 8684

VI Hans Holbein, *The Ambassadors*. London, National Gallery

VII The Stanzino of the Palazzo Vecchio, Florence

VIII Gian Lorenzo Bernini, *The Ecstasy of Saint Teresa*. Rome, Church of Santa Maria della Vittoria

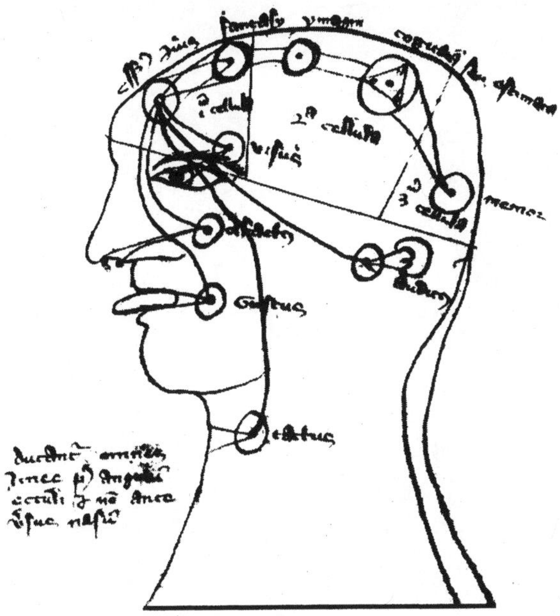

38 A map of the brain from a fourteenth-century treatise on anatomy, *De generatione embryonis*. Munich, Bayerisches Staatsbibliothek, cod. lat. 527. From *La fabbrica del pensiero. Dall'arte della memoria alle neuroscienze* (Milan: Electa 1984), also published in English as *The Enchanted Loom: Chapters in the History of Neuroscience* (New York: Oxford University Press 1991)

the art of memory means artificially reproducing the primary mechanisms of human experience.

Alongside the tradition that teaches how to build the images of memory, there also develops an actual medicine for memory.[11] In *On Memory* Aristotle writes that, in order for the movement produced by the *phantasma* of sensation to leave its imprint and to endure, it is necessary that a person not be agitated by passions or too worn by age. Memory is facilitated in a person who is not too moist and not too hard, or, in other words, not too young or too old (1.450b.1–5). There are physical and psychological dispositions that can promote or obstruct recollection. Medicine can attempt to compensate for the deficiencies and excesses by trying to create artificially the ideal conditions of humidity, heat, and temperament.

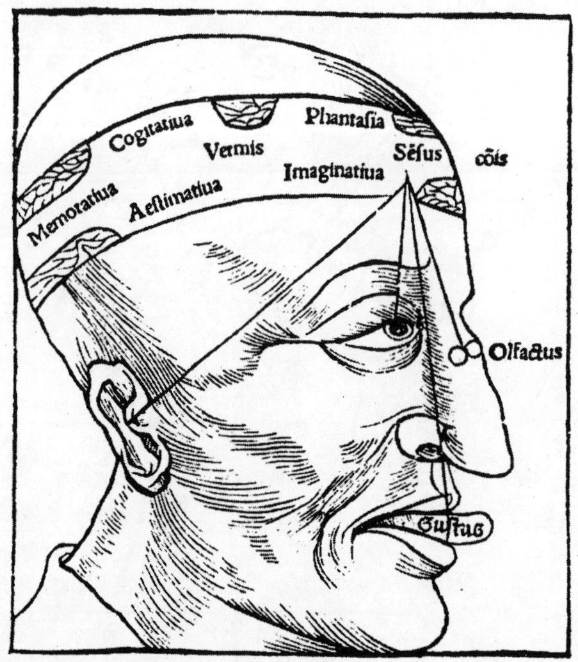

39 A map of the brain, from Guglielmus Leporeus, *Ars memorativa* (Paris: Calchographia Ioannis Fabri 1520)

The remedies and medicines for memory found in the manuals are sometimes given a secondary position with respect to the *loci* and *imagines*, while at other times they clearly dominate the text. The recommended medicines and remedies have been handed down through an uninterrupted tradition that spans the Middle Ages and the Renaissance. They encompass a rather impressive variety of features. Take, for example, the recommendations given by Iacobo Publicio in the third book of his *Oratoriae artis epitoma* [Epitome of the art of oratory] (Venice: Erhardus Ratdolt 1495). This book is dedicated precisely to memory: baths are helpful, as is moderation in drinking, eating, sleeping (it is better to sleep on your back, with your feet exposed), not to mention lovemaking. Melancholy, however, is a dangerous enemy to be avoided, and for this reason, 'at times one must ward off sadness with pleasure, bring joy back to life with sex' [tristitia nonnunquam voluptate propulsanda est, coitu laeticia revocanda] (folio 57r). It is also prudent to moderate one's diet: there are some foods to be avoided, such as leeks, garlic, and onion. Drugs that make you sneeze, however, are ideal. Other remedies are derived from natural magic. It is said that a hoopoe's tongue, for example, when worn by a forgetful person, can help her/him to remember (folio 61v).

Publicio's is a rather summary example. In other treatises there is a much richer variety of remedies: there are ointments to be applied to the head, substances with which to wash the feet, fumigations used to deodorize a room, gargles, and recipes for complex – and repulsive – mixtures to be swallowed in pills. Medicines for memory were widely used, and enjoyed a booming market in which there was no lack of dubious and alarming aspects. Evidence is provided in a manual written by a Franciscan friar, Filippo Gesualdo. 'In regard to the medications,' he writes, 'I will not hesitate to say that they are usually dangerous, especially the ointments applied to the aft of the brain (called the "occiput") in order to invigorate memory.' These substances, he explains, are too hot and dry, 'and since heat ignites the spirit of the brain, and since these ignited, burning spirits alter, irritate, and upset the *simulacra*, it follows that those who imprudently use such ointments often become agitated and go mad' (*Plutosofia* [Padua: Paolo Megietti 1592], folio 9v). Gesualdo's words open up an unsettling perspective on a medicine for memory that takes literally the idea that the *phantasmata* and *simulacra* of memory have an actual physical consistency and are located in a specific area of the brain. This type of cure and its unfortunate outcome recall the methods used to cure the malady of love. But we will return to the relationship between the images of memory and the *phantasma* of the beloved later on.

In this passage from Gesualdo we can hear an echo of the worries and reservations previously set forth by Giovan Battista Della Porta. Indeed, while Della Porta includes in his work an ample list of remedies and medicines for memory, at the same time he warns against the potential risks. In fact, in his *Magia naturale* [Natural magic] he writes that he has listed only the most widely used and efficient remedies: 'you will find the other secrets,' he adds, 'in our *Physiognomy*, and there are many of them. But I would recommend the art of remembering since it is much better than risking madness, and I have written a short book about it that has enjoyed great success.'[12] There is no doubt that Della Porta is using this opportunity to advertise his books, and his short treatise on the art of memory in particular. His position on the dangers of medicines for memory is, nonetheless, of great importance and interest, especially when considered in relation to the scope of his work. In the introduction to the sixth book of his *Fisonomia dell'uomo*

[Physiognomy of man], he extols the virtues of drugs in treating human vices and more general weaknesses (in fact, this book dedicates a great deal of space to the medicine of memory). He explains that, in the preceding books of this work, he has taught how to interpret physical characteristics, how to read the signs of the body that reveal the most secret of internal properties:

> in this last book, we must now deal with something new and most amazing, most worthy of being coveted and desired: how to completely erase your own or others' vices when they have been identified. What else would this art be good for, if it did not convert your vices, once identified, into virtues? But it does not do so with thought, imagination, or the persuasions of the moral philosophers and their mostly vain remedies, but with purgation, local remedies, and the natural virtues of herbs, stones and animals, and hidden properties.[13]

This is a highly revelatory passage. In order to insulate himself from the wrath of the Inquisition (this problem has been mentioned in chapter 3 in reference to his treatise on ciphers), Della Porta consistently maintains that his physiognomical doctrine does not run counter to his faith in free will and his belief that man can always find the road to salvation through reason and volition. This fact sheds an interesting light on the contrast between the useful discoveries of natural magic and the 'mostly vain' results obtained by the 'moral philosophers' in the face of human vice and deficiencies.

The other element that makes rather peculiar his warnings against the risk of madness that medicines for memory bring with them is Della Porta's position regarding experimentation with drugs and poisons. The second chapter of the eighth book of the *Magia naturale* is titled: 'how you can make a man go crazy for a day.' Della Porta promises a 'playful spectacle' from anyone you can persuade to gulp down a concoction made from belladonna. The victim will believe that she/he is a fish or a bird: 'I remember,' he writes, 'that as a young man I experimented with these things on the slaves of my house.' His treatment made some of them flounder about desperately, convinced that they were drowning, while one of them believed he was a ox, and 'he thought that he had been gored by the horns of another.'[14] Such experimentation on slaves was evidently a common practice: on 9 October 1608, in a letter to Federico Cesi, the founder of the Accademia dei Lincei, Della Porta extols the 'secrets' discovered by his friend Borelli: it seemed that he knew more about it than anyone, and he told me that he was buying a slave for one hundred *scudi* so he could test a type of poison, and he spoke of this with great competence.'[15] Thus, the study of certain medicines and their effects is conducted by Della Porta (and his friends) with an attitude in which are interwoven the passion for experimental research and a sort of cruel game, an uninhibited *divertissement*. This aloofness can also be found in one of the more famous passages of the *Magia naturale*, a passage that was promptly deleted in the Italian translation: it has to do with the recipe for a witch's ointment. Among the ingredients listed by Della Porta is baby fat. This prompts not repugnance in Della Porta but a technical observation: the fat is needed, he writes, to open the pores of the skin in order to facilitate the penetration of the ointment.[16]

We may then conclude that Della Porta's warning regarding the dangers of some medicines for memory is the result of a purely practical concern: they are to be avoided because they do not achieve the desired effect. At any rate, unlike the 'mostly vain' remedies of the moral philosophers, those used in the art of memory have been successfully employed for centuries. They have been proven reliable by his own experience. We will return later to the way in which Della Porta refines mnemonic technique (in chapter 3 we have already seen how he recycles Palatino's sonnet/rebus). Here we want only to note that his position regarding memory is an indicator of the complexity which the problem has assumed: interventions on the body and interventions on the images of the mind can indeed coexist and reinforce each other, but they can also enter into dangerous competition.

2 The Power of Imagination and the Toil of Forgetting

'Nor is it any wonder that I have discovered the order of these things with such great art,' writes Giulio Camillo in 1532 in *Discorso in materia del suo theatro* [Essay on the subject of his theatre], a work adressed to Triphon Gabriele and his circle of friends, 'because Avicenna's conclusions in the sixth book on nature are very appealing to me, where he says that there is a certain capacity in our soul to change things and to make them obey us, while our soul is attracted by a great affection for them. And some believe that herein are the origins of incantation and necromancy.'[17] Here Camillo is referring to Avicenna's *On the Soul* (4.4) where, among other things, he states: 'when ... the soul creates an image through imagination and becomes fixed upon it, the material body immediately receives a form that is related to that which is imagined through a similarity or mutual property.'[18] For Avicenna imagination is thus a mysterious, yet effective go-between by which the soul can directly affect things: thanks to imagination one is able to reverse the process by which things affect us internally when they leave the imprint of their images. In this theory Camillo points to the prior condition that has made his theatre of memory possible: the order of the theatre gives *place* to the *materials* of eloquence and to the artifice with which they clothe themselves, the different forms that they take. This is possible, according to Camillo, thanks to the capacity of *imaginatio* 'to change things and to make them obey us.' To build the theatre of memory would mean celebrating the entire potential of *imaginatio*; to build the images of memory would also mean recreating the world, completing an alchemical process in which the possible metamorphoses take shape and become images, that is, living *phantasmata* and *simulacra*.

Undoubtedly, Camillo's discourse is that of an insider, a member of an intimate circle of friends; the passage cited above is part of a dense network of allusions, of memories of shared readings and discussions.[19] It is important, neverthless, to emphasize that here Camillo is showing us something that goes far beyond his theatre of memory; the connection between the magical capacities of *imaginatio* and the art of memory is a legitimate element of that 'consensus' that we are outlining here. We will, in fact, also find this connection in texts that are, so to speak, above suspicion, unimpeachable – far removed from those shady zones of sixteenth-century culture frequented by Camillo.

Take, for example, the *Discorso intorno alle imagini sacre e profane* [Essay on sacred and lay images] (1582), a text in which Cardinal Gabriele Paleotti (1522–1597), archbishop of Bologna, tries simultaneously to rebut the Protestant condemnation of sacred images and to reform their use in the Catholic world. He cites the art of memory as evidence of how images can have an effect upon the faculties of the soul, that is, according to the Augustinian scheme, upon the intellect, will, and memory. 'As to memory,' he writes, 'what shall we say? We know that so-called artificial memory consists mostly in the use of images. Thus, it is no wonder that sacred images refresh the memory all the more.'[20] The theory of *imaginatio* – a commonly accepted concept according to Paleotti – provides an explanation for the extraordinary power of images: philosophers and doctors, he states, believe that, 'in accordance with the various conceptions that our imagination apprehends of things, firm imprints are made in it, and from these imprints are derived substantial alterations and signs in the body.' Since our imagination is 'thus suited to receive such imprints, there is clearly no stronger or more effective means than that of realistic images *that seem to violate our unwary senses.*'[21] This final statement is highly indicative. Laden with images of bodily violence, it betrays Paleotti's true attitude regarding his subject matter. He believes images to be a powerful and extremely dangerous force: they can be utilized and handled, but there is always the risk that they will defy our control.

The construction of images in the art of memory initiates contact with a delicate yet potent territory that shifts between body and psyche. This reflects a common mode of thought that we have seen in both Camillo and Paleotti. While medicines for memory can cause madness, images, writes Paleotti, can 'violate our unwary senses.' We will now see if the treatises on memory have conserved any traces of these concerns. The problem becomes clearer when we consider the reverse operation, that is, the ways of destroying and deleting those images that no longer serve any purpose.

The problem of forgetting is embodied by a man who lived in the twentieth century: Shereshevskij, 'the man who remembered everything,' and to whom neuropsychologist Aleksandr Luriia has dedicated a fascinating study.[22] Images became implanted in Shereshevskij's mind with such intensity that they inexorably dragged in their wake old recollections and left no space for new things. Shereshevskij supported himself by showing off his mnemonic talents, but the force of the images populating his mind created problems, and new performances became too taxing. As a result, he had to develop techniques for forgetting that entailed concealing and deleting images: 'I was forced to block off everything that wasn't essential by covering it over in my mind with a large canvas.' When he was called upon to remember a series of numbers written on a blackboard, he feared that he would confuse one performance with another:

> I'm afraid I may begin to confuse the individual performances. So in my mind I erase the blackboard and cover it, as it were, with a film that's completely opaque and impenetrable. I take this off and listen to it crunch as I gather it into a ball. That is, after each performance is over, I erase the board, walk away from it, and mentally gather up the film I had used to cover the board. As I go on talking to the audience, I feel myself crumpling

this film into a ball in my hands. Even so, when the next performance starts and I walk over to that blackboard, the numbers I had erased are liable to turn up again. If they alternate in a way that is even vaguely like the order in one of the previous performances, I might not catch myself in time and would read off the chart of numbers that had been written there before.[23]

Thus, his ritual of erasure, with its various phases, could also prove to be unreliable. The same thing happened when Shereshevskij wanted to forget some numbers that he had annotated on a piece of paper; he threw the paper into the fire, but then realized that in his memory some traces of the numbers remained on the burnt page.

The images of memory, therefore, are not just tools of memory; at times their force is overwhelming, and their vitality needs to be curbed. The pages that Luriia dedicates to the art of forgetting practised by Shereshevskij are fascinating: this man, who performed amazing feats of memory throughout the USSR during the 1930s and 1940s but had no knowledge of the age-old tradition of the art of memory, used techniques exactly similar to those the tradition taught, not only to remember, but also to forget. With great precision (and often with great tedium), the manuals of memory written during the fifteenth, sixteenth, and seventeenth centuries pass on sound advice on how to remove from the memory those images that are no longer useful. The advice they give refers to practices so widespread that they are often mentioned in abbreviated form. It is easy to see their exact correspondence to those that Shereshevskij attempted to use during the twentieth century, although, as we have noted, he did not always obtain the desired result.

Take, for example, the methods for forgetting listed in Giovanni Fontana's fifteenth-century treatise (cited in chapter 3, p. 101); in the chapter entitled 'De oblivione' [On forgetting], he notes that he commonly uses a piece of cloth to cover mentally images he wants to forget; or else, he imagines that the place where they are positioned is crumbling, or going up in flames.[24] These methods are more effective and more rapid than merely letting the images fade, or trying not to recall them to memory, or clumsily loading them with things impossible to remember.

This testimony from the fifteenth century is an indication of what would become a constant: a person's relationship with the images that he/she desires to remove becomes increasingly conflictual. You have to wage a real battle with the image because it is alive and powerful. You can also try, writes Fontana, to picture images as if 'they appeared asleep and dead' [sopite et mortue viderentur]: ideally, you have to deprive the image of all vitality.[25] The method recommended by a Dominican friar from Florence, Cosma Rosselli, is exactly like a description of iconoclasm: imagine, he writes, 'that a man comes home, that he throws all his images on the floor, and then he throws them out or tosses them out of the window' (*Thesaurus artificiosae memoriae* [Thesaurus of artificial memory] [Venice: Antonio Padovano, 1579], folio 129v). The Catholic teachers of memory thus reappropriate the techniques of their religious enemies and recycle them as useful ingredients of their little theatres of the mind. It should be remembered that these iconoclastic scenes, freely used in late-sixteenth-century memory treatises, are highly topical. The Protestant world does, in fact, reformulate the ancient accusations made by the iconoclasts and launched them against the Catholic world, that is, the accusations of an idolatrous cult of images.[26]

There are no less than eight methods of *ars oblivionalis* [the art of forgetting] recommended by Thomas Lambertus Schenckel (1547–ca 1603) – a Belgian master of memory who was famous for his public exhibitions and who was accused of performing magic. His successful treatise, published for the first time in 1595 as *De memoria liber* [Book on memory], and republished under the title *Gazophylacium artis memoriae* [Treasure-house of the art of memory], is included in an anthology of texts dedicated to mnemonics. Schenckel's eight methods for forgetting pick up right where the procedures recommended by Fontana have left off, and they are characterized by a crescendo of destructive violence:

> Sixth [method]: pretend that all the doors and windows have been flung open; there is a great wind storm and all of the images, lying about like loose paper, just fly away.
>
> Seventh: a maidservant has swept up every room and every space with a broom, and because she did not notice the images she must have thrown them away, or perhaps she put them aside because they are so precious and she did not want to get them dusty.
>
> Eighth: let us imagine that a man in a fit of rage has taken over the fields, the houses, and the rooms with the help of a band of armed men, and he has killed some images, and wounded many others; others have fled through the doors, others have jumped out of the windows, and when you enter, you find none of them left inside.[27]

As the description of the techniques used becomes more violent and detailed, the images become more animated: from paintings, papers, and precious furnishings, the images are transformed into living persons, dismayed by the enemy attack, forced to flee or to take their own lives.

The resilience and vitality of the images, which make the techniques for their removal so much more complex and violent, are the result of the care taken in their construction. Careful visualization is the indispensable first step, but at times the treatises recommend the use, although in a purely mental capacity, of the other senses so as to familiarize oneself with the images and instil life in them. Take, for example, the recommendations given by the Franciscan friar Filippo Gesualdo: first you position the images of different persons in the various *loci*; then 'with the mind, start to contemplate them in those places, as if they were there, and as you pass by, greet them, touch them, call them by name, chat with them, look at them from the front, look at them again from the sides' (*Plutosofia*, folio 23r). It is significant that Gesualdo, an expert in techniques of meditation and mental oration, among other things,[28] also dedicates a long chapter to 'L'arte di scordarse' [The art of forgetting] in which he returns to the traditional expedients, elucidates them, and varies them with touches of colour (the cloth used to cover the images become 'white curtains, or green sheets, or black fabric') and dramatic details (the enemy soldiers who provoke the flight or destruction of the images become Turks or pagans, 'since such fright creates confusion and turns everything upside down') (*Plutosofia*, folio 64r).

The techniques for forgetting handed down by the treatises are testimony to the persistence and power of the images. When one passes through the territory of memory, creating images and summoning forth emotions in order to use them, it is not always possible to control the entire process: it may assume a life of its own, as Aristotle warns in *On Memory*, one of the original texts of the tradition. A person who seeks to remember, he writes, is like someone who has thrown a dart and can no longer restrain its flight: 'just as it is no longer in people's power to stop something when they throw it, so also he who is recollecting and hunting moves a bodily thing in which the affection resides' (2.453a.20–25). This movement will not subside immediately: 'the affection is like names and tunes and sayings, when one such has come to be very much on someone's lips. For after the people have stopped, and without their wishing such a thing, it comes to them to sing it or say it again' (2.453a.29–30).[29] This is a powerful description of the automatisms of memory together with the mechanisms at the basis of improvisation and poetic memory.

3 The *Phantasmata* of Eros and Images of Memory

At the end of the sixteenth century, as we have seen, the Franciscan friar Gesualdo expresses his strong reservations about some medicines for memory, especially for an ointment (too hot and too dry) that is applied to the 'aft of the brain,' the zone where memory is believed to originate; it is spread 'on the back side of the head because experience has shown it to be the part of the brain where memory resides,' writes Della Porta in his *Fisonomia dell'uomo* after he gives the recipe.[30]

This type of medicine for memory is an exact replication, even in its more hazardous aspects, of medicine that was used in the most extreme cases of lovesickness. As Massimo Ciavolella has shown, sixteenth- and seventeenth-century medical treatises offer evidence that it was common practice to overheat the cranium of those obsessed by love. It was believed that by doing so one could '"dissolve" the image from that kind of hardened wax which was the receptacle of memory.'[31] The possibility of losing one's life along with the image of the loved one was considered an unavoidable – and to some extent secondary – risk.

These cruel practices are based on a classical tradition that was revived by medieval medicine and then merged with sixteenth-century mainstream culture. This tradition widely feeds into literature, into poetry especially, from the Sicilian school of the thirteenth century to Ariosto's *Orlando furioso*.[32] It is commonly believed that the intensity of amorous desire causes the *phantasma* – that is, the image of the beloved – to concentrate within itself all the vital forces of the lover; it occupies the entire *vis imaginativa*, it feeds upon incessant recollection, and it gathers the vital spirits together around it. The result is a grave alteration of the *virtus aestimativa*, and the zones of memory and imagination become hard and dry. If the zones of memory are like a mass of wax on which a seal leaves its imprint, lovesickness transforms them into a hard block in which the *phantasma* of the object is fixed. It may result, progressively, in melancholy, rage, madness, and even death. It is easy to understand, therefore, why medicine for memory and medicine for love have a great deal in common. 'When the temperament of the brain is halfway between one and the other, that is, hot and cold,' wrote Della Porta in the *Fisonomia dell'uomo*, 'memory becomes strong, but from cold comes absent-mindedness, and from extreme cold comes lethargy, from much heat come fevers and madness.'[33] The application of warm substances to the part of the brain considered to be the area of memory is intended to help remove images: it is supposed to render the organ of memory more receptive, or, in the case of lovesickness, it is supposed to dissolve the *phantasma* of desire from the dangerous block that it has created around itself. But this medicine, which follows the theories to the letter, ends up causing great harm, whether taken to reinforce memory or to cure presumed lovesickness. For those less fortunate than Orlando, whose friend Astolfo flies to the moon to retrieve his lost wits, the treatises of medicine offer – with disquieting indifference – a rather grim prognosis.

Thus, eros and memory are deeply related. With a much greater and more dangerous force than the images of memory, the *phantasmata* of eros occupy a space that opens up between body and psyche. Like the remedies for memory, remedies for love seek to act upon both.

If memory, by nature, plays an essential role in affixing and feeding the amorous *phantasma*, the art of memory proves to be keenly interested in reversing the process, in using it for its own ends. Sexual references are common among the examples of images of memory given by the treatises, especially in the word games used for *memoria verborum* (these games have attracted the attention of those looking for analogies between the art of memory and psychoanalysis).[34] At the same time, the use of images laden with erotic references is explicitly recommended: we have seen an example of this in Toscanella's *Retorica ad Erennio* (chapter 2, p. 73, above). In many ways these images appear as *imagines agentes* par excellence, capable of stirring and rousing one's emotions and memories. They testify, as we shall see, to a male erotic imagination; evidently the writers of the treatises are for the most part men, and they appeal to an audience made up substantially of men.

In the *Phoenix*, a treatise on memory written at the end of the fifteenth century (a text destined to be a real best-seller), the famous jurist Pietro da Ravenna offers a peculiar variant of one of the typical ingredients of mnemonics, the figurative alphabet (we have seen the examples given by Della Porta above): 'in place of letters, I generally put beautiful women since they greatly excite my memory' [ego communiter pro literis formosissimas puellas pono: illae enim multum memoriam meam excitant]. As a young man, he adds, he used the image of the woman he loved. In this way, he guarantees, it all becomes much easier and much more pleasant. Only modesty has kept him from revealing this highly effective trick before. It certainly will be of no help to anyone who hates or spurns women: 'they will have much more difficulty in obtaining good results' [sed isti fructus difficilius consequentur]. Pietro concludes this discourse by apologizing to men of religion (*Memoriae ars quae Phoenix inscribitur* [Art of memory also called the Phoenix] [Vienna: Mathias Bonhome 1541], p. 9; the first edition was published in 1491). In other words, men with a cold disposition, immune to the charms of feminine beauty, do not have available to them the avenues of the art of memory that require a malleable *imaginatio*, a receptiveness for interaction between perceptible reality and the pscyhic world within. Evidently, Pietro has no lack of these gifts, since he claims to have given performances of his prodigious memory in all of Italy. People said that it was the fruit not of a human but of a divine art, and 'there were even those who made the sign of the cross' [aliqui etiam se cruce signabant] (p. 3) in response to his feats.

The image of a beautiful female body is also featured in a system of memory devised by Leonardo Giustiniani, a Venetian humanist of the early fifteenth century. His *Regulae artificialis memoriae* [Rules of artificial memory], probably written in 1432, offers, among other things, an example of how one can remember an oration. Had he ever needed to give an oration to the Senate on the opportunity of making a truce, he writes, 'in the first place, I would have put a beautiful girl that I knew, depicted as being weary, not knowing whether or not to continue shooting arrows at a snake wearing a crown.'[35] The woman, he explains, represents the city of Venice, and the snake the duchy of Milan. Clearly, these images of memory are taken from heraldry and general iconography. They helped to create a link between iconography and rhetoric: it is easy to imagine the allegories and theatrical tricks that can be used in a deliberative oration memorized with images like these. Of course, the portrayal of Venice as a female figure is part of traditional iconography, but the fact that Giustiniani gives her the features of a beautiful girl known to him imparts to the official image a unique and unforgettable flavour: it is transformed precisely into a *imago agens*.

An erotic component makes its presence felt with great intensity in Della Porta's treatise, *L'arte del ricordare* [The art of remembering] (Naples: Marco Antonio Passaro 1566). Its power to evoke recollection is discussed in the chapter dedicated to *loci*:

Nor can I imagine a man so foolish and so silly who, when he is passing through a place, does not promptly remember, even if he does not want to, something that happened to him or something that he found there particularly pleasing or unpleasant. As the horse of Darius passed through the place where it had enjoyed the favours of a mare the night before, it remembered the event and, according to Trogus, its neighing was the reason that its rider was adorned with the crown of Persia.   (Folio A3v)

The association of place and erotic scene is highly evocative. It functions automatically in man and can be found even in the animal world. It can be used universally as a tool of the art of remembering. However, it is to be vigilantly avoided if one wants to forget. Ovid's *Remedia amoris*, for that matter, has already taught that a man should remove any portraits of his lady and stay clear of those places where he had made love with her (verses 725–730).

Della Porta boasts of the outstanding results obtained when one uses *imagines agentes* such as maidens who stimulate pleasant recollections: 'those who have experience with our rules will see with what cheer and clarity one reaches a place associated with a person whose favours he has enjoyed, or desired, for where other persons might give us the recollection of a single word, this person will show us an entire line of poetry, or even two.' Della Porta recommends that his readers position 'from ten to twenty beautiful women whom we have enjoyed, loved, or revered' in the *loci* (folio B2r). The traditional precept that images of memory have to be emotionally effective, and therefore unusual, is expanded by Della Porta to include a strong taste for the comic, the grotesque, and the obscene. To enhance the efficacy of the image all concern for decorum or stateliness is cast aside. It is easier to remember, he writes, the passion between the matron and the ass narrated by Apuleius than the heroice devices of the ancient Romans:

> if I want to remember LOVER, I do not imagine the person of the *place* as well-dressed, and wont to sigh, and other similar things typical of the gentleman in love, but I paint him like Ovid's Polyphemus in love, shaving his beard with a scythe, combing his head with a rake, looking at his reflection in the water; playing and singing with a strange musical instrument. Because this ridiculous image will awaken my memories with much greater ease.   (Folio C2r)

Even the images related to love can thus be infused by the literary tradition, but in order for them to function in the theatre of memory the literary genre has to be carefully chosen, as do the types of *mores* that they entail. For example, the lover found in comedy or love poetry will be completely ineffective; the grotesque caricature is much more functional.

It is no secret that the boundaries between rewriting, translating, and plagiarizing are rather blurred in the publishing practices of the sixteenth century. After adding some details and giving an Italianate patina to a translation of Romberch's treatise, *Congestorium artificiosae memoriae*, for example, Lodovico Dolce has the work printed as his own. One of the mnemonic tricks that he claims to have used is the alphabet composed of beautiful maidens that Pietro da Ravenna had already promulgated. The image of a maiden one has once known, fixed in a response of rejection, is useful in remembering that '"You will have everything in words, nothing in deed," and "Love has as many pains as the seashore has shells" ... I can use the image of a maiden whom I knew who always gave such an answer to those who sought her out' (*Dialogo nel quale si ragiona del modo di accrescer et conservar la memoria* [Dialogue in which ways of enlarging and conserving memory are discussed] [Venice: Heredi di Marchiò Sessa 1575], folios 6or and 46v).

The use of images of beautiful women in techniques of memory must have been common practice if, at the height of the Counter-Reformation, even an observant Minorite friar, the Calabrian Girolamo Marafioto, recommends in his *Ars memoriae* (Frankfurt: Matthaeus Becker 1603) that you walk the streets and carefully watch the most attractive women, fixing in your mind their gestures and the movements of their bodies, and using them as *imagines agentes* (p. 19). He himself, he writes, has seen that the method works; he even uses it to remember some of his sermons. Naturally he uses these techniques only for the purpose of edification: in order to remember the soul, for example, he used the image of a gorgeous young woman whom he once met (p. 66). Perhaps even here, as in other parts of Marafioto's treatise, an iconographic notion is at work, that is, the customary representation of the soul as a naked body.

There is no lack of those who keep their distance from the widespread use of images of beautiful women. An anonymous *Ars memorativa* written in Bologna in 1425, probably in a religious environment, offers a noteworthy case: great emphasis is placed here on the theme of the utility of the art of memory with regard to morality and devotion. In the part of the treatise dedicated to the different ways of remembering a narration, the story of Saint Marina (Saint Margaret of Antioch) is used as an example. Her story can be divided into twelve parts, each positioned in one of twelve places. You can use 'an honest girl that you know' [quandam honestam virginem tibi notam], writes the author, and you call her Marina.[36] Even when it is part of a safe and harmless context (the edifying story, the indisputable virtues of the woman), the female *phantasma* can create distress, and therefore it should be used only if certain precautions are taken: you have to isolate yourself and concentrate, warns the author, 'so that you do not excite carnal concupiscence which aggrieves the mind's eye with its impurity, and thus it is even safer to use generic images of men, and not persons with whom you have had close contact.'[37] Not only is the female *phantasma* to be handled with great care, but even images of familiar men may be dangerous since they can arouse emotions and feelings.

This is a concern that reappears almost two centuries later in the memory treatise that accompanies the *Arte di predicare bene* [The art of preaching well] by Paolo Arese, bishop of Tortona.[38] He knows and feels at ease with a rich tradition of rhetoric and mnemonics, and he enumerates with great lucidity the inherent advantages and risks of using the images of persons capable of arousing strong emotional reactions:

> Just as persons whom you have loved have the power to wake your memory, they also have no lesser power in holding it, wherefore it may be that when you find yourself thinking of one such person, your memory is held there, as a ship is held by a remora, and it goes no further, nor does it care to regard the image accidentally made of the beloved, but it stops at her own natural image; and since all fervent affection is contrary to memory and the imagining of such persons undoubtedly creates such affections in us, it does not seem to be a very safe undertaking. (*Arte di predicare bene ... con un trattato della memoria* [The art of preaching well ... with a treatise on memory] [Milan: Giovan Battista Bidelli 1627], p. 419)

Here the *phantasma* of eros asserts all its power. The art of memory, notes Arese, can try to use and shape the image of the beloved for its own ends, but the image's power is such that it may blur the distinction between the *accidental* image (that is, one created for mnemonic purposes) and the *natural* image, the product of sight and therefore fueled by passion. When this happens, as we have seen, it causes the process of memory to accelerate and ultimately throws it out of gear. It concentrates on the object of desire and turns it into something that occupied all the vital spaces of the psyche; it is possible that 'memory is held there, like a ship is held by a remora.' The comparison with the remora, the small fish that (according to the naturalists) can stop a great ship, is highly important. Given that Arese is an expert in the art of the device and that the image of the ship blocked by the remora is found frequently in the fifteenth- and sixteenth-century books of devices (figure 40), we can make use of the device ourselves and think of it as an emblem of the relationship between the *phantasmata* of eros and the images of the art of memory.[39]

4 The Window Opening onto the Heart

Until now we have seen the amorous *phantasma* localized in the head, wholly intent on occupying, indeed devouring, the space of imagination and memory. But now the moment has arrived to return it to the place where we still position it spontaneously today, that is, the heart.

We have mentioned above (chapter 4, p. 132) that there are both heart-centred and brain-centred traditions in Greek medical thought. As we have seen, the techniques used to cure lovesickness as well as deficiencies of memory are based on the idea that the *phantasmata* are located in the brain. The literary tradition, which in many ways interacts profoundly with medical and philosopical speculation, proves to be more receptive to the idea that they are located in the heart. It is there, according to commonly accepted theory, that the image arouses love. The process begins with sight; and according to the Platonic model, revived and renewed at the end of the fifteenth century by the Florentine Neoplatonists, the visual process takes place through 'spirits' that come out of the eyes. They are produced by the most delicate and warmest part of the blood, and they act as intermediaries between the soul and the body. These spirits, writes Baldassarre Castiglione in *Il Cartegiano*,

> being generated near the heart, enter in through [the] eyes (at which they are aimed as an arrow at a target) and penetrate naturally to the heart as if it were their proper abode, and, mingling with those other spirits there and with the very subtle kind of blood which these have in them, they infect the blood near the heart to which they have come, and warm it, and make it like themselves and ready to receive the impression of that image which they have brought with them.[40]

40 The remora that blocks ships, from Johannes Sambucus, *Emblemata* (Antwerp: Christoph Plantin 1564)

These concepts – along with the tradition relating to love that we mentioned earlier – fuel a literary topos that enjoyed renewed success in the sixteenth century because it lent itself perfectly to the play of variations and intellectual complications. This is the topos of the image of the beloved painted or sculpted in the heart. 'Oh, Love,' exclaims Gismondo in Bembo's *Gli Asolani*, 'may I always bless your hands with which you have painted, written, and imprinted in my soul so many things of my sweet lady that I carry a large canvas with me at all hours, filled with numberless portraits of her.'[41] Or take for example the 'variations on the theme' that Della Porta dedicates to this topos in one of his comedies, *La Sorella* [The sister]: 'It pains me,' says the character Erotico, 'that I cannot show her the inside of my heart; for there she would see her beautiful image shine, as in a sparkling, polished mirror; and she would see how it is entirely occupied by this image, and how there is no space for any others, and the entrance is closed to all.' Even if he does not see his lady, he says a little later, he still speaks with her, thanks to the 'continuous memory that I have of her, and that portrait

that love painted in my heart with the brush of imagination is so alive
that there is no room for the soul itself.'[42]

There are also interesting elaborations of this topos in sixteenth-
century lyric poetry: Luigi Cassola (ca 1480–1560), for example, writes
that, since he is not able to see his lady in person, he has asked an artist
to paint a portrait of her:

> and in order not to seem foolish before such a noble task, the painter
> opened my heart with immeasurable art: the drawing copied from it was
> as natural as what nature herself made.[43]

Thus, this topos interacts with the enduring theme of the 'portrait of
the lover' that is used in mysterious, and at times disturbing, ways to
fill her/his absence.[44] The play of reflection between the portrait and
the image painted in the heart is already present in the poetry of the
Sicilian school. We see it in a poem by Giacomo da Lentini:

> As a man who has his mind on
> another model, paints
> a picture similar to it,
>   so, fair lady, do I,
>   for deep inside my heart
>   I bear your image.
>
> It seems that I bear you in my heart
> depicted as on a wall,
> but outwardly nothing shows ...
>
>   Feeling a great desire,
>   I painted a picture,
>   fair lady, which has your likeness;
>   and when I do not see you,
>   I look upon that image,
>   and it seems that I have you before me.[45]

We can imagine that there is a strong impulse in the sixteenth century to interpret this topos literally, an impulse related to the canon of
imitation/emulation and *concettismo* [conceit], as well as the medical
and philosophical tradition that we have discussed: for one accustomed to believing in the miracles of *imaginatio*, it is not so farfetched to

think that the *phantasma* of the beloved can take on shape and texture to the point that it becomes visible. Pregnant women, writes Ficino, using one of the more common examples, impress the image of what they most desire onto the foetus (like the image of wine): 'Is there anyone so inexperienced that he does not know that someone in love craves the beloved even more than a pregnant woman desires such refreshment? Therefore he ponders her more strongly and firmly, and consequently it is no wonder that the face of the beloved, chiselled in the heart of the lover, paints itself in the spirit, and from the spirit imprints itself in the blood.'[46] In the tradition of mysticism, for that matter, we also find analogous procedures translated mostly into meticulous iconographic realism: more than once, in fact, we read that the hearts of women mystics, once opened, reveal the intensely cherished engraved images of the crucifix and the Passion.[47]

The context that we have briefly evoked here – a context in which philosophical ideas are intertwined with the practices of medicine, with the images of poets and painters, and with mystical experiences – is essential to understanding how an ancient image acquires a new meaning during the sixteenth and seventeenth centuries: the image of the window opening onto the heart. As Mario Andrea Rigoni has demonstrated, in the Greek tradition this image is derived from one of Aesop's fables: when called upon to judge what some of the gods have built, Momus criticizes Prometheus for having fabricated man without giving him a window through which one can see what he has in his heart.[48] This is not, however, the principal tradition of the sixteenth century. Generally, the image of the window onto the heart is attributed to Socrates, a tradition based on the preface to the third book of Vitruvius' *De architectura*. Here the source cited is not Aesop but the Delphic oracle, which alludes to this image as proof of Socrates' extraordinary knowledge. Rigoni has offered the thesis that Vitruvius has been influenced by the Platonic representation of Socrates as Silenus: if one could open a window onto his heart, he would discover the beautiful image of a god that hides beneath the skin of a coarse, ridiculous body.

Like the image of the Silenus, the image of the window opening onto the heart enjoys great popularity in the sixteenth century, so much so that it is consecrated and at the same time ossified in iconographic repertories: for example, in Pierio Valeriano's *Hieroglyphica*, which introduces the variant of the man carrying his heart dangling from a necklace in order to indicate the *viri probo sermo* [the speech of a righteous man], that is, the correspondence between words and thoughts, between actions and the heart; or in Ripa's *Iconologia*, where Reality and the Love of God (figure 41) display an open heart, while Sincerity places the heart in the left hand (figure 42).[49] The latter is the visualization of an image still present today as a common idiomatic expression, that is, when we say 'con il cuore in mano' [with heart in hand].

The image of the window opening onto the heart thus corresponds to an ideal of transparency; it expresses the dream that one is able to visualize directly the internal dimension where, according to an ancient tradition, truth has its *place*, that is, where it resides. Rigoni has seized upon this aspect as an exemplar of the metaphysical myth in the western tradition, 'of its profound vocation and its unattainable *telos*: to abolish the separation and to dissipate the ontological opacity in which body, language, and interpretation *take place*, or, in other words, the world itself as the eternal realm of the mask.'[50] We will now examine other occurences of this image in the sixteenth and seventeenth centuries and show how they are related to those zones of experience to which we have referred earlier, zones that are not dominated, to use Rigoni's expression, by the 'condemnation of appearances, *phantasma*, and *simulacra*.'[51] The aim, instead, is to make use of them, to penetrate and operate within a dimension in which interior and exterior, visible and invisible, are mixed together, one translated into the other. As we have seen, internal mental images possess a complex status in the sixteenth century. They are interpreted through a tradition of Neoplatonism that lives together with and is contaminated by other traditions and experiences. To open a window onto the heart thus means constructing, perhaps artificially, an observatory onto the *phantasmata* that inhabit the body and the psyche. To use the repertory of images and ideas to which we have referred above, we can think of the window onto the heart as an observation point that allows one to see the inside of a gallery in which paintings and sculptures make feelings and thoughts visible.

This image enjoys substantial and widespread popularity. Rigoni has cited its presence on a triumphal arch raised in Brussels in 1594 in honour of the entrance of Archduke Ernst of Austria: a naked man trampling on masks, holding a dove in his left hand, pointing with his right to his heart, which appears through the bars of a window on his chest. According to the apparatus, the image represents the sincerity of the Catholic faith that characterizes the inhabitants of the city. The man's chest is revealed 'so that through the bars, all of the furnishings

41 Love of God, from Cesare Ripa, *Iconologia* (Rome: Lepido Faci 1603)

of the heart were in plain sight' [ut per cancellos universi pectoris *supellex* visendam se praeberet].[52] In addition to its importance with regard to the diffusion and the level, so to speak, of the use and consumption of the image, the example of the arch in Brussels is also noteworthy because of the term used to indicate the contents of the heart: *supellex*. The window seemingly opens onto a chamber in which have been amassed furniture, provisions, or treasures. The notion of the heart as a warehouse (as we will see in chapter 6), overlaps with that of the gallery or the collection to describe the spaces of human interiority.

The fact that the image of the window onto the heart is a component of mainstream culture and sixteenth-century imagery is evidenced by its presence in two works dedicated to games that we have already mentioned. In the presentation of the Game of Trickery Innocenzo Ringhieri uses the technique of praising women *e contrario*: 'I firmly believe that if you were all made of transparent crystal, or glass, or if

42 Sincerity, from Cesare Ripa, *Iconologia* (Rome: Lepido Faci 1603)

there were true *openings or windows in your bodies* so that the thoughts and secrets of your souls could be seen,' there would be only innocence, candour, and faith.[53]

In one of the games mentioned by Girolamo Bargagli, the Game of the Sorceress, a judgment is made in the case of a lover who, desperate because his lady doubts the sincerity of his feelings, asks the sorceress that *'in his chest and in her breast a window might be born, whereby they could see each other's hearts as they pleased,* so that she can be certain of his love and he could clarify that which she claimed to hold for him.' But the judge gives a negative verdict, and says that *'giving lovers a window through which one could see the images sculpted in the heart* would take away all the beautiful trials of love and every remarkable amorous action.'[54] Bargagli's version clearly highlights the close connection, discussed above, between the theme of the image painted or sculpted in the heart and the image of the window. However, the motif of sculpture ('one could see the images sculpted in the heart') is a detail added by the judge to the dynamic of the game. He thus becomes an annotator of, a commentator on, the text/game, and his mode of interpretation is clearly influenced by his literary memory.

The motivation behind the judge's sentence is also most interesting: the ideal of transparency makes things too simple, it takes away the fascination and mystery, and it sweeps away simulation, doubt, and risk; it leaves no room for ingenuity. The objection posed by Bargagli's judge is not very different from that expressed by Emanuele Tesauro in his *Cannocchiale aristotelico*: he writes that it is wrong for Socrates to blame

> Nature for not having opened a window in the chests of men in order to see their original concepts face to face, without the interpretation of a lying tongue whose renditions were often unfaithful. Nature could have composed her apology to this complaint by answering that she would at the same time have defrauded those who were ingenious of the pleasure of so many wondrous arts of discourse.

It is in fact the property of 'human genius to love that which one admires, and to admire the clothed rather than the naked truth.'[55]

If we look back, using Tesauro's criticism as well as the polite reservations expressed by Bargagli's judge in the Game of the Sorceress, we could say that for a certain period, perhaps paradoxically, the image of the window opening onto the heart is the condensation of different needs and myths: the idea of an absolute transparency of being, of which it emblematically expresses the weakness and contradictions; but also the notion that it is possible to make visible the way in which, as Tesauro would say, ideas take shape (the way they become 'archetypal wit') when they are deposited in the imagination, the way in which language dresses up concepts and gives them form. In some ways, therefore, the image of the window onto the heart is well adapted to what we have discussed in this chapter: it ably expresses the attempt to build an observatory onto the *phantasmata*, the anxiety to *see* the spaces that open up between the soul and the body, and the search for suitable techniques for this purpose. We will let this image guide us as we attempt to form an idea of what these techniques are and how they are related.

We can find the image of the window onto the heart in the middle of the comedy of errors that for some years marked the relations between Erasmus and Camillo. After being violently attacked by Julius Caesar

Scaliger in 1531 for his *Ciceronianus*, Erasmus erroneously suspected that it was Camillo who had authored the attack, and he entrusted an inquiry into the matter to a friend, Viglius Zuichemus, who was in Padua.[56] Viglius finally managed to meet Camillo in Venice and see his theatre. He writes to Erasmus on 8 June 1532:

> The author has different names for his theatre: *artificial soul and mind, or endowed with windows*. He says, in fact, that all the things that the human mind conceives but that cannot be seen with the eyes of the body can, however, with careful consideration, be expressed with some bodily signs, so that everyone can see directly with his own eyes all that which otherwise is submerged in the depths of the human mind. And he has called it a theatre because it can be seen with the eyes of the body.[57]

Although Viglius reports Camillo's words with strong scepticism, he does so very accurately. They are echoed in a passage by Camillo himself in *Pro suo de eloquentia theatro ad Gallos oratio* [Oration to the French in defense of his theatre of eloquence]:

> Nature has thus given us a mind that embraces the impressions that all things leave in us, impressions that are common to all peoples, so much so that all nations conceive things according to one, identical form ... analogously, I too have constructed a great mind, outside us, that contains the forms of all things and of all words.

Camillo's theatre projects outside the soul those images with which, universally, man perceives the world, regardless of linguistic differences. 'Our artificial mind,' he adds, 'this contruction of ours, fruit of such great labour, is so *endowed with windows* that Socrates himself could have not desired it to be more open.'[58]

From Camillo's perspective the relationship between interiority and the external world is thus turned upside down (this is made possible, as we noted above, through the magical capacities of the *imaginatio*): in the theatre of memory it is the spectator/user who is on the stage and who sees, touches, and uses the forms of the images no longer enclosed in the secret recesses of the heart but artificially recreated. The image of the window is thus extended to that of the theatre, which becomes a sort of heart turned inside out and set on display.

Besides the art of memory, another ancient art that flourishes during the sixteenth century asserts its right to open a window onto the heart:

physiognomy.[59] It teaches how to read in the physical features of man images and signs of his moral and psychological attributes, and it relies principally on resemblances between men and animals. In a work that would enjoy immense popularity Della Porta proposes and elaborates this art, partly by putting it under the sign of the Socratic window onto the heart. More than any other animal, Della Porta writes in the *Proemio* to the Italian version of *Fisonomia dell'uomo*, man desires the company of his own kind, but he has the problem of not falling snare to the wicked, who are often difficult to recognize because of dissimulation.

> For this reason, so that no man would ever be fooled, Socrates desired above all that there be a window in the chest so that a duplicitous heart could not be hidden and so that everyone would be allowed to discover the will, the thoughts, the truth, and the lies. Physiognomy, indeed, thoroughly fulfils Socrates' righteous desire and meets the challenge of such iniquity: using signs that can be discovered in a man from a distance, it reveals his intentions and behaviour, seemingly penetrating the darkest and most hidden places of the heart.

In 1616 Giovanni Bonifacio (1547–1635), a great admirer of Della Porta's *Fisonomia* published the *Arte dei cenni con la quale formandosi favella visibile si tratta della muta eloquenza, che non è altro che un facondo silenzio* [Art of gestures with which, by forming a visible language, one can learn a mute eloquence, nothing less than a voluble silence (Vicenza: Francesco Grossi 1616).[60] This work furnishes a repertory of more than six hundred gestures, and it indicates the moral or psychological disposition that each one represents. The *Art of Gestures*, like physiognomy, relies on the principle whereby the interpretation of the body allows one to penetrate the secrets of the soul, but at the same time it asserts its greater accuracy and different dynamics: 'with physiognomy,' writes Bonifacio, 'one can discover the natural inclination of others ... But with the ability to read the gestures, the movements and gesticulations of man, one can easily find out what is present in everyone's soul at any given moment' (p. 516). Through a sort of dictionary of the meanings of the gestures and movements of the body one can attempt to construct a guide to the interior self. It is no wonder that the image of the window onto the heart reappears here. 'And those who have complete knowledge of this art,' he writes, 'will have no need to desire that *Socratic window to see the heart* in a man's chest, because with the ability to read these gestures, the most secret thoughts and most hidden sentiments of the human soul are revealed' (p. 11).

Camillo Baldi (1550–1637), a professor of literature and philosophy at the university of Bologna, a commentator on the pseudo-Aristotelian *Physiognomy*, and the author of works on the same subject, published in 1622 a short work entitled *Come da una lettera missiva si conoscano la natura e qualità dello scrittore* [How one can know the nature and qualities of the writer from one of his letters] (Carpi: Girolamo Baschieri). In this work, considered to be a precursor of graphology, Baldi examines not only handwriting but other components of the text such as the selection of words, the expressions used, the style, and the concepts. In each of these elements he tries to see the signs of the character of the writer as defined according to traditional models of the temperaments. 'With apparent inanity,' writes Armando Petrucci in a recent edition of this text, 'Camillo Baldi brought his critical discourse to an intersection between the study of the propensities of bodies and handwritings and the study of the structures of texts and of rhetoric.'[61] In effect, the text needs to be considered in its entirety, from its study of elements at the most visible and physical level – that is, handwriting – to the most abstract – style and concepts. Each of these is the offshoot of something that is imprinted not just on the soul but also on the body. The techniques proposed by Baldi teach how to retrace the chain of connections, to see this hidden dimension. The choice of the letter is related to the conviction that it uses less artifice, and therefore it enhances, so to speak, the conditions of visualization. Baldi's authorities in this field are Demetrius, author of *De elocutione* [On style] and his sixteenth-century commentator, Pietro Vettori:

> Demetrius says that the letter would not be a letter if one could not discern in it the ways of the writer ... wherefore if actions show us everyone's customs and habits, and the latter are expressed in speech, and speech can be seen in writing, we can know the qualities of the writer from the writing. It is for this reason that Vittorio [Vettori] says that those who read a letter – if they have a discerning eye – *see at the same time the heart inside the chest of the writer.*   (P. 8)

In his commmentary on Demetrius, in fact, Vettori writes that 'it is as if those who read [the letter] could see the heart of the writer and know his most intimate feelings.'[62] Although there is no image of a window, we are in a similar context. This is confirmed by the fact that not much earlier in the text Baldi cites the Socratic maxim so dear to Erasmus: 'Socrates also said, "speak that I may know you"' (p 7).[63]

It is clear that during the sixteenth and seventeenth centuries there are numerous arts that claim to have the secret for opening a window onto the heart: the art of memory, physiognomy, the art of gestures, graphology and rhetoric (the technique used to analyse literary texts). We will now try to see how the art of memory utilizes and augments this multifaceted attempt to construct a map of the territory that connects the body and the soul.

5 The Theatre of Passions between Memory, Rhetoric, and Physiognomy

Della Porta is a good place to start: he uses only images of persons as *imagines agentes*, and this choice characterizes the strong theatrical aspect of his techniques of memory. It was a matter of constructing an actual mental theatre in which one places the characters that are needed. There are two essential requirements. The first is the variety of the characters. Besides the ten or twenty beautiful women mentioned earlier, we use 'ridiculous persons, like clowns or other similar characters, and here we will mix in matrons, noble and base persons, with friars, young and old, priests, boys, and others' (*L'arte del ricordare* [Naples: Marco Antonio Passaro 1566], folio C2r). The second requirement is that these characters be in a certain sense types, or masks. In other words, they have to have strong characteristics, well-defined attitudes. In this way, writes Della Porta, when we encountered 'a person standing in that place and *know all of his customary behaviour and temperaments* ... we quickly adapt him to the desired gesture, and we can undress him, and dress him, and depict him in all those *temperaments and ways* that we need" (folio C11v). We will come back to the phrases in italics, but first we must note that even Della Porta (like Gesualdo, who copies from him) recommends establishing a close, very 'physical' relationship to the images: 'now, once we have positioned them in the places, it is necessary to contemplate them for a while with the eyes of the mind, as if they were alive, to pass by them very closely, and to touch them with our hands, and to call them from the front and the back' (folio C2v).

Those who practise the art of memory have to function like directors or playwrights. Their fundamental task is to make each character act in accordance with his/her type. At the beginning the different characters, writes Della Porta, are to be lined up in order according to a specific criterion (as, for example, age or social status), standing, with their backs leaning on the wall and their arms at their sides. Their degree of expression is reduced to zero in order to erase the recollections that have been associated with them. But in order for the show to begin, for the actors (or puppets) to become *imagines agentes*, they have to be animated by giving them gestures, expressions, and attitudes, by dressing them with clothes of different designs and colours, by putting certain objects in their hands. As Della Porta states in the passage cited above, the fundamental rule of the game is that all of this must happen in a suitable fashion, in a way that respects 'all the customary behaviour and temperaments' of the characters. Artificial memory is thus supported by an association based on the psychological and moral types of the characters themselves. It has to reflect the set of characteristics that makes the character into a type. This is the reason why it is essential for those who practise the art of memory to know the customary behaviour and temperaments of different characters.

This task is not very difficult in the sixteenth and seventeenth centuries when rigid divisions among different social and sexual roles are precisely reflected in outward appearances. Different arts, moreover, pass on and use a grid of *mores*, a typology of human *characters* and of the gestures, attitudes, and behaviours, connected to them. Those who practise the art of memory according to Della Porta's teachings, for example, could make use of works on rhetoric and poetics. According to Aristotelian tradition, in fact, in order to move the listener orators have to exhibit passions that they deem useful and suitable to their cause, and, at the same time, they have to appeal to the passions felt by their audience. For this reason treatises of rhetoric transmit a psychological and moral classification differentiated according to the age and social and political conditions of the audience: one has to arouse or subdue different passions in audiences made up of young people or old, the powerful or the poor, citizens of a free republic or subjects of a tyranny.[64]

An analogous grid is used in the treatises on poetics, especially in the part dedicated to comedy. The return to the classical model creates a need for stock characters: the young and impulsive lover; the jealous, miserly old man; the parasite obsessed with food, etc. Della Porta, an author of a number of comedies, knows this repertory well and manages it with great skill.

Besides the treatises on rhetoric and poetics and the sixteenth- and seventeenth-century theatre, there is another source available to those who need to know the typology of *mores* and the language of gestures in order to practise the art of memory: treatises on art, and, of course, the knowledge of works of art. The movement of the mind is understood through the movement of the body, writes Leon Battista Alberti in *De pictura* [On painting], a work that would enjoy great success in the sixteenth century: 'all the movements of the body should be closely observed by the painter.'[65] The painter has the task of depicting his characters in such a way that their perceptible image conveys their interior state. He has to be able to communicate their emotions and feelings. Through the gestures and attitudes of their characters, in other words, even painters open a window onto the heart. At the height of the cinquecento the different types of characters in the figurative arts grew immensely: artists demonstrate an acute interest in the ugly, in the deformed, in exaggerated caricatures, in those *pitture ridicole* [ridiculous paintings] that Barry Wind has associated with the *low* characters of comedy.[66] The authors of the treatises are also interested in these problems. In his *Disegno* [Drawing] (1549), Anton Francesco Doni emphasizes the importance of the *colours* in physiognomy, and he recommends that the painter carefully study the *air* of his characters so as to know how to adapt it to each profession: 'the doctor,' for example, 'has to have a fresh, colourful face, otherwise people will say that he does not know how to cure himself, let alone others. The hermit ought to be lean and pale.'[67]

Gian Paolo Lomazzo (1538–1600) dedicates the entire second book of his *Trattato dell'arte della pittura, scultura et architettura* [Treatise on the art of painting, sculpture, and architecture] (1584) to a rich typology of *moti* [movements], a term that 'covers the entire range of meanings of motion, gesture, expression, passion and character,' writes Robert Klein.[68] It is important to note that among the painters who have expertise in this difficult field, Lomazzo cites not only Leonardo, Raffaello, Mantegna, and Titian, but also his 'old tutor' (p. 101), Gaudenzio Ferrari, especially in his depiction of the scenes of the Passion in the Sanctuary of Sacro Monte at Varallo, a veritable gallery of types, an extraordinary theatre of passions (plate III).

True and proper repertories of gestures, gesticulations, and characters also begin to appear in manuals dedicated to mnemonics. The *Ars memorativa* written in Bologna in 1425 explains that 'images can be formed using the movements and actions of the body' [per motus

corporis et actus ymagines formantur], and it furnishes a dictionary of
the meanings of hand gestures and the various positions of the head.[69]
At the end of the fifteenth century Iacobo Publicio teaches that biting
one's fingers and nails [digitorum et unguium mordicatio] is a sign of
forgetfulness (*Oratoriae artis epitoma* [Epitome of the art of oratory]
(Venice: Erhard Ratdolt 1485), (folio 56r). Dolce also dedicates ample
space to this question when he plagiarizes Romberch: 'We must form
the image that we have in our mind with certain lines and attitudes of
the body suitable to their qualities and temperaments, in such a way
that they represent even the interior self.' Old age, for example, should
appear 'sad, a youth should be prodigal, a woman greedy, a man
generous, and hunger pale. In this manner, one can take an almost
infinite number of qualities of such images from poets, who describe
them in detail' (*Dialogo nel quale si ragiona del modo di accrescer et conservar
la memoria*, folio 48r).

Beyond the different arts and their specific needs, the typology of
mores, the language of gestures, the ways in which the body speaks are
all part of a common heritage. It is not difficult to understand why this
exchange is so easy and natural. We have just seen that Dolce recommends that the practitioner of the art of memory use the poets. Della
Porta, in the chapter of his *Ars reminiscendi* entitled 'Quomodo ex gestu
recordari possumus' [The ways in which we can remember using ges-
tures], resorts to a true collage of sources, and it is their very variety
that opens up varied and noteworthy vistas beyond the text:

> like painting, a silent work that represents things always with the same
> attitude, the gesture is capable of expressing intimate feelings with such
> efficacy that sometimes it seems to surpass the expressive force of the
> word. The mute use gestures instead of speech, and with their hands and
> their gestures they display their will. Even the feelings of speechless
> animals, like wrath, joy, or adulation, are understood by means of the eyes
> and some other signs of the body. (*Ars reminiscendi* [Naples: Giovan
> Battista Sottile 1602], p. 27)[70]

The first sentence is copied from Quintilian (11.3.67), from the section
dedicated to *actio*, that is, the way in which the orator has to move and
pose when speaking in public.[71] As we mentioned earlier (chapter 3,
p. 94), Della Porta draws from this section of the *Institutio oratoria* when
he discusses the expressiveness of the hands in his treatise on ciphers.
In the second sentence cited here Della Porta synthesizes and, in part,

reproduces a passage that comes just before in Quintilian's text (11.3.66).[72] Della Porta continues by giving examples of how gestures express the passions: 'Do you not think him to be full of grief whose forehead is bent over, whose head is bowed, in short whose every limb seems downcast? Who does not think someone to be overwhelmed by anger whose face and eyes are swollen and red, who in all the parts of his body is violently shaken by the fury of wrath?' (*Ars reminiscendi*, pp. 27–28).[73] The source of this passage, not cited by Della Porta, is Alberti's *De pictura*. As proof of the connection between the movements of the body and the movements of the soul discussed in the passage cited above, Alberti has written:

> In the grieving the forehead is bent, the head bowed, all members sag as if tired and neglected. In the angry, because anger ignites the soul, the face and eyes are swollen red, and all the parts of the body are violently shaken by the fury of wrath.[74]

The association between Quintilian and Alberti probably comes about because the passage copied from Quintilian begins with an example from painting.

The identification of the sources used in this text allows us to understand in detail the way in which Della Porta's literary memory functions, the way in which it assembles textual fragments. It helps us to understand the rich mixture of notions that come together in his theatre of memory: someone who builds *imagines agentes* is like an orator who needs to inscribe in his body the passions that he wants to comunicate. At the same time, he is like a painter who needs to master the semantics of gestures in order to make the emotions visible.

Another passage from Alberti's *De pictura*, again related to the representation of the movements of the mind, is recycled by Della Porta in his treatise on memory, but this time the meaning is turned upside down. In the name of composure and decorum Alberti condemns movements that are too violent [nimium acres], and he comments that some believe 'that those figures appear most lively which most throw about all their members,' and for this reason 'without heeding the dignity of painting, they imitate actors.'[75] Della Porta, however, recommends that the images of memory 'be larger than necessary, decorated with lively colours and shining light; the characters should move their limbs in a very obvious way, and they should imitate the movements of actors' (*Ars reminiscendi*, p. 16).[76]

Alberti's work on painting is thus profoundly present in Della Porta's treatise on memory, as we shall also see below. However, it is significant, first, that Della Porta's work is also closely linked to Quintilian's text on rhetoric, from which it appropriates the section dedicated to gestures, bodily 'movements,' and, secondly, that Alberti is inverted precisely here, where the imitation of actors is at stake, that is, when there is reference to the theatre, the province of Della Porta the playwright.

There is yet another art that traditionally boasts of direct competence regarding the *mores* of men, the various moral and pyschological types, and thus is able to provide a useful reference point for the animation of the theatre of memory: physiognomy. It is helpful, therefore, to re-examine the section of *Fisonomia dell'uomo* that Della Porta dedicates to the *mores* in order to get an idea of how the art of memory and physiognomy interact.

What are the sources utilized by Della Porta? First of all, he uses direct observation, especially of galley-slaves, prisoners, the wretched sick who are rotting away in the public hospitals, witches, and highwaymen sentenced to be executed. Della Porta's macabre interests have aroused the curiosity of some critics who see in him a precursor to Cesare Lombroso. The other type of source, just as famous, is the animal world. The comparison of the profiles of animals with human portraits is based on the conviction that there is a single substrate that connects the animal and human worlds. Starting with the animal world to identify the physical signs of the *mores* and then applying them to men thus becomes a correct and practical operation. On the animal level, in fact, the identification of meaningful elements is much easier and clearer because the relationship between the physical figure of the animal (that is, its belonging to a particular species) and its character is a transparent and visible one, and therefore the connection between signifier and signified – established by nature once and for all – is more reliable. The search for these signs on the human level is more difficult, not only because of the greater complexity and diversification of the human organism, but also because the world of man plays with the signs, dragging them through the vortex of masks, disguises, and deceptions. Physiognomy interacts with Della Porta's theatre not only because it is used to classify the individual characters but also because, once it becomes a component of the world of comedy and therefore subject to the play of appearances, it is jumbled and comically overturned.[77]

Since the animal world offers reliable models by making the connec-

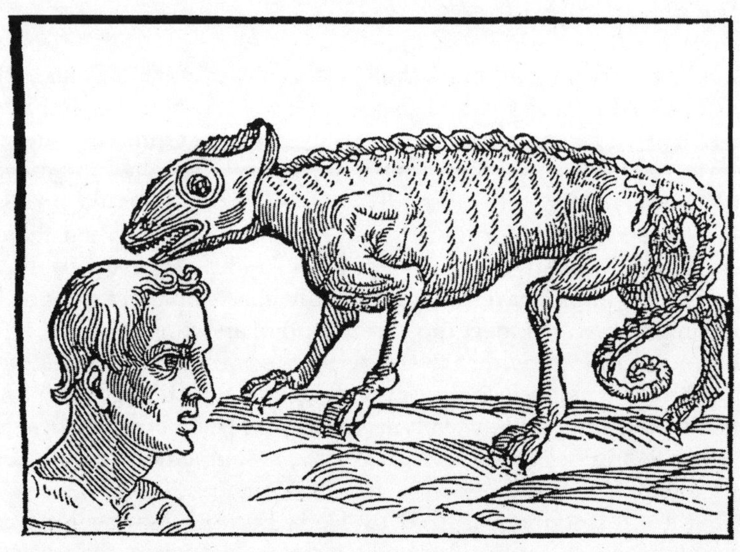

43 The coward and the chameleon, from Giovan Battista Della Porta, *Della fisonomia dell'uomo* (Padua: Pietro Paolo Tozzi 1627)

tions between inside and outside directly visible, we can understand why Della Porta is so concerned that the illustrations in his *Fisonomia dell'uomo* faithfully reproduce the different animals. 'With labourious effort,' he writes, 'we have sent to Florence for the portrait of the leopard, and dissatisfied with this, we had a portrait made in Naples from a live leopard brought here in 1584 in order to show how its features resemble those of a woman' (*Fisonomia dell'uomo*, [Padua: Pietro Paolo Tozzi 1627], folio 131v). For the same reason, writes Della Porta, he has raised a chameleon in his home: its image ('taken from a live chameleon, maintained in my home just for this purpose,' folio 17v) is matched with the profile of a frightened man (figure 43). Fidelity in the portraits of animals is sought, not in the name of modern scientific accuracy, but because it serves to make the physiognomic signs visible and consequently applicable to the human world.

The same methods are used with regard to Egyptian hieroglyphics read through the canonical sources: the text of the pseudo-Horapollo and the commentary by Pierio Valeriano. The image of the leopard mentioned above is cited, for example, and then followed by this obser-vation: 'when they wished to denote one who seeks to conceal his evil, wicked spirit so it will not be found out by others, the Egyptian sages depict the leopard because it stealthily pursues other animals, nor does it allow the speed and impetus used in the pursuit to be perceived' (folio 32r); 'when they wished to show a impudent man, the Egyptians depicted the frog, which has no blood in any part of the body except in the eyes, and for this reason, those who have blood in their eyes are called impudent' (folio 127v).[78] In other words, hieroglyphics faithfully reproduce a moral classification deduced from the animal world and thus act as a figurative dictionary of physiognomy. Because of the capacity of hierglyphics to condense a network of associations into a perceptible image, we often find them recommended in the treatises as images of memory. Della Porta, in fact, dedicates an entire chapter of his *Ars reminiscendi* to hieroglyphics (chapter 18).

But there are other sources, generally overlooked by scholars, for the types of *mores* described in the *Fisionomia dell'uomo*. Alongside the earlier tradition of treatises devoted to physiognomy we find the treatises devoted to rhetoric (cited because they describe the framework of different kinds of human behaviour and temperament in relation to different ages), as well as literary and artistic sources. Among these a pre-eminent position is taken up by descriptions – and their corresponding visual representations – that can be subdivided in the following manner:

1 *Descriptions of stock characters, taken from writers and poets.* Plautus is cited, for example, for the way he *paints* or *shows* the pimp, the lover, the cheater, etc.
2 *Descriptions of allegorical images, taken mostly from Dante and Ovid.* These images could be used in a number of ways. They can function as iconological models or as topical sources for the description of individual characters – the image of envy, described by Ovid (*Metamorphoses* 1.760–782), for example, can be used by anyone who wants to represent an envious character – or as images of memory. In the chapter of *Ars reminiscendi* entitled 'De aliquibus vitiorum et virtutum imaginibus' [Some images of vices and virtues], the author recommends the use of the allegorical descriptions of the poets because they provide *imagines agentes* of the vices and the virtues, and he gives Ovid's description of envy as an example. This mixture of cultural planes, of perspectives, can help us to understand the function of the image of jealousy that monopolizes the prologue of one of Della Porta's best comedies, the *Fantesca* [The wench].[79]
3 *Descriptions of great persons from the past, taken from historical works*

and/or portraits, and passed on to us in the form of statues, medallions, or coins. These descriptions offer an advantageous opportunity for observation: the stories of these characters have already been completed, and their destinies can be interpreted in terms of their psychological and moral characteristics, which in turn can be associated with their physiognomical features as passed on by historians, poets, and artists. The double gallery of Della Porta's physiognomy has its origins here: the gallery of illustrious men and the gallery of animals that mirror each other. For example, Della Porta associates the 'large head of the owl and the disproportionate head of the emperor Vitellius that we have had drawn, using the marble statue conserved in the museum of Adriano Spatafora, my most learned uncle and scholar of ancient things' (folio 36v; figure 44). Naturalist and antiquarian collecting are brought together because their images mirror each other and are easily combined. For this reason Della Porta cites some of the major collections of the era – naturalist and antiquarian – that he has seen in Naples, Rome, and other cities.[80]

4 *Descriptions (and images) of mythological characters, gods, and constellations.* When using these diverse sources Della Porta is very careful to underline their points of convergence. Take, for example, the label for the image of Mars and Saturn: 'On the right-hand side of this picture, one can see Mars, on the left-hand side Saturn; we have drawn them using marble statues and bronze medallions as well as astrologers' descriptions' (folio 23v). Emphasizing the points of convergence means establishing the validity of his work. Each source brings with it a link useful in the construction and consolidation of a network of correspondences, of meaningful analogies – that great network of signs deposited, in a dispersed and fragmentary way, in the world of nature and in the literary and artistic tradition. They need to be extracted in order to be put back together, made visible and functional.[81]

Della Porta's physiognomy thus helps us to understand how collecting functions as a depository of memory: it is capable of offering *imagines agents* that can put into motion a powerful chain of associations. We will return later to the relationship between collecting and the art of memory.

If we consider, moreover, the importance of naturalist and antiquarian illustration on the one hand and literary description on the other, it

44 The emperor Vitellio and the owl, from Giovan Battista Della Porta, *De humana physiognomonia* (Vico Equense: Giuseppe Cacchi 1586)

is easy to understand the analogous role played by the combination of the two in the illustrated book: the continuous alternation between text and image liberates from the image its deposits of knowledge and its fabric of possible associations.

The fifth book of *Fisonomia dell'uomo*, dedicated to the images of vices and virtues, reorganizes the material distributed in the previous books by using a vast classification of characters: the gambler appears, for example, next to the sponger and the glutton. The taste for particularly meaningful images (*forms* or *figures* in Della Porta's terminology), images capable of condensing an entire topos, is clearly present in the comment accompanying the image of the Farnese *Hercules*: 'We have reproduced here the figure of Hercules, drawn from the ancient figures in the palace of the illustrious prince of Parma, where it is possible to contemplate *all* the signs of fortitude in *one*' (folio 184v). The fifth book is thus an attempt at an exhaustive survey of the *mores*: it offers a great theatre of passions in the sense that each human passion is embodied by a type of character, in a gesture, in a trait, where the passion thus finds form and visibility. The theatre and its repertory are intended for use by literati, artists, and anyone who practises the art of memory. This perspective allows us to reconsider the audience for whom *Fisonomia dell'uomo* is intended. As we mentioned earlier, the book boasts that it has opened a window onto the heart. For this reason it helps one to choose one's friends wisely, and in a well-ordered society it can serve to distribute roles and functions rationally. But physiognomy, writes Della Porta, also has a rhetorical function:

> It is also the art of poets and painters: by including in their poems and paintings persons with different customs and describing their features, they give them to us in a proper manner. We have seen it used by Homer, Virgil, Ovid, by Plautus and Terence in the their comedies, by Euripides and Sophocles in their tragedies, and especially by ancient artists in their bronze medallions and marble statues.   (*Proemio*)

In a certain sense we have come full circle: the types of sources used by the method coincide with its destined audience.

If, on the one hand, physiognomy places before the eye the masks of the different passions and makes them into visible forms that can be used in the theatre of memory, it also, on the other hand, provides a convenient storehouse for artists and writers. This had already been recognized by Pomponio Gaurico (ca 1480–1530), a man of letters who lived between Padua and Naples, and the author of a commentary on Horace's *Ars poetica*. A large part of his book *De sculptura* [On sculpture], published in Florence in 1504, is devoted, in fact, to physiognomy. It is presented as an art that every good sculptor needs to know, as a science that allows one to visualize the great men of the past. It makes it possible to translate into images the words that have been written about these individuals.[82]

Thus, Gaurico believes that the artist could use physiognomy as a *topica*, a repertory of models. This is a cue that is only marginally taken up by the tradition. The idea is present, as we have seen, in Della Porta's work, and at the end of the century it is revived by Giacomo de Gaeta.[83] A jurist from Cosenza, a member of the Accademia Telesiana, a friend of the young Tommaso Campanella, Giacomo was the author of *Ragionamento detto l'academico overo della bellezza* [An essay titled the academic, or on beauty] (Naples: Giuseppe Cacchi 1591), a work in which traditional aesthetic models interact with new notions derived from the naturalism of Telesio and the research carried out in the circle of the Della Porta brothers.[84] Giacomo praises Della Porta's work on physiognomy and calls it the basis of a new science that teaches how to create perceptible images capable of expressing all the *mores*, of giving form, therefore, to the different aspects of the inner self. It is a science, he writes, that 'could find and give suitable lineaments and bodily features to the behaviour and inclinations of the mind.' Although this science has no name, 'it should, nonetheless, be practised all the time by painters, and it is highly suitable for poets' (p. 49).

The art of memory and physiognomy thus opens a window onto the heart: they build a gallery of images in which the invisible takes shape and becomes usable in the theatrical play of representation and metamorphosis. The relationship among the different arts is not unidirectional but circular: thanks to physiognomy, the theatre of memory can be modelled in such a way as to crystallize and reanimate recollections. At the same time, *remembering* physiognomy leads to the construction of texts and images that are, in turn, effective and memorable.[85]

6 The Body and the Text

There is another aspect that makes mnemonics comparable to a theatre of passions, an aspect that is recognized and thoroughly exploited in preaching, theatre, and painting.[86] We can start yet again with Della Porta. He teaches that in order for a memory play to begin, in order for the various *personae* positioned in the places to be transformed into *imagines agentes*, it is necessary to animate them in different ways, with costumes and props, but above all they need to be given passions and feelings and their bodies need to be adjusted according to the gestures and expressions suitable to express those desired feelings.

To do this, those who practise the art of memory have to pretend to feel the same passions. In a certain sense they have to lose themselves in the role. The resulting analogy with the profession of the actor is already present in the tradition. 'Nonetheless, we can situate the images of such unseen things using the example of those who normally act in comedies or tragedies,' writes Dolce in 1575 in his dialogue on memory (*Dialogo nel quale si ragiona del modo di accrescer et conservar la memoria*, folio 85r).

As we mentioned earlier, the orator is also required to impersonate the different *mores*, to express the different passions. Invaluable recommendations are found in the section of Quintilian's *Institutio oratoria* dedicated to *actio* and *pronuntiatio*, an actual treatise on body language, on how the orator needs to use it in order to captivate his audience. The game is played above all, he writes, by arousing passions [maxima ex parte praestant motus animorum]. The orator needs to communicate feelings that are both true and false:

> But there is a difference between true emotion on the one hand, and false and fictitious emotion on the other. The former breaks out naturally, as in the case of grief, anger or indignation, but lacks art, and therefore requires to be formed by methodical training. The latter, on the other hand, does imply art, but lacks the sincerity of nature: consequently in such cases the main thing is to excite the appropriate feeling in oneself, *to form a mental picture of the facts, and to let oneself be moved by it as if it were true.*[87]

This shows us that the procedures recommended for an effective *actio* are identical to those necessary for those who practise the art of memory: the orator has to construct a sort of *tableau vivant* and then immerse himself in it and lose himself in the corresponding passions. It is no wonder, as we saw earlier, that Della Porta copies Quintilian's recommendations on *actio* in the part of his treatise on memory dedicated to the language of gestures.

The emotional immersion recommended by Quintilian greatly influences late-sixteenth-century theorists of preaching. An author whom we have already encountered, Bishop Arese, author of the massive *Arte di predicare bene*, and expert in the art of memory and sacred devices, cites the same passage from Quintilian before giving some practical examples to the preacher:

> For example, if one wants to feel compassion for the misery of Lazarus the beggar or some other wretched fellow, one ought to imagine seeing him seated on the ground, half-naked, with putrid blood running from his sores ... one should imagine hearing his lamenting voice and moans, imagine approaching him and touching the nudity of his limbs with one's hands ... or one should actually attempt to become the beggar and imagine the pain that one would feel if one were to suffer the pains and ailments that afflict the poor man. (*Arte di predicar bene ... con un trattato della memoria*, p. 584)

Thus, the techniques of *actio* and the techniques of memory converge and overlap in the creation of an actual theatre of passions: this passage from Arese describes well the progressive involvement of all the senses, even to the point of imagining total identification. Here, rhetorical techniques are mixed with techniques of meditation and silent prayer.

Of course, we are far from the spirit of uninhibited experimentation that characterizes Della Porta's research, but the procedures and techniques are the same. Indeed, Della Porta's treatise on memory enjoyed widespread popularity in the sixteenth and seventeenth centuries among theorists of an art of memory for use in preaching: besides Arese, we must also remember the work of Gesualdo. The strong theatrical component of Della Porta's treatise and its close connection to the techniques of *actio* undoubtedly play an important role in creating the great interest in his work.

As we have seen above, the representation of the *movements* of the mind is also essential to the images created by painters. Lomazzo dedicates the entire second book of his *Trattato dell'arte della pittura, scoltura et architettura* to this question. His ideas are very similar to those that we have seen in Quintilian and Arese concerning the need for emotional identification on the part of the creator of images. Lomazzo's starting point is a passage from Horace's *Ars poetica* (verses 99–104), which explains how poetry can enchant the mind of the audience:

It is not enough for poems to be fine; they must charm, and draw the mind of the listener at will. As the human face answers a smile with a smile, so does it wait upon tears; if you would have me weep, you must first of all feel grief yourself; then and not till then will your misfortunes, Telephus or Peleus, touch me. If the part assigned you is not in character, I shall fall asleep or laugh.[88]

Like Alberti before him, Lomazzo finds evidence in Horace that there is a natural urge towards imitation and emotional identification. He discovers, moreover, that this is true in both poetry and painting: 'using movements depicted from nature,' he writes, a painting 'will undoubtedly make one laugh with those who laugh, make one think with those who think, make one grieve with those who cry.' This urge towards imitation, moreover, has an almost magical dimension because it is connected to the theory of imagination that we discussed earlier (chapter 4, p. 139). Everyone knows, writes Lomazzo, that the mind 'and, similarly, the imagination alter and transform the body in different ways, with visible changes.'[89]

This is the first reason why the actor or orator (and any practitioner of the art of memory) is able to evoke passions that, on the one hand, imprint their form on the body as well as the mind and, on the other, can communicate that form to the audience by transmitting the same passion with the strength and directness of magical empathy (in fact, Lomazzo's *Trattato dell'arte della pittura, scoltura et architettura* owes a great deal to the *De occulta philosophia* [Three books of occult philosophy], a treatise on magic by Cornelius Agrippa).[90] In the chapter entitled 'Come il corpo ancora si muta per moto d'imitazione' [How the body can also be changed through imitated movements], Lomazzo constantly refers to the example of the actor: 'for this reason we see that one who recounts an amazing event to others is first of all moved himself by the nature of what is being recounted, and the listeners – some more than others – moved with him by those same emotions, will experience similar effects on their bodies' and burst into tears or laughter, for example. With its immediate effect on the viewer, painting can more effectively exploit the 'power and almost occult strength' that impels us to reflect the represented emotion. 'Therefore,' begins Lomazzo's last recommendation to the painter, 'those who master these things and who have *firmly imprinted them in their memory*, and who then use them in creating their figures, are guaranteed to produce not just praiseworthy but marvellous works.'[91] Because knowledge of the movements of the soul – an essential component in the creation of great works – requires an identification that is at once physical and emotional, memory thus becomes a depository of the movements, a network of correspondences between body and spirit, a sort of living archive.

There is one last aspect of this question with which I wish to conclude. Traditionally *actio*, or body language, is not a mere accessory added to the text. It is not just something that helps the text to be effective. In many ways it is a double of the text; like mnemonics, techniques of *actio* are not tools that supplement the text, but another way of creating the text, of presenting it. The passages from Cicero cited by Quintilian at the beginning of his chapter on *actio* are extremely important in this regard: 'for delivery is a kind of language of the body' [est enim actio quasi *sermo corporis*] (*De oratore* 3.222); and 'for delivery is a sort of bodily eloquence' [est enim actio *quasi corporis quaedam eloquentia*] (*Orator* 55).[92] We also note here a phenomenon to which we have already referred: the model of the text and that of the body overlap. Quintilian's observations on how to define the rhetorical figure are also most important. The comparison with the body comes precisely into play: the figure, in the true sense of the word, that is, the *schema*, means something that introduces a movement, a particular aspect of the form of the text. It is like a particular position assumed by the body (9.1.10–11). The figures, therefore, may be thought of as gestures of language [habitus quidem et quasi gestus] 9.1.13). It is a comparison that enjoys a certain popularity in sixteenth-century manuals of rhetoric. Francesco Robortello (see chapter 2, p. 23), for example, revives it and comments on it in his courses at the university.[93] But if the rhetorical figure marks the body of the text with a gesture, it is not without consequences on the level of emotive communication: we have seen, in fact, that gestures are carriers of feelings and passions. Quintilian introduces the section dedicated to the connection between figures and passions, between the rhetorical artifice to be used and the emotive content that one wanted to transmit, in the following manner: 'Further, there is no more effective method of exciting the emotions than an apt use of figures. For if the expression of brow, eyes and hands has great efficacy in stirring the mind, how much more effective must be the face of our discourse itself [orationis ipsius vultus] when disposed to produce the result at which we aim?'[94] Rhetorical figures are thus the gestures with which one can arrange the body of the text, the expressions with which one can animate the face of language.

As bearers of the passions, rhetorical figures can acquire within the space of the text an almost autonomous presence, magically endowed with life, just like the phantasmata inside the mind. A similar notion seems to have appeared in a Greek text on rhetoric that was widely read during the sixteenth century: the treatise On the Sublime, attributed to Longinus. According to a passage of this text – to which Jean Starobinski has called attention – the sublime is generated by those images (φαντασίαι) in which, 'as a result of enthusiasm and emotion, it appears that you are gazing at the things that you are describing and that you are setting them before the eyes of your listeners' (15.1).[95] This context is very similar to a passage in Quintilian's sixth book in which, once again, he discusses the ways of artificially provoking/arousing the passions. It is possible, he writes, to transform daydreams – hallucinations that may also be considered a sickness of the soul [animi vitium] – into something positive:

> There are certain experiences which the Greeks call φαντασίαι and the Romans visions, whereby things absent are presented to our imagination with such extreme vividness that they seem actually to be before our very eyes. It is the man who is really sensitive to such impressions who will have the greatest power over the emotions. Some writers describe the

possessor of this power of vivid imagination, whereby things, words and actions are presented in the most realistic manner, by the Greek word εὐφαντασίωτον, and it is a power which all may readily acquire if they will.[96]

One aspect of Camillo's theatre thus appears in a new light and acquires new importance: his promise to offer the user, not just all possible subjects, but all the rhetorical devices and passions that artifice can produce. Camillo distinguishes, in fact, between *materia ignuda* [naked matter] which, for example, is treated by the philosopher, and passionate matter that is found in the works of orators and poets, in other words, matter dressed with rhetorical figures and expressing the feelings that the figures are capable of arousing.[97] The theatre of memory, therefore, as a theatre of passions, helps to produce/remember the rhetorical artifice suited to a given situation. It shows how to engrave the gestures that express each passion on the face of language.[98]

CHAPTER FIVE

How to Translate Words into Images: Memory and Invention

1 The Memory of Images and Iconological Repertories

In the villa at Asolo, a splendid backdrop for a queen in exile, the different faces of love and the complex, and at times playful, nature of poetry are enacted in a ritualistic celebration: this is the subject of Pietro Bembo's *Gli Asolani*, as we have seen in chapter 3. In the second book of the dialogue Gismondo explains that the poets who describe themselves as prey to a rain of tears and overwhelmed by a wind of sighs – even though they are happily in love – do so 'in order to give various subjects to the ink of their pens, so that by varying their inventions with these colours, the picture of Love is all the more graceful in the eye of the beholder.'[1] The final metaphor, inspired by the rules of *ut pictura poesis*, is an example of a way of thinking that we have already encountered, that is, the tendency to perceive poetic images in visual terms and, vice versa, to translate visual images into words. Passages like this one should be placed beside those in which words and images directly correspond, in which they translate one into the other, that is, beside the iconological passages dedicated to the *figure* of Love (1.18), to the way in which it is represented, and by which it is given a body and, indeed, made visible.[2] In this manner another dimension of that playful component that we have seen in the classical canon comes to light: if writing means imitation (and variation), then both memory and interpretation are required. The creation of a new text (*inventio*, to use the terminology of traditional rhetoric) requires the mobilization of a heritage of memory that brings together both words and images. It is a hermeneutic game that makes words and images mutually translatable, and that makes it possible to enrich and vary the respective topical *repositories*.

We can form some idea of this procedure by examining the way in which the great figures of mythology are evoked and interpreted in the three books of *Gli Asolani*. In the first book, for example, Perottino, after an analytic description of the symptoms of lovesickness, says that:

the lover feeds his misery, with his pains overflowing. Such is Tityus whose liver is fed upon by vultures until his heart is renewed after a thousand bites of unbearable agony. Such is Ixion who spins on the wheel of his suffering, now at the top, now at the bottom, never released from his torment, and with every hour that he is bound and nailed there, his torture becomes greater as he is bound ever tighter and he spins more and more. My ladies, I could not match with words the torments used by this cruel master to afflict us unless I were to penetrate into the extremities of hell and *not keep from your eyes* the examples of the greatest miseries of the damned; for, as you can see, they are perhaps not as harsh.   (P. 256)

This passage is laden with literary memory: scholars have shown, in fact, that the presence of Boccaccio's *Fiammetta* is very strong here.[3] Bembo emphasizes the visual and exemplary dimensions of these images (by which they call to mind the magical force of those $\phi\alpha\nu\tau\alpha\sigma\acute{\iota}\alpha\iota$ discussed by Quintilian and the author of *On the Sublime*). Bembo produces these images in a game of diffraction. They reappear in the second book, interpreted from a different point of view. It is Perottino, says Gismondo, who is the cause of his ills: he has been following a path where he has run 'into those Tityuses, those Tantaluses, and those Ixions, among whom, almost as if gazing into clear water, he saw himself' (p. 283). Mythological images are part of cultural memory, and, consequently, they are part of everyone's internal landscape. According to the traditional rules of allegorical interpretation, they furnish the clothes of our passions, and they are thus transformed into meaningful images of the human condition. The risk, says Gismondo, is of projecting one's own image onto them and not recognizing their otherness, mirroring oneself in them ('almost as if gazing into clear water, he saw himself'). The myth of Narcissus thus becomes a model of deviant hermeneutics. While in the second book there are only allusions to Narcissus, in the third book the hermit – who teaches Lavinello the 'true' doctrine of love – explicitly cites the myth as an example of improperly directed love: 'What are you raving about, you fools? You, who are blind, concerned with your false beauties, like

Narcissus you feed upon vain desires, and you do not realize that they are just the shadows of the true beauty that you have abandoned' (pp. 336–337).

The same mythological figures are disposed differently in the *places* of the three books of *Gli Asolani*: the game of interpretation transforms them by turns into emblematic images of the different conceptions of love. Thus, allegory plays an important role in the creation of a circular relationship between memory and invention and in a mirroring relationship between words and images. Passages like the one we have cited here – generally overlooked in literary criticism – help us to understand how the image of a mythological character can become an image of memory (and, therefore, a topical place, capable of setting into motion and enriching the process of invention): the figure of the hero, visually represented or described in words, presents in a condensed form not only the narrative of his story but the different possible interpretations, the different texts that could be derived from it. In a culture like that of the sixteenth century, in which the tendency for syncretism is very strong, the practice of allegory is nourished by traditional biblical exegesis as well as by Neoplatonic and hermetic theories of 'hidden knowledge,' of the hidden wisdom that lies beneath the surface of mythology and poetry. There is thus a tendency to construct a unified heritage, a great gallery of images capable of condensing, and thus expressing, various meanings, and capable, moreover, of reactivating them in different forms, in memory and in the text. Take, for example, one of the last chapters of Castiglione's *Il Cortegiano*, where Bembo – this time a character in the dialogue – describes the fire that is ignited in the soul at the moment that it falls in love with divine beauty: 'This is the Pyre whereon the poets record that Hercules was burned atop Mount Oeta, and through such flames became divine and immortal after death. This the Burning Bush of Moses, the Cloven Tongues of Fire, the Fiery Chariot of Elias.'[4] This passage could easily be transformed into a monothematic series of emblems. At the same time, it shows us how an abstract idea (the love of divine beauty) can take different perceptible forms from iconological memory.

We have chosen examples from texts considered to be classics in order to show the depth and scope of this phenomenon. As we observed above (chapter 4, p. 172), there is a circular relationship between the sources and the readers in Giovan Battista Della Porta's work on physiognomy, in the sense that on the one hand he makes references to artistic and literary works, while on the other hand he lists artists and writers among those who could benefit from his work. There is an analogous circular relationship in Cesare Ripa's *Iconologia*. This work, says the author, is essential for 'orators, preachers, poets, designers of emblems and devices, sculptors, painters, draughtsmen, actors, architects, and creators of scenery to represent all that can befall human thought with the proper symbols.'[5] The *Iconologia* is thus intended for those who work with words, those who practise the figurative arts, and those who produce works in which words and images interact. But the heterogeneous nature of the readership of this work is nothing more than a reflection of the composite nature of its sources. Ripa claims, in fact, to have drawn from literary traditions as well as artistic ones, both ancient and modern.

The examples that we have taken from Bembo and Castiglione allow us to understand how the circularity of late-sixteenth-century repertories is only the endpoint – and a simplification – of the rich process that shapes cultural memory. Indeed, Bembo's friend Giulio Camillo wants to entrust the literary memory of classicism to a system of images, in large part mythological ones.

In the course of the century, therefore, the techniques of memory play an important role in the practices and experiences in which words are translated into images and images into words. Let us look at some examples of the different aspects of this procedure and the different forms that it assumes.

The art of memory constructs its images in internal mental space. They are connected by a dense network of relationships to images created both by words, evoked from writers and poets, and by perceptible images, especially those produced by the figurative arts. This mixture seems to be suggested already by the Greek myth that recounts the origin of the art of memory. Its founder was supposedly Simonides of Ceos, a pre-Socratic poet who was the first to note the deep analogy between painting and poetry; according to Plutarch, in fact, Simonides was the first to maintain that painting is silent poetry and poetry spoken painting (*De gloria Atheniensium* 2.346f–347c).[6]

The coupling of these discoveries attributed to Simonides seems to be upheld by what little evidence has survived concerning the practice of the art of memory in ancient Greece. The pre-Socratic fragment of Δισσοὶ λόγοι reveals two types of mnemonics.[7] One is based on a word game, on the dismantling of the word itself and the visualization of its parts (a procedure similar to what we have seen in relation to the sonnet/rebus in chapter 3, p. 91): to remember *Chrysippus*, for example, you can think of a gilded horse, obtained by dismantling the word into χρυσός 'chrysos' [gold] and ἵππος 'hippos' [horse]. Another technique is based on metonym: to remember an abstract concept (a vice, a virtue, or a profession) you go back to the god or hero to whom the concept is related. Ares and Achilles, for example, bring to mind courage; Hephaestus, the art of the blacksmith; while Epeius, builder of the Trojan horse, reminds you of cowardice.

Alongside the possibility of taking images from words, the ancient art of memory utilizes the gods and the heroes. Their images are everywhere, thanks to the representations made by painters and sculptors, and it is probable that they feed and support the images of memory.

In ancient Greece the art of memory is practised above all by orators. Beyond the variety of cases and arguments, there are some constants, recurring images and patterns of thought (topics understood as a full grid, to use Roland Barthes's definition).[8] Over time the result is the formation of a *thesaurus*, a treasure-house of things that can be said, which is ultimately transformed into a *thesaurus* of things to be remembered. It is, so to speak, a dictionary of images of memory, an inventory or an archive, always ready for use. It is modelled – the fragment of Διssoὶ λόγοι would seem to indicate – on the iconology of the gods and the heroes. We are dealing with a great gallery, an extraordinary museum, carefully organized in the space of the mind.

There is evidence in Latin texts of such an inventory and its diffusion in the cultural world of the ancient Greeks. According to the *Rhetorica ad Herennium* (3.23), the Greeks used a repertory of images for *memoria verborum* [memory of words] (the most difficult part of the art). This solution, however, is criticized by the author of the *Rhetorica ad Herennium* in the name of the irreducible variety of words and the necessity of bearing in mind the individual reactions of the audience. It is better, he claims, to teach a method for composing images rather than to furnish a sampling that may not function for all users. Analogous criticism can be found in Quintilian (9.2.26): the memorization of a fixed repertory of images, he notes, requires twice the effort. It is like someone who uses a ciphered language: in the end he doubles the amount of time and effort required for both writing and reading.

As the art of memory passes from the world of the ancient Greeks to the Latin world, an antagonistic relationship begins to take shape between two components of the art, an antagonism that is destined to be of long duration: on the one hand, the need to respond to the spontaneity of individual reactions – certainly effective but unpredictable and hard to control; and, on the other, the necessity to establish, in correspondence with rhetoric, a standardized repertory of images capable of being adapted to particular situations. Throughout the centuries the treatises on memory develop an actual iconological inventory in response to this latter need. In so doing, it is commonly held, they make the practitioner of the art of memory very similar to other creators of images, that is, painters and poets. For example, in his fifteenth-century treatise Giovanni Fontana writes:

> there is no art or science that is more similar to painting than artificial memory. Both need places and images, and one follows the other, and for this reason it is helpful to use examples taken from painting. Indeed, we are painting when we construct images to be positioned in the places.[9]

Iacobo Publicio also stresses the effectiveness of taking images of memory from the allegorical descriptions of the poets. The good images, he writes, are hidden in the texts [signa latitant], and they need to be extracted in order to be used again (*Oratoriae artis epitoma* [Epitome of the art of oratory] (Venice: Erhardus Ratdolt 1495], folio 54r). Publicio, as we have mentioned, is a master of both rhetoric and memory. Here, we see again how techniques of literary imitation and mnemonics are very similar. Lodovico Dolce clearly and pragmatically observes that these techniques are of enormous help to painters and poets in the practice of the art of memory so that they are already well disposed to this art: 'Every good poet and painter will use the office of this art with greater ease for the readiness that he will have in forming such images for memory' (*Dialogo nel quale si ragiona del modo di accrescer et conservar la memoria* [Dialogue in which ways of enlarging and conserving memory are discussed] [Venice: Eredi di Marchiò Sessa 1575], folio 86v).

If we put together the parts that the treatises on memory dedicate to the construction of images, we can see that various pictorial typologies begin to emerge during the sixteenth and seventeenth centuries. They belong to a rich iconological inventory that is, at times, encyclopedic in ambition. In these typologies we can see how the art of memory recycles the artistic and literary heritage, and how it is situated on the border between two camps of experience: it has built a channel through which words and images are translated (flowing back and forth) one into the other. It would be stimulating to make a comparative analysis of the images recommended by the treatises on memory and those realized in literature and the visual arts: the result would be an interesting picture of correpondences and, perhaps, of significant divergence. But let us now examine some of the principal iconological typologies that took shape in the tradition of mnemonics.

We can begin with sacred iconography, a traditional meeting place for painting, writing, memory, and devotional and mystical practices. In a Venetian manuscript of the late fifteenth century, *De nova ac spirituali quadam artificialis arte memorie* [A new and spiritual art of artificial memory], there is a description of a system of memory based on seven altars, each of which is decorated by numerous sacred images. According to this text, they need to be constructed very carefully, with great care given to the variety of clothes, attitudes, and attributes: 'therefore, those who wish to achieve such a wonderful effect in their work must very carefully establish in the eyes of their minds the variety and forms of the above-mentioned images by means of painting or imagination.'[10]

'By means of painting or imagination' [Aut per picturam aut per fantasiam]: these two roads are actually destined to meet and intersect. We see this clearly in another anonymous fifteenth-century treatise, *De memoria artificiali adipiscenda tractatus* [Treatise on the ways of obtaining artificial memory], in which techniques of memory are closely tied to the quest for inner, spiritual elevation. Here, sacred images are constructed using both official models of iconography and imaginative variations. The latter, nourished by literary memory – especially by Dante – decisively take the upper hand; they constitute a repertory of images with which one can memorize everything needed for penitence and prayer. A decrepit, naked old man, for example, represents inevitable death; a leper, naked as well, 'horribly consumed' [ac turpiter devoratum], and afflicted by Saint Anthony's fire, is meant to remind us of the different sufferings that life has in store for us. Of course, there are also biblical characters: 'Esau, all hairy like a savage' [Esau pilosus more hominis silvestris], Judas, 'a man with a crooked neck, naked, with his belly and innards in pieces' [hominem torto collo nudum, ventre ac visceribus scissum].[11] Thus, a gallery of naked, old, and tormented men is proposed for meditation and memory.

The images for remembering the saints are generally characterized by the attributes used to identify them in iconography. The treatises of memory pass on lists of the names of saints and their respective attributes that vary in length and that can be extended at will. An analogous technique is used to remember the different trades and professions:

each is represented with a characteristic tool of the trade or the typical attire of the profession. Countries, cities, and social classes are memorized in the same way. To construct these typologies of images the memory treatises evidently interact with the richly illustrated works dedicated to the customs of different peoples: for example, *Habiti di diversi paesi* [Customs of different countries] by Cesare Vecellio (Venice 1589), or *De omnibus artibus* [On every profession] by Hartmann Schopper (Frankfurt, 1574), or even the grotesque inventions of Arcimboldo of the professions, printed by Nicolas Larmessin at the end of the seventeenth century.

An analogous procedure is part of the construction of images used to remember ancient gods: from lists of characteristic attributes (which vary in length) to the recommendation given by the ever-pragmatic Dolce that one use the repertories of the mythographers (*Dialogo nel quale si ragiona del modo di accrescer et conservar la memoria*, folio 86v).

Rich iconological instructions regarding the different images for remembering various divisions of time – the seasons, the months, and the days of the week – are scattered throughout memory treatises in the fifteenth and sixteenth centuries. The anonymous *Ars memorativa* written in Bologna in 1425 gives exact and concise instructions: for August, fix grapes in your mind; for October, Saint Francis' girdle; and so on.[12] Publicio recommends that one remember the days of the week using the metals with which each day is associated, while the months can be memorized through the descriptions of their effects passed down by the poets (*Oratoriae artis epitoma*, folio 55r). Publicio cites only Latin poets, such as Virgil and Ovid, but vernacular texts also come to mind: first of all, the cycles of sonnets by Folgore da San Gimignano (died 1332), dedicated to the months and the days of the week. At the end of the sixteenth century Cosma Rosselli furnishes the practitioner of the art of memory with various illustrated mental calendars, including an analytical description of twelves scenes with a central character of varying age characterized by gestures and trades. These scenes have been reconstructed, he writes, by collecting fragments scattered in the ancient texts. The first two months of the year are depicted in the following manner:

> January was represented with a picture of a man seated at a splendid and plentiful table. He eats greedily and stretches out his hand towards a goblet filled to the rim, as if he wanted to drink. This is in the season when, according to Hippocrates, the stomach is very warm, it easily digests the

foods that have been swallowed, and it is eager to swallow others, with similar success. February was represented with the image of an old man who warms himself at a fire, and the reason for such a representation is that this month often conserves the remnants of the cold, of the wind and the bad weather belonging to January, and also that it consumes the old age of winter. (*Thesaurus artificiosae memoriae* [Thesaurus of artificial memory] [Venice: Antonio Padovano 1579], folio 116r)[13]

There are also recurrent lists of images useful for remembering the vices and virtues in the memory treatises. They are generally either female figures with the relative attributes or figures of animals. The traditional associations between animals and certain moral and psychological characteristics (for example, wolf/greed, rabbit/fear, fly/impudence) are thoroughly treated and therefore enjoy a renewed popularity in the *Hieroglyphica* [Hieroglyphics] by the Pseudo-Horapollo. In correspondence with the dissemination of the text and its related commentaries and translations, lists of so-called Egyptian hieroglyphics become rather frequent in the memory treatises. They can be used as *imagines agentes* of the vices and virtues or other abstract concepts (we have already discussed Della Porta's use of them in chapter 4, p. 168). The hieroglyphics lead to formation of a sort of moral alphabet based on animals.

The memory treatises also help to form a repertory of human *types*, a gallery of images that represent the different moral and psychological personalities, the different ages and conditions of man. The description of types is often accompanied by a lively attention to the language of gestures, to the expressive capacity of bodily posture, to the semantics of physical traits. We have already noted, in regard to Della Porta, how this aspect of the art memory is related to theatre. Filippo Gesualdo's treatise on memory, *Plutosofia* [Plutosophia] (Padua: Paolo Megietti 1592), provides further confirmation. He writes that he prefers stable and immobile places of memory, 'and therefore, although I admire and praise their invention, I would not follow the practice of those who take one hundred persons of different age, condition, status, and country, and position them in a feigned and imaginary theatre by places: then they attach the images to these persons' (folios 14v–15r). Gesualdo is an invaluable witness: in the time-honoured practice of the art of memory there has developed a rich typology of characters ('one hundred persons,' according to Gesualdo), so articulated and commonly used that it is able to furnish the system of places, the basis, that is, on which to construct the single images of memory. These 'one hundred persons,' therefore, when properly positioned, furnish a troupe of actors capable of improvising on any subject matter, of performing all possible plays, of representing all necessary scenes in the theatre of memory.

We have previously noted that, in the great repertories of the late sixteenth century – especially in Ripa's *Iconologia* – the classification of sources and the corresponding readership mirror each other. Now we can understand how, on the one hand, the *Iconologia* is the heir of a long practice of constructing repertories of images, a practice also related to the art of memory, and how, on the other, the *Iconologia* can be swallowed up by mnemonic practices, how it can become, in turn, a convenient reference point for the construction of *imagines agentes*.

2 The Places of Memory and Topical Places

The role played by the art of memory in mediating between words and images, in creating bridges and modes of translation from one to the other, not only affects the construction of an iconological repertory, but also pervades all the components of the art: the use of places, their ordered disposition, the fact that images are deposited in them.

In the sixteenth century the word *luogo* or *loco* [place] acquires multiple meanings of which we have already seen some examples: in the documents of the Accademia Veneziana *luogo* refers to the physical place – of the library, of the palazzo – and at the same time it is the place in the diagram, the *tree*, in which the single discipline, the single book, can be positioned according to the given rules of classification (chapter 1, p. 16). In the texts of Orazio Toscanella, Ludovico Castelvetro, and Francesco Panigarola *luogo* is the place in the text, on the printed page, that may correspond to the *luogo* of the repertory, of the apparatus, or it is the topical place, the source of *inventio* (chapter 2). The places of the text thus take on an ideal, material texture: they are spaces into which one can enter and become master of the treasure that they contain; they are places in a mechanism that is put into action. Multiple factors come together in the construction of this dense mass of meanings and notions that coagulate around the word *luogo*: the ancient tradition of topics, understood as both a collection of places ready to use and a method for producing argumentation; the modern re-elaboration of this tradition, from Rudolf Agricola to Giulio Camillo and Peter Ramus; and the new sensibility produced by the art of the printing press and the new possibilities that it offers. The places used by the art of memory also come into play and contribute to the growth of that network of superimpositions, of similarities between interior and external experience, between mental and material dimensions, between the invisible and visible, that, as we have seen, constitutes an age-old source of fascination.[14]

In the Greek tradition topical places and the places of memory have already been brought together and tend to overlap. Take, for example, a passage from Aristotle's *Topica*:

> You should also try and grasp the categories into which the other arguments most often fall. For as in geometry it is useful to have been trained in the elements, and in arithmetic to have a ready knowledge of the multiplication table up to ten times helps much to the recognition of other numbers which are the result of multiplication, so too in arguments it is important to be prompt about first principles and to know your premisses by heart. For just as to a trained memory the mere reference to the places in which they occur causes the things themselves to be remembered, so the above rules will make a man a better reasoner.[15]

This powerful association of the places of memory and topical places has by no means escaped the notice of commentators on Aristotle, and they have indeed taken a great step forward in identifying one with the other. This is an interpretation to which Della Porta, for example, is opposed. He underscores instead the physical, material, spatial sense of the Aristotelian places of memory: 'In his book on memory Aristotle says that the mind moves wilfully through the places and is excited by them. It is true that some commentators interpret places as topical places, but Themistius, an excellent Peripatetic, understands them as material places' (*Ars reminiscendi* [Art of remembering] [Naples: Giovan Battista Sottile 1602], p. 5).[16] Retracing the places in order to put the procedure of memory in motion thus means retracing a material path: it, in turn, is mirrored in the places of the text and in the order with which they follow each other in the *dispositio* [order], according to rhetorical terminology. For this reason, writes Della Porta, in the *Aeneid* Aeneas tells Dido of his adventures by remembering first the places in which they happened, in successive order (p. 4). According to Della Porta, this allows for the creation of a network, a series of mirroring relationships among material places, topical places (from which the *inventio* of the text is derived), and places of memory. The rhetorical need for an ordered *dispositio* perfectly coincides with the mnemonic need for the construction of an ordered route of places.

As we have already observed, topics may also become a repertory of textual fragments, of formal solutions ready to use. Even Bembo (see chapter 3, p. 86), has prepared a collection of places to facilitate memory and *inventio*. We have seen in chapter 2 how, through the course of the century, mnemonics is intertwined with the ever more widespread use of repertories, illustrative and encyclopedic collections, charts, indexes, and different types of apparatuses. The memory treatises confirm the fact that the enormous labour expended on the compendia and catalogues that pervaded Europe is related to the tradition of mnemonics, that it is perceived more precisely as part of the construction of the places of memory.

Camillo's theatre, indeed, feeds upon a detailed *anatomy* of exemplary Latin and vernacular texts to which he dedicates great effort. The places of the theatre are at once places of memory and topical places, capable of furnishing matter for content and formal solutions suitable to any need.

Alessandro Citolini (ca 1500–1583), a friend and student of Camillo – and accused, in fact, of having copied Camillo's theatre – is the author of *Tipocosmia* [Model of the cosmos]; published in 1561, this work is at once an encyclopedia, a system of memory, and a dictionary.[17] Its organization of knowledge is based on a system of topical places, arranged within a tree-shaped structure that is explained in a short work entitled *I luoghi* [The places] (in *Lettera in difesa della lingua volgare* [Letter in defense of the vernacular language] [Venice: Al Segno del Pozzo 1551; the first edition was published in 1541], folios 24r–31r). This structure is influenced by the new directions of dialectics and rhetoric; it is interesting to note that one of the interlocutors in the work is Domenico Venier, friend of Federico Badoer, the founder of the Accademia Veneziana. While Camillo fills the places of his theatre with the results of a meticulous dismantling of texts to which he has dedicated a good part of his life, Citolini offers a structure in which the user can reposition *his own* repertory of commonplaces, a grid to use in the organization of the fruits of his reading: 'I will leave everyone with the freedom to fill it with the possessions that he prefers' (folio 24v). The places of memory thus become the safest deposits of places taken from the texts. They offer the ideal card catalogue in which one may insert information that can be put to use in the moment of need.

Gesualdo compares the mental places used by the art of memory to the physical spaces of a bookshelf in a library. He recommends that, 'besides the full places, the builder should have empty places that he can use day by day. And in the same way that he takes thoughts and puts them on paper while studying books, he can use the places in which he can position his concepts' (*Plutosofia*, folio 58v). Once again the places of memory are associated with the places on paper where citations are transcribed. Together they are a depository, an ideal repertory of all reading, a library in epitome.

3 The Text as a Building

In the age of the printing press – more so than during the age of writing – the text is perceived as a set of places, as something that is positioned in space. The human faculties that generate the text (that is, the mind, memory) are perceived in an analogous fashion. It is easy to understand, therefore, how the term *luogo* acquires multiple meanings. The text is constructed (and read) in the space of the book in the same way that one constructs in the spaces of memory a set of places to which images are assigned, and in the same way an architect erects a building in physical space.[18] Indeed, the building is one of the classical models for systems of memory. Many treatises teach how to position the places in houses, palaces, convents, and churches.

While the architectural model (and consequently the comparison of the text and the building) is an ancient one, it assumes renewed importance in the age of the printing press. Let us consider some examples.

We can distinguish two models for this kind of thinking: the first encompasses the various forms in which the text is compared to a building, and the work of the writer to that of the architect; in the second the influence of topics is stronger, and the places of the text and its different parts are compared to the places and different components of a building.

In the *Prose della volgar lingua* [Discussions of the vernacular language] by Pietro Bembo (1525), one of the interlocutors mentions that Pietro has been reproached because he writes in Italian. His brother Carlo says to his detractors:

> he customarily responds briefly, and says that those men displease him just as much who, inversely, dedicate great care and study to the languages of others and, while they masterfully practise their ability in those languages, do not care if they do not know how to converse in their own; and he compares them to those who, in some far-off and lonely countryside, seek to build great costly palaces made of marble and shining gold while in their cities they live in the most wretched homes.[19]

Writing elegantly in the vernacular thus corresponds to the construction of a splendid home in one's own country, among one's fellow citizens.

An analogous architectural model, inspired by the splendours of contemporary sixteenth-century architecture, is also present even in *Gli inferni* [Hells] the second part of Anton Francesco Doni's *I mondi e gli inferni* [Worlds and hells] (1552–1553), but the tone and context are profoundly different. The character Momus regrets that he has remained among the academics (of the Accademia Pellegrina):

> Who would ever believe that these noble literary spirits have such bizarre whims? Their works are just like the construction of the beautiful façade of a temple where numberless figures in marble and bronze are to be placed. Celestial spheres, terrestrial worlds, histories of the living, of the dead – in short, a great number of statues, and while the architect is attending to the construction, the statues are already finished and they are shown to the whole world so that everyone can judge them in detail. Those who do not know the architect's plan rack their brains, and they speculate and ponder to what end each figure has been made, and they say to themselves: 'Where will this one go? for what reason are they shaped like that? I do not understand this order: I would like to know the purpose, the mind of the master,' and often they pass judgment and go as far from the order as one can go.[20]

With a tone somewhere between complacency and anxiety Doni often writes that the modes and rhythms of the printing press are overly hasty.[21] There is the risk that they will compromise the vision of the whole that is guaranteed by the book/edifice: just as the structure of the text is dismantled by the capricious flow of discourse, the statues meant to decorate the façade are put on display in a fragmented and random succession that upsets the order and makes judgment and interpretation random and uncertain.

An example that dates back to an earlier moment in time allows us to understand the easy transition from the first to the second model of architectural analogies. In 1512–1513 Giovan Francesco Pico della Mirandola and Pietro Bembo engage in a debate – destined to become famous – on the models to be followed when one writes in Latin.[22] Pico, on the side of writing that knows how to reflect the individual nature of its author, maintains that Virgil did not imitate the ancients, 'although here and there he did not so much steal as borrow something; and he used it as a sign, as a chiselled bit of antiquity *to decorate the buildings of his poems*; nonetheless, his poems are remarkable and absolutely the greater for the decorations that are their own.'[23]

The imitation of ancient literary models is thus implicitly associated with that reappropriation of ancient works that so strongly characterizes architectural practice. Ancient findings are inserted (quoted, so to speak) in the different parts of a building according to their type. In the same way, the different parts of the text require suitable rhetorical artifice. They require, that is, the selection and variation of the ancient textual fragment that is to be imitated.[24] The image of the text as an edifice thus develops very easily into a plurality of images in which the places of the text are compared to the places of the building, to its different components. For example, in his rhetorical treatise Francesco Sansovino writes:

> The preface of the oration is similar to the beautiful and rich entrance hall of a well-planned palace: as soon as it presents itself to the eyes of the beholders, they begin to discuss it and they pass judgment that the inside of the palace must be well decorated, composed with perfect architecture, with each part corresponding to the whole. In the same way, the entrance to the oration is the image and the demonstration of that which needs to be said and discussed.[25]

One enters a text, therefore, the way one enters a palace. The reception of the different parts of the text is represented in visual terms.

Now let us take an example from a dialogue on love that was published in 1544, *Il Raverta*, by Giuseppe Betussi (ca 1512–ca 1573). Dedicated to Vicino Orsini, the prince who built the garden of Bomarzo, this dialogue is set in the home of Baffa, a learned courtesan and friend of the author, who examines the definition of love given by Leone Ebreo in his *Dialoghi d'amore* [Dialogues on love]. There emerge, as is the custom of the times, various doubts and questions relating to love. Enough of this particular question, says the lady of the house with some urgency:

> nor should we do what many others do: when they go to see a beautiful palace, they enter a beautiful room and they stay there so long without going ahead that the other places become occupied, or something interrupts them, and the result is that, even though they have come to see much, they have become lost in a small space of happiness, and they leave

discontented and unsatisfied. And, therefore, before evening is upon us or
something else gets in the way, I want us to pass through all of this palace
without missing any of the quarters.[26]

Thus, the various doubts regarding love examined by this text are like
the rooms of a palace: they need to be visited in the suitable places of
the text in order for the result to be satisfactory. Only in this way, as
Bembo might have said in *Gli Asolani*, will the picture of love be 'all the
more graceful in the eye of the beholder.'

An example taken from a seventeenth-century text, *Arte di predicare
bene* [The art of preaching well] by Paolo Arese (see chapter 4, pp. 150,
174), gives us an idea of how one can unfold the game of architectural
associations. The reader, writes Arese, should not stop at the preface
(which is rather long). Of course, here he says something regarding the
nature of sacred rhetoric:

> but those who believe, from the little they have learned there, that they
> have perfect knowledge of it, are like those who arrive before a royal
> palace and stop at the door to gaze at its frontispiece; and, after having
> considered with not a little amazement the height of the roof, the breadth
> of the site, the refinement of the marble, the detail of the work, the
> proportion of its parts, and all of that which is seen to be beautiful and
> elegant in the first encounter, they believe that there is nothing else to see,
> nor do they attempt to penetrate further inside to see the rooms, the
> apartments, the porticos, the gardens, and other beautiful things that are
> enclosed in the bosom of the palace; and if they were to see these things in
> their beauty and wonder, they would erase from their minds that which
> they had first admired as beautiful in the frontispiece.
>
> Such would be the reader, I say, who contents himself with what he has
> learned in the preface and does not attempt to penetrate further into the
> knowledge of this art. For one can say that it is a royal palace, even that it
> is the most noble and superb palace ever built: a palace built by Wisdom
> on towering columns, so that it would be a worthy room in which a table
> could be prepared with the celestial and delicate victuals that are the word
> of God for souls redeemed with the blood of Christ; we have just shown
> the frontispiece of such a palace in the preface by discussing its height and
> dignity, the difficulty and detail of its works in general, and other such
> things.
>
> But we will introduce the reader to much more in its most secret rooms
> and we will show him not only all of the rooms and the chambers, one by

> one, but also the riches that they contain and the purpose of each thing that he will see, and, moreover, we will make a gift to him of everything for which he shows a liking.   (*Arte di predicare bene ... con un trattato della memoria* [The art of preaching well ... with a treatise on memory] [Milan: Giovan Battista Bidelli 1627], pp. 51–52)

Sacred rhetoric and the book that describes it are like a royal palace. The façade of the palace corresponds to the preface of the book, and the reader is invited to enter, to pass through the places, the internal rooms (the various parts of the work). Other notions and other images intersect with that of the royal palace: the image of the house of Wisdom, which, as Solomon said (Proverbs 9:1), is built on seven pillars (which here have become extremely high), and the image of a palace that hides extraordinary treasures, arranged in an orderly fashion in its most secret rooms.[27] This image of a palace that contains a splendid collection is superimposed on that of the mystical house of Solomon: in chapter 6 we will see other examples that are in some ways analogous. All these images refer back to a book, actually to the greatest book, the Bible, source of all treasures, inexhaustible archive in which one can find the answer to all of one's problems, even those regarding rhetoric. The image of the text/building thus refers back to the topos of *Deus artifex* – God, architect and writer of the world.[28]

The architectural model inspires a veritable fashion as can be seen in the titles of various works published between 1540 and 1560: *Tempio d'amore* [Temple of love] by Niccolò Franco (Venice: Marcolini 1536), a work that is actually a plagiarized version of a poem by Iacopo Campanile that had circulated in manuscript form;[29] *Tempio della Fama in lode d'alcune gentil donne venetiane* [Temple of Fame in praise of some Venetian gentlewomen] by Girolamo Parabosco (Venice: Comin da Trino 1548); *Del tempio alla divina signora Giovanna d'Aragona, fabricato da tutti i più gentili spiriti, et in tutte le lingue principali del mondo* [On the temple of the divine Lady Giovanna of Aragon, built by all the most noble spirits, in all the principal languages of the world], edited by Gerolamo Ruscelli (Venice: Plinio Pietrasanta 1555); Giuseppe Betussi's dialogue dedicated to *Le imagini del tempio della signora donna Giovanna d' Aragona* [The images of the temple of Lady Giovanna of Aragon] (Venice: Giovanni de' Rossi 1557) – and this is just a partial list.[30] Poems are united in the places of the book as if to construct a temple decorated with statues, paintings, exemplary and memorable images. The model of the temple oscillates between that of a church and that of a pagan temple, a structure where triumphs are celebrated, where spoils are hung, and where one can fulfil one's vows.

In Bembo's *Gli Asolani* the review of unhappy cases of love is compared to a collection of votive offerings: I have drawn only from 'the memory of the least part of my ills,' says Perottino to Lisa: 'if I had wanted to tell and paint the stories of a hundred thousand lovers that one can read – as is often done in churches where before the altar one sees the faith, not of one man, but of infinite men, depicted and told in a thousand little paintings – you would certainly be amazed.' This comparison – the projection of the pages of the text onto the wall of the church – is taken up again and reversed by Gismondo in the second book: 'in some famous temples one sees paintings of many ships, some with the mast limp and broken and the sails entangled, some pushed towards the rocks.' Although these bear witness to the misfortunes of an ill-fated journey, this does not mean that many others have not happily completed the voyage without leaving any remembrance behind.[31]

These comparisons reflect a widespread sensibility, as we can see in the *Dialogo de' giuochi* [Dialogue on games] by Girolamo Bargagli, in which he mentions, among others, the Game of the Pilgrimage: 'pretending to have made a votive offering at the temple of Venus, for delivery from some danger or for some avoided disgrace in love, one declares that which others going to fulfil a vow would carry painted on a little canvas; in most cases, it will result in nothing other than an *impresa* [device].'[32] If the text of *Gli Asolani* finds a mirror image of itself – or at least of the topos of ill-fated love – in a collection of votive offerings, in Bargagli words and images are brought closer together: on the walls of the temple of Venus it is mostly *devices* that will be hung, objects, that is, characterized by the co-presence and interplay of a linguistic fragment and an iconic fragment.

4 Doni's Theatre: An Illusionistic Game

The text and the building thus tend to correpond: the places and the images of the former are mirrored in the places and the images of the latter. It is in this intellectual climate, in the early 1560s, that Anton Francesco Doni's similar project to construct a temple, or a theatre of Fame, matures in all of its ambiguity.[33] As we shall see, the texts that describe the project contain a mixture of illusionistic play, a captivating quest for financial support, and a visionary component. Not only is the nature of the project ambiguous, but the identity of its promoter is uncertain and ever-changing: at times it is Doni himself, at others the Accademia Pellegrina; at others it is Doni as secretary of the Academy.[34]

In 1561 the image of the theatre of Fame appears – in a context close to that which interests us here – in an autograph manuscript of Doni's work entitled *Una nuova opinione circa all'imprese amorose e militari* [A new opinion regarding amorous and military devices] (Florence: Biblioteca Nazionale, N.A. 267). In the introduction Doni states that he has decided to construct a device for himself:

> I know that many busybodies will say that it is wrong for me to enter with my bag of tales into the theatre of Fame, which seems to have barred its door and posted outside the emblems of many great writers and learned men ... and also because Fame's trumpet has proclaimed everywhere that its first place has been occupied both admirably and rightfully. Should this trumpeter not want that I sit in her house on a barrel or a chair, I will sit on a stool or stand, and when I have finished my harangue, she can throw me out for I do not care to meddle in her affairs ... I will leave the epitaph attached to the wall of her building for a few weeks in spite of her because the privilege of freedom that I hold in my breast permits me, just as it does others, to speak, and why should I not use it? All the more so since I live freely and in a land of freedom.[35]   (Folio 6r–v)

As we have seen in the examples taken from Bembo and Bargagli, the literary work is something that can be visualized and hung on the wall of a temple. The fact that Doni's is a work dedicated to devices facilitates this transposition into iconic and spatial terms.

The following year, in 1562, the theatre of Fame began to take on material substance. It is transformed into a architectural project intended for an exceedingly important location: Arquà, Petrarch's home at the time of his death, one of the topical places of literary memory. In his *Cancelliere* [The chancellor] Doni makes Fame speak: she invites everyone to participate in the 'undertaking at Arquà,' to contribute to the project of the Accademia Pellegrina, and to

> erect a new temple outside the ... old church of Arquà in a front portico, something like a theatre, above the cemetery, with a high loggia and colonnade; under the latter we will place the tomb of Petrarch, a man of truly heavenly spirit, and around it we will place all the statues of illustrious Italian writers, with their epitaphs and Latin and vernacular verses

below them, cut in marble, as required, decorating the theatre with wonderful architecture, with all the body of the sacred temple adorned with
rare capitals, honourable cornices, fluted shells, with histories in bas-
reliefs, friezes, grotesques, and stucco-work.   (*Cancelliere* [Venice: Giolito
1589], p. 6; the first edition was published in 1562)

The project thus sanctions the cult of Petrarch (actually exploiting it for
the publicity) that Doni has often ferociously derided. There are also
other components of sixteenth-century tastes and culture that come
together here: for example, the theme of Mount Parnassus that enjoyed
great popularity in art and literature in the first half of the century (one
need think only of Raphael's fresco in the Vatican);[36] or the widespread
notion of a gallery of illustrious men with accompanying inscriptions
that has its most famous materialization in Paolo Giovio's Museum at
Como. The building, however, is thought of as a system of images so
complex that it becomes 'something like a theatre.' Various elements
suggest that Giulio Camillo's theatre of memory has strongly influenced Doni's theatre, and Camillo is a friend of Doni.[37] Doni's project,
in fact, is presented for the first time in the *Cancelliere* (an allusion to
Doni himself, as *cancelliere* of the Accademia Pellegrina), subtitled *Libro
della memoria dove si tratta per paragone della prudenza de gli antichi, con
sapienza de' moderni in tutte le attioni del mondo* [Book of memory in
which the prudence of the ancients is compared with modern wisdom
in all the deeds of the world]. The work presents an exmplary *topica*,
arranged in alphabetical order, a list of the 'sayings and gestures' of the
ancients and the moderns, mostly copied from Erasmus' *Adages*.[38] The
Cancelliere is thus a repertory that filters literary memory, classifies it,
reorganizes it, and makes it ready for *inventio*.

Doni visited Giovio's Museum, and he has written two descriptions
of it, one of which is a burlesque parody.[39] In these texts it is clear that
the celebrated gallery is part of a complex iconographic system. Giovio's
entire villa – with its lodgings, gardens, rooms decorated with paintings, inscriptions, and devices – is a great theatre of memory of which
the gallery of portraits is just one component. The fact that such an
interpretation comes naturally to Doni is evidenced by the burlesque
version of his description of it, contained in a letter originally adressed
to Domenichi and then to Tintoretto. 'I wanted to make a *marmoria
luogale* [local marmory] but there was such a commotion of letters that I
could not drink them with my brain' (*Lettere* [Letters] [Venice: Marcolini
1552], p. 79). *Marmoria luogale* – a collection of places made of marble –

is the invention of the same deformation of names that pervades the text (the name D'Avalos became *Diavolos* [Devils], for example, while Pontano is twisted into *Pottano*, an allusion to a rather vulgar slangword for the female genitals). *Marmoria luogale* is a play on *memoria locale* [local memory], one of the names of the art of memory.

In 1563 Doni writes to Alfonso II d'Este and Cosimo I de' Medici in the hope of receiving financial backing for his project.[40] He presents himself as president of the Accademia Pellegrina, in charge of the construction of a theatre in Arquà surrounding Petrarch's tomb, with the statues of twenty illustrious writers. If the princes are willing to finance the undertaking, their coats-of-arms will be sculpted next to the statues of the writers whom they have protected or who have brought fame to a city in their dominions. The Estensi arms are, of course, to be placed next to the statue of Ariosto, while those of the Medici family are to be sculpted next to the statues of Dante, Petrarch, and Boccaccio.

From writing to stones: the theatre of Fame seems about to take physical form. But, then, the following year, things become rather clouded and unclear. Doni publishes a work entitled *Pitture nelle quali si mostra di nuova inventione Amore, Fortuna, Tempo, Castità, Religione, Sdegno, Riforma, Morte, Sonno e Sogno, Uomo, Repubblica e Magnanimità* [Paintings showing new inventions of Love, Fortune, Time, Chastity, Religion, Disdain, Reform, Death, Sleep and Dreaming, Man, Republic, and Magnanimity] (Padua: Grazioso Percaccino 1564) that will be incorporated in successive editions of his *Zucca* [The pumpkin].[41] Dedicated to the Accademia degli Eterei of Ferrara (which counted Torquato Tasso among its members), this work is closely related to the theatre of Fame: its subtitle is, in fact, *Il Petrarca composto in Arquà* [Petrarch composed in Arquà]. Yet the beautiful palace decorated with images that fulfils the author's extraordinary and new *inventions* seems here to live in the unlimited space of the word rather than the three-dimensional space of marble and stone. It seems to be one of those visions (like the utopian city in the *Mondo savio/pazzo* [Sagacious/crazy world], for example) that Doni loves to represent in such a way that they play on truth and unlikelihood, and are open to the interplay of different interpretations: 'My paintings will be like airy grotesques because I am not such a fool not to know that depictions of wit and madness, representations of memory ... are nothing but castles in the sky. But I do so in order to be admitted myself among madmen' (folio 6r).[42] While the proclamation of the *Cancelliere* and the letters of the previous year ask for money and specify a location and architectural project, here the temporal coordinates immediately create a sense of estrangement. 'When my house (actually, my palace) was built, in the same period in which the great Ficino had laid the foundation of his museum,' writes Doni, 'I got the crazy idea of having the inside entirely painted. I had been prompted by his saying that he wanted to do the same in his palazzo, both because the images could decorate it with little expense and in order to show new inventions' (*Pitture*, folio 6r) – Ficino died in 1499, and Doni was born in 1513. But it is not just the time frame that makes the image shimmer and dismantle itself and reassemble as if seen through a kaleidoscope: here a new term, *museum*, is associated with *temple* and *theatre*. Every allusion to the statues of illustrious men has disappeared, both from the introduction from which we have taken this passage and from the text that follows. The reference to Arquà and Petrarch's tomb appears, instead, not only in the subtitle, but in the letters dedicated to the single *inventions*:

> I am certain that those who presently see my theatre are few with respect to the infinite number who will see it in the future; for I am even more certain that the written version, by means of the printing press, will endure many centuries. For this reason I intend to make a short copy with my pen so that someone will find it, if not useful, then at least amusing: amusing by virtue of the new invention and perhaps useful, considering the things in themselves, for their meanings and life, as well as for human behaviour and actions. Those who will come after us (even if the house is ruined) will see it still standing inside their minds because writing has the ability quickly to build every great edifice and instantly to paint all that one says about it and designs for it.   (Folio 6r–v)

At the heart of this passage is the play between the visible image – fulfilled by the painter and architect – and the image described with the pen – the image entrusted to the greater safe-keeping of the printing press. A traditional component of the comparison between painting and poetry is the greater endurance of the written word with respect to the work of art. Here this topos is influenced by the theme – very important in Doni – of the new possibilities offered by the printing press. At the same time, he pretends to describe a building that actually exists (or that is, at least, under construction) and the paintings with which it is decorated, but this fiction is at once concealed and revealed, acknowledged and justified, by the final observation: it is in the mind (and therefore in memory) that images find their most stable manifestation, free from the ruinous effect of time. As far as these internal images are concerned, the act of writing is more direct than that of painting and architecture: *ecphrasis*, the description of the image, has an immediacy of realization that artists will never know.[43] This brings to mind the *Orlando furioso* (a text very dear to Doni, and also a strong influence in his *Pitture*) and its palaces magically created in one night (and described/realized in just a few stanzas), with its paintings, with its characters evoked, as if in a theatre or a gallery of statues, 'to paint the future.'[44]

Published by Doni in 1564, the *Pitture* is thus a book that describes (and is constructed like) a building. The palace is positioned atop a great mountain. One arrives there by climbing a staircase of forty-two steps associated with the vices and virtues. Halfway to the top there is a circular *loggetta* where the images of the rewards of each virtue are painted. The *inventions*, that is, the way of making visible various abstract concepts, thus create images that are positioned within a well-defined system of *places*. It was not always this way. The first version of the *Pitture*, contained in an autograph manuscript of 1560 entitled *Le nuove pitture* (figure 45), presents the same *inventions* (only Chastity and Magnanimity are missing), but the order of succession is different, and, above all, the grid of *places* is missing; the images follow each other in random order and their number is destined to grow indeterminately (according to a formula typical of Doni). The manuscript of the *Pitture* alco includes a letter addressed to the Venetian painter Battista Franco, in which Doni asks him to prepare drawings for many of his works. One of these is

a book of more than a hundred inventions of paintings, divided into various sections which are something like Time, Fortune, Disdain, Religion, Death, Reform, Love, and others never before made or seen. A stairway of the virtues, where there is no step that is not based on Plato, Seneca, Plutarch, and other stupendous, wise, and prudent men.[45]

The inventions that he sends are just the first in a long series (they were eventually to number more than a hundred). The only organizational element is the stairway of virtues, an iconography from medieval memory but rewritten with classical material.[46]

The printed version of the *Pitture* positions the images within an architectural structure. The theme of mnemonics and classification in the stairway of virtues is translated into an actual stairway (or, at least,

45 Frontispiece in Anton Francesco Doni, *Le nuove pitture*. Città del Vaticano, Biblioteca Apostolica Vaticana, codice Patetta 364

it is delineated as such in words) of forty-two steps associated with the vices and virtues. At the moment in which the printed version transforms the disorderly series of *inventions* into an ordered system of places in a building, it takes from them one of their dimensions: their iconic, visual dimension. The printed text does not include illustrations, while the autograph manuscript is a refined product in which Doni shows his abilities as calligrapher and artist. However, as we have seen in the letter to Battista Franco, he is planning to entrust the fulfilment of his *inventions* to a painter.

In 1561, however, Franco died. Various clues lead us to believe that his place is taken by Federico Zuccari. Thanks to this painter, in fact, at least some of Doni's *inventions* would become visible; they take shape and place in real buildings. In 1564 (the same year as the publication of the *Pitture*), Zuccari made a drawing in red ochre (now at Windsor

Castle, identified by Heikamp) in which a listener (perhaps Zuccari himself) is standing near a figure who is playing a harpsichord.[47] According to Zuccari's autograph annotation on a copy conserved in the Louvre, the musician is Doni: 'Anton Francesco Donni in Arquà. 1564.' On the other side of the folio there is a sketch for the painting of the Cappella Grimani in San Francesco della Vigna in Venice on which Zuccari has been working since 1563.

In the letter with which Doni dedicates the painting of Time to Archbishop Altoviti, he thanks the archbishop for his visit to Arquà and promises to return the favour by sending him a

> copy of the painting of Time that was to be placed at the top of the room. It was coloured by the hand of a young man of great talent and profound valour, matched by few: master Federigo [Zuccari] da Urbino, the next Raphael. He is painting the chapel of the most reverend Monsignor Grimani. This painting is one of the most beautiful things that can be seen. (*Le nuove pitture* [New paintings], folio 22r)

Doni and Zuccaro thus met in Venice in the early 1560s, and it is here that we find Zuccari celebrated by characters whom we have previously encountered. In 1564 a collection of poems was published by Dionigi Atanagi, a member of the Accademia degli Sdegnati in Rome (see chapter 3, p. 87). One of these poems is a sonnet written in praise of Zuccari by Giovan Mario Verdizzotti (chapter 2, p. 32), a sonnet that Atanagi comments on in words very similar to Doni's: the worth of the twenty-four-year-old Zuccari, he writes, is so great 'that he could deservedly be called the next Raphael of Urbino' (*De le rime di diversi nobili poeti toscani* [Poems by various noble Tuscan poets] [Venice: Lodovico Avanzo 1565], folio 164r and illustration).[48]

Just a few years later Zuccari would paint (or oversee the painting of) the image of Time according to Doni's invention in the splendid villa that Cardinal D'Este was having built in Tivoli. Alongside this painting we also find other *pictures* by Doni: Nobility, Glory, Fortune, Magnanimity, and Religion.[49] Later, in 1577, Zuccari revives Doni's iconography of Time in one of the rooms of his home in Florence; the fact that it is used in the decoration of a private space is a sign of its enduring appeal.[50]

The temple of Fame that is to be erected in Arquà and that lives in the literary space of the *Pitture* is partially achieved at the Villa D'Este at Tivoli. As we will see later, this villa is built, in its turn, as a text, as a great visualized oration in praise of the cardinal, and in its planning there is no lack of notions related to the art of memory.

We have analysed the way in which Doni reappropriates the images created in the manuscript of the *Pitture* for the printed version; the story of their subsequent iconographic fortune is significant. On the one hand, it is the closing of a circle, in the sense that the individual images are autonomously revived outside the architectural framework, just as they had originally been conceived; on the other hand, their placement in various real palaces, in different iconographic contexts, is confirmation that they are allegorical images open to the play of interpretation and also *imagines agentes* of the art of memory. They can thus be recycled in multiple systems of places. They will indeed reappear on the scene in still other contexts.

5 Poems and Galleries: The Metaphors Used by Galileo the Literary Critic

In the same year that Doni died, 1574, there is a new episode of what we have called an illusionistic game. Some of the images described in the *Pitture* (Love, Fortune, Disdain, Death, Sleep and Dreams) appear in another text: Orazio Toscanella's commentary on Ariosto's *Orlando furioso*.[51] Here Doni is not cited. The passages on images, writes Toscanella, come from an unknown manuscript of Camillo's theatre which Luigi Alamanni had taken from the library of Cardinal Giovanni di Lorena. Toscanella leaves us with a true mystery: who has copied whom? Doni, of course, has a record of plagiarism, and in style the passages in question are closer to his work than to Camillo's. Toscanella, at any rate, seems to have been incapable of contriving a forgery. Thus a third character enters the scene, unidentified, at least for the moment.[52]

Resolving this mystery is not as important as seeing in which *places* the images reappear. We need to try to reconstruct the mode of their further dissemination. They are inserted in a text that, following a widespread fashion, gives an allegorical reading of *Orlando furioso*.[53] Allegory has above all a moral bearing. In accordance with an image dear to the Middle Ages, the poem becomes a universal mirror. The action and characters of the poem flow past us in a sort of allegorical theatre, only to be suddenly frozen in a scene pregnant with moral teachings: they are thereby transformed into allegorical images. This type of interpretation is closely related to the theme of sight. In the introduction Toscanella writes of Ariosto's extraordinary evocative power: 'In his poems *one does not read but sees* the fire that burned the city, the blood of the dead, the blades of the weapons, the wings of the wind and the horses.' For Toscanella, *Orlando furioso* – the work of 'our most erudite Ariosto' – is thus 'a mirror in which we see the actions of men worthy of praise and reproach' (p. 4).

Beyond the moral teachings that it provides, this type of interpretation tends to transform the poems into a series of topical places, to divide it into textual fragments observed through a lens that makes them into models for the writing of other texts. Take, for example, the commentary on canto 15, stanza 101:

> All of this stanza was written by our poet to describe the disloyalty and evil nature of a woman described in the person of Origille: when we need to reproach a woman of this sort, this stanza will be highly useful for the effect. It is, moreover, a mirror in which men can see the kind of woman from whom they should flee, however beautiful she may be.   (P. 131)

This gloss closely ties moral allegory to the construction of a topical image that can be imitated and utilized in the moment of need ('when we need to reproach a woman of this sort ...'). The stanza is thus transformed into a mirror both for morality and for writing (or painting). Through allegorical interpretation, in other words, the text is transformed into a series of images of the art of memory. This dimension becomes visible, for example, in Toscanella's analysis of the verse that describes Melissa (3.8.6–7): 'ungirdled, barefoot, and with loosened hair.' Toscanella observes:

> An ungirdled barefoot woman signifies deliberation, or rather firm and unexpected purpose, and it signifies furor which in turn signifies deliberation ... See the images placed by Giulio Camillo under the Gorgons of Mars in his *Idea del theatro* [Idea of the theatre], where he affirms that Virgil used such a figure, in Dido's prompt and firm deliberation to die; Virgil wrote that she had

> one foot free from all fastenings and her dress ungirdled.

> The fact that it further signifies furor is clearly shown by the thing itself. And in the sixth book, we read that having unbound hair is a sign of rage; when the Sibyl's furor begins to mount, she is described by him in the following manner:

her face was transfigured, her colour changed, her hair fell in disorder about her head.[54]

In this passage we can clearly see the connection between mnemonics and the *theatre of passions* that we discussed in chapter 4: the image in Camillo's theatre of memory gives unified form to something that has previously been deposited in the literary tradition, where it takes on the masks of different characters and the forms of different expressions. The intersection of references in Toscanella's commentary helps us to see how the line from the *Orlando furioso* could be translated into an image of memory. The representation of Melissa condenses in itself *memoria verborum*, that is, the memory of words (the network of intertextual relationships, especially the verses from books 4 and 6 of the *Aeneid*), and *memoria rerum*, that is, the memory of things, the force and the immediacy of a decision inspired by furor. Thus, allegorical interpretation – as practised by Toscanella – stitches back together the ties between memory and invention. It establishes a correspondence between Camillo's theatre of memory and Ariosto's poem, which is, in turn, transformed into a gallery of topical images.

The images of Love, Fortune, and so on, that Toscanella attributes to Camillo (some of which correspond, as we have observed, to images in Doni's *Pitture*) are inserted in the commentary on *Orlando furioso* by an analogous procedure that aims, however, at a more universal dimension. Here Toscanella isolates a single word (love, fortune, death, etc.) and translates it, so to speak, into images that represent it, into inventions that make it visible. The play between images and different kinds of places is particularly stormy: from Ariosto's text he passes on to mental images (images of memory that come from Camillo's text), then to real images, painted or sculpted: 'I once saw a painting in the Wardrobe of the king,' writes Camillo (according to Toscanella), on the depiction of Love in painting, 'by the hand of Rosso [Fiorentino], where there was a tree with a certain type of large and extravagant leaf' (p. 24). Introducing the painting of Fortune, Toscanella writes that 'Giulio Camillo claims to have seen in the hands of King Francis a figure of Fortune diligently sculpted in the following manner: a woman without eyes on the top of a tree who knocked down its fruit using a pole' (p. 89). Of great interest is the nature of the place that contains these works of art that in a certain sense interpret and illustrate Ariosto's poem: the Wardrobe [*Guardaroba*] of King Francis I, or, in other words, the collection of the French king who has protected and financed Camillo.

Here, we do not have entirely dependable information and reliable documentation: in Doni's writings the tie between his *pitture* and pre-existing works of art is already the object of a precipitous game of variations and combinations that makes his testimonies of these works all the more dubious.[55] But, in any case, Toscanella has created a highly interesting association. Ariosto's poem has been dismantled and divided into a series of places in which exemplary and memorable images are positioned. It can thus be mirrored in the Wardrobe of the king of France, the place where the king conserves his art collection. The splendid rooms of Fontainebleau may thus be barely glimpsed (like a watermark) through the page of Ariosto as commented on by Toscanella.

The mode of reception of the literary text that we have attempted to reconstruct here (the text as building and/or building decorated with statues and paintings, the poem as collection, as gallery) is so strong and widespread that it is present even in an author who is not interested in the art of memory: Galileo Galilei. It is well known that Galileo's *Considerazioni al Tasso* [Commentary on Tasso], probably written in his youth, between 1589 and 1592, is a passionate indictment of Tasso's *Gerusalemme liberata* and a celebration of Ariosto's *Orlando furioso*, the poem Galileo loved so much that he memorized it almost in its entirety.[56] In Galileo's pages of criticism the canon of *ut pictura poesis* plays a leading role, even lending itself to highly personal and fascinating variations. In the following passage Galileo compares an allegory that seems to him ineffectual and awkward to an anamorphic image:

> But, Signor Tasso, I would like you to know that stories and poetic narrative must serve the allegorical meaning in such a way that they show no sign of being strained: otherwise they will be given over to the awkward, to the forced and disproportionate, and the result will be one of those paintings, that, when viewed from the side from a predetermined position, show a human figure; but they are painted with such a rule of perspective that when viewed from the front – in the way other paintings are naturally and commonly observed – they represent nothing other than a confused and disorderly mixture of lines and colours from which one could barely make out images of winding rivers or trails, empty beaches, clouds, and chimeras.

In the same way that anamorphosis made little sense when seen from in front, in poetic narrative it is even more reprehensible that – in order to accommodate an allegory that can only be seen obliquely and covertly understood – the unfolding story which appears directly and openly to the reader should be extravagantly encumbered by chimeras and fantastic, superfluous fabrications. (*Considerazioni al Tasso*, in *Opere* [Florence: Barbera 1899], IX, 130)

This type of criticism is a splendid illustration of the procedures that we have looked at above: the literary text is something that is viewed, that offers itself to the eye, that is constructed according to certain rules of perspective. Allegory is carefully inserted in this play of glances directed at the text. It suggests other planes; it creates new spatial depth, and, consequently, new dimensions of the imagery. The example of anamorphosis is thus used by Galileo with regard to the various points of view that a text creates for itself. One might see in it a suggestive confirmation of the parallel drawn by Stephen Greenblatt between the structure of More's *Utopia* and Holbein's painting *The Ambassadors*: the painting introduces into a splendid scene, constructed and moderated by the human arts, an unsettling anamorphic image of a skull (plate VI).[57]

But not only the single images inside Tasso's poem are read by Galileo in terms of their visualization. The entire poem is projected into space, and, in different forms, it is compared to a building. In his disgust with stanza 14 of canto 2 of the *Liberata*, for example, Galileo makes an analogy between the places of the text and the places of a house, empty places of little value in this case, perhaps the places of a storeroom: 'this insipid, wretched, and usually pedantic rubbish is useful only to fill empty corners' (p. 75). The topical comparison between poetry and food inspires yet another architectural image. The excessive use in 2.60.8 of the adjective *grande* [great], writes Galileo, is 'pedantic and bombastic: I can only see that the hand is reaching for the box of "grande" to season, as we will progressively see, many, many soups of great heads ... great bulls ... great bodies' (p. 79). Tasso's masterpiece is thus projected into a place that is not really appropriate for an epic poem, that is, the kitchen. The topical places from which Tasso takes his stylistic ingredients (for example, the connotation of *grande* suggests an elevated register) are compared to jars containing seasonings for various foods.

Another architectural comparison, again in a negative light, is inspired by 14.30:

> This book is a workshop made of different scraps gathered from a
> thousand ruins of other buildings, among which one can sometimes find
> a good piece of a cornice, a capital, or some other fragment. If these
> pieces were situated in their places, they would create a fine effect, but
> placed here, out of order and disproportionately, they break the order
> of architecture and, in short, they make the building irregular and
> disorderly.   (P. 128)

We see a similar notion in the passage from Pico della Mirandola (p. 192
above), where literary imitation is compared to the reappropriation of
components from ancient buildings. While barely broached in Pico, this
theme is lavishly developed in Galileo.

A passage from the *Considerazioni al Tasso* in which the parallel
between poem and building is developed with greater complexity is
also the most famous and most often cited portion of the text:

> It has always seemed to me that this poet is infinitely stingy, poor, and
> wretched in his inventions, and the opposite of Ariosto, who is magnifi-
> cent, rich, and wonderful; and when I consider the knights, with their
> actions and deeds, together with all the other tales in this poem, it appears
> to me as if I enter into the little study [*studietto*] of some curious little man
> [*ometto*] who has entertained himself by decorating it with things that
> have, either for their antiquity or for their rarity, something uncommon
> about them, and yet they are in effect trifles [*coselline*]: things such as a
> petrified crab, a dried chameleon, a fly or a spider in gelatin in a piece of
> amber, some of those clay puppets that they say are found in the ancient
> tombs of Egypt, and then, in the form of painting, some sketches by Baccio
> Bandinelli or Parmigianino, and other similar little things. But just the
> opposite happens when I enter the *Furioso*: I see a wardrobe open, a
> tribune, a royal gallery adorned by a hundred ancient statues by the most
> famous sculptors, with infinite complete stories, and the best, by illustri-
> ous poets, with a vast number of vases, of crystals, agates, lapis lazuli, and
> other jewels, and in sum filled with rare, precious, and wonderful things,
> all excellent.   (P. 69)

Two places, and two different forms of late-sixteenth-century collecting, are compared in order to visualize the contrast between the *Orlando
furioso* and the *Gerusalemme liberata*: on the one hand, a splendid gallery,
orderly and brilliant, where the excellence of the works of art is matched
by the precious quality and rarity of the objects; on the other hand, a

Wunderkammer, disorderly and pretentious, dark, closed onto itself, its pettiness mercilessly marked by the list of objects and by the use of diminutives (*studietto, ometto, coselline*). In the latter, the weakness of intellectual motivation (amateurism, curiosity) is accompanied by poor taste and a distorted perception of the value of things.[58] While we can see the gallery of Fontainebleau behind Toscanella's commentary on Ariosto, this passage from Galileo projects the *Orlando furioso* into the rooms and hallways of the Uffizi gallery.

Great attention has been given to this passage for its richness of notions and ideas. We need, however, to emphasize one particular aspect: from the moment in which Galileo begins to express his point of view in such a visual way, so charged with his humours and literary and artistic tastes, he borrows metaphors from a well-defined and consolidated tradition. The text is something that is situated in a spatial dimension ('when I enter the *Furioso*'). Its places and its images are reflected in the places and images of the mind and in material places and images constructed by architects, decorated by painters and sculptors. Galileo, in other words, works at using topical models. He constructs a splendid and highly personalized variation of the theme.

There is further confirmation of this reading. As Paola Barocchi has noted, architectural metaphors also come into play in another moment in the *querelle* [debate] regarding the *Orlando furioso* and the *Gerusalemme liberata*: in the dialogue by Camillo Pellegrino, *Il Carrafa overo dell'epica poesia* [Carrafa, or on epic poetry] (Florence 1584), defender of Tasso; in the response written in the name of the Accademia della Crusca by Lionardo Salviati, *Difesa dell'Orlando furioso contra Camillo Pellegrino* [Defence of the *Orlando furioso* against Camillo Pellegrino] (Florence 1584); and in the *Replica* [Response] that Pellegrino published in the following year.[59] For Pellegrino, Ariosto has chosen 'beauty and delight' over utility. The *favola* [story] of the poem, he claims, lacks unity. It is a chaotic accumulation of episodes and digressions. For this reason the *Orlando furioso* is like a very rich and splendid palace, but its richness and splendour are all superficial, able to please only the *semplici* [the simple], that is, those who judge things by their appearance, guided by 'imperfect sight,' by the eye of the body, who are unable to grasp the impropriety of the poem's model, the shortcomings of its structure. The *Gerusalemme liberata*, however, with its 'well-formed' story, is like an 'edifice, not so great in size, but well planned, with architectural measure and proportion.'[60] It satisfies, therefore, 'the masters and professors of that art,' who are 'experts of perspective,' who use 'the eye of the mind,' and who judge things as they really are and not how they appear. The response of the Accademia della Crusca appropriates all the architectural metaphors, all the visual implications contained in Pellegrino's text, and turns them upside down. Here we can clearly see how the tendency to project the poem, with its different components, onto an architectural space is part of a common mental habit, above and beyond the different options of literary taste.

A final example brings us to a typology of images very close to that of Galileo, as Massimiliano Rossi has shown. In the brief discourse *Dell'unità della favola* [On the unity of story], given in 1599 in Florence, at the Accademia degli Alterati, Giovanbattista Strozzi (1551–1634) maintains that the multiplicity of actions of the *Orlando furioso* can be 'reduced to true unity.'[61] The poem thus achieves the universal model of perfection, the model in which plurality returns to the one, in which the diversity of the components make for an elaboration, an expansion, of the unitary principle. To those who point out that variety is entertaining, Strozzi responds by saying:

> the mind is pleased by [unity]; when the mind sees different and dissimilar things, it always seeks to find the similarity between them, and, if you will, it seeks to shape them with a form that it produces; in the same way, when in some study or chamber there are paintings, statues, minerals, petrified things, and other objects of this kind, if they are not organized among themselves, the mind organizes and arranges them on its own, and if they are organized, it is pleased by this, and however different they may be, the mind considers them as similar and assembled to make the unity that it desires, and it includes them under the category decoration and marvels.[62]

Thus, once again we find ourselves in the middle of a typical late-sixteenth-century collection, where works of art are mixed with objects found in nature, *artificialia* are classified together with *naturalia* and *mirabilia*. By analysing the wholly intellectual pleasure of giving order to the diverse objects of a collection, or rather of being pleased with their ordered arrangement, Strozzi elegantly describes an essential aspect of the taste for collecting in the sixteenth century: the artificial reconstruction of the whole above and beyond the multiplicity of the objects, or, rather, through the multiplicity of the objects. Strozzi invites us to see Ariosto and Tasso's poems from a complex viewpoint, to categorize them according to the places, the images, the objects of a collection, and to determine whether or not their order will hold, whether or not the mind can play its favourite game, that is, the reconstruction of the unitary plot of things.

We have thus seen how widespread is the tendency to perceive the text in architectural terms, as a building, perhaps decorated with images, or as a depository of disparate artefacts, the object of the sixteenth-century collector's varied desires. The projection of the text within a system of places remains a constant, even with the variations in architectural and urbanistic models: the texts can be constructed (or seen) as palaces, temples, theatres, galleries, or as kitchens, storerooms, dark Mannerist studies. Some of the titles of works by the canon Tommaso Garzoni (1549–1589) – *Piazza universale di tutte le professioni del mondo* [Universale square of all the professions of the world] (1585); *La sinagoga de gl'ignoranti* [The synagogue of the ignorant] (1589); *L'hospidale de' pazzi incurabili* [The hospital of the incurably mad] (1586); *Il serraglio de gli stupori del mondo* [The seraglio of the wonders of the world] (1613) – are enough to show that the spatial and architectural model answered multiple needs, whether it was used for encyclopedic enumeration or debased for grotesque and moralizing ends.[63]

How does the art of memory interact with this widespread mode of perception? We can say that it simultaneously uses and augments it. A text constructed (or received) as a set of places in which images are arranged is in a certain sense a text already *treated* in accordance with mnemonic requirements. It is a text ready to be translated and reorganized in the mental places and images of the art of memory. However, all of the ingredients of this mode of perception are the same as those on which the art of memory is based: visualization, the dimension of space, the ordering of places. It is safe to say, therefore, that mnemonics helps to sustain this mode of perception, to nourish the set of images that we have discussed. We are once again faced with the problem of the relationship between memory and invention, that is, between memory and writing. It is somewhat impoverishing and reductive to think of the techniques of memory as functioning in a dimension separate from and subsequent to the composition of the text. In a certain sense these techniques help us to understand characteristics internal to the text. They prompt us to cast our gaze on the way in which the text is both constructed and received. In this light a passage from a letter by Camillo, written in the late 1520s, to Marcantonio Flaminio takes on great significance: retracing the route he has followed in the search for a set of places suitable for his system of memory, Camillo writes that he had first considered the models used by the ancients, especially the building proposed by Cicero and the places of the zodiac used by Metrodorus, 'but seeing in the former little dignity, and in the latter much difficulty, and both perhaps more suitable for reciting than for composition, we turned our thoughts to the wonderful edifice of the human body.'[64] Camillo is clearly aware that the system of places of memory serves not only in the reciting of a text, that is, to remember a text already prepared, but also in the composition of the text itself. It can thus contribute to *inventio*. In Camillo's definitive project the different models with which he has experimented will ultimately combine: the human body, yes, but also the celestial places; the container, however, will be a building, albeit of a rather particular type: his theatre, built on the seven pillars of divine Wisdom, the machine that guarantees and at the same time mobilizes the relationship between memory and invention.

6 How to Translate a Narrative into a Cycle of Images

The memory treatises of the fifteenth and sixteenth centuries are filled with recommendations on how to remember an oration, a sermon, and, in particular, the narrative sequences that they may contain. The *Ars memorativa* written in Bologna in 1425 is rich with instructions of this nature. The model of writing and reading is powerful in this treatise: thanks to the art of memory, it claims, one reads what one wants to remember 'as in a mental book' [tamquam in libro mentali]. Places can be ordered in any fashion, but it is better to have an order that moves from left to right, 'like that which we follow when we write and read a physical book' [qualem tenemus in descriptione litterarum et lectione in libro materiali].[65] In the part entitled 'de ymaginibus sentenciarum' [the images of sentences], the author explains that in order to remember a narration, you need to divide it into different parts that reflect the essence of the things narrated. Each of the parts is then translated into an image: 'when you want to work with the images of the sentences, it is not necessary to use the single expressions of which the sentence is made up, but you must fully understand the substance of the thing and make a summary of it and compose an image of the summary.'[66] At this point the images are positioned in the places of memory. The example given is that of Saint Marina (Saint Margaret of Antioch): her life is divided into twelve parts, each with a corresponding image. The figure of Saint Marina entering the monastery is to be positioned in the first place of memory; in the second place, her dying father, who forbids her to reveal that she is a woman; and so on.

It is clear that the mnemonic procedure used here is identical to the procedure that a painter would follow if he wanted to represent the life of Saint Marina in twelve paintings. In the spaces of memory the model of writing lives alongside and overlaps with a model from the figurative arts.

There is another very interesting comment in the manuscript about the perception of time that is best suited for the translation of a narration into a series of mental pictures. It is foreseen that the order of mnemonic places will reflect the order of events in the story. The spatial succession, therefore, visually translates the time of the story. 'Note, however,' warns the author, 'that everything must appear, not as belonging to the past, but almost as if it were to happen in the future or as if it were present in the mind.'[67] It would seem that at the moment that the time of the narration is translated into the space of the image, there is a sort of temporal distortion: the image is more effective if it does not refer to a past event but puts the event in the present, or even makes the event into a representation of the future. This mode of perceiving images that tell (and recall) a story makes us think of a time game played by Ariosto a century later in the *Orlando furioso*: in the castle of Tristan in canto 33 the tragic events of contemporary history are represented in a cycle of paintings. In this way, they are transported into the past, projected into the age of the paladins, and recounted through images thanks to the prophetic abilities of Merlin, the only painter who knew how to 'paint the future' (33.3.6). Ariosto thus plays with time by using the artifice of a feigned *ecphrasis*: the words are presented as if suggested by the images to which they themselves have given life, images that exist only in the space of the poem.[68]

From this perspective, Della Porta's treatise on memory once again proves to be most interesting. The comparison between memory and painting shows up in the nodal points of the text. In the first chapter, for example, the process by which the imagination transmits perceptible images to memory is described in the following manner: 'it takes in images of perceptible things and, as if it were an excellent painter, it uses its brush to draw them in the memory, which has been made into a blank canvas for this purpose' (*Ars reminiscendi*, p. 1).[69] The intellect, which subsequently recalls to itself the images of memory, is compared to a painter who restores an image that has been ruined and faded by time. In the seventh chapter Della Porta cites the famous words of

Themistocles to Simonides, the inventor of the art of memory, who has offered Themistocles his services: 'I would rather that someone taught me the art of forgetting,' Themistocles supposedly answers. Della Porta removes any symbolic or polemical charge from this answer in order to offer it as an option in his *ars memorativa*.[70] He will teach even the art of forgetting, how to do what painters do when they dispose of a painting that they no longer like by using a sponge to erase the figures and the paint and make the canvas white again (p. 12). At any rate, the art of memory and painting have something fundamental in common, that is, the creation of images; for this reason, says Della Porta in the tenth chapter, the hardest thing is to remember words that are not translatable into images: 'given that this art does not consist in anything else but the representation in memory of the image of things to be remembered, then how can a great painter represent the image of something of which he does not know the form?'[71] The model of painting, this time nourished by references to the great paintings of the sixteenth century, can be discerned even in the passage (already discussed in chapter 4, p. 166), in which Della Porta copies Alberti's *De pictura* while turning its advice upside down. Della Porta recommends using images of persons characterized by pronounced gestures, by histrionic expressivity; he notes: 'We remember the paintings of Michelangelo, Raphael, and Titian more readily than the paintings of a mediocre artist. In the latter we find only common gestures; in the former we see strong, unusual gestures' (p. 16).[72] While, as we have seen, the framework of conventions and signs that teaches how to read and construct the theatre of passions enjoys wide cultural usage throughout the course of the sixteenth century, there is also an appreciation of the great painters who – from the point of view of mnemonics, at least – push the limits of the grid, who break down the boundaries of the norm.

In Della Porta's treatise the traditional canon of *ut pictura poesis* intersects with a sort of *ut pictura memoria*, with a constant emphasis on the analogies that tie painting to mnemonics. The fruitful intersection of these planes appears as a particular theme in the sixth chapter, which is dedicated for the most part to the construction of images capable of helping us to remember a story. There are two possibilities, according to Della Porta: if the story is *simple*, reducible to a single character and a single action, then it can be concentrated into a single image. 'If we wish to remember the story of Andromeda,' for example, 'we will pretend that the person of the place is nude, tied to the rocks with chains of iron, trembling and in tears' (p. 10).[73] If, however, the story is *composite*, that is, contains a plurality of actions and characters, it is a matter of making a summary of the principal narrative sequences and freezing them in a series of paintings positioned in the places of memory. As an example Della Porta shows how one can remember the story of the expulsion of the kings from Rome by reducing it to five basic scenes: in the first, there is Tarquin dressed in royal garb; in the second, Lucretia in tears, with the appearance of someone who has been the victim of violence; and so on. This is the same procedure, we realize, that is recommended in the anonymous fifteenth-century treatise. But even as Della Porta recycles traditional techniques, he rewrites them from the perspective of modern literary and pictorial experience. This can be seen in the way he introduces the section dedicated to the images of memory of composite stories:

> but if we wish to remember a history or fable where different characters appear, we will reduce the story in a compendium that contains persons and things, and we will adapt it to the places. I greatly appreciate the rule followed by writers of tragedies and comedies who represent their work with the smallest number of characters possible, and there is no story so full of a variety of things that it cannot be excellently represented with nine or ten characters.   (P. 10)[74]

As we have already seen, Della Porta's experience as a playwright helps to shape his treatise on memory: the play that takes place on the stage and the play positioned in the spaces of the mind correspond and tend to overlap. Especially here the theatre seems to offer useful parameters for mnemonics because of its ability to play out all stories with a limited number of characters. We might say that Della Porta has been influenced by the sixteenth-century renewal of classical theatre and its regulation by treatises on poetics.

Actually this is somewhat misleading: we are forced to correct our perspective of the text by the discovery that Della Porta is plagiarizing. One part of the second book of Alberti's *De pictura* is dedicated to *istoria*, to what the painter has to do when he wishes to represent the story of an event. The painter, writes Alberti, has to use an intermediate number of characters and try to avoid the double risks of overcrowding and solitude. He adds: 'I strongly approve in an *istoria* that which I see observed by tragic and comic poets. They tell a story with as few characters as possible. In my judgment no picture will be filled with so great a variety of things that nine or ten men are not able to act it with dignity.'[75] This passage coincides – almost word for word – with the passage cited from Della Porta.

What is interesting here is not so much the customary practice of plagiarism but rather what has made it possible. Della Porta is able to recycle Alberti for two convergent reasons: the first is that Alberti's treatise is inspired by the canons of *ut pictura poesis* and tends to inscribe the artistic experience within a rhetorical framework. In the passage cited above, the theatrical tradition becomes a point of reference for the painter who has to paint an *istoria*. The second reason is that, in the code used and elaborated by Della Porta, those who have to remember a narration are faced with the same basic problem as the painter who has to represent a narration in a cycle of paintings: in both cases, in fact, it is a matter of subdividing the narrative sequence of the story into a series of scenes. Something that originally possesses a temporal dimension has to be arranged in space, physically or mentally. It is a common practice in the tradition of the art of memory to translate poems into buildings, galleries, and cycles of paintings. By the height of the cinquecento the play of similarities among mental processes, literary experience, and artistic practice has become truly dizzying.

7 The Illustrated Book

All of this has some fallout on sixteenth-century publishing, on the techniques for *packaging* a book. We can get some idea of this by examining a work by Lodovico Dolce (1508–1568), a protagonist in Venetian publishing. In Venice in 1572 Giolito published Dolce's *L'Achille et L'Enea ... dove egli tessendo l'historia della Iliade d'Homero a quella dell'Eneide di Virgilio, ambedue l'ha divinamente ridotte in ottava rima con argomenti et allegorie per ogni canto* [Achilles and Aeneas ... in which the author has woven the story of Homer's *Iliad* to that of Virgil's *Aeneid*, and he has divinely reduced both in rhymed octaves with subjects and allegories for each canto], and in the following year his *Ulisse* [Ulysses]. Dolce has deftly synthesized and translated the poems of Homer and Virgil into rhymed octaves. As the title promises, the text is accompanied by an allegorical interpretation in which moral teachings are combined with a sort of book of etiquette for the politician and the courtier.[76] For example, Thersites beaten into silence teaches what happens to the stupid and imprudent who speak 'without making distinctions among persons, places, and occasions' (folio 71r). Telemachus is the 'wise son'

preoccupied with the honour of his father (*Ulisse*, folio 127r), and
Penelope is a 'gentlewoman and honoured princess' (*Ulisse*, folio 136v).
Ulysses is the image of the good prince, capable of marrying revenge
and clemency with Machiavellian cunning. The text is preceded by a
large portrait of Dolce (accompanied by a device) and an alphabetically
ordered list of verse maxims that, it is claimed, can be derived from the
narrated events.

In Dolce's poem there are many echoes of Ariosto's *Orlando furioso*
that the reader can easily recognize. In his oration *Delle lodi della poesia
d'Omero e di Virgilio* [In praise of Homer's and Virgil's poetry], published as an appendix to Dolce's text of the *Iliad* and the *Aeneid*, Andrea
Menechini claims that Dolce has made Homer and Virgil modern and
Italian, and has 'adorned and sweetened' them 'in the beginning of
each canto with those graceful morals and beautiful inventions found
in the glorious and divine Ariosto in order to complete them with every
beauty and bring them to the height of every perfection, whereby he
has accommodated the poem for the use accepted and favoured by
modern poetry' (folios unnumbered). While the use of the octave has
given a modern, vernacular form to Homer and Virgil, the allusions to
the *Orlando furioso* rounds out the topical character of the text. Reviving
one of the initial images evoked in this study, we might say that this
book by Dolce becomes a text/archive, a cornucopian text, the product
of a game of combinations: it offers the reader-user not only a unified
narration of the basic texts of the epic tradition, but also allegories and
didactic sayings that interpret the whole and multiply the possiblities
for reappropriation.

An iconic component fits perfectly in this operation. At the beginning of each canto, in fact, we find the argument – an octave that
synthesizes the content – inserted in a richly decorated frame; the
allegory; and in the same frame used for the argument, an image that
illustrates a salient episode. Even on this last level the game of combinations comes into play: the illustrations recycle visual matter that was
used by Giolito for the editions of the *Orlando furioso* edited by Dolce.
This results in some discrepancies, or at least some rather forced visual
translations of the story: for example, the image of a naked character in
the act of uprooting trees (figure 46), perfect in its place in canto 23 of
the *Orlando furioso,* is recycled to illustrate the return of Ulysses to
Ithaca in canto 17 of Dolce's *Ulisse.*[77] There is undoubtedly a principle
of economy functioning here: for Giolito it is a good solution to use pre-
existing matrices for the illustrations. But there is also a cultural code

46 Illustration recycled from *Orlando furioso,* in Lodovico Dolce, *Ulisse*
(Venice: Giolito 1573)

that makes all of this possible, perhaps at the price of misrepresenta-
tion. The recycled images that had originally illustrated the *Orlando
furioso* act as a counterpart of the imitation of Ariosto's text in a poem
that combines Homer and Virgil. In this way, too, Dolce's book becomes a book/archive, a book/cornucopia: it unifies and concentrates
a heritage of memory, textual and iconic, that is presented as already
arranged for memorization, ready for different types of reuse.

This mode of *packaging* the book transforms epic narration into a
cycle of images/illustrations. Because of the way it is constructed, this
cycle of images can find a place in different spaces: on the page of the
book, on the walls of a building, or in the internal dimension of a
system of memory.

Dolce's book, in fact, is cited in a manuscript by Ulisse Aldrovandi
(1522–1605) in a context pertinent to our study. Around 1585 this
celebrated Bolognese naturalist decided to decorate his country villa
with a cycle of paintings based on the stories of his namesake Ulysses, a
theme that had developed into a rich allegorical tradition over the
centuries. In the complex work accompanying the *invention* of the
thirteen paintings (each accompanied by an inscription) that are to

decorate the walls of the villa, Aldrovandi uses and cites Dolce's poem.[78] Besides the synthesis of the material, he also finds in Dolce's book an example of visual translation. The illustrated book prefigures the operation that Aldrovandi intends to entrust to the artists.

In addition to a cycle of frescoes, Dolce's book could also be translated into a cycle of mental images, into a system of the art of memory. The author, in fact, is aware of this aspect of the question. In 1562 he published a treatise on memory that is actually a translation of a text by Joannes Romberch. Among the Italianate additions are the following recommendations on how to prepare effective images of memory:

> those who wish to remember the story of Europa could use the example of the painting by Titian, and also the story of Adonis, and of any fictional story, profane or sacred, by especially choosing those figures that delight and excite memory. Illustrated books, so commonly printed today, are useful for this, like most of those that issue from the press of the most accurate Giolito.   (*Dialogo nel quale si ragiona del modo di accrescer et conservar la memoria*, folio 86r)

Like images made by painters, the illustrated book, Dolce informs us, offers models and materials for images of memory. It is one of the ways a paradoxical balance is achieved between the art of memory and the printing press. It is this collaboration of ancient techniques and modern technology that will ultimately render the former meaningless. At any rate, it is important to note that Dolce offers an interpretative key that we can apply to some of his more successful works: his Italian translation of Ovid's *Metamorphoses*, for example, not to mention *L'Achille et l'Enea*. At the same time, his words confirm our observations (chapter 4, p. 168) on Della Porta's illustrated books.

Dolce, of course, is not the only one to associate illustrated books with systems of memory. Treatises more interested in the religious dimension of memory offer evidence of just how widespread this association and use actually are. In *Thesaurus artificiosae memoriae* Cosma Rosselli, for example, recommends that one take inspiration from illustrations in the Bible and in other books of devotion ('you will find varied and beautiful figures in the illustrated editions of the sacred books' [varia autem et pulcherrima schemata in Bibliis sacris et figuratis invenies], p. 31). In the *Gazophylacium artis memoriae* [Treasure-house of the art of memory] by Thomas Lambertus Schenckel (Strasbourg:

Antonius Bertramus 1610), the Belgian author claims that it is good to form images of memory based on the Bible, 'and for this reason, the illustrated Bibles [printed] in folio are highly useful' [ad quod valde iuvabimur editione Bibliorum per imagines in folio] (p. 141). The author also recommends that one often review mentally the set of places and images. To do this, he writes, very little time is needed:

> In fact, if, using our eyes, we can rapidly retrace and review all of a Bible illustrated with material images in the course of an hour, it will not take long for us to turn the pages and see with a glance what it is about, on the condition, naturally, that we are already familiar with it, so it must be for the things that we have positioned in the places. How much more can one do with the eyes of the mind, which operate with much greater speed!   (P. 122)[79]

Perhaps the richest and most fascinating example of how mnemonics and the illustrated book can intersect is found in *Rhetorica christiana* [Christian rhetoric], a manual of sacred oratory published by the Franciscan friar Diego Valadés in Perugia in 1579.[80] He equips the text with a series of images that, as he explains in great detail, help one to remember it: he provides, therefore, the text and its own system of memory. The illustrated book is the ideal container for both. Valadés uses a plurality of mnemonic tools: for example, a table that reduces all of rhetoric into a tree, accompanied by a note on how memory, an absolutely essential talent, is cultivated through reading, toil, and meditation, 'but perfected also through the positioning and arrangement of the things that we wish to remember' [sed etiam perficiatur collocatione dispositioneque eorum, quae in memoria habere cupimus] (p. 48). Valadés shows, moreover, that he is familiar with the use of diagrams, which – as we mentioned in chapter 2, pp. 76–82) – characterize Borromeo's circle; in fact Valadés cites Agostino Valier's *Rhetorica ecclesiastica* (p. 292).

A wealth of meanings and functions never seen before accumulates around Valadés' use of images. At first sight they appear to have been constructed according to rather simple and traditional pedagogic principles; for example, the image accompanying the chapter dedicated to the talents of the Christian orator (p. 10; figure 47) is a *summa* of the teachings presented there. Each of them is recalled by a letter of the alphabet and visualized in a direct manner by taking a metaphor literally. The globe upon which the priest rests his feet is there to remind

47 The model Christian orator, from Diego Valadés, *Rhetorica christiana* (Perugia: Pietro Giacomo Petrucci 1579)

one to put the wealth of the earth under one's feet. The situation becomes more intense when Valadés recalls the decades that he has spent in Mexico and exalts, against their detractors, the human and cultural values of the peoples of the New World. It is true that they do not know writing, he says, but they use images to communicate and to remember, exactly as the ancient Egyptians had done, and as Europeans do today when they use the art of memory. To those who deny the human dignity of indigenous peoples, Valadés offers a reinterpretation, a new cultural translation: the mysterious and unsettling images of pre-Columbian civilization in Mexico are contained in a framework that makes them accessible to Western culture. It does so by associating them with a remote antiquity that the West regards with reverential fear (the hieroglyphics of ancient Egypt), as well as with a modern and commonly accepted component of Western culture, the art of memory. This process is in some ways similar to the attempt of the Jesuit Matteo Ricci in China in the last years of the century to create a parallel between Chinese ideograms and European images of memory.[81] Valadés' situation, however, is very different and more dramatic: for him it is a matter of defending peoples who have been subject to domination. His attempt at cultural translation is addressed, in fact, more to the *conquistadores* than to the indigenous people who are to be evangelized. Valadés himself probably lived out in his person the problematic relationship between the two worlds: it appears that he was a *mestizo*, born of the union between a Spanish noble and an American Indian woman. There is a special meaning behind the care that has been given to the images that illustrate his *Rhetorica christiana* and entrust it to the memory of the reader. Those images are, in fact, the bridge between two cultures. They are the tools of communication and memory by which the Old and New Worlds could meet.[82] The fact that the Franciscans used images to evangelize the Mexican peoples, to make them recognize the ugliness of sin and the evils of the devil (figures 48, 49), is witnessed in the iconography of Valadés' text and is presented as a way of adapting to a cultural practice already deep-rooted among the native peoples. Highly indicative is the large-scale image of memory, found at the end of the second part of the work, that serves to recall all the books of the Bible. It starts with the tabernacle that God ordered Moses to construct (Exodus 26:15–30). The biblical description is embellished with many details that generate new images. The pillars decorated with precious gems are a good example: alongside gems known to the Western world (their properties have been illustrated by a long literary tradition), there are also the new precious stones of the West Indies (pp. 101–124). These, too, contribute to the construction of a grand internal edifice in which one can remember the Bible, the starting point and *summa* of all sacred rhetoric.

The system of memory and the illustrated book coincide perfectly in Valadés' book: here the art of memory is called upon to create the conditions of translatability, not only between words and images, between the invisible and the visible, but also between two cultures, between two worlds, that have suddenly and dramatically come into contact.

8 Biography and Portraiture

Behind all the practices that we are examining there is great trust in the synthetic and evocative powers of the image. 'In very little space, without turning pages or volumes, images embrace wide-reaching and weighty concepts,' writes an admiring Gabriele Paleotti in his *Discorso intorno alle imagini sacre e profane* [Essay on sacred and profane images].[83] The capacity of the image to synthesize is perhaps clearest in the case of the portrait: the art of memory, in fact, helps us to understand that portraits not only illustrate biographies but also, in a certain sense, substitute for them.[84]

We have already seen in chapter 4 how physiognomy is used to

48 The torments of hell, from Diego Valadés, *Rhetorica christiana* (Perugia: Pietro Giacomo Petrucci 1579)

decipher portraits and to reconstruct them. Pomponio Gaurico's *De sculptura* [On sculpture] (1504) has already recommended that sculptors use physiognomy to visualize the great figures of the past, to translate into images the words that have been written about them. In this way, for example, we are able to see Homer himself, whom we desire so greatly to see ('illum ipsum qui tantopere desideratur Homerum'): a component of desire thus comes into play in this procedure, a desire that has to do with our need to consider the great figures

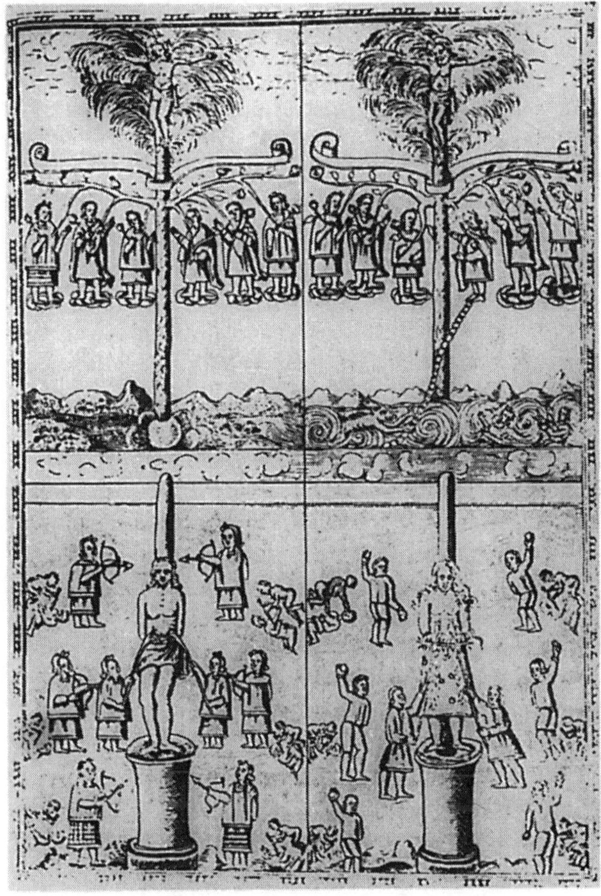

49 The punishment of the adulterers, from Diego Valadés, *Rhetorica christiana*
(Perugia: Pietro Giacomo Petrucci 1579)

whom we want to imitate as living persons, so as to enter into dialogue
with them, just as Machiavelli wrote in his famous letter to Francesco
Vettori on 10 December 1513.[85]

The mixture of fascination and diffidence that images arouse becomes highly visible in Paleotti's *Discorso intorno alle imagini sacre e
profane*. In the part dedicated to portraits, he proposes a severe limita-
tion on their use because he is convinced that the portrait is immediately transformed into an internal model, into a *phantasma* that tends to

mould behaviours and thought in its own image and likeness. But Paleotti makes an exception for portraits of virtuous persons, like popes and kings:

> similarly there are images of other noteworthy men of various professions in the chambers and wardrobes of great gentlemen and other persons, which have been collected with great praise and with benefit for others; just so the virtue and diligence of Vasari willed that the memories of the painters and sculptors discussed here remain for future generations, not only in writing, but also in the form of drawings, which today can be seen and read with much honour to his name.

In this passage Paleotti is referring to the 1568 edition of Vasari's *Lives*, in which each biography is preceded by a portrait of the artist. Barocchi writes of this passage that 'the historical indifference of the Bishop [Paleotti] was such that he seemed to put the *Lives* and the portraits on the same level.'[86] In effect, this association seems strange and paradoxical to the modern reader, but it helps us to understand just how strong was the faith in the extraordinary synthetic and exemplary force of the image. For Paleotti the portrait becomes the equivalent of biographical narration inasmuch as it visually transmits the sense, the moral meaning, of the whole narrative. It functions, we may say, as an image of memory.

There is a continuation of this last idea in Rosselli's *Thesaurus artificiosae memoriae*. He recommends preparing an archive of images of memory among which there would be an alphabet made up of different persons (whose names, in other words, would follow each other in alphabetical order). Besides friends and relatives, one can resort to people seen in portraits, or people read about in biographies:

> Consequently, it is highly useful to see in various authors, and in particular Diogenes Laertius, the sayings, inscriptions, devices, and biographies of the men discussed above. When, in fact, you know their sayings and actions, it is not difficult to conceive and mentally construct a figure, a likeness, a *simulacrum* corresponding to each of them.   (Folio 61v)[87]

The two passages, by Paleotti and Rosselli, are virtually reflections of one another: the portraits that accompany Vasari's *Lives* condense the narration and crystallize it in memory, thus making it possible both to see and to read the memories, as Paleotti notes. Rosselli proposes an analogous mental operation: using the portraits of great men outlined in words in their biographies, one can construct corresponding visual images, an ideal gallery of portraits placed beside the biographies. Vasari's *Lives* is one case of a rather widespread practice. The most famous example is that of Paolo Giovio, author of biographies, of *Elogia*, and tireless collector of portraits of illustrious men for his villa at Como.

The passage from Rosselli helps us to understand once again how the art of memory is perfectly at ease in this back and forth relationship between words and images, between the duration of biographical narration and the exemplifying synthesis of portraiture.

9 Memory and Invention: Francesco Sansovino and Pirro Ligorio

We will now transpose the analysis and see if the themes that we have been discussing are to be encountered among those who are involved in the creation of images, that is, those who participate directly in the figurative arts.

Let us begin with the celebrated guide to the splendours of Venice that Francesco Sansovino (1521–1586) – son of the famous architect and sculptor Iacopo Sansovino – compiled in the form of a dialogue between a Venetian and a foreigner. After arriving at the Piazza San Marco, the two interlocutors direct their attention to the Loggetta and especially to the four bronze statues that decorate it. The Venetian explains to the foreigner that the first figure is that of Minerva (figure 50), and that it is there to represent the wisdom of the Venetian legislators, thanks to whom republican government has been preserved in Venice throughout the centuries, and by which 'this city has greatly surpassed all the others in its government.' The statue of Mercury (figure 51) signifies eloquence, the cherished companion of wisdom, and a talent particularly appreciated in free republics. According to the Venetian, the meanings of the statue of Apollo (figure 52) are somewhat more varied:

This one ... was made to express the fact that, just as Apollo means the Sun – and there is only one Sun, and no more, and for that reason it is called Sun [Sole] – so this republic is the only one [sola] in the world so wisely and justly governed. Besides this, every man knows that our nation enjoys music, and for this reason Apollo is depicted for Music. But because from the union of the Magistrates, who have joined so wonderfully

50 *Minerva*, in the Loggetta of Iacopo Sansovino, Piazza San Marco, Venice

together, an unusual harmony emanates, perpetuating this immortal government, for this reason also Apollo has been depicted for he signifies the Harmony that I have told you about.

The last statue represents Peace (figure 53), so dear to Venice that it is incorporated into its emblem and its evangelic greeting: *Pax tibi, Marce Evangelista meus* ['Peace be with you, Mark my Evangelist'].[88]
Sansovino's guide for tourists explains the *inventio* that had guided his father: the statues of the Loggetta are part of a visualized panegyric of the Venetian government, of the wisdom and beauty of its order and the effects that it has produced. In effect, as Manfredo Tafuri has shown, the works that Iacopo Sansovino was commissioned to create – the Library, the Zecca [Mint], the Loggetta – are laden with precise political values and ideals.[89] They were destined to renew the face of Piazza San

51 *Mercury*, in the Loggetta of Iacopo Sansovino, Piazza San Marco, Venice

Marco, the emblem of Venetian power, and they were decided upon while Andrea Gritti was doge, in a phase in which Venice was trying to present itself as a new Rome: the Sack of Rome had made the myth of a *translatio urbis* credible. Sansovino came from Rome, and the grafting of his classicism onto the nerve centre of the city of Venice is in accord with the idea of a *renovatio urbis* that is more than just city planning. Especially the Loggetta, writes Tafuri, is a 'triumphal arch in miniature,' a definition that corresponds to Francesco Sansovino's allegorical interpretation of his father's work.

The pages of the guide to Venice examined here reiterate and expand some affirmations already present in Francesco's short treatise on rhetoric, mentioned above (p. 193): *L'arte oratoria secondo i modi della lingua volgare* [The art of oratory according to the modes of the vernacular language], published for the first time in 1546, the same year in which

52 *Apollo*, in the Loggetta of Iacopo Sansovino, Piazza San Marco, Venice

the Loggetta was finished. After his treatment of *inventio, dispositio,* and *actio*, Sansovino discusses, as a practical matter, memory and the techniques used to reinforce it. As an example, he gives the statues that his father has positioned in the Loggetta:

> We can say that they are like the places of memory because, just as soon as a man lays his eyes on the image of Minerva, he understands through that sign all the things that according to the poets have been taken from her, besides the significance that she has here: that the Great Venetian Senate is most wise both in governing and in deed. The same happens when we see Apollo: we are immediately reminded what the ancients said of him; the same for Mercury and the others.[90]

Sansovino gives us precious evidence for our study: a dimension of the

53 *Peace*, in the Loggetta of Iacopo Sansovino, Piazza San Marco, Venice

art of memory comes into play in the reception of works of art, and it does so on more than one level. The statue of Minerva, for example, concentrates and therefore easily evokes in the mind of the viewer a rich heritage of literary tradition ('according to the poets'). At the same time, it is laden with allegorical meaning and therefore with a political function: it signifies – and therefore brings to mind – one of the components of the myth of Venice, that is, the wisdom of its governors. It is very clear that memory and invention correspond to one another here: to show that the statues of the Loggetta are images of memory, Sansovino uses the same arguments by which he has explained the artistic creations of his father to the *foreigner*.

In the tourist guide the commentary that concludes the explanation of the figures of the top *bas-relief* of the Loggetta is also very significant for our purposes. The islands of Cyprus and Crete are depicted by

Venus and Jupiter, while Venice is represented by the figure of Justice, and her dominions on land by old men who correspond to rivers – 'in such a way,' says the Venetian, 'that in this small façade you see the empire of this Signory, both on sea and on land, collocated in figures' (*Della cose notabili della Città di Venetia* [On points of interest in the City of Venice], pp. 57–58). The expression 'collocated in figures' is laden with a particular meaning having to do with memory. It is clear that there is a close link between *imagines* and *loci*: the statues develop their political function and remind one of the merits of Venice because they are located in a place already laden with meanings: Piazza San Marco, in fact, is the calling-card of Venice, the *preface* to the city – to use one of the metaphors from Sansovino's treatise on rhetoric. It is the place where the government constructs (and renews) its own representation.

The last case that we will examine offers us a much closer vantage point: it provides evidence that comes not from a commentator but from an artist, the author of the invention of an iconographic program. This time the place is Tivoli, and, to be more precise, the splendid villa built by Cardinal Ippolito d'Este in the mid-sixteenth century.[91] As we mentioned above (p. 203), it is in this villa that, thanks to Zuccari, the project of Doni's *Pitture* is partially fulfilled.

Fascination with the ancient world and the reappropriation of antiquity had a large part in the construction of the villa. A great deal of archeological material was collected – often taken from churches and private citizens – to be inserted into the grand *text* constituted by the villa and its extraordinary gardens.

A fundamental role was played by Pirro Ligorio (ca 1510–1583), an antiquarian and architect who served the pope and the Este family during the 1550s. David Coffin cites Ligorio as the principal planner behind the complex symbolism of the gardens. According to the documents, the gardens are meant to be an extraordinary theatre in praise of the cardinal. They are to be presented as the new Garden of the Hesperides, in accordance with the myth of Hercules, a hero associated with the Este dynasty and with the three golden apples that appear in the device of the cardinal. At the same time the gardens of the villa are intended to be a new Mount Parnassus, to become the place par excellence for the exaltation of the arts and the virtues, where, in particular, the Greek hero Hippolytus – the cardinal's namesake – would be celebrated.

In 1569, according to a manuscript published by Coffin, Ligorio prepared sixteen drawings for the cardinal, probably meant to be reproduced on tapestries to decorate the rooms of the villa. The theme is the life of Hippolytus. The manuscript allows us to penetrate into the artist's laboratory: he reactivates an extraordinary archive of mythological and antiquarian knowledge, often extremely rare and refined. He chooses materials that he then recombines and recomposes. Thanks to this method, Ligorio is able to reincarnate the Greek hero Hippolytus in the figure of Virbius, the mythical founder of Ariccia, and he chooses to illustrate and comment upon those stages of his legendary career that in some way can be associated with various moments in the cardinal's life. For each *quadro* [scene] Ligorio explains the moral allegory that informs the details and the whole. In his comments on the scene in which the young Hippolytus is entrusted to Pittheus for his education (figure 54), Ligorio writes:

> The present scene shows how Pittheus explained the image of Minerva and Diana, and how he revealed that virtue and the liberal arts were those which greatly benefited man, especially when they were accompanied by things relating to Diana like the hunt, chastity, and honest fame, and this supremely benefited Hippolytus. This is the sum of the morality of this scene. The ancients had the custom of keeping and looking at virtuous images as *local memory*; when Caesar looked at the image of the young Alexander, placed as a man of valour in the temple of Hercules, he sighed to see such a youthful figure, who had already accomplished many heroic deeds at that early age.[92]

The story of Caesar in front of the statue of Alexander the Great is a rhetorical topos. It can be found, for example, in Dolce's *Dialogo della pittura intitolato l'Aretino* [Dialogue on the painting entitled 'Aretino'] (1552) in a very interesting context: it is used by the speaker, Piero Aretino, to combat the iconoclastic tenets of the Protestants. Images, he says, urge one to consider what they represent:

> whereby one reads that Julius Caesar, when he saw a statue of Alexander the Great in Spain and was prompted to consider that Alexander at his age had almost conquered the world, and that he, Caesar, had not done anything worthy of glory, he cried; and his desire for immortality burned so greatly that he dedicated himself to the great endeavours by which he

54 Pittheus showing the statues of Athena and Diana to Hippolytus, from
Pirro Ligorio, *Vita di Virbio*, in D.R. Coffin, *The Villa d'Este at Tivoli*
(Princeton: Princeton University Press 1960)

not only equalled Alexander but surpassed him. Sallust wrote that Quintus
Fabius and Publius Scipio used to say that when they observed the images
of their forefathers, they felt kindled to virtue. Not that the wax or marble
of the image had such great force: but the flame of the soul rose in those
great men by the *memory* of those illustrious deeds.[93]

In Dolce the episode of Caesar in front of the statue of Alexander is
linked, on the one hand, to the exemplary function of images and, on
the other, to the fact that such a function is achieved through memory,
through all that images internally create and suggest.

In Ligorio the reference to memory is more specific and technical: the
theme of *local memory* and the art of memory come into the limelight
right in the middle of the invention of his iconographic program, and in
close connection with its allegory.[94] In an image intended for moral
instruction he shows Hippolytus himself being given moral instruction

by Pittheus through images of Minerva and Diana. We can see how this informs the heart of Ligorio's work: his imitation, his reappropriation of antiquity, tends to endow his own images with the same functional capacity that classical images, when positioned in predetermined places, are able to develop. The statue of the young Alexander, placed in the temple of Hercules, functions exactly as an image of memory, according to Ligorio, in the sense that it recalls to Caesar not only the historical character of Alexander but an *exemplum* of precocious heroism to be imitated and emulated.[95] The scenes in which Ligorio captures the most important moments of the life of Hippolytus/Virbius carry out an identical function through the mediation of the allegorical meanings that the artist himself wishes to explain to the cardinal.

In this way, the tapestries, once they are arranged along the walls of a room in the villa, will construct, through images, not only a story of the ancient hero but also a panegyric of the cardinal and a gallery of images of memory.

CHAPTER SIX

The Art of Memory and Collecting

1 Samuel Quicchelberg's Theatre and the Metaphors of Memory

In Munich, in 1565, Adam Berg published a short work with a long title by Samuel Quicchelberg (1529–1567), a young doctor from Antwerp who was interested in libraries and collecting and who worked for the wealthy Fugger family and Albert V, duke of Bavaria: *Inscriptiones vel tituli theatri amplissimi, complectentis rerum universitatis singulas materias et imagines eximias, ut idem recte quoque dici possit promptuarium artificiosarum miraculosarumque rerum, ac omnis thesauri et pretiosae supellectilis, structurae atque picturae, quae hic simul in theatro conquiri consuluntur, ut eorum frequenti inspectione tractationeque singularis aliqua rerum cognitio et prudentia admiranda, cito, facile ac tuto comparari possit* [Inscriptions or captions of a large theatre that embraces the single subjects and most important images of all things, so much so that it can rightfully be called a reference book of artistic and extraordinary objects, and of every treasure and precious furnishing, structure, and painting, all of which have been gathered together in the theatre in such a way that by continuously seeing them and handling them, one can quickly obtain a singular knowledge and wonderful experience of things].[1] In this book Quicchelberg describes an ideal system of universal cataloguing: just as Cicero had outlined the model of the perfect orator, Quicchelberg wishes to describe how to organize a *theatrum sapientiae* in which all the products of the arts, the sciences, and nature are arranged in order. This short work is intended to be the prologue to a *theatrum sapientiae* that Quicchelberg would never write: it is an endeavour fundamentally analogous to that of Giulio Camillo, who promised a grand 'theatre of knowledge,' fulfilled only in his *Idea del theatro* [Idea of the theatre]. But it is not just in their similar destiny that the works of these two authors recall and reflect each other. In Quicchelberg's text there are numerous and important citations from Camillo that can guide us by pointing out at least some of the fascinating, yet often fleeting, issues in which the art of memory and collecting come together and interact.

In his first reference to Camillo Quicchelberg explains that he uses the term *theatrum* not in the metaphorical but the physical sense of the word: 'The term *theatrum* is used here not in an improper sense, but in the literal sense, to indicate a large structure, curved like an arch or an oval, or in the shape of a corridor ... It is important to note here that even Giulio Camillo's museum, by virtue of its semicircular shape, was rightfully called a theatre' (folio D4r).[2] The association of the theatre of the collection and Camillo's theatre of memory – significantly termed a *museum* – is based on their physical dimensions, their visibility. This marks a clear-cut difference with respect to the use of the term *theatre* in sixteenth-century publishing. Quicchelberg cites a few examples, such as the *Theatrum humanae vitae* [The theatre of human life] by Theodor Zwinger (an encyclopedia of *exempla* organized in Ramist-style diagrams) and the collection of emblems by Guillaume de la Perrière entitled *Le théatre des bons engins* [Theatre of fine devices], and he notes that these are books capable of speaking to us of human life and history, 'not buildings to look at' [non autem spectandi aedificii], (folio D4r).

The way in which Quicchelberg speaks of Camillo's theatre makes us think of the wood model that Viglius Zuichemus had seen in Venice in 1532 and that he described in a letter to Erasmus (see chapter 2, p. 30, and chapter 4, p. 159). Quicchelberg's familiarity with Camillo's work does not seem strange if we consider that, because of his interests and his work for the great German collectors, he made many journeys to Italy. He greatly praises, for example, the museum of Ulisse Aldrovandi that he had visited in Bologna, as well as that of the Paduan professor Marco Mantova Benavides (folio E2r). He also claims to have stayed in Venice where he publicized his work: 'learned men have analysed the manuscript exemplar of our theatre' [viri docti manuscripti exemplar theatri nostri conspexerunt] (folio F1v). These were milieux in which Camillo's fame was greater than ever, and these were also the years that saw the remarkable editorial success of his works.

Beyond this biographical background, the allusion to Camillo opens an important window onto how the art of memory and collecting interact, mirror each other, and exchange models and ideas. In a certain sense this is the culminating moment of a long story that we have watched unfold in the course of our study, of the tendency, that is, to make mental and physical places overlap, to make the map of the mind and the map of things coincide.

It is also a story linked to the profound transformations that are taking place first with writing and then with the printing press. These tools of communication, in fact, remove words from the temporal and ephemeral dimension of oral communication and arrange them on the space of the page; they make words become things, transforming them into an artificial product that will endure through time and that can be taken apart and analysed. In direct relation to this process the mode of perceiving human faculties changes: the mind is represented as something that is situated in space, and the processes of perception and the intellect are viewed and described in terms of motion. We have seen important examples of this in chapter 2, in the works of Castelvetro and Toscanella.

Even memory is conceived in terms of space, as a set of places where one can deposit the images of recollections. The enduring metaphors inspired and given life by this mode of perception are of prime importance for our theme, and we will, therefore, give some examples.

In some of the essential texts of Latin rhetoric memory is represented as a closed, circumscribed space in which there is an accumulation of precious material that can be used in the moment of need. 'Now let me turn to the treasure-house of the ideas supplied by Invention, to the guardian of all the parts of rhetoric, the Memory,' writes the author of the *Rhetorica ad Herennium* (3.16).[3] Quintilian praises the definition of memory as a 'treasure-house of eloquence':

> it is the power of memory alone that brings before us all the store of precedents, laws, ruling, sayings and facts which the orator must possess in abundance and which he must always hold ready for immediate use. Indeed it is not without good reason that memory has been called the treasure-house of eloquence.   (11.2.1)[4]

The model of the archive thus tends to be superimposed on that of the treasure-chamber.

In the famous passages dedicated to memory in book 10 of Saint Augustine's *Confessions*, the images handed down by the tradition find a new and extraordinary vitality. Chapter 8 of book 10 begins with an enormous expansion of the internal space and the relative amplification of the image of the treasure-house: 'I come into the fields and spacious palaces of memory, where there are treasures of countless images' (10.8.12). This widening of perspective is repeated at the end of a long journey that winds through the vast territory of memory: from physical perception to abstract notions, memories of the past, and expressed feelings: 'Here are the expanses and caves, the innumerable caverns of my memory, filled with innumerable varieties of innumerable things ... I pass through all these things, wandering here and there' (10.17.26).[5] The space of memory is divided into its various parts, and this idea is expressed through a display of metaphorical fireworks. In a scene laden with theatricality, in which Saint Augustine evokes images of recollections one after another, he claims that some make themselves desired as if 'they had to be drawn out from some even more hidden repositories' [tamquam de astrusioribus receptaculis eruuntur] (10.8.12). Immediately following this, a darker and more secret dimension enshrouds the terrority of memory. It is a great cavern in which recollections are deposited and hidden in mysterious recesses: 'Memory takes all these things into its limitless recesses, into I do not know what mysterious and indescribable crevices, to be called up and brought forth when there is need for them' (10.8.13). Further on, the way in which abstract notions are arranged in memory and then extracted at the moment of need suggests the image of a depository or archive: 'It is clear that these things indeed do not have access to memory: it is only their images that are seized with marvellous speed and put away in niches no less marvellous, and in a way just as wonderful are made newly present in the act of recollection' (10.9.16).[6]

The image of the vast spaces of memory and the treasures that they contain is also developed in an architectural direction, whereby memory becomes a grand palace: 'These acts take place within myself, in the immense court of my memory' [intus haec ago, in aula ingenti memoriae] (10.8.14). As the commentators have observed, in the Christian tradition 'aula' means not only a princely court but also the seat of God, the interior of the soul.[7] The two meanings tend to overlap in this text as a result of the skill with which Saint Augustine develops the traditional image of the senses as the door to the edifice of the body, as the places through which the world communicates with man's inner self.

Like a game of Chinese boxes, the image of the treasure-house can evoke that of the coffer, that is, a smaller and more precious version of the container of riches. As the tradition develops, this double version of memory as either a large or a small container of objects and precious images enjoys great popularity. In a refined elaboration, for example, Petrarch speaks of the small cracks and chinks that forgetfulness can make in the coffer of memory, in which the man of letters has placed the fruits of his vast reading and long meditations.[8]

Yet another precious container is associated with memory in the *Ars memorativa* written in Bologna in 1425: to remember memory, it claims, you construct the image of 'a golden bowl that generates and contains the mind and will.'[9] In a mid-sixteenth-century text that we have already encountered, Alessandro Citolini's *Tipocosmia* (Venice: Vincenzo Valgrisi 1561), we find linked to memory, more specifically the art of memory, the image of the treasure-house, the collection, and the coffer (pp. 2, 29).

Should we wish to take part in the game of associations, this tradition helps us to understand why Francesco I de' Medici's *Stanzino*, or Treasure-Room, in the Palazzo Vecchio – in which the most rare and precious objects of his collection were deposited – is in the shape of a coffer (plate VII).[10] As we will see later, it is a small area divided and decorated in such a way that it functions as a system of memory for the collection itself.

But let us return to the spatial metaphors of memory. In the Middle Ages the image of the *thesaurus* enjoys great popularity (it is used, for example, by Saint Thomas Aquinas [*Summa theologica* 1, q. 78, art. 4]), and it is intertwined with the analogous, although more prosaic, image of the wardrobe. On the subject of Fra Bartolomeo di San Concordio, a promulgator of the rules of memory who lived in the late thirteenth and early fourteenth centuries, the chronicle of the Convent of Saint Catherine of Pisa claims that 'his memory and his intellect' have become 'a sort of wardrobe of the Scriptures.'[11] Using the image of the wardrobe, the text underlines the fact that the *loci* of the Scriptures have been placed in a fixed and ordered manner in the *loci* of his mind.

The book and memory thus tend to overlap and coincide. This can be seen in the famous *incipit* of Dante's *Vita nuova*: 'In that part of the book of my memory before which little can be read, there is a rubric saying "Here begins a new life" [Incipit vita nova]. Under this rubric I find written the words that I intend to transcribe in this little book; if not all of them, at least their substance.' The little book [libello], that Dante is writing – and that we are reading – is the visible manifestation, the copy, of an inner book, and the recollections have been arranged in its places, in its 'rubrics.'[12]

In his studies of the metaphors used for memory Harald Weinrich has identified two different groups that correspond to two models of the mind: the 'metaphors of the warehouse' and the 'metaphors of the wax tablet,' or, in other words, the metaphors of an architectural nature and those linked to the experience of writing and of the book.[13] From our point of view, we can see, however, that the two metaphorical fields converge inasmuch as they both refer to the dimension of space – and of an ordered space at that. In chapter 5 we have seen numerous examples of the book/building. We can observe that the fourteenth-century image cited above – the erudite Dominican friar who is a walking wardrobe, so to speak, of the places of the Scriptures, a living book/library – has a long tradition behind it.

Such notions come from the classical world, from Pliny (*Naturalis historia* 7.24) and Seneca the Elder (*Controversiae* 1.17–19), who speak of men capable of memorizing entire books and even an entire library. Memory is the ideal library, an internal space sheltered from the wear and tear and all the drawbacks of the physical world, a space in which knowledge is conserved, organized, and catalogued so that it is ready for reappropriation. This model is used by Petrarch, and continuously into the sixteenth century and beyond.[14] It is present, for example, in two texts that we have already encountered: in Lambert Schenckel's treatise on memory and, above all, in the *Plutosofia* [*Plutosophia*] (Padua: Paolo Megietti 1592), by the Franciscan Filippo Gesualdo.[15] In the latter an entire chapter full of conceits is dedicated to the virtues, magnitude, and superiority of the 'library of memory' (folios 55v ff.).

In sixteenth-century texts the wealth of metaphorical invention related to memory is extraordinary. The architectural model is clearly dominant: the space of memory seemed to be constructed, controlled, and delimited through the human arts. We have already seen in Camillo and Quicchelberg how the image of the theatre is reinterpreted in its etymological sense: the theatre is that which makes visible, which projects outward, the stage spectacle overseen by memory inside of man. In the early seventeenth century Robert Fludd also teaches how to build theatres of memory, and the illustrations used to depict them have prompted Frances Yates to suggest an association with the Globe Theatre.[16]

Earlier we mentioned Citolini's *Tipocosmia* (1561). The structure of this work is explained in a short work of his entitled *I luoghi* [The places] (1541), in which the encyclopedia of words and things is reduced to a tree: the roots represent the unified dimension of reality, while the opening out of the branches is a visualization of the passage from the general to the particular. The tree allows one to give places to the different arts and sciences, as well as to the structure of the world. As in many other cases, the sources cited in this procedure are the philosophers and rhetoricians of antiquity, but it is highly likely that the actual models are much closer to the author in space and time: Camillo's *topica* and the new dialectics, the line of thought from Rudolf Agricola to Peter Ramus.

Of particular interest to us are the metaphors and models used by Citolini to describe a system of the art of memory that is somewhere between an encyclopedia and a dictionary. We can see in this work how the three-dimensional model of architecture intersects with the two-dimensional models of the tree and the page of the book. The memory techniques are described in terms of an ordered and functional space that is capable of receiving and preserving a rich heritage. The image of the countryside – an ample but disordered and undependable space – is contrasted with that of the house, with its rooms that have been carefully filled with goods: in order to preserve and augment memory, writes Citolini, 'one should imitate a good father of a family who first obtains a house that meets his needs and then goes to buy the necessary things, and thus, he places them in the different rooms of the house according to their diversity, and later he can find everything he might need ready to hand' (*I luoghi* [Venice: Al Segno del Pozzo 1551], folio 25v; the first edition was published in 1541). The building, in which all space is controlled, is thus contrasted with the rich but unreliable dimensions of nature: we have already seen in Francesco Panigarola (chapter 2, p. 78) how the use of places is associated with the garden as opposed to the abundant and dangerous wealth of the forest. Another negative spatial model in Citolini's text is the labyrinth. It is the image of a system that is not accessible to all and that consumes time and energy.

The well-ordered house in which treasures can be placed is what Citolini describes in his *Tipocosmia*. Here, natural memory is represented as a dangerously narrow room. Knowledge risks being piled up in a disorderly fashion; it can become jumbled and even disappear. To avoid this, Citolini attempts to construct a system of artificial memory that uses the entire world as a point of reference. In its structure the text refers back to an architectural model: its cognitive route passes from room to room; in each one the character who acts as guide shows the contents to his interlocutors. The pathway through the places of the edifice thus coincides with those of the writing, and reading, of the *Tipocosmia*. It is a narration (or, rather, a description) of an intellectual journey in which the scholastic and somewhat boring pace of enumeration gradually picks up and takes on the traits of an adventure of initiation. The work is a new world that Citolini – a sort of new Atlas – has to support on his shoulders. At the same time, the work is also the fruit of a long and difficult birth that brings one to the threshold of death; it generates something that has not yet assumed a definitive shape, like bear cubs that the mother licks into shape after giving birth to them (*Tipocosmia*, introduction). These are images that can be found in the most popular emblems and devices. The final destiny of the voyage corresponds, in a certain sense, to a *mise en abyme* of the structure of the text: in the end the characters/visitors find a large book.

Most interesting for our purposes is the play between the point of arrival and the three-dimensional model that the reader/visitor finds in the seventh room. The master of the house invites the whole company 'to see with their own eyes that world already formed that for six days he had painted with words' (p. 546). He then leads them into a large room where 'he showed them an enormous ball in which they could enter; and when they entered, they saw the heavens around them; and in the middle, they saw the earth, and they saw things ordered there in a way more pleasing to the eye of the body than to the eye of the mind' (p. 548). This type of didactic museum leaves the visitors unsatisfied: 'they all finally concluded that these things were more childish than worth knowing. Then the count took them into his study, and he opened an extremely large book and began to show them this new and artificial world of his' (p. 549). Only then was the 'eye of the intellect' satisfied as well as the 'eye of the body.' The type of vision offered by the book allows for an identification with nature and with the principles of things: 'they saw rivers, not just from the outside, but inside in the bowels of the earth.' It seemed to them that they were entering 'the most complete garden that they had ever seen,' where all animals and plants could be found, 'and seeing them in this way, they arrived at understanding not only their names but their true essence and form' (pp. 550–551).[17]

What has made this miracle possible? We may imagine that the great book makes visible the diagram, the tree, that reproduces the relationship between the one and the many, and that this is the true foundation of the pathway through the six rooms of the world. The great book, in turn, is positioned, not in the room of the immense but disappointing didactic globe, but in the little study, in the most secret and personal place in the house. One has to arrive there to find the actual treasure, to find out what makes it possible to pass from the outside to the inside, to see things from the inside.

In the second half of the sixteenth century old and new metaphors blend together. In the *Dialogo nel quale si ragiona del modo di accrescer et conservar la memoria* [Dialogue in which the way of enlarging and conserving memory is discussed] (Venice: Eredi di Marchiò Sessa 1575; originally published in 1562), in which Lodovico Dolce extensively plagiarizes Romberch's treatise on memory, we find familiar images, like the wardrobe and the coffer of memory (folio 90r). In 1579 the work by Dominican friar Cosma Rosselli from Florence is entitled *Thesaurus artificiosae memoriae* [Treasure-house of artificial memory]; its subtitle guarantees the readers that their memory will become 'a sturdy and safe coffer of celestial and earthly things' [rerum terrestrium atque caelestium tenax ac tutum scrinium]. Gesualdo explains that he has called his work *Plutosofia* because artificial memory is the 'treasure and wealth of all human knowledge.' Later on, the traditional image of man as a microcosm or small kingdom prompts the metaphor of 'a public treasury in which the treasures and wealth of the knowledge of things would be faithfully conserved' (*Plutosofia*, folio 1v).

The revised and expanded version of Schenckel's treatise on memory (Strasbourg: Antonius Bertramus 1610), is given the title *Gazophylacium artis memoriae*, that is, the ark or treasure-chamber of the art of memory. After reminding the reader of the old definition whereby 'memory was the treasury that conserved forms perceived by the soul' [memoria est thesaurus specierum ab anima perceptarum et retinaculum] (p. 1), Schenckel cites other commonly used metaphors: 'others call it a warehouse, a treasure-house, and a treasure-room of the sciences' [alii promptuarium, aerarium et gazophylacium vocant scientiarum] (p. 2). A little later he uses the image of the art of memory as 'a sturdy and safe coffer of celestial and earthly things' [rerum terrestrium atque caelestium tenax ac tutum scrinium], which may be a direct citation of Rosselli, but more likely picks up a widely used topos.

2 Collecting and the Art of Memory: Shared Mythology

At the height of the sixteenth century a new reality infuses renewed vitality into the old metaphors of memory. A combination of different factors contributes to this situation: the changes related to the most innovative systems of memory on the one hand, the spread of collecting on the other, and the fact that the two types of experience have in common an anxious desire to know, to master, and to control all of reality. The importance of collecting in the second half of the sixteenth and the seventeenth centuries, its specific characteristics, and its most significant manifestations give consistency and new credibility to the old metaphors of memory like the treasury, the archive, the universal library, and the coffer of knowledge. In a certain sense those metaphors can now be taken literally. Thus, there emerges a play of correspondence and exchange between *intus* [inside] and *extra* [outside] – between inner constructions and external practices, between the invisible and the visible – that exerts an extraordinary fascination in this period.

At the basis of this phenomenon are some myths shared by the art of memory and by collecting. The art of memory in the sixteenth century conserves the traditional basic ingredients (*loci*, order, images), but it also undergoes radical transformations.[18] The renewed popularity of Lullism and the reform of logic related to Ramism open up new horizons. There is a search for a method capable of reproducing the profound rhythm of reality, a method that is able to offer a *clavis universalis*, a guarantee of the possibility of knowing and remembering everything. Many masters of memory are fascinated, moreover, by doctrines of hermetic, cabbalist, and Neoplatonic leanings. The art of memory becomes part of a complex set of procedures whereby one seeks to decipher the dense network of correspondences that link the microcosm to the macrocosm. The hope is to master the powers that come from access to the deepest and most secret levels of reality.

The search for encyclopedic knowledge and the attempt to obtain magical and alchemical powers – to fulfil a profound inner metamorphosis that leads to transformation into divinity – are elements that intersect with the practices of the art of memory in the sixteenth and seventeenth centuries. But, at the same time, they are also part of a cultural context that nourishes the most significant experiences of European collecting.[19] The collection, the single objects it contains, its organization, and its accompanying images all act as guides in an intellectual journey that winds through the vast pathways of the world. Both the collection and the practice of the art of memory, as we have seen in the treatises by Gesualdo and Schenckel, promise to show the way back to the state of Eden, to recover that direct and immediate relation to the knowledge of things that belonged to man before the Fall.[20]

This intellectual climate also gives rise to the tone that characterizes Quicchelberg's work. It is the tone of one who sees himself as part of a grand intellectual adventure to be carried out on a universal scale, and who invites other participants to collaborate and exchange experiences (Quicchelberg asks all those who have 'in some way outfitted museums, theatres, or treasuries' to write to him); and also one who feels a kind of mission: 'in the coming years I hope,' he writes, 'to impel many kings, princes, and lords to construct theatres and treasuries of knowledge.'[21]

Quicchelberg's reference to Camillo's theatre, cited above, is precious evidence of the fact that, at the height of the sixteenth century, collecting and the art of memory not only have shared aspirations, mythologies, and cultural patterns, but in some cases actually interact directly. The examples of such interactions that we will now discuss are by no means exhaustive. The fact that they come from different texts and experiences, however, gives us an idea of the complexity and diffusion of the phenomenom.

3 The Collection as a Theatre of Memory

We have seen that the appearance of Camillo's theatre is invoked by Quicchelberg as an intellectual backdrop for the splendid collection belonging to Albert V, duke of Bavaria. But Camillo's theatre – by virtue of its ideals and the tastes that inspired it, and above all, the logical and rhetorical procedures upon which it is based – also lies behind the precious and highly personalized collection of Francesco I de' Medici in the Stanzino of the Palazzo Vecchio (plate VIII).[22] This can be seen in an analysis of the letters, written in 1570 and 1571, in which Vincenzio Borghini explains to his friend Vasari the invention that he has elaborated and the iconographic program to be followed by the artists who are to decorate the Stanzino:

> The invention, I believe, must conform to the material and the quality of the things to be placed there so that it makes the room elegant and not entirely removed from this purpose; it should actually serve in part as a sign and sort of inventory for finding the things by making the figures and paintings that will be on top of and around the cupboards allude in a certain way to what is preserved inside.[23]

The idea, therefore, is to construct a system of images that functions as a visual catalogue of the collection. In order to activate it one needs a secret key: through his explanation of the *invention*, Borghini is giving that key to Vasari so that he, in turn, can pass it on to the patron who has commissioned it, Francesco de' Medici.

What procedures does Borghini use to complete this project? He is faced with fragmentary and chaotic material: those 'rare and precious things' that Francesco I has chosen from his collection to be placed in the Stanzino. With regard to this material he uses methods and patterns that bring to mind those used by Camillo when he is faced with the *forest* of Italian and Latin literary texts. Camillo's procedures can be described in the following manner:

1 selection of the material, identification of exemplary texts, models to be imitated, that correspond to the ideals of Petrarchism and Ciceronianism;
2 dismantling of the exemplary texts into their deepest structures, in search of the *topical places* that have generated the *artifice* of the texts, and in search of those logical and rhetorical mechanisms from which the beauty of the texts ultimately derives;
3 recomposition of the material obtained within an order that has two characteristics: it must be universal (capable of containing all words and things), and it must not be arbitrary but based on the nature of the things, on the secret structure of the world. The order of the theatre, in its secret dimension, thus makes visible the play between unity and plurality that characterizes the world, and hence acts as a guide to *deification* and to the fulfilment of the alchemical *opus*.

Borghini, too, seeks to create an order that embodies both unity and multiplicity, an order capable of reflecting the 'great chain of being.'[24] The project for the *invention*, he writes, seems 'well linked and chained together, and all the parts correspond not only to the whole, but also to each other.' The figures that embrace each other in the corners of the room, he adds, are intended to represent 'the link and the suitability that each element has with the others, and through which they come to be united and linked together and to form that wondrous chain of nature that preserves the whole' (II, 889). Alchemical notions are also at work here.[25]

But now let us see how Borghini proceeds to realize his project. In the chaotic set of objects in the collection he identifies a basic unifying order (the convergence of nature and art in their formation) that can be divided into a limited number of structures: the four elements, with their different attributes, linked, according to an ancient tradition, with human temperaments. Borghini writes, in reference to the objects in the collection:

> Considering that such things are not all from nature, nor all from art, but both play their part, helping each other: for example, nature provides the diamond or carbuncle or crystal, with other raw and unshaped material, while art polishes, frames, and cuts them, etc.; and for this reason I have decided that all of this invention should be dedicated to nature and art ... and, therefore, in the tondo in the middle on the ceiling will be depicted Nature and she will have Prometheus as her companion ... And since nature principally has as its subject in its operations and effects, the four elements ... and since there are four walls, I would station one on each. (Pp. 886–887)

This basic structure and the constant attention given to maintaining the network of associations and correspondences in each image and in the respective placement of each transforms the places of the Stanzino (the partitions of the vault, the walls, and single compartments) and the images (the paintings and sculptures) into places and images of memory of the collection. A measure of this operation is the plurality of meanings that Borghini gives to the term *luogo* [place]. He writes, for example, that in correspondence with the figure of water painted on the ceiling, 'two statues of women' will be positioned there 'because water is very generative'; the statues are of Venus and Amphitrite, or of another nymph who will have ambergris and coral in her hand, 'and if there are other things that depend on water, this will be their *place*' (p. 887). In the second redaction of the *invention*, he suggests painting a scene of fishing for pearls and coral in the empty space between the statues. Further, underneath Vulcan, writes Borghini, 'strong minerals, like steel and iron, will be positioned, where fire has its principal *place* of operation' (p. 888). The *place*, therefore, marks a dense network of correspondences just as it does in the documents of the Accademia Veneziana (see chapter 1 and chapter 5, p. 188): it is both a physical place (it indicates the part of the room in which certain objects of the collection will be located) and a conceptual place: it thus makes visible the generative process by which the objects came into being and, through that process, their position in the chain of nature and the order of the universe.

An analogous process is used for the images: they are constructed in such a way that they can condense the meanings to be transmitted to the observer as a result of their position in the grand chain of signs that characterizes the Stanzino: 'it is almost a continuous story,' notes a proud Borghini (p. 888).

4 Treatises on Memory and the Model of the Collection

Some experiences of collecting in the sixteenth century, from Bavaria to Florence, seem to rely, therefore, on procedures and models typically used in the art of memory. Now we will see if it is possible to complete a journey in the opposite direction, starting from the treatises on memory.

Let us begin with Citolini's *Tipocosmia*, published in in 1561. This work is based on the classification of knowledge according to the model of the tree. In the introduction Citolini writes that the reduction of a plurality of things under a single heading, 'the world,' is very useful because, 'as you descend the steps,' you will easily find what you need, 'since once you have found the foot of the tree, you can surely find all its branches, leaves, flowers, and fruit' (p. 20). He proceeds by 'reducing ... (as you can see) all of my things to their most general genus, and then I descend from species to species as necessary' (p. 134). The connection between this method and the art of memory is explicitly affirmed in a passage in which memory is positioned among the parts of rhetoric: 'then follows memory, where you will see artificial memory with all of its artifices, by which you see how much these orders of mine can be useful' (p. 532). These are analogous positions to those we looked at in chapter 2.

The model of the tree intersects, as we have noted earlier, with the architectural model. Words and things are grouped in six rooms corresponding to the six days of creation. The interlocutors – and the readers – are guided from room to room so that they can learn and memorize the order of the world. The author's spokesman is Count Collaltino. Citolini ascribes to him a defence of the system of classification that he adopts:

He then showed how useful such divisions can be; however much confusion they create when narrated aloud, they offer so much the more contentment, utility, and convenience to the reader who can enjoy them, well ordered, in his books; he gave the example of someone who has bought a jewel and takes it home but does not put in the courtyard, nor the drawing room, nor the bedroom, in order more easily to find it when necesssary: rather, not content with just having it in the house or the courtyard, he puts it in the study, or his most secret chamber; and, still dissatisfied, he puts it into an iron strongbox, in the most hidden and secret compartment of the box, and then in a jewellery case, and in one of the compartments of the case, and thereafter he has no confusion or difficulty in finding the jewel when he wants it, but rather facility, contentment, and greater security.   (Pp. 290–291)

This passage enacts an exemplary process: the protagonist's progressive search for a suitable place for the jewel is solved by following a course through a series of smaller and smaller places. Among these, the 'study, or his most secret chamber' holds a pre-eminent position, and then the strongbox, its secret compartment, the jewellery case, and its internal compartment. Citolini emphasizes that the multiplicity of the places makes it possible to facilitate and speed the recovery of the single object. This function becomes more important as the number of the objects in play grows. However, the large quantity of things to be handled is an undeniably positive aspect, and it is a point of pride, as he reiterates with a somewhat ironic comparison in the passage that follows the previous citation:

the poor man, since he has only one garment, spends much less time looking for his clothes than the rich man who searches for one suit among the many that he owns; but there is no one who does not desire rather the great toil of the rich man than the little toil of the poor man; in the same manner, one has much more to be happy for in the small difficulty of finding things held in so much abundance than for much ease in a great scarcity of things.[26]   (P. 291)

Citolini's system of memory thus brings collecting into play in the name of the ordering and classification of the material: they have to be as well articulated as the material is valuable and important. Here, too, as in Borghini's text, the term *luogo* takes on multiple meanings. It stands for both the physical place (of the palace, or single room, or single piece of furniture) and the mental place of the art of memory. Here we are very far removed, however, from the rich variations on mythological themes that characterize Camillo's theatre and Borghini's *invention*: the place of memory tends to correspond to the topical place. It marks, that is, a determinate point, a determinate division in the tree of sciences. It closely correponds, moreover, to the type of art of memory that Citolini uses. What remains constant is precisely the system of references back and forth between collecting and the art of memory, the mirroring of their relative experiences in the name of effective cataloguing and collocation of the material.

This problem becomes the point of departure for a passage in the manuscript treatise *Arte della memoria locale* [The art of local memory], written by Agostino Del Riccio, a Dominican friar from Florence, in 1595. After inviting practitioners of the art of memory to choose the places according to their own individual 'caprice,' and to keep them, once chosen, stationary and distinct from one another, Fra Agostino writes:

> do as wealthy and powerful kings do with the many rooms in their palaces; in one room there will be antiques, in another tapestries, in another the silverware, in another the jewels, in another weapons of warfare, both offensive and defensive, in other rooms the provisions used to maintain the armies, etc. This is what you must do if you wish to be universal in your knowledge: have many rooms in which to place sermons, speeches, concepts, sayings, histories, and whatever you choose to profess.   (Florence, Biblioteca Nazionale, cod. Magl. II, 1, 13, folio 13v)

Clearly we have here the elaboration of the classical image of memory as a *thesaurus eloquentiae*. For a friar who lived at the end of the sixteenth century, the problem is that of memorizing conceits, maxims, and everything that will be useful in preaching. It is interesting that even a traditional system of memory like Del Riccio's, so alien to the encyclopedic aspirations that characterize his contemporaries, at a certain point describes itself and represents its own procedures through a comparison to collecting. As in Citolini, the theme of ordered arrangement intersects with an emphasis on the abundance and wealth of the material ('if you wish to be universal,' writes Del Riccio). The *loci* of memory are superimposed on the rooms of royal palaces. A clear division of material to be remembered – so as to have it ready for any rhetorical need – suggests the kind of correspondence between a room and the type of its contents that is to be found in an ideal and very rich collection. Here the complicated organizational structure of the *Wunderkammer* has given place to the simpler and more rational division of objects through classification by type.

We have already seen that Schenckel, in his list of the most common

55 The *places* of memory arranged in a city, from Johannes Romberch,
Congestorium artificiosae memoriae (Venice: Melchiorre Sessa 1553)

metaphors for memory, cites treasure, the treasure-room, and the treasury. Moreover, the human body, seen as a microcosm, is compared to a
perfect edifice, to a city, to a small kingdom, all perfectly arranged and
organized, as Gesualdo writes in *Plutosofia* (folio 152r–v). In Schenckel's
treatise this extension of the spatial model – from the single palace to
the entire urban context (figure 55) – brings about a renewal of and
variation on the theme which sees a correspondence between the art of
memory and the collection because both have the problem of ordering
their material. Schenckel invites his readers to construct an ordered city
of knowledge in their memories:

> once you have formed the places, you must give each subject matter a
> house or quarter, as, for example, a house for grammar, a house for rheto-

56 The house of grammar, a woodcut attributed to Voghterr (1548), reproduced in R. van Marle, *Iconographie de l'art profane au Moyen Age et à la
Renaissance* (New York: Hacker Art Books 1971)

ric, for dialectics, etc. ... a house for the Bible ... a house for words, a house
for sacred conceits, a house for profane ones, a house for sermons, a house
for holy days, a house for controversies, and, to say it in a word, every
subject should be entrusted to determined quarters and houses, just as in a
well-ordered city. If, in fact, someone wanted to buy or sell books, cloth,
wine, meat, etc., he would head towards those houses in which those things
are bought and sold.[27] (*Gazophylacium artis memoriae* [Treasure-house
of the art of memory], 119–120)[27]

These are elements linked to the tradition and the iconography of an art
of memory that is animated by pedagogy (as, for example, in the *house
of grammar*; figure 56).[28] At the same time, the image of the well-ordered

city and its territory divided into places that respond to different needs reminds us of the projects for utopian, ideal cities (Anton Francesco Doni's *Mondo savio/pazzo* [Sagacious/crazy world], for example). At any rate, redesigning the city often means, in the sixteenth-century utopia, redesigning the encyclopedia.[29]

In another passage Schenckel explains how to use the art of memory to dictate letters. According to the tradition the composition of a written text or the so-called improvisation of an oral discourse depends on the use of a memorized repertory. Schenckel invites his readers to arrange epistolary formulas in the rooms of memory appositely prepared for them, and to position in each of them the images suitable for memorizing the inventoried material. When a letter is to be dictated, one has only to retrace the path through the rooms and recover what is needed for it. 'Once we have returned to the museum,' writes Schenckel, 'we will begin with the first place, with the first image' [Reversi in musaeum, a prima incipiemus, ex primo loco] (*Gazophylacium artis memoriae*, p. 134); the use of the word *museum* is indicative of the cultural model that spontaneously comes into play.[30]

5 Dolls and Wax Images

We have seen the art of memory and collecting establish a series of reciprocal connections in terms of relationships between internal and external reality; a correspondence is created, in fact, between the *loci*, the order, and all the *imagines* that mnemonics constructs in the interior space of memory, on the one hand, and the places, the organization, and the objects in the collection positioned in physical space, on the other.

Even this distinction, however, is to some extent flawed. The art of memory freely adopts everything which could be useful in the construction of effective internal images capable of making a lasting impression. For this reason it borrows from the figurative arts. But, at times, it does even more: it actually builds images to be projected into the spaces of the mind. There are examples in the *Thesaurus artificiosae memoriae* by the Dominican Cosma Rosselli (Venice: Antonio Padovano 1579). For example, in the chapter in which he gives useful recommendations for the formation of images, he notes that 'many have experimented and found that it is very useful to construct images for memory out of wax or other similar material' (folio 132r).[31]

Quicchelberg offers similar advice about collecting. He observes that a good collection should have a rich assortment of clothes from different peoples and that the dolls commonly exchanged as gifts by queens and princesses can be used carry out an analogous function, that is, as documentation and as images of memory. It is necessary, he claims, to have dolls, 'similar to those that queens and princesses commonly send to one another, in order to examine carefully the singular clothes of other nations. Thanks to these dolls, one can also observe the customs of different peoples which manifest themselves in precise detail in the dolls: how they dress, especially the nobility, at home and in public, at weddings or funerals.'[32]

Treatises on memory often recommend using as images of memory the clothes of other nations or the garments belonging to various trades, professions, ages, and social conditions: there are richly illustrated repertories that can easily be used for this purpose. The passage from Quicchelberg gives us an example of how that gallery of internal images, perhaps modelled on book illustrations, can be translated into a delightful collection of objects: in this case, dolls furnished with extraordinary wardrobes that provide an effective encyclopedia of customs. Quicchelberg continues:

> It happens that the daughters of princes conserve, for the purposes of memory and in miniature form, the national dress that they are accustomed to wear. For example, Mary and Mary Maximiliana, the daughters of Lady Anne, duchess of Bavaria, and Albert [Albert V, duke of Bavaria], her dear husband, had hundreds of them, together with a great deal of tiny, silver furniture; and their Duchess mother's granddaughters had even more of them ...; these things were arranged according to an order that reflected the tasks and the events of each place in such a way that whoever looked at the single objects seemed to know perfectly all the rooms of a royal palace, the ceremonies, and the customs of the court.[33]

The rich collection of clothes and toys – 'hundreds of them' – is thus transformed into a book of manners, a working repertory, easily memorizable, of court etiquette.

6 The *Wunderkammer* and the Internal Castle

In some sixteenth-century systems of memory there is a component of magic and alchemy that is linked, in turn, to the search for profound inner transformation and divine metamorphosis. In figures such as

Giulio Camillo and Giordano Bruno this aspect takes on connotations hard to contain within models of religious orthodoxy. In other masters of memory the work that mnemonics develops in the imagination is explicitly oriented to the goals of devotion, prayer, and the spiritual ascent to God, all the way to the heights of mystical ecstasy.[34] This is part of a long tradition that began in the Middle Ages and culminates in its most important and best-known formulation in the Spiritual Exercises of Saint Ignatius Loyola.[35] We have seen some examples of this tradition in previous chapters: in Federico Borromeo (chapter 2, p. 79) or in sixteenth- and seventeenth-century manuals in which mnemonics and the methods of preaching are closely related (chapter 4, p. 174). Techniques of memory and techniques of devotion and of guidance for mystical experiences have been blended together throughout the centuries. With this in mind, a passage from the *Castillo interior* [Interior castle], written by Saint Teresa of Avila in 1577, takes on new meaning: it deals with the way in which Saint Teresa tries to describe the culminating moment of the mystical experience to her companions.[36] She claims to have received favours from God that were

> deeply imprinted in the most intimate part of the soul; they cannot be expressed but cannot be forgotten.
>
> How can they be remembered if no image is seen and the powers of the soul do not comprehend them? I, too, do not understand this ... I wish I could find some suitable comparison to illustrate what I say, yet none seems to suit the purpose. Let us, however, use this one.
>
> You enter into the rooms of a king or great lord, which I believe they call the treasure-chambers, where there are countless kinds of crystal and porcelain vesels and other things so arranged that they are seen immediately upon entering. Once I was brought to a room like this in the house of the duchess of Alba where, while I was on a journey, my superiors ordered me to stay because of this lady's insistence. I was amazed on entering and, wondering what gain could be had from that conglomeration of things, I saw that so many different kinds of objects could serve to praise the Lord. But now I am very happy when I realize how that experience has helped me in my present circumstance. Although I was in that room for a while, there was so much there to see that I soon forgot it all; none of those pieces has remained in my memory any more than if I had never seen them, nor would I know how to explain what they were like. I can only say that I remember seeing them.
>
> The same is true here. The soul has become one with God and is placed in this room of the empyreal heaven that we must have inside ourselves.

57 Noah guiding the animals into the ark, from Athanasius Kircher, *Arca Noe*
   (Amsterdam: Janssonius 1675)

God, she continues, allows the soul to have a glance, 'and after it returns to itself, the soul is left with that impression of the grandeurs that it saw, but it cannot describe any of them.'[37] The image of the princely treasure-chamber – more specifically a *Wunderkammer* – is thus associated with both the mystical experience and the problem of memory. Faced with the phantasmagoric wealth of the duchess of Alba's collection, memory is subjected to a gruelling trial, and, indeed, it succumbs. It confesses its failure just as the soul, in an encounter with God in the most secret chamber of its 'interior castle,' is able to retain only a confused impression, so strong that it cannot be expressed, or remembered – or forgotten. At the same time, however, the treasure-chamber and the splendid collection that she had seen long ago become for Saint Teresa both a metaphor and the image of memory of an experience that cannot otherwise be expressed or remembered. In the culminating moment of the mystical experience the image of the castle is not enough; it is a particular place full of treasures and wonders – the collection – that intervenes to help *express* human interiority, the inner realm of the soul.[38]

But it is not only here, in Saint Teresa's extraordinary story, that the model of the collection is used to describe and give shape to the spaces of the inner world. Another example is found in the letters of that singular seventeenth-century figure, the Jesuit Athanasius Kircher (1602–1680), author, among other things, of a reconstruction of Noah's ark that transforms it into a universal system of memory (figure 57), and organizer of a grand encyclopedic museum.[39] In a letter sent to Kircher on 9 September 1672, his fellow-Jesuit and student Eusebius Truchses writes:

> I find this otherwise delicious crater of Naples little to my liking because I see myself in a much more esteemed place, that is, in the memory of Your Reverence; it is a gallery in which the most rare and exquisite things of the world are conserved, and I begin to swell with pride when I see that I have been put here.   (Rome, Pontificia Università Gregoriana, *Kircher*, cod. 565 [XI], folio 292r)

I am grateful to Father Eusebius for having written these words, and to Paula Findlen for having made me aware of them: they allow me, in a certain sense, to conclude this journey. We have seen how literary texts, especially Ariosto's and Tasso's poems, are perceived as galleries, as collections. We have used different examples to show how collecting and the art of memory tend to mirror one another. Father Eusebius' letter shows us how, a century later, memory itself and the internal spaces inhabited by it have become a gallery. They have been transformed into a collection of statues. Kircher is also an expert designer of wonderful optical machines. We can thus say that the letter from his student shows us how the play of viewpoints, of diffraction and of reflection between places and images of different natures, has become more and more polyhedric and, at the same time, closed unto itself.

In the same period in which the image of the gallery of the soul is so widespread that it is used even in private correspondence, there are also signs of a restive dissent. 'Memory does not possess a silent gallery of variable paintings,' writes Giovanni Ciampoli (1589–1643), poet and friend of Galileo, protector of Campanella (philosopher, poet, and utopian writer), secretary to Pope Urban VIII, but soon to fall into disgrace.[40] 'They are not printed there; they are not fixed there. It is a population of living *simulacra*; they live there noisily, untamed, in constant uproar.' This polemic is directed against an Aristotelian tradition that he sees still operating in the mentality of his contemporaries; the idea of memory as wax upon which seals can be impressed has generated the image of the mind as a gallery of paintings. This perspective appears to Ciampoli to be reductive and inadequate because it condemns the mind to a purely passive role. He prefers a distinction between a theatre and a prison-house of memory. In the prison-house perceptible images are amassed and deposited; but in the small space of the theatre of memory they are called forth by the mind to reanimate themselves:

> On first entering, the watchful mind sees that they are peaceful; then new troops of foreign *phantasmata* arrive; the former ones, once they have had their audience, retire to the cells of memory in which they rest unseen, waiting for their turn to be led back to the operations of the theatre.

But the borders between the confused mass in the prison and the illuminated scene of the theatre are not always clear-cut and under control:

> But during slumber, when the guards are sleeping, they boldly burst out. What commotion is made by these unguarded phantoms inside our heads without our consent? They sing, they sigh, they dance, they war, they plunder the altars, they violate the gods, without distinction, without law, recklessly, unregulated, furiously, surpassing the works of nature with the inventions of dreams; they show us a world gone mad with the impossibilities of disproportion.

At the same time that Ciampoli distances himself from the tradition, he also uses its topical images, beginning with architectural notions (theatre, prison-house, gallery), either to negate them or to place them in a new context. But, of course, the point of view has changed: the review of the disorderly, vital, and creative activities to which the phantoms of our mind dedicate themselves during sleep seems to suggest that the secrets of memory can be revealed by scrutinizing the dark world of dreams rather than by creating an orderly gallery of images.

Notes

Preface

1 Girolamo Muzio, *Lettere* (Florence: Bartolomeo Sermartelli 1590; reprint, Bologna: Forni 1985), pp. 66–67, letter to Francesco Calvo.

2 The play in Italian on the words *penne* [wings] and *pene* [sorrows] is lost in the English translation.

3 For further bibliographical information on Giulio Camillo, see Lina, Bolzoni, *Il teatro della memoria: studi su Giulio Camillo* (Padua: Liviana 1984); Corrado Bologna, 'Il "theatro" segreto di Giulio Camillo: l'Urtext ritrovato,' *Venezia Cinquecento: studi di storia dell'arte e della cultura* 1, no. 2 (1991): 217–271; Bologna, *Tradizione e fortuna dei classici italiani* (Torino: Einaudi 1993), I, 19 ff.

4 Carlo Dionisotti, *Geografia e storia della letteratura italiana* (Torino: Einaudi 1967); Amedeo Quondam, 'Il letterato in tipografia,' in *Letteratura italiana* (Torino: Einaudi 1983), II, 555–686; Giancarlo Mazzacurati, *Il Rinascimento dei moderni: la crisi culturale del XVI secolo e la negazione delle origini* (Bologna: Il Mulino 1985); Andrea Battistini, and Ezio Raimondi, *Le figure della retorica: una storia letteraria italiana* (Torino: Einaudi 1990), pp. 115 ff.; Paolo Trovato, *Con ogni diligenza corretto: la stampa e le revisioni editoriali dei testi letterari italiani (1470–1570)* (Bologna: Il Mulino 1991); Brian Richardson, *Print Culture in Renaissance Italy. The Editor and the Vernacular Text 1470–1600* (Cambridge: Cambridge University Press 1994).

5 On the theory of *ut pictura poesis*, see Rensselaer W. Lee, *Ut pictura poesis: A Humanistic Theory of Painting* (New York: Norton 1967). On hieroglyphics, see *Hiéroglyphes, languages chiffrés, sens mystérieux au XVIIe siècle*, monographic issue of *XVIIe siècle* 40, no. 1 (1988). On the device and the emblem, see Mario Praz, *Studi sul concettismo* (Florence: Sansoni 1946); Praz, *Studies in Seventeenth-Century Imagery*, 2nd ed. (Rome: Edizioni di Storia e Lettera-

tura 1964); Robert J. Clements, *Picta poësis: Literary and Humanistic Theory in Renaissance Emblem Books* (Rome: Edizioni di Storia e Letteratura 1960); Robert Klein, 'La théorie de l'expression figurée dans les traités italiens sur les "imprese" (1555–1612),' in *La forme et l'intelligible* (Paris: Gallimard 1970), (English translation, 'The Theory of Figurative Expression in Italian Treatises on the *Impresa*,' in *Form and Meaning*, trans. M. Jay and L. Wieseltier (New York: Viking 1979). On the construction of images in the sixteenth century and its relation to literature, see Ernst H. Gombrich, *Symbolic Images: Studies in the Art of the Renaissance* (London: Phaidon 1972); Carlo Ossola, *L'autunno del Rinascimento. Idea del tempio dell'arte nell'ultimo Rinascimento* (Florence: Olschki 1971); Andrea Gareffi and Gennaro Savarese, *La letteratura delle immagini nel Cinquecento* (Rome: Bulzoni 1980; Donald D. Gordon, *The Renaissance Imagination* (Berkeley/Los Angeles: University of California Press 1975); Giovanni Pozzi, *Sull'orlo del 'visibile parlare'* (Milan: Adelphi 1993); Marc Fumaroli, *L'école du silence: le sentiment des images au XVIIe siècle* (Paris: Flammarion 1994). Also important are Michael Baxandall's studies on the modalities of the reception of images; see his *Painting and Experience in Fifteenth Century Italy: A Primer in the Social History of Pictorial Style* (Oxford / New York: Oxford University Press 1972).

6 On this interpretation of classical imitation, see Terence Cave, *The Cornucopian Text: Problems of Writing in the French Renaissance* (Oxford: Clarendon Press 1979); Thomas M. Greene, *The Light in Troy: Imitation and Discovery in Renaissance Poetry* (New Haven, Conn.: Yale University Press 1982); Greene, *The Vulnerable Text: Essays on Renaissance Literature* (New York: Columbia University Press 1986).

7 *Orlando furioso* 460.12.5–7: 'e quei che per guidarci ai rivi ascrei / mostra piano e più breve altro camino, / Iulio Camillo' [And he who, to guide us to the Ascrean banks / shows us another road, level and shorter, / Giulio Camillo']; Torquato Tasso, *La Cavaletta overo de la poesia toscana*, in *Dialoghi*, ed. E. Raimondi (Florence: Sansoni 1958), II, 2, pp. 615–682, especially pp. 662–663.

8 See Roland Barthes's elegant definition of topical places in *L'ancienne rhétorique* (Paris 1970.) See also: 'Testi umanistici su la retorica,' *Archivio di filosofia* (Rome/Milan), 23 (1953): 3; *Topik: Beiträge zur interdisziplinaren Diskussion*, ed. D. Breuer and H. Schanze (Munich 1981); Wilhelm Schmidt-Biggeman, *Topica universalis: Eine Modellgeschichte humanistischer und barocker Wissenschaft* (Hamburg 1983).

9 The printed work in which Camillo describes the theatre is *L'idea del theatro* [The idea of the theatre], published posthumously in 1550. See *L'idea del theatro*, ed. L. Bolzoni (Palermo: Sellerio 1991).

10 Paolo Rossi, *Clavis universalis: Arti della memoria e logica combinatoria da*

Lullo a Leibniz, (Milan/Naples: Ricciardi 1960); Frances A. Yates, *The Art of Memory* (London: Routledge and Kegan Paul 1966); Mary Carruthers, *The Book of Memory: A Study of Memory in Medieval Culture* (Cambridge: Cambridge University Press 1990). See also *La fabbrica del pensiero: Dall'arte della memoria alle neuroscienze* (Milan: Electa 1989) especially 16–65, English translation, *The Enchanted Loom: Chapters in the History of Neuroscience* (New York: Oxford University Press 1991); *La cultura della memoria*, ed. L. Bolzoni and P. Corsi (Bologna: Il Mulino 1992); *Ars memorativa: Zur kulturgeschichtlichen Bedeutung der Gedächtniskunst 1400–1750*, ed. J.J. Berns and W. Neuber (Tübingen: Max Niemeyer 1993).

11 Marshall McLuhan, *The Gutenberg Galaxy: The Making of Typographic Man* (Toronto: University of Toronto Press 1962); Walter J. Ong, *Orality and Literacy: The Technologizing of the Word* (London / New York: Methuen 1982). See also Elizabeth L. Eisenstein, *The Press as an Agent of Change: Communications and Cultural Transformations in Early-Modern Europe* (London: Cambridge University Press 1979); the bibliography in Quondam, 'Il letterato in tipografia'; Roger Chartier, *L'ordre des livres: Lecteurs, auteurs, bibliothèques en Europe entre XIV et XVIII siècle* (Aix-en-Provence: Alinea 1992), English translation, *The Order of Books: Readers, Authors and Libraries in Europe between the Fourteenth and Eighteenth Centuries* (Stanford, Calif.: Stanford University Press 1994).

12 Eric A. Havelock, *Preface to Plato* (Cambridge, Mass.: Harvard University Press 1963); Jean Pierre Vernant, *Mythe et pensée chez les Grecs: Êtudes de psychologie historique* (Paris: Maspero 1965), English translation, *Myth and Thought among the Greeks* (London: Routledge and Kegan Paul 1983); Jesper Svenbro, *La parola e il marmo: Alle origini della poetica greca* (Torino: Boringhieri 1984).

13 See chapter 3, p. 277, n. 2.

1 Making Knowledge Visible: The Accademia Veneziana

1 See Pietro Pagan, 'Sulla Accademia "Venetiana" o della "Fama,"' *Atti dell'Istituto Veneto di scienze, lettere ed arti* 132 (1973): 359–392; Paul Rose, 'The Accademia Venetiana: Science and Culture in Renaissance Venice,' *Studi veneziani* 11 (1969): 191–242; Lina Bolzoni, 'L'Accademia Veneziana: Splendore e decadenza di una utopia enciclopedica,' in *Università, Accademie e Società scientifiche in Italia e in Germania dal Cinquecento al Settecento*, ed. L. Boehm and E. Raimondi (Bologna: Il Mulino 1981), 117–167; Bolzoni, 'Rendere visibile il sapere: L'Accademia Veneziana fra modernità e utopia,' in *Italian Academies of the Sixteenth Century*, ed.

D.S. Chambers and F. Quiviger (London: Warburg Institute 1995), 61–78; Manfredo Tafuri, *Venezia e il Rinascimento: Religione, scienza, architettura* (Torino: Einaudi 1985), pp. 172–184; Barbara Marx, 'Die Stadt als Buch: Anmerkungen zur Academia Venetiana und zu Francesco Sansovino,' *Studi: Schriftenreihe des Deutschen Studienzentrums in Venedig* 9 (1993): 223–260; *La ragione e l'arte. Torquato Tasso e la Repubblica Veneta*, ed. G. Da Pozzo (Venice: Il cardo 1995).

2 Angelo Stella, 'Federico Badoer' [entry], in *Dizionario biografico degli italiani* (Rome: Istituto dell'Enciclopedia italiana 1963–), V, 106–108.

3 See Bernardino Pino, *Della nuova scielta di lettere di diversi nobilissimi huomini, et eccellentissimi ingegni* (Venice: Andrea Muschio 1582), I, 124, II, 99–109, 206–214; Claudio Tolomei, *Lettere* (Venice: Domenico and Cornelio Nicolini 1559), VII, folios 275r, 288v; Pietro Bembo, *Lettere* in *Opere* (Milan: Editrice dei Classici italiani 1809), V, 368–371; Pietro Aretino, *Lettere* (Paris: Matteo il Maestro 1609), folios 38v, 223r.

4 Niccolò Franco, *Le pistole volgari* (Venice: Antonio Gardane 1542), folio 64r; Franco also dedicated his *Dialoghi piacevoli* to Badoer; Anton Francesco Doni, *I marmi*, ed. E. Chiorboli (Bari: Laterza 1928), I, 68–69; in 1558 Doni dedicated his *Libraria* to Badoer and recalled having been helped by him in 1544. Also dedicated to Badoer is Ludovico Dolce's *Lettere di diversi eccellentissimi huomini* (Venice: Giolito 1554).

5 Francesco Sansovino, *Lettere sopra le diece giornate del Decamerone di Boccaccio* (Venice: Costantini 1543), folio 40v. The term *carnivalesque* is used here with reference to M.M. Bakhtin's *Rabelais and His World* (Bloomington: Indiana University Press 1984). These pages from Sansovino bring to mind an unpublished poem that was read at the Neapolitan Accademia del Lauro sometime in the mid-sixteenth century: masks, it says, allow women to reclaim the free love typical of the first age of the world; see Nicola Badaloni, 'Vita religiosa e letteraria tra Riforma e Controriforma,' in *Letteratura italiana: Storia e testi* (Bari: Laterza 1973), IV, part 2, 457–484. Other examples of the connection between the golden age and sexual freedom in the sixteenth century are reported by Carlo Ginzburg in 'Montaigne, Cannibals, and Grottoes,' *History and Anthropology* 6, nos. 2–3 (1993): 125–155.

6 Antonio Brucioli, *Dialoghi della morale philosophia* (Venice: Francesco Brucioli e fratelli 1544), folio 36r. On the various editions of the *Dialoghi*, see Giorgio Spini, 'Bibliografia delle opere di Antonio Brucioli,' *La bibliofilia* 42 (1940): 129–180. On the interlocutors of the *Dialoghi*, see Carlo Dionisotti, 'Tiziano e la letteratura,' *Lettere italiane* 28 (1976): 401–409.

7 Andrea Calmo, *Le lettere*, ed. by V. Rossi (Torino: Loescher 1888),

pp. 146–147; see also Ludovico Zorzi, 'Andrea Calmo' [entry], *Dizionario biografico degli italiani*, XVI, 775–781.

8 Girolamo Tiraboschi, *Storia della letteratura italiana* (Venice: Fontana 1824), VII, part 1, 232–236, VII, part 5, 1547.

9 Pietro Aretino, *Lettere*, ed. F. Flora (Milan: Mondadori 1960), p. 351; on Doni, see n. 4; Girolamo Parabosco, *I diporti* (London: Poggiali 1795), p. 7 (the date of publication of the first edition is unknown; the second was published in 1552).

10 See 'Capitoli e conventioni fatte e sottoscritte di propria mano da alcuni de' signori academici, a 13 d'agosto 1559,' in Rose, 'The Accademia Venetiana,' pp. 222–224. On this literary environment, see Edoardo Taddeo, *Il manierismo letterario e i lirici veneziani del tardo Cinquecento* (Rome: Bulzoni 1974); Giovanni Pozzi, *La parola dipinta* (Milan: Adelphi 1981), pp. 180–189; Francesco Erspamer, 'Petrarchismo e manierismo nella lirica del secondo Cinquecento,' *Storia della cultura veneta* (Vicenza: Neri Pozza 1983, IV, 189–222.

11 'Supplica ai Procuratori di San Marco, 12 luglio 1560,' in Rose, 'The Accademia Venetiana,' pp. 228–233 (the passage cited is on 229).

12 In 'Accordo della Ditta e Fratelli co'l Tasso,' reprinted in Antoine-Auguste Renouard, *Annales de l'imprimerie des Alde, ou histoire des trois Manuce et de leurs éditions*, 3rd ed. (Paris: Jules Renouard 1834), p. 278; there were provisions not only for the father's stipend, but also for the lodging and protection of his son Torquato, even if he chose not to participate in the Academy's projects.

13 Bernardo Tasso, *Lettere* (Padua: Giuseppe Comino 1733), II, 458.

14 Carlo Sigonio, *Opere* (Milan: Stamperia Palatina 1737), p. 999.

15 Bernardo Tasso, *Lettere*, II, 459.

16 The 'Supplica alla Serenissima Signoria' (Manchester, John Rylands Library, folios unnumbered) states: 'We again proffer our desire to guide those young men who work in the chancellery *down the easy and speedy path* to true and perfect mastery of the Latin and Italian languages.'

17 See Ezio Raimondi's introduction to *Università, Accademie e Società scientifiche*, ed. Boehm and Raimondi, pp. 14–15.

18 Bernardo Tasso, *Lettere*, II, 359–360, and 'Concessione dell'eccelso Consiglio di Dieci all'Accademia, a dí ultimo di maggio 1560,' in Renouard, *Annales*, p. 279.

19 On Aldo Manuzio [Aldus Manutius] see Martin Lowry, *The World of Aldus Manutius: Business and Scholarship in Renaissance Venice* (Oxford: Blackwell 1979); Carlo Dionisotti, *Aldo Manuzio: Umanista e editore* (Milan:

Il polifilo 1995). On Paolo Manuzio [Paulus Manutius] and Badoer, see
Ester Pastorello, *L'epistolario manuziano: Inventario cronologico-analitico
1483–1597* (Florence: Olschki 1957); Pastorello, *Inedita manutiana: 1502–
1597. Appendice all'epistolario* (Florence: Olschki 1960). See also Paul
Grendler, *The Roman Inquisition and Venetian Press* (Princeton: Princeton
University Press 1977), especially pp. 23–24.

20 Bernardo Tasso, *Lettere*, II, 359–360.

21 On Francesco Giorgio Veneto, see Cesare Vasoli, *Profezia e ragione. Studi
sulla cultura del Cinquecento e del Seicento* (Naples: Guida 1974), pp. 129–403.
'I too believe that Cabal of his, on which we have debated at length,' writes
Bembo to the archbishop of Salerno in 1533, 'is very suspect and danger-
ous': Pietro Bembo, *Lettere, Opere* (Milan: Editrice dei Classici italiani 1809),
V, part 1, 174).

22 Amedeo Quondam, 'Nascita della grammatica,' *Alfabetismo e cultura scritta
nella storia della società italiana*, ed. A. Petrucci, (Perugia: Università degli
studi 1978), p. 275; Carlo Dionisotti, 'Tradizione classica e
volgarizzamenti,' *Geografia e storia della letteratura italiana* (Torino: Einaudi
1967), pp. 140 ff.; *Libri, editori e pubblico nell'Europa moderna: Guida storica e
critica*, ed. A. Petrucci (Bari: Laterza 1977).

23 For example, there is also a promise of '*Pymander* and *Asclepius* by
[Hermes] Mercurius Trismegistus, translated from the Greek,' with an
'erudite and lengthy commentary, from which one can understand all that
this amazing author has taken from Mosaic doctrine and knowledge: and
how also all of the ancient theology of Pythagoras, Eudoxus, Plato, and
others derived from him': *Somma delle opere che in tutte le scienze et arti più
nobili et in varie lingue ha da mandare in luce l'Accademia Venetiana, parte
nuove et non più stampate, parte con fidelissime tradottioni, giudiciose correttioni
ed utilissime annotationi riformate* [Compendium of the works of all the most
noble sciences and arts and various languages that are to be brought out
into the light by the Accademia Veneziana; in part new, and in part never
before printed, in part with faithful translations, judicious and useful
corrections, and reformulated annotations] (Venice: Accademia Veneziana
1558), folio 10r. I have consulted the copy in the Biblioteca del Seminario
Arcivescovile di Udine. On the rebirth of hermetism in the fifteenth and
sixteenth centuries, see Eugenio Garin, *Ermetismo del Rinascimento* (Rome:
Editori Riuniti 1988).

24 *Somma della opere*, folios 29r, 28r, 28v.

25 See Vittorio Cian's review of Pierre de Nolhac, 'Fac-similes de l'écriture de
Pétrarque et Appendices au "Canzoniere" autographe avec des notes sur

la bibliothèque de Pétrarque,' *Mélanges d'archéologie et d'histoire publiées par l'Ecole Française de Rome* 8 (1887): 1, in *Giornale storico della letteratura italiana* 5 (1887): 441.

26 *Somma della opere*, folio 29r.

27 Ibid.

28 Modena, Biblioteca Estense, Cod. Alpha M.8.12 (It. 729), folios 1r–49v (the cited passages are on folios 29v, 47r). This manuscript is mentioned by Aldo Vallone *Aspetti dell'esegesi dantesca nei secoli XVI e XVII* (Lecce: Milella 1966), 11, n. 7. The date of 1588 that Vallone gives to this manuscript is in conflict with the praise of the Academy on folio 2v. Therefore, the manuscript should be dated between 1557 and 1561.

29 See Cesare Vasoli, 'Osservazioni su alcuni scritti "religiosi" di Giulio Camillo,' in 'Giulio Camillo Delminio e altri autori,' *Quaderni utinensi* 3, nos. 5–6 (1985): 11–35.

30 Celio Magno, *Prefatione sopra il Petrarca*, in Taddeo, *Il manierismo letterario*, pp. 199–244.

31 Bernardo Tasso, *Ragionamento della poesia*, *Lettere*, II, 513–523 (the passage cited is on p. 521); a more recent edition has been published *Trattati di poetica e retorica del Cinquecento*, ed. B. Weinberg (Bari: Laterza 1970), II, 567–584.

32 *Instrumento di deputatione di Federico Badoer*, Accademia Veneziana, Venice, folio 1v. This document is dated 30 December 1560.

33 Paolo Manuzio, *Lettere volgari* (Venice: Manuzio 1560), pp. 38–39.

34 See Antonio Foscari and Manfredo Tafuri, *L'armonia e i conflitti: La chiesa di San Francesco della Vigna nella Venezia del '500* (Torino: Einaudi 1983).

35 See Lina Bolzoni, *L'universo dei poemi possibili: Studi su Francesco Patrizi da Cherso* (Rome: Bulzoni 1980), pp. 83–85. On Rudolf Agricola and the renewal of rhetoric, see n. 43 below.

36 Marcantonio Luigini, *Fabrica intellectualis* (Padua: Grazioso Percacino 1560). On Luigi Francesco and Marcantonio Luigini, see Gian Giuseppe Liruti, *Notizie delle vite ed opere scritte da i letterati del Friuli* (Venice: Modesto Fenzo 1762), II, 133–158. On their relations with Giulio Camillo, see Lina Bolzoni, *Il teatro della memoria: studi su Giulio Camillo* (Padua: Liviana 1984), pp. 22–23. On Federico Luigini's interest in Erasmus, see Silvano Cavazza, 'Inquisizione e libri proibiti in Friuli e a Gorizia tra Cinquecento e Seicento,' *Studi goriziani* 43 (1976): 29–80, especially p. 63; Silvana Seidel Menchi, *Erasmo in Italia: 1520–1580* (Torino: Bollati Boringhieri 1987), pp. 319, 397, 456.

37 Paolo Rossi, *Clavis universalis: Arti della memoria e logica combinatoria da Lullo a Leibniz* (Milan / Naples: Ricciardi 1960); Cesare Vasoli, *L'enciclopedismo del Seicento* (Naples: Bibliopolis 1978).

38 *Somma delle opere*, folios 23r, 30v.

39 Ibid., folio 24r.

40 See n. 30 above.

41 *Somma delle opere*, folio 24v.

42 'Lettere agli studiosi delle buone arti,' in Rose, 'The Accademia Venetiana,' pp. 227–228.

43 Walter J. Ong, *Ramus: Method and the Decay of Dialogue. From the Art of Discourse to the Art of Reason* (Cambridge, Mass.: Harvard University Press 1958); Ong, *Interfaces of the Word* (Ithaca, NY: Cornell University Press 1977); Cesare Vasoli, *Dialettica e retorica dell'Umanesimo* (Milan: Feltrinelli 1968); Luciano Artese, 'Antonio Persio e la diffusione del ramismo,' *Atti e memorie della Accademia toscana di scienze e lettere La Colombaria* 46 (1981): 83–116; Nelly Bruyère, *Méthode et dialectique dans l'œuvre de la Ramée: Renaissance et âge classique* (Paris: Vrin 1984); Guido Oldrini, *La disputa sul metodo nel Rinascimento. Indagini su Ramo e sul ramismo* (Florence: Le lettere, 1997). On the influence of the new logic on education, see Eugenio Garin, *L'educazione in Europa (1440–1600)* (Bari: Laterza 1957), pp. 160–187; Anthony Grafton, and Lisa Jardine, *From Humanism to the Humanities* (Cambridge, Mass.: Harvard University Press 1986), chapters 6–7.

44 See chapter 2, p. 52.

45 Ong, *P. Ramus*.

46 'Supplica ai Procuratori di San Marco,' in Rose, 'The Accademia Venetiana,' p. 231.

47 See Alfredo Serrai, *Storia della bibliografia* (Rome: Bulzoni 1988), vol. I; (1991), vol. II.

48 'Instrumento,' folio 4v.

49 On 'topical places' and 'origins,' see Preface, n. 7.

50 'Instrumento,' folio 11v.

51 Giusto Fontanini, *Biblioteca dell'eloquenza italiana* (Rome: Rocco Bernabò 1736), p. 540; Marco Foscarini, *Della letteratura veneziana ed altri scritti intorno ad essa* (facsimile, Bologna: Forni 1976), p. 92.

52 See Michel Plaisance, 'Une première affirmation de la politique culturelle du Côme Iᵉʳ: La transformation de l'Académie des "Humidi" en Académie Florentine (1540–1542)' and 'Culture et politique à Florence de 1542 à 1551: Lasca et les "Humidi" aux prises avec l'Académie Florentine,' in *Les écrivains et le pouvoir en Italie à l'époque de la Renaissance*, ed. A. Rochon (Paris: Université de la Sorbonne Nouvelle 1973), I, 361–438; (1974), II, 148–242.

53 Tafuri, *Venezia e il Rinascimento*.

54 See Nicola Ivanoff, 'Il ciclo allegorico della Libreria sansoviniana,' *Arte antica e moderna* 4 (1961): 248–257; Ivanoff, 'Il ciclo dei filosofi della Libreria

Marciana a Venezia,' *Emporium* 70 (1974): 207–211; Ivanoff, 'I cicli allegorici della Libreria e del Palazzo Ducale di Venezia,' in *Rinascimento europeo e Rinascimento veneziano*, ed. V. Branca (Florence: Olschki 1967), pp. 281–297; Thomas Hirthe, 'Die Libreria des Iacopo Sansovino,' *München Jahrbuch der Bildenden Kunst* 37 (1986): 131–176.

55 'Supplica ai Procuratori di San Marco,' in Rose, 'The Accademia Venetiana,' 230. The text of the *invention*, as far as I can determine, has not been found. Charles Hope conjectures that the text may still be in existence because Girolamo Bardi copied at least a part of it after 1577; see Charles Hope, 'Veronese and the Venetian Tradition of Allegory,' *Proceedings of the British Academy* 71 (1985): 398–428, especially pp. 402–404.

56 Francesco Barberi, *Paolo Manuzio e la stamperia del popolo romano, 1561–1570* (reprint, Rome: Gela 1985).

57 Claudia Di Filippo Bareggi, *Il mestiere di scrivere: Lavoro intellettuale e mercato librario a Venezia nel Cinquecento* (Rome: Bulzoni 1988).

58 Stella, 'Federico Badoer,' p. 106.

59 Marcantonio Magno, who would translate Valdés' *Alfabeto cristiano* in 1545, was the father of Celio Magno, a member of the Academy; see Juan Valdés, *Alfabeto cristiano*, ed. M. Firpo (Torino: Einaudi 1994).

60 Grendler, *The Roman Inquisition*; Paolo Simoncelli, *Evangelismo italiano del Cinquecento: Questione religiosa e nicodemismo politico* (Rome: Edizioni di Storia e Letteratura 1979); Conor Fahy, 'The Index librorum prohibitorum and the Venetian Printing Industry in the XVI Century,' *Italian Studies* 45 (1980): 52–61; Silvano Cavazza, 'Libri in volgare e propaganda eterodossa: Venezia 1543–1547,' *Libri, idee e sentimenti religiosi nel Cinquecento italiano*, ed. A. Prosperi and A. Biondi (Modena: Panini 1987), 9–28; John Martin, *Venice's Hidden Enemies: Italian Heretics in a Renaissance City* (Berkeley / Los Angeles: University of California Press 1993).

61 'Lettera agli studiosi delle buone arti,' in Rose, 'The Accademia Venetiana,' 227–228.

62 The text is reproduced in Pagan, 'Sulla Accademia "Venetiana" o della "Fama,"' pp. 387–391.

63 For a complete bibliography, see Bolzoni, *L'universo dei poemi possibili*; Cesare Vasoli, *Francesco Patrizi da Cherso* (Rome: Bulzoni 1989). On Patrizi's relations with the Academy, see Lina Bolzoni 'Il "Badoaro" di Francesco Patrizi e l'Accademia Veneziana,' *Giornale storico della letteratura italiana* 158 (1981): 71–101.

64 Jakob Zwinger, the son of Theodor Zwinger, wrote to Giovan Vincenzo Pinelli in 1596 asking for news of the books that the Academy had printed or was planning to print: see Anna Laura Puliafito, 'Due lettere del Pinelli

e l'Accademia della Fama,' *Studi veneziani* 18 (1989): 285–295. On the relations between Patrizi and Theodor Zwinger, see Antonio Rotondò, *Studi di storia ereticale italiana del Cinquecento* (Torino: Giappichelli 1974), I, 404–413. On Zwinger, see Ong, *Interfaces of the Word*, 180 ff.

2 Trees of Knowledge and Rhetorical Machines

1 On Robortello, see Gian Giuseppe Liruti, *Notizie della vita ed opere scritte da i letterati del Friuli* (Venice: Modesto Fenzo 1762), II, 413–483. On his method, see Lina Bolzoni, 'Alberi del sapere e macchine retoriche,' in *Omaggio a G. Folena* (Padua: Editoriale Programma 1993), pp. 1131–1152. See also Antonio Carlini, 'L'attività filologica di F. Robortello,' *Accademia di scienze, lettere e arti di Udine* 7 (1967): 5–36.

2 'Quod faustum fortunatumque sit. Franciscus Robortellus Utinensis hoc anno rhetoricam facultatem Venetiis Gymnasiarchum iussu explicaturus, ex antiquorum rhetorum praescripto tabulam hanc auditoribus suis spectandam offert, in qua omnia, quae ad artem pertinent dicendi, tum a Cicerone et Quintiliano, tum ab Hermogene et Aristotele scripta, suis locis disposita cernere quivis potest, et singulae questiones unde ortum habent, ad quodve caput sint referendae, cognoscere, ut cum interpretando aliqua controversia orta fuerit, omnis de ea disputatio suo loco apte collocata videatur.'

3 See chapter 1, n. 43, p. 267.

4 On Antonio Bellone, see Liruti, *Notizie delle vite*, II, pp. 225–237. Bellone's letters to Camillo are preserved in Udine, Biblioteca Comunale, Cod. 565, folios 73, 81v–82r.

5 *Excerpta ex lectionibus domini Francisci Robortelli in Topica Ciceronis*, Biblioteca Apostolica Vaticana, Vat. Lat. 6528, folios 156r–191v.

6 Ibid., folios 183v, 185v.

7 Francesco Robortello, *Discorso in materia delli luoghi topici*, Biblioteca Apostolica Vaticana, Vat. Lat. 6528, folios 192r–195r (the passage cited is on folio 192v). There is another copy of this work in Paris, Bibliothèque Nationale, Lat. 8764, folios 71r–78v.

8 Even Speroni uses 'reduction to trees,' but in the eighteenth century, the diagram is expunged from the text. See Giancarlo Mazzacurati, *Il Rinascimento dei moderni: La crisi culturale del XVI secolo e la negazione delle origini* (Bologna: Il Mulino 1985), pp. 258–259.

9 For a complete bibliography on Triphon Gabriele, see *Annotationi nel Dante fatte con M. Trifon Gabriele in Bassano*, ed. L. Pertile (Bologna: Commissione per i Testi di Lingua 1993).

10 On Partenio, see Liruti, *Notizie delle vite*, II, 113–126; Silvano Cavazza, 'Inquisizione e libri proibiti in Friuli e a Gorizia tra Cinquecento e Seicento,' *Studi goriziani* 43 (1976), 29–80, especially pp. 59–60.

11 Bernardino Partenio, *Pro lingua latina oratio* (Venice: Aldi filios [Paolo Manuzio] 1545), folio F4r: 'quod theatrum appellavit, quoniam in omnium conspectu atque oculis non unius tantum hominis divitias, sed universi illius aurei seculi quasi spectaculum proposuit.'

12 Viglius gives a description of the theatre in a letter to Erasmus dated 8 June 1532. See Erasmus of Rotterdam, *Opus epistolarum*, ed. P.S. Allen (Oxford: Oxford University Press 1941), X, 29–30.

13 Partenio, *Pro lingua latina oratio*, folio F4v: 'tam aperte ... notatis locis, ut nihil ab humano ingenio planius, nihil illustrius possit excogitari. Ad summam talem verborum vel moltitudinem, vel varietatem Venetiis eodem monstrante in magnis suis voluminibus repositam collectamque vidisse memini, ut (tametsi antea mecum reputassem, non nihil essem ipse aliquando expertus) miratus sum tanta copia, totque ornamentis unum redundare potuisse.'

14 Dionisio [Dionigi] Atanagi, *Lettere di XIII homini illustri* (Venice: Francesco Lorenzini 1560), book 7, p. 280.

15 Bernardino Partenio, *Dialoghi della imitatione poetica* (Venice: Giolito 1560), p. 148. The Latin version, *De poetica imitatione libri V*, was published in 1565 and again in 1577. The Italian text is reprinted in *Trattati di poetica e di retorica del Cinquecento*, ed. B. Weinberg (Bari: Laterza 1970), II, 521–558. See Partenio's *Pro lingua latina oratio*, folio F4v: 'non iam hominem, sed vix deum quendam dicere aut scire potuisse existimabam.'

16 Partenio, *Dialoghi della imitatione poetica*, 34, 70.

17 Giulio Camillo, *Topica delle figurate locutioni* (Venice: Francesco Rampazetto 1560), folios 54v–55r (I have consulted the copy in Venice, Library of Museo Correr, Op. Cicogna 6.6).

18 On Verdizzotti, see Giuseppe Venturini, *Saggi critici: Cinquecento minore: O. Ariosti, G.M. Verdizzotti e il loro influsso nella vita e nell'opera del Tasso* (Ravenna: Longo 1970); and Lina Bolzoni, 'Variazioni tardocinquecentesche sull'*ut pictura poësis*: La "Topica" del Camillo, il Verdizzotti e l'Accademia Veneziana,' in *Scritti in onore di E. Garin* (Pisa: Scuola Normale Superiore 1987), 85–115.

19 Giovan Mario Verdizzotti, 'Del quadripartito uso de' luoghi topici,' in Camillo, *Topica delle figurate locutioni*, folios 78v, 79r.

20 Ibid., folio 80v.

21 Giovan Mario Verdizzotti, 'Vita di Girolamo Molino,' *Rime* (Venice: n.p. 1573), folios unnumbered.

22 Giason Denores, *Breve trattato dell'oratore* (Padua: Simon Galignani 1574). The text is reprinted in *Trattati di poetica e retorica del Cinquecento*, ed. Weinberg, III, 101–134 (the *Discorso* and the pertinent tables, however, are not included).

23 Giason Denores, *Breve institutione dell'ottima republica raccolta in gran parte da tutta la philosophia humana di Aristotile, quasi come una certa introduttione dell'Ethica, Politica, et Economica ... Introduttione ... ridotta poi in alcune tavole sopra i tre libri della Rhetorica d'Aristotile* (Venice: Paolo Megietto 1578), folio 50v.

24 Giason Denores, *Della rhetorica libri tre, ne' quali, oltra i precetti dell'arte, si contengono venti orationi tradotte de' più famosi et illustri philosophi et oratori: con gli argomenti loro, discorsi, tavole et ruote, ove si potrà facilmente vedere l'osservatione et l'essecutione di tutto l'artificio oratorio, utilissimo a predicatori, a giudici, ad avvocati* (Venice: Paolo Megietto 1584). Not all of the printed copies include the illustrations with the *wheels*; they are missing, for example, in the copy preserved in Pisa, Biblioteca Universitaria, D'Ancona II.4.24, but they can be found in Paris, Bibliothèque Nationale, X 3851.

25 Ibid., folios 260r, 264r.

26 On Valier, see Giovanni Ventura's biography of 1604, in Agostino Valier, *Opuscula duo, Episcopus et Cardinalis* (Venice: Petrus Valvasensis 1754), xiii–xlv; Iacopo Morelli's biography, in Agostino Valier, *Memoriale a Luigi Contarini sopra li studii ad un Senatore Veneziano convenienti* (Venice: Antonio Curti 1803); Gaetano Cozzi, 'Cultura, politica, religione nella "pubblica storiografia" veneziana del Cinquecento,' *Bollettino dell'Istituto di storia della società e dello stato veneziano* 5–6 (1963–1964): 215–294, especially pp. 244–255; Cecilia Tomezzoli, 'Agostino Valier (1531–1606) fra "humanitas" e "virtutes": il periodo dal 1554 al 1561,' *Studi storici Luigi Simeoni*, 45 (1995): 141–172. On Valier's relations with Borromeo and the typeface of his *Rhetorica ecclesiastica*, see Marc Fumaroli, *L'âge de l'éloquence: Rhétorique et 'res literaria' de la Renaissance au seuil de l'époque classique* (Geneva: Droz 1980), pp. 142 ff.; Carlo Delcorno, 'Dal "sermo modernus" alla retorica "borromea,"' *Lettere italiane* 39, no. 4 (1987): 465–483, especially pp. 470 ff.). On the Academy of 'Noctes Vaticanae,' see Michele Maylender, *Storia delle Accademie d'Italia* (Bologna: Cappelli 1929), IV, 78–81; Giuseppe Alberigo, 'Carlo Borromeo e il suo modello di vescovo,' *S. Carlo e il suo tempo*, Atti del Convegno Internazionale nel IV Centenario della morte, Milan, 21–26 May 1984 (Rome: Edizioni di Storia e Letteratura 1986), pp. 181–208, especially pp. 191 ff.

27 'Omnia quamvis abstrusa et recondita percipiebat, et in mente memoria, qua semper excelluit, omnes Aristotelis locis distincte admodum retinebat;

cuius rei periclitandi gratia nonnunquam, ut ipse postea dixit, in arenam, ut de quibuscumque Aristotelis disputaret locis, lacessebat magistros, ipsosque quodammodo celeritate et memoria praestare videatur' (from Giovanni Ventura's introduction to Valier, *Opuscula duo*, p. xx).

28 'Qua ratione versandum sit in Aristotele ad Leonardum Donatum,' in Anna Laura Puliafito, 'Filosofia aristotelica e modi dell'apprendimento: Un intervento di Agostino Valier su "Qua ratione versandum sit in Aristotele,"' *Rinascimento* 30 (1990): 153–172, especially p. 166.

29 Valier, *Memoriale a Luigi Contarini*, p. 46.

30 Agostino Valier, *Libri tres de rhetorica ecclesiastica, synopsis eiusdem rhetoricae ab ipso authore contexta* (Paris: Thomas Brumennius 1575), folio 120v: 'Coniunctio est etiam (ut optime nosti, quandoquidem huiusmodi artium et disciplinarum distinctionibus maxime delectaris) praeclarissimo huic methodo mirabilis quaedam voluptas, ut animus res, quasi viva quadam pictura expressas, magis cernere, quam discere videatur, et nos similitudinem Dei, ad quam effecti sumus, hac ratione exprimentes quatenus humana infirmitas patitur, ut uno intuitu ille omnia cognoscit, sic uno aspectu singulas artes et scientias possimus animo perlustrare.'

31 Federico Borromeo, *De sacris nostrorum temporum oratoribus libri quinque* (Milan: Typographia Collegii Ambrosiani 1632), p. 103: 'In omni preparanda concione utebatur arte quadam, ut arbore constituta, disponeret in ramis argumenta et locos, memoriae credo causa, quam ordo ille non parum adiuvaret. Has arbores ego in octo volumina degerendas curavi.'

32 On the Ambrosian mss., see *Discorsi inediti di San Carlo Borromeo nel IV Centenario della sua entrata in Milano*, ed. C. Marcora (Milan: 1965), pp. 25–50. On his techniques of visualization, see Carlo Borromeo, *Arbores de Paschate*, ed. C. Marcora (Milan: Biblioteca Ambrosiana 1984). On the sacred rhetoric of Borromeo and his circle, in addition to the works by Fumaroli and Delcorno, see Giovanni Farris, 'L'arte della persuasione religiosa tra il popolo nelle "Instructiones" di s. Carlo Borromeo,' in *Cultura popolare e cultura dotta nel Seicento*, Atti del Convegno di studio di Genova, 23–25 November, 1982 (Milan: Angeli 1983), pp. 199–214; John W. O'Malley, 'Saint Charles Borromeo and the "Praecipuum Episcoporum Munus": His Place in the History of Preaching,' *San Carlo Borromeo: Catholic Reform and Ecclesiastical Politics in the Second Half of the Sixteenth Century*, ed. J.M. Headley and J.B. Tomoro (Washington: The Folger Shakespeare Library / London and Toronto: Associated University Press 1988), pp. 139–157. See also *Stampa, libri, e letture a Milano nell'età di Carlo Borromeo*, ed. N. Raponi and A. Turchini (Milan: Vita e Pensiero 1992).

33 On Castelvetro's life, see Ludovico Antonio Muratori's prefatory biography in Ludovico Castelvetro, *Opere critiche inedite* (Berne: Pietro Foppens [printed by Stamperia Palatina, Milan] 1727); Valerio Marchetti and Giorgio Patrizi, 'Ludovico Castelvetro' [entry], *Dizionario biografico degli italiani*, XXII, 8–21.

34 Ezio Raimondi, 'Il modello e l'eccezione,' *Poesia come retorica* (Florence: Olschki 1980), pp. 7–24.

35 Muratori is inexact when he dates the commentary on the *Rhetorica ad Herennium* towards the end of Castelvetro's life (*Opere critiche*, p. 73). I have used the only printed edition available: Ludovico Castelvetro, *Esaminatione sopra la ritorica a Caio Herennio* (Modena: Andrea e Girolamo eredi del Cassini 1653). I collated this edition with the autograph ms. preserved in Reggio Emilia, Biblioteca Municipale, Vari B 26, identified by Giuseppe Frasso in 'Per Lodovico Castelvetro,' *Aevum*, 65, no. 3 (1991): 453–478, especially 453. I found no discrepancies in the passages I have cited. The folio number in the manuscript is given along with the page number in the printed edition.

36 Ludovico Castelvetro, *Poetica d'Aristotele vulgarizzata et sposta*, ed. W. Romani (Bari: Laterza 1978), I, 309. The passages that follow are also from this edition.

37 One example of the medieval wheel is the *rota Virgilii* [wheel of Virgil], which visualizes the tripartite division of styles using Virgil as a model. Camillo's wheel appears in Giulio Camillo, *Trattato delle materie*, in *Opere* (Venice: Domenico Farri 1579), pp. 147–196 (the passage cited is on 166).

38 On his relations with Camillo, see Valentina Grohovaz, 'A proposito di alcuni frammenti manoscritti d'opere di Giulio Camillo Delminio e Lodovico Castelvetro,' *Aevum* 67 (1993): 519–532.

39 Michael Evans, 'The Geometry of the Mind: Scientific Diagrams and Medieval Thought,' *Architectural Association Quarterly* 12, no. 4 (1980): 32–55.

40 Another image used to visualize a system of opposites is the yoke; see Castelvetro's *Poetica*, I, 105, and his *Esaminatione sopra la ritorica ...*, pp. 34–35.

41 This illumination comes from Guillaume Peyraut's *Summa de vitiis*, London, British Library, Harleian ms. 3244, folio 28r. See Michael Evans, 'An Illustrated Fragment of Peraldus's "Summa" of Vice: Harleian Ms. 3244,' *Journal of the Warburg and Courtald Institutes* 45 (1982): 14–68; Lina Bolzoni, 'Il "Colloquio spirituale" di Simone da Cascina: note su allegoria e immagini della memoria,' *Rivista di letteratura italiana* 3, no. 1 (1985): 9–65, especially pp. 47 ff.

42 Luciano Artese, 'F. Patrizi e la cultura delle imprese,' *Atti e memorie dell'Accademia toscana di scienze e lettere La Colombaria* new series 36 (1985): 181–207.

43 See the ninth dialogue, 'Il Cornaro ... overo della retorica perfetta,' in Francesco Patrizi, *Della retorica dieci dialoghi* (Venice: Francesco Senese 1562), folios 48v–57r (reprint, Lecce: Conte, 1994).

44 Giulio Camillo, *Topica, Opere*, II, 74 (the first edition was printed in 1560).

45 See the letter from Zwinger to Cratus von Crafftheim in Antonio Rotondò, *Studi e ricerche di storia ereticale italiana* (Torino: Giappichelli 1974), 407. On Zwinger, see chapter 1, n. 64, p. 268.

46 Francesco Patrizi da Cherso, *Della poetica*, ed. D. Aguzzi Barbagli, 3 vols. (Florence: Olschki 1969, 1970, 1971). See *Deca ammirabile*, II, 316. The following passage is also taken from this edition.

47 Aldo Stella, *Anabattismo e antitrinitarismo in Italia nel XVI secolo* (Padua: Liviana 1969), p. 214.

48 On Toscanella, see Amedeo Quondam, 'Dal "formulario" al "formulario": Cento anni di libri di lettere,' *Le 'carte messaggere': Retorica e modelli di comunicazione epistolare*, ed. A. Quondam (Rome: Bulzoni 1981), pp. 71 ff; Luciano Artese, 'O. Toscanella: Un maestro del XVI secolo,' *Annali dell'Istituto di Filosofia dell'Università di Firenze* 5 (1983): 61–95; Artese, 'Orazio Toscanella: Corrispondenza con il granduca di Toscana e documenti inediti,' *Atti e memorie dell'Accademia toscana di scienze e lettere La Colombaria'* 48 (1983): 29–68; Lina Bolzoni, 'Le "parole dipinte" di O. Toscanella,' *Rivista di letteratura italiana* 1 (1983): 155–186; Paul F. Grendler, *Schooling in Renaissance Italy: Literacy and Learning, 1300–1600* (Baltimore, Md.: The Johns Hopkins University Press 1989), pp. 222–229.

49 Orazio Toscanella, *Discorsi cinque. Per studiare una epistola di Cicerone. Per tradurre. Per studiare diversi autori di humanità. Per studiare un poeta volgare et latino. Per trovare materia di discorrere sopra ogni occorrente concetto* [Five essays: on the study of a letter by Cicero; on translation; on the study of different authors of the humanities; on the study of a vernarcular poet and a Latin poet; on finding material for the discussion of any concept needed] (Venice: Pietro Franceschi 1575).

50 'Et ex labore studiorum in insanabilem morbum incidi: huic tamen labori quies nulla successit: constitui enim prius extremum spiritum effundere quam scribendi laborem intermittere.'

51 Artese 'Orazio Toscanella: Corrispondenza con il granduca di Toscana e documenti inediti,' p. 57.

52 Georgius Peuerbachius, *Le nuove teoriche de i planeti* (Venice: Giambattista Melchiorre Sessa 1566); Rainerus Gemma, *Aritmetica prattica facilissima,*

coll'aggiunta dell'abbreviamento de i rotti astronomici di Giovanni Pelletario (Venice: Giovanni Bariletto 1567).

53 'Viam pene digito commostravit felicissimam caeterisque tutiorem'; 'plenius humana corpora illi cognoscunt, qui illa ipsa concidunt minutius, sic melius orationes illi cognoscunt, qui eas membratim conciderint.'

54 *Concetti di Geronimo Garimberto et di più autori, raccolti da lui per scriver familiarmente* (Venice: Comin da Trino 1562); Aldo Manuzio, Jr., *Eleganze insieme con la copia della lingua toscana e latina* (Venice: Aldi filios [Paolo Manuzio] 1566).

55 Johannes Romberch, *Congestorium artificiosae memoriae* (Venice: Melchiorre Sessa 1553), folios 48v–49r.

56 Anton Francesco Doni, *Mondo risibile* [Laughable world], in *I Mondi e gli Inferni* [Worlds and hells], ed. Pellizzari and M. Guglielminetti (Torino: Einaudi 1994), 135–136: 'The letters of the alphabet are a mill that turns around in every book, and we turn our lives along with them ... Is there anything in this world that is not made, remade, turned, turned again, spun about and respun over and over?' The book machine is from Agostino Ramelli, *Diverse e artificiose machine* [Various artifice machines] (Paris: published by the author 1588).

57 For the modern reader this aspect of Toscanella's work cannot help but recall some of the themes and characters so dear to Borges, such as *Pierre Menard*, absorbed in a new version of Cervantes' masterpiece that matches the original word for word. Menard, writes Borges, is also the author of a monograph on Raymond Lull's *Ars magna generalis* (Jorge Luis Borges, *Ficciones* [New York: Knopf 1993], p. 30).

58 Artese, 'O. Toscanella: Un maestro del XVI secolo.'

59 Joannes Ravisius Textor (Jean Texier), *Officina, ...* (n.d. [1552?]), pp. 509–518. On this text and the genre to which it belongs, see Walter J. Ong, *Interfaces of the Word* (Ithaca, NY: Cornell University Press 1977).

60 *Somma delle opere che in tutte le scienze et arti più nobili et in varie lingue ha da mandare in luce l'Academia Venetiana, parte nuove et non più stampate, parte con fidelissime tradottioni, giudiciose correttioni ed utilissime annotationi riformate* (Venice: Accademia Veneziana 1558), p. 13 (see chapter 1, n. 23, p. 265).

61 Rudolph Agricola, *Della inventione dialettica tradotto da Oratio Toscanella* (Venice: Giovanni Bariletto 1567), book 2, chapter 26, pp. 204–207.

62 Castelvetro, *Esaminatione sopra la ritorica*, p. 136 / folio 130.

63 Agricola, *Della inventione dialettica*, book I, *Proemio* [Introduction], p. 3.

64 'Si quis quotidie Luciferum / exorientem viderit, multa / pollet memoria.'

65 Agricola, *Della inventione dialettica*, pp. 204, 288–289.

66 Artese, 'Orazio Toscanella: Corrispondenza con il granduca di Toscana e documenti inediti,' p. 51.

67 Francesco Patrizi da Cherso, *Lettere ed opuscoli inediti*, ed. D. Aguzzi Bargagli (Florence: Olschki 1975), pp. 13–14.

68 Francesco Patrizi da Cherso, *Amorosa filosofia*, ed. J.C. Nelson (Florence: Le Monnier 1963).

69 On Panigarola, see Giovanni Pozzi, 'Intorno alla predicazione del Panigarola,' in *Problemi di vita religiosa in Italia nel Cinquecento: Atti del Convegno di Storia della Chiesa in Italia*, Bologna, 2–6 September 1958, (Padua: Antenore 1960), pp. 315–322; Lina Bolzoni, 'Oratoria e prediche,' *Letteratura italiana* (Torino: Einaudi 1984), III, part 2, 1041–1074, especially pp. 1057–1063; Carlo Delcorno, 'Dal "sermo modernus" alla retorica "borromea,"' pp. 471–472.

70 Torquato Tasso, *Le lettere*, ed. C. Guasti (Florence: Le Monnier 1855), V, 145.

71 See Paolo Prodi, 'Federico Borromeo' [entry], *Dizionario biografico degli italiani*, XIII, 33–42; Alessandro Martini, *'I tre libri delle laudi divine' di Federico Borromeo: Ricerca storico-stilistica* (Padua: Antenore 1975). On Federico's artistic and cultural interests, see Arlene Quint, *Cardinal Federico Borromeo as a Patron and a Critic of the Arts and His Museum of 1625* (New York: Garland 1986); *Storia dell'Ambrosiana: Il Seicento* (Milan: Cassa di Risparmio delle Provincie Lombarde 1992); Pamela M. Jones, *Borromeo and the Ambrosiana: Art Patronage and Reform in Seventeenth-Century Milan* (Cambridge / New York: Cambridge University Press 1993); Barbara Agosti, *Collezionismo e archeologia cristiana nel Seicento. Federico Borromeo e il Medioevo artistico tra Roma e Milano* (Milan: Jaca Book 1996).

72 'Vel per loca sola, vel cum tabula, vel sine tabula per figuras.' Further evidence of Federico Borromeo's interest in problems of rhetoric can be found in the advice he sought in this area from Giovan Battista Strozzi, man of letters and animating spirit of the Florentine Accademia degli Alterati: see Adrasto S. Barbi, *Un accademico mecenate e poeta: Giovan Battista Strozzi il giovane* (Florence: Sansoni 1900). See also Silvia Morgana, 'Gli studi di lingua di F. Borromeo,' *Studi linguistici italiani* 29, no. 7 (1988): 191–216.

73 'Res in sua capita distribuit, quae difficile in ordinem redigerentur. Multorum librorum lectionem facile reddit.'

74 'Ad prudentiam in rebus humanis; ad futurorum coniecturam, prudentiae ductu et ratione; ad secreta invenienda; ad augendam memoriam, aciem ingenii, ratiocinativam. Inventionem auget.'

75 Federico Borromeo, *De suis studiis commentariis* (Milan: Typographia

Collegii Ambrosiani 1627), p. 127: 'Ardebam etiam peregrinorum scientiarum cupiditate; ... valdeque consectabar artificia memoriae et eiusmodi alia, quae iuvenes insita curiositate admirantur.' See Martini, *'I tre libri delle laudi divine' di Federico Borromeo*, p. 28. Federico Borromeo cultivates this interest throughout the course of his life. The *Miscellanea adnotationum variarum*, for example, reveals a great admiration for Girolamo Cardano.

76 See Rodolfo Maiocchi and Attilio Moiraghi, *L'almo Collegio Borromeo: Federico Borromeo agli inizi del collegio* (Pavia 1912), p. 48.

77 Federico Borromeo, *De cabbalisticis inventis*, ed. F. Secret (Nieukoop: De Graaf 1978), p. 38: 'Sed et Iulium Camillum rarum hominem ingenio credimus ideam theatrumque suum ad Hebraicam Cabbalam accommodare voluisse, sive ad Raimundi artem; quod fuerit ne assecutus, an frustra tentaverit incertum est.'

78 Ibid., p. 56: 'Iulius Camillus *Theatro* suo similis quiddam spectavit, videturque cabbalistica inventa contrectasse, sed sensit postea idem, inania esse, neque usum alium habere, quam expoliendae et variandae paulisper orationis.'

3 Memory Games

1 Luciano Artese, 'Orazio Toscanella: Corrispondenza con il granduca di Toscana e documenti inediti,' *Atti e memorie dell'Accademia toscana di scienze e lettere La Colombaria* 48 (1983): 29–68 (the cited passage is on p. 51).

2 On the relationship between culture – and literature in particular – and play, see Johan Huizinga, *Homo Ludens: Versuch einer Bestimmung des Spielelmentes der Kultur* (Amsterdam: Pantheon 1939), English translation, *Homo ludens: A Study of the Play Element in Culture* (Boston: Beacon Press 1962); Gregory Bateson, *Steps to an Ecology of Mind* (New York: Chandler 1972); Roger Caillois, *Les jeux et les hommes: La masque et la vertige* (Paris: Gallimard 1958), English translation, *Man, Play and Games* (New York: Free Press of Glencoe 1961); 'Carte: Gioco, divinazione, scrittura,' *Lectures* 18 (1986): 103–121. On play in the Renaissance, see *Les jeux à la Renaissance*, ed. P. Ariès and J.-C. Margolin (Paris: Vrin 1982); Jean-Michel Mehl, *Les jeux au royaume de France: Du XIII au début du XVI siècle* (Paris: Fayard 1990); *Passare il tempo: La letteratura del gioco e dell'intrattenimento dal XII al XVI secolo*, Atti del Convegno di Pienza, 10–14 September 1991 (Rome: Salerno editrice 1993).

3 Marco Girolamo Vida, *De arte poetica*, in *Opere* (Antwerp: Christopher Plantin 1567), book III, pp. 257–258, 443; English translation, *The 'De arte*

poetica' of *Marco Girolamo Vida,* trans. Ralph G. Williams (New York: Columbia University Press 1976), p. 103.

4 On the relationship between intertextuality and modes of reception, see (among others): Giovanni Nencioni, 'Agnizioni di lettura,' *Strumenti critici* no. 2 (1967): 191–198; Gian Biagio Conte, *Memoria dei poeti e sistema letterario: Catullo, Virgilio, Ovidio, Lucano* (Torino: Einaudi 1974); Antoine Compagnon, *La seconde main, ou le travail de la citation* (Paris: Seuil 1979); Cesare Segre, 'Testo letterario, interpretazione, storia: Linee concettuali e categorie critiche,' in *Letteratura italiana* (Torino: Einaudi 1985), IV, 21–140.

5 On *Gli Asolani,* see Piero Floriani, *Bembo e Castiglione: Studi sul classicismo del Cinquecento* (Rome: Bulzoni 1976), pp. 78–79; Francesco Tateo, 'La disputa dell'amore: Retorica e poetica del contrario,' in *Il dialogo filosofico nel Cinquecento europeo,* ed. D. Bigalli and G. Canziani (Milan: Angeli 1990), pp. 209–228; Pasquale Sabbatino, 'Gli "Asolani": La letteratura sulla scena del giardino di corte,' in *La 'scienza' della scrittura: dal progetto del Bembo al manuale* (Florence: Olschki 1988), pp. 13–45; Riccardo Scrivano, 'La forma del dialogo: Pietro Bembo,' *Il modello e l'esecuzione* (Rome: Bulzoni 1993), pp. 103–112; Lina Bolzoni, 'La letteratura e il modello del gioco: Esempi cinquecenteschi,' *Studi offerti a Luigi Blasucci dai colleghi e dagli allievi pisani* (Lucca: Pacini Fazzi 1996), pp. 115–132; Claudia Berra, *La scrittura degli 'Asolani' di Pietro Bembo* (Florence: La Nuova Italia 1996).

6 Pietro Bembo, *Asolani,* ed. G. Dilemmi (Florence: Accademia della Crusca 1991), II, 270.

7 Ibid., p. 261.

8 Emanuele Tesauro, *Cannocchiale aristotelico* (Torino: Bartolomeo Zavatta 1679), facsimile, ed. A. Buck (Berlin / Zürich: Gehlen-Bad Homburg 1968), p. 82. See Ezio Raimondi, *Letteratura barocca: Studi sul Seicento italiano* (Florence: Olschki 1991), 1–49; Mario Zanardi, 'Metafora e gioco nel "Cannocchiale aristotelico" di Emanuele Tesauro,' *Studi secenteschi* 26 (1985): 25–99.

9 Bembo, *Asolani,* p. 313.

10 Vittorio Cian, 'Contributo alla storia dell'enciclopedismo nell'età della rinascita: il "methodus studiorum" del card. Bembo,' *Miscellanea di studi storici in onore di Giovanni Sforza* (Lucca: Baroni 1920), pp. 289–330. Giancarlo Mazzacurati, as far as I know, is the only other scholar who has mentioned it; see his *Misure del classicismo rinascimentale* 2nd ed. (Naples: Liguori 1990), p. 227, n. 1. He associates it with the cultural climate of the 1530s.

11 Pietro Bembo, *Methodus studiorum,* Archivio Segreto Vaticano, Arm. II, 78, folios 44r–49v: 'Hic usus est locis, ut vocant communibus sed, ut verius

dixerim, propriis singularum rerum quae in optimis quibusque libris legerat, memoriae adminiculis'; 'his inquam locis memoriam, quam natura eum minus felicem fecerat, exercebat' (folio 44r).

12 Emanuele Casamassima, *Trattati di scrittura del Cinquecento italiano* (Milan: Il Polifilo 1966), p. 9. See also Armando Petrucci, 'La scrittura fra ideologia e rappresentazione,' in *Storia dell'arte italiana* (Torino: Einaudi 1980), III, 2, pp. 5–123, especially 18–31; *Alfabetismo e cultura scritta*, monographic issue of *Quaderni storici* 13 (1978), ed. A. Bartoli Langeli and A. Petrucci; Stanley Morison, *Early Italian Writing Books: Renaissance to Baroque*, ed. N. Barker (Verona: Edizioni Valdonega 1990).

13 On Palatino, see James Wardrop, 'Civis Romanus sum: Giovambattista Palatino and His Circle,' *Signature* 7, no. 14 (1942): 3–38; Lina Bolzoni, 'Riuso e riscrittura di immagini: Dal Palatino al Della Porta, dal Doni a Federico Zuccari, al Toscanella,' in *Scritture di scritture: Testi, generi, modelli nel Rinascimento*, ed. G. Mazzacurati and M. Plaisance (Rome: Bulzoni 1987), pp. 171–206, especially pp. 171–179.

14 On the Accademia dello Sdegno and the Accademia della Virtù, see Michele Maylender, *Storia delle Accademie d'Italia* (Bologna: Cappelli 1930), V, 141, 478–480. On the relationship between the Roman academies of the 1530s and "burlesque" literature, see Silvia Longhi, *Lusus*: Il capitolo bernesco nel Cinquecento (Padua: Antenore 1983), pp. 44 ff.

15 In his anthology of poetry, *De le rime di diversi nobili poeti toscani* (Venice: Lodovico Avanzo 1565), Dionigi Atanagi includes a sonnet of his own addressed to the Accademia dello Sdegno (folio 208). In the commentary he associates its birth with the golden age created by Pope Paul III for the literati.

16 See Grgo Gamulin, and Maria Cionini Visani, *Giorgio Giulio Clovio: Miniaturist of the Renaissance* (New York: The Alpine Fine Arts Collection 1980).

17 On ciphers, see André Muller, *Les écritures secrètes* (Paris: Publications universitaires de France 1971); *Hiéroglyphes, languages chiffrés, sens mystérieux au XVIIᵉ*, monographic issue of *XVIIᵉ siècle*, 40 (1988): 1.

18 I have taken the image of 'playing utopia' from Bronislaw Baczko, 'Utopia' [entry], *Enciclopedia* (Torino: Einaudi 1981), XIV, 856–920, especially p. 865. The alphabet of the Utopians appears in the 1516 edition of Thomas More's *Utopia*, and in the definitive edition of 1518, published in Basel by Froben.

19 Giovan Battista Palatino, *Libro nel qual s'insegna a scrivere ogni sorte di lettera* (Rome: Valerio Dorico 1561), folio E6v (the passages that follow are from this edition). I consulted the copy preserved in the Biblioteca Universitaria of Pisa. As noted above, the first edition, *Libro nuovo d'imparare a scrivere*

tutte sorte lettere antiche et moderne di tutte nationi ..., was published in
1540.

20 On Trifone Benci, see Wardrop, 'Civis romanus sum,' pp. 7–10; Adriano Prosperi, 'Trifone Benci' [entry], *Dizionario biografico degli italiani*, VIII, 203–204.

21 This work by Modio is reprinted in *Trattati del Cinquecento sulla donna*, ed.
G. Zonta (Bari: Laterza 1913), pp. 309–370.

22 See Giovanni Pozzi's observations on Palatino's sonnet in *Poesia per gioco:
Prontuario di figure artificiose* (Bologna: Il Mulino 1984), pp. 84, 89–90. See
also Giancarlo Innocenti's analysis in *L'immagine significante: Studio
sull'emblematica cinquecentesca* (Padua: Liviana 1981), pp. 165–171.

23 On the relationship between the letter and the image, between the visible
and the invisible, see Michel Butor, *Les mots dans la peinture* (Geneva:
Editions d'Art Albert Skira 1969); Jean-François Lyotard, *Discours, figure*
(Paris: Klincksieck 1971), on the rebus see 295–311; Louis Marin, *Etudes
sémiologiques: Ecritures, Peintures* (Paris: Klincksieck 1971); Giorgio
Agamben, *Stanze: La parola e il fantasma nella cultura occidentale* (Torino:
Einaudi 1977), English translation, *Stanzas: Word and Phantasm in Western
Culture* (Minneapolis: University of Minnesota Press 1993).

24 On the rebus, see Jean Céard and Jean-Claude Margolin, *Rébus de la Renaissance: Des images qui parlent* (Paris: Maisonneuve et Larose 1986). On
Giovio's omission of the rebus, see Paolo Giovio, *Dialogo dell'imprese
militari e amorose*, ed. M.L. Doglio (Rome: Bulzoni 1978; the first edition
was published in 1551), pp. 43, 53–54. On the relationship between the
device and the rebus, see Innocenti, *L'immagine significante*, 155 ff.

25 Pietro Aretino, *Marescalco, Teatro*, ed. G. Petrocchi (Milan: Mondadori
1971), 7: *amo* [I love]; *del fino* [with a pure]; *core* [heart]; *delfino*, when
written as one word, means [dolphin]. See also *The Marescalco*, trans. L.G.
Sbrocchi and J.D. Campbell (Ottawa: Doverhouse 1986), p. 114, n. 18.

26 See Giovanni Pozzi, 'Il ritratto della donna nella poesia d'inizio
Cinquecento e la pittura di Giorgione,' in *Sull'orlo del 'visibile parlare'*
(Milan: Adelphi 1993), pp. 145–172.

27 Innocenti, *L'immagine significante*, pp. 167–168; Lyotard, *Discours, figure*.

28 On Della Porta, see *Giovan Battista Della Porta nell'Europa del suo tempo*, ed.
M. Torrini (Naples: Guida 1990). His book on memory was originally
published in Italian, *L'arte del ricordare* [The art of remembering] (Naples:
Mattio Cancer 1566). The Latin version, with its revisions and additions,
was published in 1602. The sonnet/rebus is part of an iconographic appa-
ratus that appears for the first time in this edition. See Giovan Battista
Della Porta, *Ars reminiscendi aggiunta L'arte del ricordare tradotta da
Dorandino Falcone da Gioia*, ed. R. Sirri (Naples: Edizioni Scientifiche
Italiane 1996).

29 *The Institutio Oratoria of Quintilian*, trans. H.E. Butler (Cambridge, Mass.: Harvard University Press 1961), IV, 289.

30 For example, the secret language of gestures is illustrated by Bartolomeo Gottifredi *Specchio d'amore nel quale alle giovani s'insegna innamorarsi* (1547), *Trattati d'amore del Cinquecento*, ed. G. Zonta (Bari: Laterza 1912), facsimile edition, ed. M. Pozzi (Bari: Laterza 1980), pp. 300–301.

31 Iacobo Publicio, *Oratoriae artis epitoma* (Venice: Erhard Ratdolt 1585), folio 63r. The first edition was published in 1482. I consulted the copy preserved in Venice, Biblioteca Marciana, Misc. 2674, 12. See also Thomas Murner, *Logica memorativa, chartiludium logice sive totius dialectice memoria* (Strasbourg: Iohann Gruninger 1509), folio C4r.

32 'Altera [similitudo] ex verbi significatione, altera ex scriptura, quemadmodum literae iacent. Ab ultima exordiemur, velut a certiori.'

33 I derive this expression, taking a certain liberty, from Louis Marin, *Utopiques: Jeux d'espaces* (Paris: Editions de Minuit 1973); English translation, *Utopics: Spatial Plays* (Atlantic Highlands, NJ: Humanities Press / London: Macmillan 1984).

34 'Nos ad tyrones facile in exercitationes introducendos, aliquos italicos versus adducimus cum suis figuris, ut hoc exemplo in aliis uti possis.'

35 The anthropomorphic alphabet, for example, originated and enjoyed popularity in the Germanic countries. The alphabet with work tools seems to have originated instead in Venice. On figurative alphabets, see Ludwig Volkmann, 'Ars memorativa,' *Jahrbuch des Kunsthistorischen Sammlungen in Wien* new series 4, no. 30 (1929): 111–203, especially pp. 149, 168–173); Dietman Debes, *Das Figurenalphabeth* (Munich-Pullach: Verlag Dokumentation 1968); Massin, *La lettre et l'image: La figuration dans l'alphabet latin du huitième siècle à nos jours* (Paris: Gallimard 1970).

36 See *Alphabets (1470–1700) à lire, à dire, à écrire, à broder*, catalogue of the exhibition held at the Musée de l'Imprimérie et de la Banque, Lyon, 25 April–10 June, 1990. See also Danièle Alexandre-Bidon, 'Abécédaires et alphabets éducatifs du XIIIᵉ à la fin du XVᵉ siècle,' *Nouvelles de l'Estampe* 23, no. 90 (1986): 6–10; Alexandre-Bidon, 'La lettre volée: Apprendre à lire à l'enfant au Moyen Age,' *Annales Economies Sociétés Civilisations* 44, no. 4 (1989): 953–992.

37 Franca Petrucci Nardelli, *La lettera e l'immagine: Le iniziali 'parlanti' nella tipografia italiana (secoli XVI–XVIII)* (Florence: Olschki 1992).

38 Paolo Rossi, *Clavis universalis: Arti della memoria e logica combinatoria da Lullo a Leibniz* (Milan / Naples: Ricciardi 1960), pp. 179–238; Claude-Gilbert Dubois, *Mythe et langage au seizième siècle* (Bordeaux: Ducros 1970), Italian translation, *La lettera e il mondo* (Venice: Arsenale 1988), with an introduction by Lina Bolzone; Gerahard F. Strasser, *Lingua universalis:*

Kryptologie und Theorie der Universalsprachen im 16. und 17. Jahrhundert (Wiesbaden: Harrosowitz 1988); Umberto Eco, *La ricerca della lingua perfetta nella cultura europea* (Bari: Laterza 1993), English translation, *The Search for the Perfect Language* (Oxford: Blackwell 1997).

39 This expression is used in reference to techniques that combine cabbalistic notions with the traditions of figurative poetry: The word (usually a proper name) is dismantled and its single letters are arranged in such a way that they create a chain of associations. See, for example, Giulio Camillo, *Lettera a Lucrezia*, in *Opere* (Venice: Domenico Farri 1579), I, 300–311. See also Giovanni Pozzi, *La parola dipinta* (Milan: Adelphi 1981), p. 202; Mario Turello, 'Lucrezia anagrammata e il cosmo programmato,' *Anima artificiale: Il teatro magico di Giulio Camillo* (Udine: Aviani 1993), pp. 115–136); Orazio Toscanella, *Franciscus Serenissimi Magni Etruriae Ducis nomen*, in Lina Bolzoni, 'Le "parole dipinte" di O. Toscanella,' *Rivista di letteratura italiana* 1 (1983): 155–186, especially pp. 166–186.

40 Carlo Ossola, '"Vedere le voci,"' in *Figurato e rimosso: Icone e interni del testo* (Bologna: Il Mulino 1988), chapter 1, 169.

41 Anton Francesco Doni, *Mondo misto*, in *I Mondi e gli Inferni* [Worlds and hells], ed. Pellizzari and M. Guglielminetti (Torino: Einaudi 1994), p. 120.

42 See Eugenio Battisti, and Giuseppe Saccaro Battisti, *Le macchine cifrate di Giovanni Fontana* (Milan: Arcadia 1984); the text of *Secretum de thesauro experimentorum* is on pp. 143–158 (the passages that follow are from this edition). See also Eugenio Battisti, 'Schemi geometrici, artifizi retorici, oggetti di meraviglia nel trattato quattrocentesco sulla memoria di Giovanni Fontana,' in *La cultura della memoria*, ed. L. Bolzoni and Corsi (Bologna: Il Mulino 1992), pp. 117–138.

43 'Artifitium enim meum, vel ferreum, aut ex alia re formatum, materia nempe dicitur. Formatio vero et situatio literarum per ordinem, forma in ipso consistit.'

44 'Propter hanc et alias causas inventa fuisse horologia visum est, cum praeteritorum temporum et motuum nobis memoriam servant. Ego quidem persepe feci horologia, quandoque rotis, quandoque fumo egencia, que me ad opus vocabant immemorem, *ac si veram haberent memoriam in se ipsis.*'

45 See Daniel P. Walker, *Spiritual and Demonic Magic from Ficino to Campanella* (London: The Warburg Institute 1958), pp. 96–106; Ioan P. Couliano, *Eros et magie à la Renaissance* (Paris: Flammarion 1984), English translation, Ioan P. Culianu, *Eros and Magic in the Renaissance* (Chicago: University of Chicago Press 1987); and for an account of the cultural environment in France, Frances A. Yates, *The French Academies of the Sixteenth Century* (London: The Warburg Institute 1947).

46 Jacques Gohory, *De usu et mysteriis notarum liber in quo vetusta literarum et numerorum ac divinorum ex Sibilla nominum ratio explicatur* (Paris: Sertenas 1550), folio A3v: 'Sunt autem haec instar Sileni Alcibiadis prope ridicula rerum admirabilium integumenta, tanquam vilis vestis pulcherrimae virginis. At introite, hic dii sunt, dicebat Heraclitus.' The passages that follow are from this edition.

47 Carlo Ossola, 'Les devins de la lettre et les masques du double: La diffusion de l'anagrammatisme à la Renaissance,' in *Devins et charlatans au temps de la Renaissance*, ed. M.T. Jones-Davies (Paris: Centre de Recherche sur la Renaissance 1979), pp. 127–157; Nuccio Ordine, *La cabala dell'asino: Asinità e conoscenza in Giordano Bruno* (Naples: Liguori 1987), pp. 107–108, English translation, *Giordano Bruno and the Philosophy of the Ass* (New Haven: Yale University Press 1996).

48 'Quae sapiens nomenclator debet diligenter intueri. Ars autem eloquentiae, quae sibi inter caeteras principatum vendicat, quantam quaeso diligentiam adhibet in literis ipsis componendis, ne asper, ne horridas aut hiulcus sit concursus vocalium et consonantium? quantam in syllabis propemodo numerandis et metiendis?'

49 'I enim litera (autore Alberto Durero) velut recta linea, fundamentum est compositionis omnium literarum.'

50 'Miro ordine condebat velut copiae quoddam cornu quod promere promptum esset ad de quacumque re proposita ornate copioseque dicendum.' It is interesting that Gohory uses the same metaphor to describe Camillo's theatre that Terence Cave borrows from Rabelais to describe the mechanisms of interpretation and imitation employed during the Renaissance (see Preface, p. xvi above).

51 Gerolamo Ruscelli, *Del modo di comporre in versi nella lingua italiana* (Venice: Giovan Battista e Melchiorre Sessa 1559), pp. xxix–xxx; see Lina Bolzoni, *Il teatro della memoria: Studi su Giulio Camillo* (Padua: Liviana 1984), pp. 93–94.

52 On Nazari, see Anna Zenone, 'I sogni alchemici di Giovan Battista Nazari,' *Esperienze letterarie* 10, nos. 2–3 (1985): 82–111.

53 See Francesco Colonna, *Hypnerotomachia Poliphili*, ed. G. Pozzi and L.A. Ciapponi (Padua: Antenore 1980).

54 The cited passages are taken from the second edition: Giovan Battista Nazari, *Della tramutatione metallica sogni tre* (Brescia: Pietro Maria Marchetti 1559, reprint, Genoa: Phoenix 1978).

55 See Walter Benjamin, 'Das Kunstwerk im Zeitalter seiner technischen Reproduzierbarkeit,' *Schriften* (Frankfurt am Main: Suhrkamp 1955), English translation 'The Work of Art in the Age of Mechanical Reproduction,' *Illuminations* (New York: Harcourt, Brace and World 1968).

56 Leon Battista Alberti, *Libelli de cifra proemium*, in *Opera inedita et pauca separatim impressa*, ed. G. Mancini (Florence: Sansoni 1898), p. 310; and *Dello scrivere in cifra* (Torino: Galimberti 1995). See Amedeo Quondam, 'La letteratura in tipografia,' *Letteratura italiana* (Torino: Einaudi 1983), no. 2, pp. 555–686, especially 567.

57 Geofroy Tory, *Champfleury auquel est contenu l'art et science de la deue et vraye proportion des lettres attiques, qu'on dit autrement lettres antiques et vulgairement lettres romaines proportionnées selon le corps et visage humain* (Paris: sold by Geofroy Tory and Giles Gourmont 1529). See Kurt Reichenberger and Theodor Berchem's introduction to the facsimile, ed. G. Cohen (Geneva: Slatkine Reprints 1973), pp. v–xx.

58 Sigismondo Fanti, *Triompho di fortuna*, folio 12v: 'In this place, the author condemns the leniency given these days to those who commit large robberies in the belief that the gallows are only for the wretched and the poor.' On Fanti, see Albano Biondi's introduction, 'Sigismondo Fanti e i libri de la sorte,' in Sigismondo Fanti, *Triompho di fortuna* (facsimile, Modena: Edizioni Aldine 1983), pp. 5–20. The cited passages are from this edition.

59 There are also elements of religious polemic in the *Triompho di fortuna*: 'wherefore the author says that he believes that learned men, however much they lack in devotion, can better find salvation than ignorant men, however devoted they may be. And consequently God keeps them in his grace all the more, although this is contrary to what some say from the pulpit, who maintain that a simple man better and more easily saves himself than an investigator of the secrets of God' (*Triompho di fortuna*, folio 10r).

60 Antonio Libanori, *Ferrara d'oro imbrunito* (Ferrara: Marasti 1665), part 3, pp. 172–173 (this passage is from Biondi, 'Sigismondo Fanti e i libri de la sorte,' 17, n. 4).

61 Robert Eisler, 'The Frontispiece to Sigismondo Fanti's "Triompho di Fortuna,"' *Journal of the Warburg and Courtauld Institutes* 10 (1947): 155–188. *La forme et l'intelligible* (Paris: Gallimard 1970), p. 181, Robert Klein mentions an association between the stars and painters that connects Fanti's *Triompho della fortuna* to Lomazzo's work.

62 See Donatino Domini, 'Giochi di percorso,' in *Giochi a stampa in Europa dal XVII al XIX secolo* (Ravenna: Longo 1985), pp. 7–17.

63 The most famous *libro delle sorti* was written by Lorenzo Spirito and published for the first time in 1482, in Perugia.

64 See Massimiliano Rossi, '"Res logicas ... sensibus ipsis palpandas prebui": Immagini della memoria, didattica e gioco nel "Chartiludium logice"'

(Strasburgo 1509) di Thomas Murner,' *Annali della Scuola Normale Superiore di Pisa*, Classe di lettere e filosofia, 3rd series, 20, no. 4 (1990): 831–877; Rossi, 'Arte della memoria e codici letterari nei giochi didattici dall'Umanesimo a Comenio,' *La cultura della memoria*, ed. Bolzoni and Corsi, pp. 139–168.

65 See Francine Daenens, 'Superiore perché inferiore: Il paradosso della superiorità della donna in alcuni trattati italiani del Cinquecento,' in *Trasgressione tragica e norma domestica: Esemplari di tipologie femminili della letteratura europea*, ed. V. Gentili (Rome: Edizioni di Storia e Letteratura 1983), pp. 11–50. On the concept of the 'formation of the compromise,' see Francesco Orlando, *Per una teoria freudiana della letteratura* (Torino: Einaudi 1973) English translation, *Toward a Freudian Theory of Literature: with an Analysis of Racine's 'Phèdre'* (Baltimore: The Johns Hopkins University Press 1978).

66 See Italo Calvino, *Il castello dei destini incrociati* (Torino: Einaudi 1973), English translation, *The Castle of Crossed Destinies* (New York: Harcourt Brace Jovanovich 1977).

67 On Marcolini, see Marion K. Epstein, *Francesco Marcolini, Antonfrancesco Doni and Pietro Aretino: Facts, Figures and Fancies* (New York, 1979; Amedeo Quondam, 'Nel giardino del Marcolini: Un editore veneziano tra Aretino e Doni,' *Giornale storico della letteratura italiana* 97 (1980): 75–116; Augusto Gentili, 'Il problema delle immagini nell'attività di Francesco Marcolini,' *Giornale storico della letteratura italiana* 97 (1980): 117–125.

68 The cited passages are from the 1550 edition. The frontispiece of *Le sorti ...* is signed by Giuseppe Porta. The illustrations are also attributed to him: see Rodolfo Pallucchini, 'Per la storia del Manierismo a Venezia,' in *Da Tiziano a El Greco: Per la storia del Manierismo a Venezia, 1540–1590*, Palazzo Ducale, September–December 1981 (Milan: Electa 1981), pp. 17–18, 322–323.

69 Lucia Nadin has shown that the images of the philosophers were inspired by Diogenes Laertius' *Lives of the Eminent Philosphers*: Lucia Nadin, *Carte da gioco e letteratura fra Quattrocento e Ottocento* (Lucca: Maria Pacini Fazzi 1997), pp. 62–65. On the appeal of Laertius' work for theoreticians of images and masters of memory, see chapter 5, n. 82, p. 296.

70 Amedeo Quondam, 'La scena della menzogna: Corte e cortegiano nel "Ragionamento" di Pietro Aretino,' *Psicon* 3, nos. 8–9 (1976): 4–24.

71 Tesauro, *Cannocchiale aristotelico*, 58.

72 Giulio Bertoni, *L''Orlando furioso' e la Rinascenza a Ferrara* (Modena: Orlandini 1919), pp. 211–212. See also *Le carte di corte: I tarocchi, gioco e magia alla corte degli Estensi* ed. G. Berti and A. Vitali (Bologna: Nuova Alfa Editoriale 1987).

73 Angelo Mercati, *Il sommario del processo di Giordano Bruno* (Città del Vaticano: 1942), Biblioteca Apostolica Vaticana 1942), p. 60. I owe this reference to Rita Pagnoni.

74 Francesco Petrarca, *Familiares* 4.1.

75 On Ringhieri, see François Lecercle, 'La culture in jeu: Innocenzo Ringhieri et le pétrarchisme,' *Les jeux à la Renaissance*, ed. Ariès and Margolin, pp. 185–200; Roberta Lencioni Novelli, 'Un trattato in forma di giuoco: I "Cento giuochi liberali" d'Innocenzo Ringhieri,' *Passare il tempo*, pp. 691–706.

76 On Bocchi, see Delio Cantimori, 'Aspetti della propaganda religiosa nell'Europa del Cinquecento (1957),' *Umanesimo e religione nel Rinascimento* (Torino: Einaudi 1975), pp. 164–181, especially pp. 175–178; Antonio Rotondò, 'Achille Bocchi' [entry], *Dizionario biografico degli italiani* XI, 67–70; Carlo Ginzburg, *Il nicodemismo: simulazione e dissimulazione religiosa nell'Europa del Cinquecento* (Torino: Einaudi 1970), pp. 179–181; Samuele Giombi, 'Umanesimo e mistero simbolico: La prospettiva di Achille Bocchi,' *Schede umanistiche* 1 (Bologna 1988): 167–216; Elizabeth S. Watson, *Achille Bocchi and the Emblem Book as Symbolic Form* (Cambridge / New York: Cambridge University Press 1993).

77 The *symbol* dedicated to Camillo recounts the story of a nightingale competing with itself: it sees its reflection in the water and, fearing that it will be the loser in a singing competition, it chases after its own image, falls into the water, and comes out drenched. The *symbol* refers to the problem of ideas, forms, the way they become visible, and the mistakes that can arise in this process.

78 Giulio Camillo, *Trattato dell'imitazione*, *Trattati di poetica e retorica del Cinquecento*, ed. B. Weinberg (Bari: Laterza 1970), I, 161–185, especially pp. 179–181. On this text, see Lina Bolzoni, 'Erasmo e Camillo: Il dibattito sull'imitazione,' *Filologia antica e moderna* 4 (1993): 69–113.

79 The cited passages are from the critical edition, ed. D'Incalci Ermini, with an introduction by Riccardo Bruscagli (Siena: Accademia degli Intronati 1982).

80 See Bruscagli's introduction to Bargagli, *Dialogo de' giuochi*, pp. 23–24.

4 Body and Soul: The Nature of Images

1 Aristotle, *On Dreams*, in *On the Soul, Parva Naturalia, On Breath*, trans. W.S. Hett (Cambridge, Mass.: Harvard University Press 1957), p. 351.

2 See *La fabbrica del pensiero: dall'arte della memoria alle neuroscienze* (Milan: Electa 1989), especially Anne Harrington's essay, 'Oltre la frenologia:

teorie della localizzazione in età contemporanea,' pp. 206–215, English translation, *The Enchanted Loom: Chapters in the History of Neuroscience* (New York: Oxford University Press 1991).

3 Aristotle, *On Memory*, trans. Richard Sorabji (Providence, RI: Brown University Press 1972), pp. 49–50. See also Sorabji's introduction, pp. 1–46.

4 Aristotle, *De Anima*, trans. D.W. Hamlyn (Oxford: Clarendon Press 1993), p. 53.

5 Avicenna, *Liber de anima*, Editions Orientalistes (Louvain / Leiden: E.J. Brill 1972), 5.2.20: 'solet semper rimari duos theasuros formalis et memorialis et semper repraesentare formas, incipiens a forma sensata aut memorata procedit ab ea ad contrariam vel ad consimilem vel ad aliquid inter quod et illam sit aliqua comparatio.'

6 When Jakobson's model is applied, metaphor corresponds to association based on likeness and difference, while metonym corresponds to association by contiguity: Roman Jakobson, *Essais de linguistique générale* (Paris: Les Editions de Minuit 1964).

7 On cerebrocentrism and cardiocentrism in ancient thought, see Paola Manuli and Mario Vegetti, *Cuore, sangue e cervello: biologia e antropologia nel pensiero antico* (Milan: Episteme 1977).

8 Avicenna, *Liber de anima*, 4.8.177: 'in cerebro autem perficitur complexio spiritus, qui est aptus ad vehendum virtutes ad sensus et motus ad corpora, ad hoc ut fiant apta ad exercendum suas actiones ... cor potest esse principium virtutum nutrivarum, quarum actiones sunt in epate, et virtutum imaginationis et memorialis et formalis, quarum actiones sunt in cerebro.'

9 Ibid., 4.8.182–183: 'virtus vero formalis et sensus communis fiunt in prima parte cerebri spiritu replente ipsum ventriculum; quae omnia non fuerunt ita, nisi ut despiciant super sensus, quorum plures non derivantur nisi ex priore parte cerebri. Cogitatio vero et memoria fiunt in aliis duobus ventriculis, sed memoriae locus est posterior ideo ut spiritus cogitationis sit in medio, scilicet inter thesaurum formarum et thesaurum intentionum et spatium quod est inter utrumque est aequale, et ut illae et aestimatio dominentur in toto cerebro.'

10 For a modern interpretation of the medieval concept of *phantasma*, see Giorgio Agamben, *Stanze: La parola e il fantasma nella cultura occidentale* (Torino: Einaudi 1977), pp. 5–38, 73–158, English translation, *Stanzas: Word and Phantasm in Western Culture* (Minneapolis: University of Minnesota Press 1993). For the Renaissance tradition, see Donald P. Walker, *Spiritual and Demonic Magic from Ficino to Campanella* (London: The Warburg Institute 1958); Robert Klein, *La forme et l'intelligible* (Paris: Gallimard 1970),

p. 83; E. Ruth Harvey, *The Inward Wits: Psychological Theory in the Middle Ages and the Renaissance* (London: The Warburg Institute 1975); Eugenio Garin, *Relazione introduttiva a Spiritus: IV Colloquio internazionale del Lessico intellettuale europeo*, ed. M. Fattori and M. Bianchi (Rome: Edizioni dell'Ateneo 1984), pp. 4–14; Ioan P. Couliano, *Eros et magie à la Renaissance (1484)* (Paris: Flammarion 1984), English translation, Ioan P. Culianu, *Eros and Magic in the Renaissance* (Chicago: University of Chicago Press 1987); Eugenio Garin, '"Phantasia" e "imaginatio" fra Marsilio Ficino e Pietro Pomponazzi,' in *Phantasia-Imaginatio* (Rome: Atti del V Colloquio internazionale del Lessico intellettuale europeo (Rome: Edizioni dell'Ateneo 1988), pp. 3–20.

11 On medicines for memory, see Mary Carruthers, *The Book of Memory: A Study of Memory in Medieval Culture* (Cambridge: Cambridge University Press 1990), pp. 46–79.

12 Giambattista Della Porta, *Della magia naturale* (Naples: Antoine Bulifon 1677), p. 281 (the first edition was published in 1558). The theme of the dangers of medicines for memory is an ancient one: it is discussed by Raymond Lull in *Liber ad memoriam confirmandam* (1308), in Paolo Rossi, *Clavis universalis: Arti mnemoniche e logica combinatoria da Lullo a Leibniz* (Milan / Naples: Ricciardi 1960), p. 71.

13 Giambattista Della Porta, *Della fisonomia dell'uomo* (Padua: Pietro Paolo Tozzi 1627), folio 205v. The first edition, *De humana physiognomia*, was published in 1586.

14 Della Porta, *Della magia naturale*, 280.

15 Giuseppe Gabrieli, 'Giovan Battista Della Porta Linceo: da documenti per gran parte inediti,' *Giornale critico della filosofia italiana* 8 (1927): 360–387 (the passage cited is on p. 365).

16 Germana Ernst, 'I poteri delle streghe tra cause naturali e interventi diabolici: Spunti di un dibattito,' in *Giovan Battista Della Porta nell'Europa del suo tempo*, ed. M. Torrini (Naples: Guida 1990), pp. 167–197 (the passage cited is on 184–185).

17 Giulio Camillo, *Discorso in materia del suo theatro*, in *Opere* (Venice: Domenico Farri 1579), p. 11.

18 Avicenna, *Liber de anima*, 4.4.62: 'cum ... imaginat anima aliquam imaginationem et corroboratur in ea, statim materia corporalis recipit formam habentem comparationem ad illam aut qualitatem.'

19 Camillo's comment on Contarini's work, for example, is indicative of this: 'It has not yet left our minds, Sir, that while we were all reading those divine books on Metaphysics by the excellent Gasparo Contarini, it was just a few days before we came upon the part taken from Plato's *Timeus*'

(Camillo, *Discorso in materia del suo theatro*, p. 13). The work that Camillo is reading with his friends is *Primae philosophiae compendium*, which Contarini completed in 1527. See Gigliola Fragnito, *Gasparo Contarini, un magistrato veneziano al servizio della cristianità* (Florence: Olschki 1988).

20 Gabriele Paleotti, *Discorso intorno alle imagini sacre e profane* (Bologna: Alessandro Benacci 1582), in *Trattati d'arte del Cinquecento fra Manierismo e Controriforma*, ed. Barocchi (Bari: Laterza 1961), II, 208. On Gabriele Paleotti, see Paolo Prodi, *Il cardinale Gabriele Paleotti* (Rome: Edizioni di Storia e Letteratura 1959); Prodi, 'Ricerche sulla teorica delle arti figurative nella Riforma cattolica, in *Archivio italiano per la storia della pietà*, vol. IV (Rome: Edizioni di Storia e Letteratura 1984), pp. 123–212; Giuseppe Olmi and Paolo Prodi, 'Gabriele Paleotti e la cultura a Bologna nel secondo Cinquecento,' *Nell'età di Correggio e dei Carracci: Pittura in Emilia dei secoli XVI e XVII*, Bologna, 10 September–10 November 1986 (Bologna: Nuova Alfa Editoriale 1986), pp. 213–236.

21 Paleotti, *Discorso intorno alle imagini*, 230.

22 See Jerome S. Bruner's introduction to Aleksandr R. Luriia, *The Mind of a Mnemonist: A Little Book about a Vast Memory*, 2nd ed. (Cambridge, Mass.: Harvard University Press 1987), ix–xix , xxii–xxv; and Giuseppe Cossu's introduction to the Italian translation, *Viaggio nella mente di un uomo che non dimenticava nulla* (Rome: Armando 1979), pp. 7–14.

23 Luriia, *The Mind of a Mnemonist*, pp. 66, 69.

24 Giovanni Fontana, *Secretum de thesauro experimentorum ymaginationis hominum*, in Eugenio Battisti and Giuseppa Saccaro Battisti, *Le macchine cifrate di Giovanni Fontana* (Milan: Arcadia 1984), pp. 143–158 (the passage cited is on 155).

25 Ibid.

26 See Moshe Barasch, *Icon: Studies in the History of an Idea* (New York: New York University Press 1992). On sixteenth-century iconoclasm, see John Phillips, *The Reformation of Images: Destruction of Art in England, 1535–1660* (Berkeley: University of California Press 1973); David Freedberg, *Iconoclasm and Painting in the Revolt of the Netherlands, 1566–1609* (New York: Garland 1988); Christin Olivier, *Une révolution symbolique: L'iconoclasme huguenot et la reconstruction catholique* (Paris: Editions de Minuit 1991); Adriano Prosperi, 'Teologi e pittura: La questione delle immagini nel Cinquecento italiano,' in *La pittura in Italia: il Cinquecento* (Milan: Electa 1988), pp. 581–592; Giuseppe Scavizzi, *The Controversy of Images from Calvin to Baronius* (New York and San Francisco: Peter Lang 1992).

27 Thomas Lambert Schenckel, *Gazophylacium artis memoriae* (Strasbourg: Antonius Bertramus 1610), p. 124: 'sextus, apertis ianuis et fenestris omni-

bus, exorta vehementissima ventorum procella, omnes [imagines] quasi chartaceae leviter affixae, remotae fingantur. Septimus: Ancilla omnia cubicula et castra scopis purgaverit, atque invisibiles sibi imagines deposuerit, aut propter preciositatem e loco moverit, ne pulvere maculentur. Octavus, fingimus furore percitum hominem, comitatum armata corona, castra, domos, cubicula occupasse, alias imagines occidisse: Multa percussisse, timore alias per ianuas fugisse, alias per fenestras se praecipitasse, ac intrantes nullas invenire.' Also included in this edition, in addition to Schenckel's text, are the memory treatises of Johann Magirus [Ioannis Austriaci], Girolamo Marafioto, and Johann Spangenberg.

28 See Filippo Gesualdo, *Metodo della oratione delle quaranta ore* (Padua: Paolo Meietto 1593). The intense fusion of mental and sensory perceptions in meditation techniques has a long tradition behind it: see, for example, *The Meditations of the Life of Christ* by the Pseudo-Bonaventure, widely used in the fifteenth century by successful preachers like San Bernardino da Siena (see *Meditaciones de passione Christi olim Sancto Bonaventurae attributae*, ed. M.J. Stallings (Washington: The Catholic University of America Press 1965); the most important and innovative application of this procedure during the sixteenth century was made by Saint Ignatius of Loyola (see Pierre-Antoine Fabre, *Ignace de Loyola: Le lieu de l'image* (Paris: Vrin 1992). On this tradition, see James H. Marrow, *Passion Iconography in Northern European Art of the Late Middle Ages* (Kotrijk: Van Ghemmert 1979); David Freedberg, *The Power of Images: Studies in the History and Theory of Response* (Chicago: University of Chicago Press 1989).

29 Aristotle, *On Memory*, pp. 59–60.

30 Della Porta, *Fisonomia dell'uomo*, folio 208r.

31 See Massimo Ciavolella, 'Eros e memoria nella cultura del Rinascimento,' in *La cultura della memoria*, ed L. Bolzoni and P. Corsi (Bologna: Il Mulino, Bologna, 1992), pp. 319–334 (especially p. 331).

32 See Massimo Ciavolella, *'La malattia d'amore'* dall'antichità al Medioevo (Rome: Bulzoni 1976); Marina Beer, *Romanzi di cavalleria: Il 'Furioso' e il romanzo italiano del primo Cinquecento* (Rome: Bulzoni 1987), pp. 83–140; *Eros and Anteros: The Medical Traditions of Love in the Renaissance*, ed. D. Beecher and M. Ciavolella (Toronto: Dovehouse 1992).

33 Della Porta, *Fisonomia dell'uomo*, folio 10r–10v.

34 Patrick H. Hutton, 'The Art of Memory Reconceived: From Rhetoric to Psychoanalysis,' *Journal of the History of Ideas* 48 (1987): 371–392; Jean-Philippe Antoine, 'The Art of Memory and Its Relation to the Unconscious,' *Comparative Civilization Review'* 18 (1988): 1–21.

35 Leonardo Giustiniani, *Regulae artificialis memoriae*, in Aldo Oberdorfer, 'Le

"Regulae artificialis memoriae" di L. Giustiniani,' *Giornale storico della letteratura italiana* 60 (1912): 221–281 (especially p. 256).

36 *Ars memorativa* (1425), in Roger A. Pack, 'An "Ars memorativa" from the Late Middle Ages,' *Archives d'histoire doctrinale et littéraire du Moyen Age* 46 (1979): 221–281; the passage cited is from p. 256.

37 Ibid.: 'nec ita cito excitatur concupiscencia carnalis, que mentis oculum impuritate turbat, unde et securius est operari cum ymaginibus hominum in commune conceptorum et non notorum tibi in speciali.'

38 See Francisco Andreu, 'Paolo Arese' [entry], *Dizionario biografico degli italiani* IV, 84–85.

39 There are examples of devices with the image of the remora and the ship in Giovanni Ferro, *Teatro d'imprese* (Venice: Giacomo Sarzina 1623), pp. 598–599.

40 Baldassare Castiglione, *Il libro del Cortegiano*, ed. A. Quondam and N. Longo (Milan: Garzanti 1987), 3.66 p. 346, English translation, *The Book of the Courtier*, trans. Charles S. Singleton (Garden City, NY: Anchor 1959), p. 271.

41 It would be interesting to reconstruct the entire history of this topos. For the passage cited here, see Pietro Bembo, *Asolani*, ed. G. Dilemmi (Florence: Accademia della Crusca 1991), p. 436.

42 Giovan Battista Della Porta, *Sorella*, in *Teatro*, ed R. Sirri (Naples: Istituto Universitario Orientale 1985), III, 144–145.

43 Luigi Cassola, *Madrigali* (Venice: Giolito 1544), I, 351. This edition, ed. Giuseppe Betussi, is dedicated to Pietro Aretino. I owe the reference to Luigi Milite. On Cassola, see Giuseppe Gangemi, 'Luigi Cassola' [entry], *Dizionario biografico degli italiani*, XXXI, 518–520.

44 On this theme, see Agamben, *Stanze*, pp. 73–83, 130–158; Maurizio Bettini, *Il ritratto dell'amante* (Torino: Einaudi 1992).

45 *Poeti del Duecento*, ed. G. Contini (Milan / Naples: Ricciardi 1960), I, 55–56, English translation, *The Poetry of the Sicilian School*, ed. and trans. Frede Jensen (New York: Garland 1986), pp. 11–13. See Franco Mancini, *La figura nel cuore fra cortesia e mistica: Dai Siciliani allo Stilnuovo* (Naples: Edizioni Scientifiche italiane 1988).

46 Marsilio Ficino, *El libro dell'amore*, ed. S. Niccoli (Flornece: Olschki 1987), 7.8.201. See the story of Clorinda's birth in Tasso's *Gerusalemme liberata* [Jerusalem delivered], canto 12.

47 The following are two examples from the fourteenth century: All of the tools of the Passion (the three nails, the whip, the column, etc.) were found in the heart of Chiara da Montefalco; three stones on which there were engraved images of a small nativity scene fell from the heart of Margherita

di Città di Castello. See Chiara Frugoni, 'Le mistiche, le visioni e l'iconografia: Rapporti ed influssi,' *Atti del Convegno su 'La mistica femminile del Trecento'* (Todi: Accademia Tudertina 1982), pp. 5–45, especially pp. 27–28; see also *Scrittrici mistiche italiane*, ed. G. Pozzi and C. Leonardi (Genoa: Marietti 1988).

48 Mario Andrea Rigoni, 'Una finestra aperta sul cuore (Note sulla metafora della "Sinceritas" nella tradizione occidentale),' *Lettere italiane* 4 (1974): 434–458.

49 Pierio Valeriano, *Hieroglyphica* (Basel: Michael Isingrinius 1556), p. 241F; Cesare Ripa, *Iconologia* (Rome: Lepido Faci 1603), p. 429, p. 18, pp. 455–456.

50 Rigoni, 'Una finestra aperta sul cuore,' 458.

51 Ibid., 445.

52 *Descriptio et explicatio Pegmatum, Arcuum et Spectaculorum ... sub ingressum ... Ernesti archiducis Austriae* (Brussels 1594) in Rigoni, 'Una finestra aperta sul cuore,' p. 437.

53 Innocenzio Ringhieri, *Cento giuochi liberali et d'ingegno* (Bologna: Anselmo Giaccarelli 1551), folio 119v.

54 Girolamo Bargagli, *Dialogo de' giochi che nelle vegghie sanesi si usano di fare*, ed P. D'Incalci Ermini (Siena: Accademia degli Intronati 1982), p. 108.

55 Emanuele Tesauro, *Cannocchiale aristotelico* (originally published Torino: Bartolomeo Zavatta 1679), ed. A. Buck (Berlin / Zurich: Gehlen-Bad Homburg 1968), p. 16. Rigoni gives a different interpretation of this passage from Tesauro: on the one hand, Rigoni identifies here the capacity to understand and grasp the philosophical nucleus of the image; on the other hand, he points out the presence of Neoplatonic notions in the treatment of the problem of expressing truth (Rigoni, 'Una finestra aperta sul cuore,' pp. 457–458).

56 See Lina Bolzoni, 'Erasmo e Camillo: Il dibattito sull'imitazione,' *Filologia antica e moderna* 4 (1993): pp. 69–113.

57 Erasmus of Rotterdam, *Opus epistolarum*, ed. P.S. Allen (Oxford: Oxford University Press 1941), X, 29–30: 'Hoc autem theatrum suum auctor multis appellat nominibus, aliquando *mentem et animum fabrefactum, aliquando fenestratum*: Fingit enim omnia quae mens humana concipit, quaeque corporeis oculis videre non possumus, posse tamen diligenti consideratione complexa signis deinde quibusdam corporeis sic exprimi, ut unusquisque oculis statim percipiat quicquid alioqui in profundo mentis humanae demersum est. Et ab corporea etiam inspectione theatrum appellavit.'

58 Giulio Camillo, *Pro suo de eloquentia theatro ad Gallos oratio* (Venice: Giovan Battista Somaschi 1587): 'Natura igitur fecit in nobis mentem rerum om-

nium impressiones complectentem, easque ita omnibus gentibus communes, ut omnes nationes res sub una eademque forma conciperent ... ad cuius similitudinem ego quoque magnam mentem extra nos feci, rerum omnium verborumque formulas continentem' (p. 39). 'Nostra haec manufacta mens, nostra haec tanti operis fabrica, ita *fenestrata* est, ut apertiorem non potuisset desiderari a Socrate' (p. 40). On the image of the *mens fenestrata* in Camillo and its relationship with the preface to the third book of Vitruvius, see Corrado Bologna, 'Esercizi di memoria: Dal "Theatro della sapientia" di Giulio Camillo agli "Esercizi spirituali" di Ignazio di Loyola,' *La cultura della memoria*, ed. Bolzoni and Corso, pp. 169–221. Camillo develops this image with conceits at the beginning of *Oration seconda al re Christianissimo*, in *Opere*, pp. 242 ff.

59 On physiognomy see Graene Tyler, *Physiognomy in the European Novel: Faces and Fortunes* (Princeton: Princeton University Press 1982); Jurgis Baltrušaitis, *Aberrations: Essais sur la légende des formes* (Paris: Flammarion 1983); *Rhétoriques des corps*, ed. P. Dubois and Y. Winkin (Brussels: 1988); Jean-Jacques Courtine and Claudie Haroche, *Histoire du visage: exprimer et taire ses émotions, XVIe–debut XIXe* (Paris: Rivages 1988); Michela Sassi, *La scienza dell'uomo nella Grecia antica* (Torino: Boringhieri 1988); Paolo Getrevi, *Le scritture del volto: fisiognomica e modelli culturali dal Medioevo ad oggi* (Milan: Angeli 1991); Lucia Rodler, *I silenzi mimici del volto: studi sulla tradizione fisiognomica italiana tra Cinque e Seicento* (Pisa: Pacini 1991); Flavio Caroli, *Storia della fisiognomica: arte e psicologia da Leonardo a Freud* (Milan: Leonardo 1995).

60 On Bonifacio, see Mario Costanzo, *I segni del silenzio e altri studi sulle poetiche e l'iconografia letteraria del Manierismo e del Barocco* (Rome: Bulzoni 1983), pp. 47–54; Paola Casella, 'Un dotto e curioso trattato del primo Seicento: "L'arte de' cenni" di Giovanni Bonifacio,' *Studi secenteschi* 34 (1993): 331–407.

61 See Armando Petrucci's introduction to Camillo Baldi, *Come da una lettera missiva si conoscano la natura e qualità dello scrittore* (Pordenone: Studio Tesi 1992), pp. ix–xii. The passages that follow are from this edition.

62 Pietro Vettori, *Commentarii in librum Demetrii Phalerei de elocutione* (Florence: Giunti 1592), p. 201: 'qui illam [epistolam] legit eodem tempore quasi apertum aspiciat pectus illius qui scripsit, et intimos suos sensus omnes notos habeat.'

63 This theme is elaborated by Francesco Stelluti, a member of the Accademia dei Lincei, who summarizes and visualizes Della Porta's physiognomy: 'But the omnipotent right hand of the sovereign Artifice has tried thoroughly to fulfil Socrates' desire: It has opened not just one, but many,

many windows in the face of man' (Francesco Stelluti, *Della fisonomia di tutto il corpo umano del signor G.B. Della Porta ora brevemente in tavole sinottiche ridotta e ordinata* [On the physiognomy of the entire human body, now reduced and organized in brief synoptic tables] [Rome: Mascardi 1637], p. 3). There is probably also a Petrarchan influence behind this theme.

64 See, for example, Bartolomeo Cavalcanti, *La retorica* (Venice: Giolito 1559), book IV.

65 Leon Battista Alberti, *De pictura*, 2.41, in *Opere volgari*, ed. C. Grayson (Bari: Laterza 1973), III, 71 [*On Painting*, trans. John R. Spencer (Westport, Conn.: Greenwood Press 1976), p. 77]: 'Motus animi ex motibus corporis cognoscuntur ... Pictori ergo corporis motus notissimi sint oportet.' On Alberti's *De pictura*, see John R. Spencer, '"Ut rhetorica pictura": A study in Quattrocento Theory of Painting,' *Journal of the Warburg and Courtauld Institutes* 20 (1957): 26–44; Michael Baxandall, *Giotto and the Orators: Humanist Observers of Painting in Italy and the Discovery of Pictorial Composition* (Oxford: The Clarendon Press 1971), chapter 3.

66 Barry Wind, '"Pitture ridicole": Some late Cinquecento Comic Genre Paintings,' *Storia dell'arte* 4 (1974): 25–35.

67 Anton Francesco Doni, *Disegno partito in più ragionamenti, ne' quali se tratta della scoltura et pittura* [Drawing divided into multiple expositions in which sculpture and painting are examined] (Venice: Giolito 1549), folio 28v. See Paola Barocchi's commentary on Giorgio Vasari, *La vita di Michelangelo nelle redazioni del 1550 e del 1568* (Milan/Naples: Ricciardi 1962), II, 178 ff., n. 152.

68 Gian Paolo Lomazzo, *Trattato dell'arte della pittura, scultura et architettura* (Milan: Gottardo Ponzio 1584) [*A Tractate Containing the Arts of Curious Paintinge, Carvinge and Buildinge* (Farnborough: Gregg International Publishers 1970)]. On Lomazzo (and for a complete bibliography), see the excellent volume ed. Roberto Paolo Ciardi, *Scritti sulle arti* (Florence: Marchi e Bertolli 1973). Lomazzo's treatise appears in the second volume, pp. 9–589; the passages that follow are from this edition. See Klein, *La forme et l'intelligible*, pp. 174–192, especially p. 179, n. 5.

69 *Ars memorativa* (1425), p. 244.

70 'Pictura tacens opus et habitus sempre eiusdem, sic gestus intimos effectus exprimit, ut ipsam vim dicendi nonnunquam superare videatur. In mutis pro sermone sunt gestus et manu et nutu suam voluntatem declarant, animalium quoque sermone carentium ira, laetita, adulatio, oculis et quibusdam aliis corporis signis deprehenditur.'

71 Quintilian, *Institutio oratoria*, 11.3.67: 'Nec mirum, si ista, quae tamen in

aliquo posita sunt motu, tantum in animis valent, cum pictura, tacens opus et habitus semper eiusdem, sic in intimos penetret adfectus, ut ipsam vim dicendi nonnunquam superare videatur' [Nor is it wonderful that gesture which depends on various forms of movement should have such power, when pictures, which are silent and motionless, penetrate into our inner- most feelings with such power that at times they seem more eloquent than language itself]: *The Institutio Oratoria of Quintilian*, trans. H.E. Butler (Cambridge, Mass.: Harvard University Press 1961), IV, 281.

72 Ibid., 11.3.66: 'Quippe non manus solum, sed nutus etiam declarant nostram voluntatem et in mutis pro sermone sunt ... et animalium quoque sermone carentium ita, laetitia, adulatio et oculis et quibusdam aliis cor- poris signis deprehenditur' [For we can indicate our will not merely by a gesture of the hands, but also with a nod from the head: Signs take the place of language in the dumb ... and even speechless animals show anger, joy, or the desire to please by means of the eye and other physical indica- tions]: *The Institutio Oratoria of Quintilian*, IV, 280–281).

73 'Quis moerentem non iudicabit, cui pressa frons, cervix languida, denique omnia veluti defessa procidunt? quis non ira exandescendentem, cui vultus et oculus intumescant, rubeant, membrorumque omnium motus pro furore iracundiae iactabundus?'

74 Alberti, *De pictura*, 2.41, in *Opere volgari*, III, 73 [*On Painting*, trans. Spencer, p. 77]: 'est quidem maerentibus pressa frons, cervix languida, denique omnia veluti defessa et neglecta procidunt. Iratis vero, quod animi ira incendantur, et vultus et oculi intumescunt, ac rubent, membrorumque omnium motus pro furore iracundiae in eisdem acerrime et iactabundi sunt.'

75 Alberti, *De pictura*, 2.44, in *Opere volgari*, III, 77–79 [*On Painting*, trans. Spencer, p. 80]: 'sed hi, quo audiunt eas imagines maxime vivas videri, quae plurimum membra agitent, eo histrionum motus, spreta omni pictura dignitate, imitantur.'

76 'Sint praeterea plus iusto maiora, vivis coloribus et splendoribus exornata, personae robuste membra moveant atque histrionum gestus imitentur.'

77 Paola Gherardini, 'Problemi critici e metodologici per lo studio del teatro di G.B. Della Porta,' *Biblioteca teatrale* 1 (1971): 137–159; Michele Rak, 'Modelli e macchine del sapere nel teatro del Della Porta,' in *Giovan Battista Della Porta nell'Europa del suo tempo*, ed. M. Torrini (Naples: Guida 1990), pp. 387–415. On Della Porta's theatrical works, see Louise G. Clubb, *G.B. Della Porta Dramatist* (Princeton: Princeton University Press 1965); Raffaele Sirri, *L'attività teatrale di G.B. Della Porta* (Naples: De Simone 1968). See, for example, Della Porta's comedy *La Fantesca* [The wench], act IV, scene 2, in

which two victims of trickery insult each other because they both believe
the other to be guilty of the deception: 'GERASTRO: Why don't you believe
it? NATICOFORO: Why are you a liar? GERASTRO: This white beard of yours
has fooled me. NATICOFORO: Your appearance told me the truth. You have
the face of a hangman! GERASTRO: You have the face of a hanged man!'
(Della Porta, *La Fantesca, Teatro*, II, 207). In *L'Astrologo* [The astrologer], the
comic inversion of physiognomy occupies a great deal of space. Instead of
citing the conniving astrologer, however, I will limit the quotation to the
way in which Pandolfo, the eldery lover, intreprets the traits of Cricco the
servant in act V, scene 5: 'PANDOLFO: He says it loud, with a wide and happy
mouth: Sign of something happy' (Della Porta, *L'Astrologo, Teatro*, III, 205);
the servant is actually about to tell Pandolfo that his hopes have vanished.

78 See Claudie Balavoine, 'Hiéroglyphes de la mémoire: Émergence et
   métamorphose d'une écriture hiéroglyphique dans les Arts de mémoire du
   XVIe et XVIIe siècles,' *Hiéroglyphes, languages chiffrés, sens mystérieux au
   XVIIe*, monographic issue of *XVIIe siècle* 40, no. 1 (1988): 1, 51–68.

79 It begins in the following manner: 'I know full well that each of you who
   sees me dressed in yellow, with my pale and lean face, with my bewil-
   dered sunken and bruised eyes, with these torches, snakes, and goads in
   hand, will wish to know who I am and to what end I have appeared (Della
   Porta, *La Fantesca, Teatro*, II, 139).

80 The Della Porta brothers were greatly interested in collecting; see Fulco,
   Giorgio, 'Per il museo dei fratelli Della Porta,' in *Il Rinascimento meridionale:
   Raccolta di studi pubblicata in onore di Mario Santoro* (Naples: Società editrice
   Napoletana 1986), 3–73. For other references on collecting in the sixteenth
   century, see chapter 6.

81 See Michel Foucault, *Les mots et les choses* (Paris: Gallimard 1966), chapter
   2; English translation, *The Order of Things: An Archeology of the Human
   Sciences* (New York: Vintage Books 1994).

82 Pomponio Gaurico, *De sculptura* (1504) ed. A. Chastel and R. Klein (Geneva: Droz 1969). The section dedicated to physiognomy is on 129–163,
   and the passage cited here, which refers to the images of Homer, the sages
   of Greece, and the Catos, is on 131: 'Apud statuarios vero [physiognomo-
   nia] tanti erit, ut nobis illum ipsum qui tantopere desideratur Homerum,
   ipsosque Graeciae sapientes Cleobulum, Periandrum, Solonem, Thalem,
   Chilonem, Pictacum, Biantem, atque a nostris utrumque Catonem,
   ipsissimos praesentare faciliter possint' [(physiognomy) is so important
   to sculptors that it allows them to achieve easily that which they desire,
   in other words, to portray Homer himself, and the sages of Greece,

Cleobulus, Periander, Solon, Thales, Chilon, Pittacus, Bias, and, among our own, Cato (the Censor) and Cato (of Utica)].

83 Della Porta gives some examples of how physiognomy can inspire rhetorical *inventio*: at the beginning of *Fisonomia dell'uomo* there is a woodcut with a portrait of Cardinale D'Este accompanied by a description of his face; the title is 'Esempio e modo di porre in prattica le regole della fisonomia nella effigie dell'ilustrissimo et reverendissimo cardinal d'Este' [Example and method for using the rules of physiognomy in the effigy of the illustrious and most reverend Cardinal D'Este]. On the influence of physiognomy on portraits of famous persons, see P. Meller, 'Physiognomical Theory in Renaissance Heroic Portraits,' *Renaissance and Mannerism: Studies in Western Art* (Princeton: Princeton University Press 1963), 53–69.

84 On Giacomo di Gaeta, see Lina Bolzoni, 'Conoscenza e piacere: L'influenza di Telesio su teorie e pratiche letterarie fra Cinque e Seicento,' *Bernardino Telesio e la cultura napoletana* (Naples: ed. R. Sirri and M. Torrini (Naples: Guida 1992), 203–239, especially 221–226.

85 It appears that there was already a connection between physiognomy, theatre, and the arts in ancient Greece: See Giampiera Riana's introduction to Pseudo Aristotele, *Fisiognomica* (Milan: Rizzoli 1993), 5–49, especially 35–39. On the different types of *mores* and their function in the relationship between rhetoric and theatre, see Marc Fumaroli's admirable treatment of this subject in 'Lo statuto del personaggio,' in *Eroi e oratori: Retorica e drammaturgia secentesche* (Bologna: Il Mulino 1990), 29–70. On the relationship between physiognomy and the different types of *character*, see Louis Van Delft, *Littérature et anthropologie: Nature humaine et caractère à l'âge classique* (Paris: Presses universitaires de France 1993).

86 On *actio* and the relationship between rhetoric and theatre in the seventeenth century, see Fumaroli, *Eroi e oratori: Retorica e drammaturgia secentesche*.

87 Quintilian, *Institutio oratoria*, 11. 3. 61–62 [*The Institutio Oratoria of Quintilian*, trans. Butler, IV, 277]: 'sed cum sint alii veri adfectus, alii ficti et imitati; veri naturaliter erumpunt, ut dolentium, irascentium, indignantium, sed carent arte ideoque sunt disciplina et ratione formandi. Contra qui effinguntur imitatione, artem habent; sed hi carent natura, ideoque *in iis primum est bene adfici et concipere imagines rerum et tamquam veris moveri.*' On *actio*, see *Die Sprache der Zeichen und Bilder*, ed. V. Kapp (Marburg: Hitzeroth 1991).

88 'Non satis est pulchra esse poemata, dulcia sunto / et, quocumque volent, animum auditoris agunto. / Ut ridentibus adrident, ita flentibus adsunt /

humani vultus. Si vis me flere, dolendum est / primum ipsi tibi: Tunc tua me infortunia laedent, / Telephe vel Peleu; male si mandata loqueris, / aut dormitabo aut ridebo' [English translation, *Horace on the Art of Poetry*, ed. Edward Henry Blakeney (Freeport: Books for Libraries Press 1970), p. 45].

89 Lomazzo, *Trattato dell'arte della pittura*, II, 95, 103.

90 Heinrich Cornelius Agrippa Von Nettesheim, *De occulta philosophia*, in *Opera omnia* (Lyon: Beringos 1531), I, 66. Lomazzo's debt to Agrippa is noted by G.M. Ackermann, *The Structure of Lomazzo's Treatise on Painting*, dissertation, University of Michigan, 1968.

91 Lomazzo, *Trattato dell'arte della pittura*, II, 111.

92 Cicero, *De Oratore*, trans. H. Rackman (Cambridge, Mass.: Harvard University Press 1977), IV, 179; and *Orator*, trans. H.M. Hubbell (Cambridge, Mass.: Harvard University Press 1952), p. 347.

93 Francesco Robortello, *De figuris rhetoricis disputatio*, Paris, Bibliothèque Nationale, cod. lat. 8764, folios 45–70. See also the printed edition, *De artificio dicendi* (Bologna: Alessandro Benasio 1567), folios 25v–32r, especially folio 25v.

94 Quintilian, *Institutio oratoria*, 9. 1. 21 [*The Institutio Oratoria of Quintilian*, trans. Butler, III, 359]: 'Iam vero adfectus nihil magis ducit. Nam si frons, oculi, manus multum ad motum animorum valent, quanto plus *orationis ipsius vultus ad id quod efficere tendimus compositus.*'

95 Pseudo Longino, *Del sublime*, ed. G. Martano (Bari: Laterza 1965) [Longinus, *On the Sublime*, trans. with a commentary by James A. Arieti and John M. Crosset (New York: Edwin Mellen 1985), p. 87]. See Jean Starobinski, *L'œil vivant* (Paris: Gallimard 1961).

96 Quintilian, *Institutio oratoria*, 6.2.29 [*The Institutio Oratoria of Quintilian*, trans. Butler, II, 433–434]: 'Quas φαντασίαι Graeci vocant, nos sane visiones appellemus, per quas imagines rerum absentium ita repraesentantur animo, ut eas cernere oculis ac praesentes habere videamur, has quisquis bene conceperit, is erit in adfectibus potentissimus. Hunc quidam dicunt εὐφαντασίωτον, qui sibi res, voces, actus secundum verum optime finget: Quod quidem nobis volentibus facile continget.' On the theme of *enargeia*, see G. Zanker, '*Enargeia* in the Ancient Criticism of Poetry,' *Rheinisches Museum* 124 (1981): 297–311; Carlo Ginzburg, 'Montrer et citer: La vérité de l'histoire,' *Le débat* 56 (1989): 43–54. On the passage from Quintilian, see Perrine Galand-Hallyn, 'Le songe et la rhétorique de l'*enargeia*,' in *Le songe à la Renaissance*, ed. F. Charpentier (Institut d'études de la Renaissance et de l'âge classique, Université de Saint-Etienne 1990), 127–135.

97 Giulio Camillo, *Trattato delle materie*, *Opere* (Venice: Domenico Farri 1579), p. 183.

98 On the rediscovery of corporeity that has characterized recent linguistic
   and semiologic methodology, see Cesare Segre, 'Il corpo e la grammatica,' in
   Notizie della crisi: Dove va la critica letteraria? (Torino: Einaudi 1993), 241–255.

5 How to Translate Words into Images: Memory and Invention

1 Pietro Bembo, *Asolani*, critical edition, ed. G. Dilemmi (Florence: Accademia della Crusca 1991), II, chapter 8, 270. The passages that follow are also
   from this edition.
2 On the iconography of love, see Erwin Panofsky, *Studies in Iconology* (New
   York: Oxford University Press 1939).
3 See the following passage in Boccaccio, *Elegia di madonna Fiammetta* (6. 14):
   'Even in the most sizzling corner of hell, with its most terrible tortures for
   those who are damned, there is no punishment like mine. Tityus is cited as
   an example of excruciating pain by ancient authors who say that vultures
   continually peck at his ever-renewing liver, and I certainly do not consider
   this a meagre punishment, but it is nothing in comparison with mine ...
   And even the unfortunate Ixion, rotating on that fiery wheel, does not
   suffer the kind of pain that can compare with mine' (Giovanni Boccaccio,
   Elegia di madonna Fiammetta, in *Opere minori in volgare* (Milan: ed. M. Marti
   (Milan: Rizzoli 1971), III, 573–574 [Giovanni Boccaccio, *The Elegy of Lady
   Fiammetta* ed. and trans. M. Causa-Steindler and T. Mauch (Chicago:
   University of Chicago Press 1990), 113–114]. The two texts are linked by
   Amilcare Iannucci in '"L'elegia di Madonna Fiammetta" and the First
   Book of the *Asolani*: The Eloquence of Unrequited Love,' *Forum italicum* 10
   (1976): 345–359; Ianucci elaborates on an idea proposed by Dionisotti. For
   general observations on Bembo's Neoplatonic reading of mythology, see
   Ronnie H. Terpening, 'Mythological Exempla in Bembo's "Asolani":
   Didactic or Decorative?' *Forum italicum* 8 (1974): 331–343.
4 Baldassare Castiglione, *Il libro del Cortegiano*, ed. A. Quondam and N.
   Longo (Milan: Garzanti 1987), 4, 69, 450 [*The Book of the Courtier*, trans.
   Charles S. Singleton (Garden City, 1959 NY: Achor), p. 355].
5 The first edition was published in 1593. The 1603 Roman edition was
   reprinted by E. Mandowsky (Hildesheim and New York: G. Olms 1970).
6 See *Poetica pre-platonica*, ed. G. Lanata (Florence: La Nuova Italia 1963),
   68–71; *Lyra Graeca*, ed. J.M. Edmonds (London: Heinemann 1924), II, 246 ff.
   On the relationship between the art of memory and iconology, see Lina
   Bolzoni, 'Iconologia e arte della memoria,' in *Metodologia della ricerca:
   orientamenti attuali. Congresso internazionale in onore di Eugenio Battisti,
   Arte lombarda* 38, nos. 105–107 (1993): 114–118.

7 Hermann Diels, *Die Fragmente der Vorsokratiker* (Berlin: Weidmann 1922), II, 345.

8 Roland Barthes, *L'ancienne rhétorique* (Paris 1970).

9 Giovanni Fontana, *Secretum de thesauro experimentorum ymaginationis hominum, Le macchine cifrate di Giovanni Fontana*, ed. E. Battisti and G. Saccaro Battisti (Milan: Arcadia 1984), 143–158: 'neque ulla ars vel scientia est que magis artifitiali memoria sit conformis quam pictori: Proprie et ipsa locis et ymaginibus indiget sicut et ista, et una alteram multum insequitur, ideo ad illam artem depingendi quandoque pro exemplis occurrere est satis utile: Depingimus et nos cum figuramus ymagines in locis' (p. 153).

10 *De nova ac spirituali quadam artificialis arte memorie*, in Roger A. Pack, 'Artes memorativae in a Venetian Manuscript,' *Archives d'histoire doctrinale et littéraire du Moyen Age* 50 (1983): 287–298: 'Ideo, quicumque ad tam mirandum opus et effectum optaverit pervenire, studeat predictarum imaginum varietati et forme aut per picturam aut per fantasiam in mentis oculos imprimere et sigilare' (pp. 294–295).

11 *De memoria artificiali adipiscenda tractatus*, in Pack, 'Artes memorativae,' ibid., pp. 265–287, especially pp. 272–273. For the reference to Dante, see *Inferno*, 28, 22 ff.

12 *Ars memorativa*, in Roger A. Pack, 'An "Ars memorativa" from the Late Middle Ages,' *Archives d'histoire doctrinale et littéraire du Moyen Age* 46 (1979): 229–267 (the passage cited is on 251).

13 'Ianuarius significabatur per hominem pictum ad mensam splendidam opulentamque sedentem, ac avide comedentem, manusque ad crateram mere plenam, tanquam quod bibere velit, extendentem. Illo enim tempore cum secundum Hyppocratem stomachi calidissimi sunt, faciliter cibos sumptos digerunt, et ad alios sumendos fructuose anhelant. Februarius, per senem igni se calefacientem, cuius ratio signi est, vel quia mensis hic reliqua frigoris ventorum ac intemperiei, quae ianuario debebantur, saepe numero retinet, vel quia iam in eo ultima hyemis senectus advenerit.' This iconography would later be used by Ripa.

14 The role of this kind of fascination in collecting has been discussed by Krzysztof Pomian in *Collectionneurs, amateurs et curieux. Paris, Venise: XVIe–XVIIIe siècle* (Paris: Gallimard 1987); English translation, *Collectors and Curiosities: Paris and Venice 1500–1800* (Oxford: Blackwell 1990). On the physicality of topical places in relation to the printing press, see Walter J. Ong, *Interfaces of the Word* (Ithaca, NY: Cornell University Press 1977). See also Ann Moss, *Printed Commonplace Books and the Structuring of Renaissance Thought* (Oxford: Clarendon Press 1996).

15 Aristotle, *Topica*, 8.14.163b, in Aristotle, *Posterior Analytics*, trans. Hugh

Tredennick, and *Topica* trans. E.S. Forster (Cambridge, Mass.: Harvard University Press 1976), II, 735. -

16 'Ait Aristoteles libro de reminiscentia quod motus animus se ultro per loca movetur, seque ipsum excitat. Etsi utique aliqui expositores per loca, topica loca intelligant, Themistius optimus Peripateticus per loca haec materialia intelligit.' See also *L'arte del ricordare* (Naples: Marco Antonio Passaro 1566), folio A4r. For the reference to Aristotle, see *On Memory*, 2. 452a.

17 See Massimo Firpo, 'Alessandro Citolini' [entry], in *Dizionario biografico degli italiani*, XXVI, 39–46; Alfredo Serrai, *Storia della bibliografia* (Rome: Bulzoni 1988), I, 243–256.

18 In light of this, the relations between Camillo and an architect and theoretician of architecture like Serlio is highly important: see Mario Carpo, *Metodo ed ordine nella teoria architettonica dei primi moderni: Alberti, Raffaello, Serlio e Camillo* (Geneva: Droz 1993).

19 Pietro Bembo, *Prose della volgar lingua*, ed. C. Dionisotti (Torino: U.T.E.T. 1960), I, chapter 3, 79.

20 Anton Francesco Doni, *Inferni* [Hells], in *I mondi e gli inferni* [Worlds and hells], ed. Pellizzari and M. Guglielminetti (Torino: Einaudi 1994), p. 265 (this text is based on the 1568 edition). An analogous passage appears a little later in the text: 'Imagine that this Academy is a company of sculptors, and, among themselves, they have designed a theatre where numerous statues and stories will be placed. These statues and stories cannot yet be seen in place in the work. When you see all of the *Hells* and not just a part of each, then you will see a terrifying edifice' (p. 266).

21 See, for example, the letters by Pietro Maria Buoni da Rimini and Francesco Marcolini that Doni includes *Inferni*: The author of the first letter claims to have heard that Doni publishes his books in a rather hurried fashion: 'you send your books to press without having composed them, and the same day you begin to write, the books are printed' (Doni, *Inferni*, in *I mondi e gli inferni* [Venice: Gioliti 1562], p. 279). 'I understand, moreover, that you write books at the booksellers' request, just as artists paint figures. Some want you to give them this number of pages, and others that number of pages. Others tell you: Give me one for this price, give me another for that price, and you write them' (p. 281).

22 For a complete bibliography, see Remigio Sabbadini, *Storia del ciceronianismo e d'altre questioni letterarie nell'età della Rinascenza* (Torino: Loescher 1886); Angiolo Gambaro's preface to Desiderio Erasmo da Rotterdam [Erasmus], *Il ciceroniano o dello stile migliore* (Brescia: La Scuola 1965), pp. ix–cxii; Marc Fumaroli, *L'âge de l'éloquence: rhétorique et 'res literaria'*

de la Renaissance au seuil de l'époque classique (Geneva: Droz 1980), 37–46, 77–115.

23 Giovanfrancesco Pico della Mirandola, *De imitatione*, in Giorgio Santangelo, *Le epistole 'De imitatione' di Giovanfrancesco Pico della Mirandola e di Pietro Bembo* (Florence: Olschki 1953), 26: 'et quamquam mutuo si non furto quaedam hinc inde quasi signa veterum atque toreumata carpsit ad ornanda suorum poematum edificia, propriis tamen illa sunt ornamentis magis conspicua, atque omnino magis illustria.'

24 See, for example, *Colloquio sul reimpiego dei sarcofagi romani nel Medioevo*, Pisa 1982 (Marburg: Verlag des Kunstgeschichtlichen Seminars 1984); Salvatore Settis, 'Des ruines au musée: La destinée de la sculture classique,' *Annales Economies Sociétés Civilisations* 48 (1993): 1347–1380.

25 Francesco Sansovino, *In materia dell'arte libri tre, ne' quali si contien l'ordine delle cose che si ricercano all'oratore* (Venice: Sansovino 1562), folio 4v. The first edition of this brief treatise was published in 1546.

26 Giuseppe Betussi, *Raverta, Trattati d'amore del Cinquecento* ed. G. Zonta (Bari: Laterza 1912); reprint, ed. M. Pozzi (Bari: Laterza, 1980), p. 100. On Betussi, see Lucia Nadin Bassani, *Il poligrafo veneto Giuseppe Betussi* (Padua: Antenore 1992).

27 In the Middle Ages the numerous buildings mentioned in the Bible had already inspired complex symbolism: see Henri De Lubac, *Exégèse médiévale: Les quatre sens de l'Ecriture* (Paris: Aubier 1559–1564), II, chapter 2, pp. 41 ff., translated in *Medieval Exegesis* (Edinburgh: W.B. Eerdmans 1998). On the popularity of this symbolism in the late sixteenth century, see Joseph Rykwert, *On Adam's House in Paradise* (Cambridge, Mass.: MIT Press 1981). See also David Cowling, *Building the Text: Architecture as Metaphor in the Late Medieval and Early Modern France* (Oxford: Clarendon Press 1998).

28 On this topos, see Ernst Robert Curtius, *Europäische Literatur und lateinisches Mittelalter* (Bern: A. Francke AG Verlag 1948), English translation, *European Literature and the Latin Middle Ages* (New York: Pantheon 1953).

29 Antonio Altamura, *Storia di un plagio* (Naples: Società Editrice Napoletana 1980).

30 In some ways analogous to the interest in 'architectural' titles is the popularity of the term 'theatre,' which is also very much in evidence in the titles of books in the sixteenth and seventeenth centuries. See Charles Bernheimer, 'Theatrum mundi,' *Art Bulletin* 38 (1956): 225–247; Mario Costanzo, *Il 'gran theatro del mondo'* (Milan: Scheiwiller 1964).

31 Bembo, *Asolani*, 1. 17, p. 235; 2. 7, p. 269.

32 Girolamo Bargagli, *Dialogo de' giuochi che nelle vegghie sanesi si usano di fare*, ed. P. D'Incalci Ermini (Siena: Accademia degli Intronati 1982), 167.

33 This explains why the somewhat sparse bibliography on this subject often
   gives contradictory information and diverse interpretations: Detlef
   Heikamp, 'Federico Zuccari e Firenze (1575–1579),' part 2, *Paragone-Arte*
   18, no. 207 (1967); 3–34, especially pp. 18–19; Mario Pepe's introduction to
   Anton Francesco Doni, *Disegno con un'appendice di altri scritti … riguardanti
   le arti* (Milan: Electa 1970), 17. Lina Padoan Urban discusses the nature
   of Doni's theatre in 'Teatri e "teatri del mondo" nella Venezia del
   Cinquecento,' *Arte veneta* 20 (1966): 137–146 (see n. 14, 144). For a bibliography on Doni, see the 1994 edition of Doni's *I mondi e gli inferni*, ed.
   Pellizzari and Guglielminetti.

34 Many scholars have expressed doubt as to the actual existence of this
   academy, supposedly founded in 1549. Claudia Di Filippo Bareggi proposes that it did actually exist: *Il mestiere di scrivere: Lavoro intellettuale e
   mercato librario a Venezia nel Cinquecento* (Rome: Bulzoni 1988), pp. 132–148.
   Her research is based on Cosimo de' Medici's correspondence in the
   Archivio di Stato in Florence.

35 There are three mss. of the *Imprese*, two of which are autographs (Florence,
   Biblioteca Nazionale, Cod. Palat. E.B.10.8, entitled *Le dimostrationi de gli
   animi degli huomini del Doni* [Examples of the hearts of men by Doni], as
   well as the ms. cited above) and one by the hand of a copyist (Venice,
   Museo Correr, cod. Correr 1387). The text was published – with the passages believed to be obscene censored and no images – in a small tome on
   the occasion of a wedding (Venice: Gazzetta Uffiziale 1858). The manuscript *Le imprese reali* [Royal devices] (Wellesley, Mass., Library of Wellesley College, The France Plimpton Collection, n. 897) contains only the
   drawings of devices of different historical persons with their names.

36 On Mount Parnassus, see Christopher Cairns, *Pietro Aretino and the Republic of Venice: Researches on Aretino and His Circle* (Florence: Olschki 1985),
   chapter 10; Marc Fumaroli, *L'école du silence: Le sentiment des images au
   XVIIe siècle* (Paris: Flammarion 1994), pp. 19–36. It is interesting to note
   that *I mondi* Doni includes the iconographic theme of Mount Parnassus in
   the literary and artistic genre of the 'vision.' After citing Dante, Virgil, and
   Sannazzaro, Doni writes: 'There have been certain saints in the Christian
   religion who have revealed wondrous truths by means of visions. Painters
   (on a lower level) have put their minds to giving us some abstract things
   with their hands by painting Mount Parnassus for us' (*I mondi e gli inferni*,
   p. 8).

37 On the relations between Camillo and Doni, see Lina Bolzoni, *Il teatro della
   memoria: Studi su Giulio Camillo* (Padua: Liviana 1984), pp. 68–69.

38 Paolo Cherchi, 'Nell'officina di Anton Francesco Doni,' *Forum italicum* 22
   (1987): 206–214.

39 On Giovio, see the procedings of the conference 'Paolo Giovio: Il
   Rinascimento e la memoria,' *Raccolta Storica. Società storica Comense* (Como
   1985), vol. 17; Francis Haskell, *History and Its Images* (New Haven, Conn.:
   Yale University Press 1993), 43–51. The two descriptions of Doni are taken
   from Anton Francesco Doni, *Lettere* (Venice: Francesco Marcolini 1552),
   75–86. The 'serious' version was republished in Doni, *Disegno*, 98–100.

40 The letters addressed to Alfonso II d'Este, dated 25 and 27 April 1563, are
   in Modena, Archivio di Stato, Cancelleria Ducale, Particolari, Filza 406,
   and Archivio per materie, Accademie, busta 1, fasc. 22. The letter to
   Cosimo I, dated 28 April 1563, is taken from Michelangelo Gualandi,
   *Nuova raccolta di lettere sulla pittura, scultura ed architettura scritte da' più
   celebri personaggi dei secoli XV e XVI* (Bologna 1844; reprinted, Bologna:
   Forni 1983), pp. 52–62.

41 In 1565 *Pitture* was recycled, with some changes, in the fifth part of *Zucca*;
   see Cecilia Ricottini Marsili-Libelli, *A.F. Doni scrittore e stampatore*
   (Florence: Sansoni 1960), n. 56. On *Pitture*, see Julius Von Schlosser, *La
   letteratura artistica. Manuale delle fonti della storia dell'arte moderna*, 2nd ed.
   (Florence: La Nuova Italia 1956), pp. 244 ff; Carlo Ossola, *Autunno del
   Rinascimento: 'Idea del Tempio' dell'arte nell'ultimo Cinquecento* (Florence:
   Olschki 1971), 188–189.

42 On the function of the 'vision' in Doni, see Giorgio Masi, '"Quelle
   discordanze sì perfette": Anton Francesco Doni 1551–1553,' *Atti e memorie
   dell'Accademia Toscana di Scienze e Lettere La Colombaria* 53 (1988): 111–112,
   especially 46 ff.

43 For a complete bibliography and more information, see Glanville
   Downey's entry 'Ekphrasis' in *Reallexikon für Antike und Christentum*
   (Stuttgart: Hiersemann 1959), IV, 921–944; Svetlana Alpers, '"Ekphrasis"
   and Aesthetic Attitudes in Vasari's "Lives,"' *Journal of the Warburg and
   Courtauld Institutes* 23 (1960): 190–215; Michael Baxandall, *Giotto and the
   Orators: Humanistic Observers of Painting in Italy and the Discovery of Pictorial
   Composition 1350–1450* (Oxford: Oxford University Press 1971), pp. 85–87,
   90–96; Murray Krieger, *Ekphrasis: The Illustration of the Natural Sign* (Balti-
   more, Md.: The Johns Hopkins University Press 1992).

44 Atlante's palace is an example of this (2.41–43), as is Adonio's palace
   (43.13–14), not to mention the reference to the descendents of the Estensi
   and the paintings in Tristan's castle (capable of 'painting the future,' 33.3.6);
   see Lina Bolzoni, '"Ut pictura poesis" nel Cinquecento,' in Associazione
   italiana di cultura classica, *La poesia: Origine e sviluppo delle forme poetiche
   nella letteratura occidentale* (Pisa: ETS 1991), pp. 223–241, especially 234–238.

45 The manuscript of *Le nuove pitture* was identified by Paul O. Kristeller, *Iter*

Italicum (London: The Warburg Institute 1967), II, 606: Archivio Capitolare Vaticano, Archivio della basilica di S. Pietro, Fondo Patetta 18.

46 See Adolf Katzenellenbogen's classic work, *Allegories of the Virtues and Vices in Medieval Art from Early Christian Times to the Thirteenth Century* (London: The Warburg Institute 1939).

47 Heikamp, *F. Zuccari a Firenze*, 19–21, drawing reproduced in plate IV.

48 In 1565 Zuccari painted the *histories* for the scenes in a wooden theatre built by Palladio for a Compagnia della Calza, the Accesi (Padoan Urban, 137).

49 Fortune, for example, is described as follows: 'A woman with a small cloud that impedes her sight, dressed in a rich manner by the hand of Pomp with various colours, sitting on an ostrich that has the wings of an eagle; as she makes it run around, she throws treasures, sceptres and crowns that rain down into her lap from a cloud above, and she scatters them around with her left hand almost as if to show that she is not giving them out in the right manner; and in her right hand she has an iron mace with heavy, fatal balls with which she wounds, kills, and takes men to the ground, men represented as babies of little intelligence who take and steal her treasure' (Doni, *Pitture*, folio 14 r–v).

50 In *Pitture* Time is described in the following manner: 'We will represent it (should we wish to break bread with commoners) as a man, so as to not leave the path of other dreamers, and we will dress him in iridescent clothes, that is, with various and different colours depending on the point of view, his garments decorated with stars, because from time to time stars are our masters: Crowned on the head with a crown of roses, spikes, fruits, and dried branches, as king of the four seasons; he will be seated, even if he is really among us, here on earth, on top of the Zodiac, which, according to astrologers, turns year round, since his virtue is positioned above [in the constellations] ... We will put in his hand a mirror that always shows the present clearly; another mirror will be held by a withered putto, like a skeleton, almost a shadow, on one side, representing past time that is being destroyed and dissolved into nothing; and on the other side, a nice, fat putto will hold another mirror, representing the future. At their feet will be a large book in which the two putti will continuously write; the first will have a sun, meaning *day*, on his head, and the other, which will be a female, will have the moon for the night on her head' (Doni, *Pitture*, folios 21v–22r).

51 Orazio Toscanella, *Bellezze del Furioso di M. Lodovico Ariosto ... con gli argomenti et allegorie de i canti, con l'allegorie de i nomi proprii principali dell'opera, et co i luochi communi de l'autore per ordine alfabetico* [The beauties

of Ludovico Ariosto's *Furioso*, with the subjects and allegories of the
cantos, with the allegories of the principal proper names of the work and
with the author's topical places in alphabetical order] (Venice: Pietro dei
Franceschi 1574). The passages that follow are from this edition. As in the
case of other works by Toscanella, this book was probably part of one of
the Accademia Veneziana's editorial programs: The *Somma delle opere che
in tutte le scienze et arti più nobili et in varie lingue ha da mandare in luce
l'Academia Venetiana* (Venice: Accademia Veneziana 1558) lists a discourse
on 'the 'beauties of Ariosto' [*bellezze* dell'Ariosto] in which the moral and
natural allegories of the poet are explained through comparisons with
Homer and Virgil in the office of poetry' (p. 29).

52 Doni's plagiarism of Camillo is discussed in Lina Bolzoni, *Il teatro della
    memoria*, pp. 67–72.

53 See Lina Bolzoni, 'L'allegoria, o la creazione dell'oscurità,' *L'Asino d'oro* 3
    (1991): 53–69. See also Walter Benjamin's remarkable observations in
    Ursprung des deutschen Trauerspiels (Frankfurt am Main: Suhrkamp 1963);
    (English translation, *The Origin of German Tragic Drama* (London: Verso
    1985).

54 Toscanella, *Bellezze del Furioso*, pp. 34–36 (*Aeneid* 4.518 and 6.47–48). See
    Giulio Camillo, *L'idea del theatro*, ed. L. Bolzoni (Palermo: Sellerio 1991),
    141: 'Underneath the Gorgons of Mars there will be the image of a maiden
    with one foot bare and her dress ungirdled; and this will mean delibera-
    tion, or rather firm and unexpected purpose, to be distinguished from
    useful deliberation which is made after reflection and depends on Jupiter;
    and being ungirdled and barefoot is greatly understood as being related to
    Jason's loin and bare foot; and this figure was expressed by Virgil in
    Dido's unexpected and firm deliberation to die when he said that she had
    "one foot free from all fastenings and her dress ungirdled"; and we have
    taken this image from him.' The image of the Gorgons is positioned on the
    fourth level of the theatre and it represents the internal man. Toscanella
    has evidently added another reference to Virgil: the depiction of the sibyl.

55 More than once in his works, Doni described various images, but at times
    he changes the medium (painting, sculpture, cameos, etc.), the name
    of the owner, the location, etc. The only constant is the *inventio*, that is,
    the iconological description; see Lina Bolzoni, 'Riuso e riscrittura di
    immagini dal Palatino al Della Porta, dal Doni a Federico Zuccari, al
    Toscanella,' *Scritture di scritture: testi, generi, modelli nel Rinascimento*, ed.
    G. Mazzacurati and M. Plaisance (Rome: Bulzoni 1987), 171–206, especially
    pp. 198–202. On the interpretative game created by Doni with images, see
    François Quiviger, 'Arts visuels, iconographie et déraison dans l'œuvre

d'Anton Francesco Doni,' *Trois: Revue d'écriture et d'érudition* 3 (1988): 52–65.

56 See Erwin Panofsky, 'Galileo as a Critic of the Arts: Aesthetic Attitude and Scientific Thought,' *Isis* 37 (1956): 31–35; Dante Della Terza, 'Galileo letterato: "Considerazioni al Tasso,"' in *Forma e memoria* (Rome: Bulzoni 1979), pp. 197–221; Tibor Wlassics, *Galilei critico letterario* (Ravenna: Longo 1974).

57 Greenblatt, Stephen, *Renaissance Self-Fashioning: From More to Shakespeare* (Chicago: University of Chicago Press 1980), pp. 17 ff. On the comparison with anamorphosis, see Mario Costanzo, *I segni del silenzio e altri studi sulle poetiche e l'iconografia letteraria del Manierismo e del Barocco* (Rome: Bulzoni 1983), 31. On anamorphosis, see Jurgis Baltrušaitis, *Anamorphoses ou magie artificielle des effets merveilleux* (Paris: Perrin 1969), English translation, *Anamorphic Art* (Cambridge: Chadwick-Healey 1977); Lina Bolzoni, 'Tra parola e immagine: Per una tipologia cinquecentesca del lettore creativo,' *Lettere italiane* 48 (1996): 527–558.

58 On the various ideas of the value of curiosity throughout the centuries, see Krzysztof Pomian, *Collectors and Curiosities*. Galileo's position on this theme is not entirely consistent; for example, in the famous passage of *Il Saggiatore* [The assayer] that describes the search for the different causes of sound, the protagonist is a 'learned man with a naturally keen intelligence and extraordinary curiosity' (in Galileo Galilei, *Opere*, ed. F. Flora (Milan / Naples Riccardi 1953), p. 199); see Ezio Raimondi, 'Il romanzo del "curioso,"' *Forme e vicende, per Giovanni Pozzi*, ed. O. Besomi, G. Gianella, A. Martini, and G. Pedrojetta (Padua: Antenore 1988), pp. 383–398.

59 Paola Barocchi, 'Fortuna dell'Ariosto nella trattatistica figurativa,' *Studi vasariani* (Torino: Einaudi 1984), pp. 53–67; Barocchi, 'Storiografia e collezionismo dal Vasari al Lanzi,' *Storia dell'arte italiana* (Torino: Einaudi 1979), I, chapter 2, pp. 5–82, especially p. 30. See also Gerhard Goebel, *Poeta faber: Erdichtete Architektur in der italienischen, spanishen und französischen Literatur der Renaissance und des Barock* (Heidelberg: Winter 1971).

60 See 'Controversie sulla Gerusalemme,' in Torquato Tasso, *Opere* (Pisa: Niccolò Capurro 1827), vol. XVIII (the passage cited is on p. 88).

61 On Giovanbattista Strozzi, see Adrasto S. Barbi, *Un accademico mecenate e poeta: Giovan Battista Strozzi il giovane* (Florence: Sansoni 1900); Lina Bolzoni, 'Ercole e i pigmei ovvero Controriforma e intellettuali neoplatonici,' *Rinascimento* 21 (1981): 285–296, especially pp. 294–296; Franco Fido, '"L'America": Primo canto di un poema inedito di Giovan Battista Strozzi il giovane,' *Studi secenteschi* 23 (1982): 277–310; Massimiliano Rossi, 'Per l'"unita" delle arti. La poetica "figurativa" di Giovambattista Strozzi il Giovane,' *I Tatti Studies'* 6 (1995): 169–214.

62 Giovanbattista Strozzi, *Dell'unità della favola*, in *Trattati di poetica e retorica del Cinquecento*, ed. B. Weinberg (Bari: Laterza 1974), IV, 333–344, especially p. 340.

63 On Garzoni, see Carlo Ossola, 'Metáphore et inventaire de la folie dans la littérature italienne du XVIe siècle,' *Folie et déraison à la Renaissance* (Brussels: Colloque international, Fédération Internationale des Instituts et Sociétés pour l'Etude de la Renaissance (Brussels 1976), pp. 171–195, especially pp. 187 ff.; Paolo Cherchi, *Enciclopedismo e politica della riscrittura: Tommaso Garzoni* (Pisa: Pacini 1980). See also the recent editions of some of Garzoni's works: *Opere*, ed. P. Cherchi (Ravenna: Longo 1993); and *Piazza universale di tutte le professioni del mondo*, ed. P. Cherchi and B. Collina (Torino: Einaudi 1996).

64 In Giulio Camillo, *Opere* (Venice: Domenico Farri 1579), p. 290. On Marcantonio Flaminio, see Carol Maddison, *Marcantonio Flaminio: Poet, Humanist and Reformer* (London: Routledge and Kegan Paul 1965); Alessandro Pastore, *Marcantonio Flaminio: Fortune e sfortune di un chierico nell'Italia del Cinquecento* (Milan: Franco Angeli 1981).

65 *Ars memorativa*, in Pack, *An 'Ars memorativa,'* pp. 229, 234. See Giuseppa Saccaro Battisti, 'Dalla narrazione alla scena pittorica mediante le tecniche della memoria,' *Metodologia della ricerca: Orientamenti attuali; Congresso internazionale in onore di E. Battisti*, 79–83.

66 *Ars memorativa*, in Pack, *An 'Ars memorativa,'* p. 253: 'quando ergo vis operari cum ymaginibus sentenciarum, tunc non est avertere necesse singulas dictiones ex quibus illa sentencia componitur, sed comprehendere bene eius substanciam facti et reducere illam in summam et secundum hanc formare ymaginem.'

67 Ibid., p. 254: 'Nota tamen quod omnia non quasi praeterita sed quasi futura vel ac si sint presencia mente debent videri.'

68 See Lina Bolzoni, '"Ut pictura poesis" nel Cinquecento,' pp. 223–241, especially pp. 234–238. In regard to the manipulation of time made possible by feigned *ecphrasis*, Verdizzotti (see chapter 2, p. 32) offers some very interesting observations: see Giovanni Mario Verdizzotti, *Breve discorso intorno alla narrazione poetica* [A brief essay on poetic narration], ed. B. Weinberg (Bari: Laterza 1974), IV, 7–12, especially p. 10. The *Breve discorso* was read in 1588 at the Accademia degli Uranici. On feigned *ecphrasis* in sixteenth-century poetry, see Guido Baldassarri, 'Ut poësis pictura: Cicli figurativi nei poemi epici e cavallereschi,' in *La corte e lo spazio: Ferrara estense* (Rome: ed. G. Papagno and A. Quondam (Rome: Bulzoni 1982), II, 605–636.

69 'Quasi optimus pictor hausta rerum sensilium simulachra, suo penicillo
memoriae designat, quae tamquam abrasa tabula huic officio antistita est.'

70 From the outset the fascination with forgetting seems to penetrate to the
heart of the tradition that exalts memory; Hesiod, for example, claims that
Memory (Mnemosyne) bore the Muses 'to be a forgetting of troubles, a
pause in sorrow' (Hesiod, *Works and Days and Theogony*, trans. Stanley
Lombardo (Indianapolis, Ind.: Hackett 1993), pp. 55–56, 62). Themistocles'
answer is cited by Petrarch (*De remediis utriusque fortunae*, book 1.8) as
proof that memory generates pain and suffering.

71 'Unde cum nil aliud sit haec ars, quam memorandarum rerum picturam
memoriae explicare et quomodo egregius pictor alicuius rei cuius
imaginem ignorat, poterit in pictura repraesentare?'

72 'Michaeli Angeli, Raphaeli, vel Titiani picturae melius reminiscimur, quam
vulgaris pictoris, cum in his non nisi usitati gestus, in illis fortes et
inusitates aptitudines [videmus].'

73 'Si Andromedae fabulae meminisse volumus, loci personam nudam
confingemus cautibus ferreis catenis alligatam, trementem, lugentemque.'

74 'At si historiae, aut fabulae, in quibus plures personae introducuntur,
historiam in personarum et rerum compendium reducemus, locisque
accomodabimus. Id vehementer placet quod a poetis et comicis
observatum video, ut quam paucis personis possint, fabulam monstrent,
neque ulla erit tam rerum varietate referta historia, quam novem aut
decem personae optime repraesentent.'

75 *On Painting*, trans. John R. Spencer (Westport, Conn.: Greenwood Press
1976), p. 76; compare the following text with that in n. 74: 'Atque in
historia id vehementer approbo quod a poetis tragicis atque comicis
observatum video, ut quam possint paucis personatis fabulam doceant.
Meo quidem iudicio nulla erit usque adeo tanta rerum varietate referta
historia, quam novem aut decem homines non possint condigne agere'
(Leon Battista Alberti, *De pictura*, 2.40, in *Opere volgari*, C. Grayson (Bari:
Laterza 1973), III, 71).

76 See Salvatore Bongi, *Annali di Gabriel Giolito de' Ferrari* (Rome: Ministero
della Pubblica Istruzione 1895), II, 308–309, 335–336. On sixteenth-century
allegorical interpretations of Ulysses, see Marco Lorandi, *Il mito di Ulisse
nella pittura a fresco del Cinquecento italiano* (Milan: Jaka Book 1996);
Lorandi, '"Sic notus Ulysses?"' *Antichità viva* 26, no. 2 (1987): 19–33. On
Dolce, see Luciana Borsetto, 'Scrittura, riscrittura, tipografia: l'"officio" di
"tradurre" di Lodovico Dolce dentro e fuori la stamperia giolitina,' in
Il furto di Prometeo. Imitazione, scrittura, riscrittura nel Rinascimento

(Alessandria: Edizioni dell'Orso 1990), pp. 257–276; Ronnie H. Terpening, *Lodovico Dolce: Renaissance Man of Letters* (Toronto: University of Toronto Press 1997).

77 I have used the 1543 edition of Ariosto: *Orlando Furioso novissimamente alla sua integrità ridotto e ornato di varie figure ... aggiunto per ciascun canto alcune allegorie* [*Orlando furioso* newly reduced and decorated with various figures in its entirety, with allegories added for each canto] (Venice: Giolito 1543), see folio 122r (as well as Dolce's *Ulisse*, 146). See Giuseppe Fatini, *Bibliografia della critica ariostesca (1510–1596)* (Florence: Le Monnier 1958); Ugo Bellocchi and Bruno Fava, *L'interpretazione grafica dell'Orlando Furioso* (Reggio Emilia: Banca di Credito Popolare e Cooperativo di Reggio Emilia 1961); Francesco Sberlati, 'Il testo "visualizzato." Iconologia e letteratura cavalleresca,' *Intersezioni* 15 (1995): 313–334; Daniel Javitch, *Proclaiming a Classic. The Canonization of 'Orlando Furioso'* (Princeton: Princeton University Press 1991).

78 See Lina Bolzoni, 'Parole e immagini per il ritratto di un nuovo Ulisse: *l'invenzione* dell'Aldrovandi per la sua villa di campagna,' in *Documentary Culture: Florence and Rome from Grand-Duke Ferdinand I to Pope Alexander VII*, ed. E. Cropper (Bologna: Nuova Alfa Editoriale 1992), 317–348. Aldrovandi cites Dolce's work in a manuscript preserved in Bologna, Biblioteca Universitaria, cod. Aldrovandi 97, folio 435r.

79 'Nam si oculis externis una hora pervolare et repetere possumus tota Biblia imaginibus expressa materialibus, tam cito enim atque folia vertimus, uno intuitu videmus quid in iis agatur, si videlicet omnia ante nobis cognita sint, ut debent quae per artem locis affiximus: Quanto magis mentis oculis, qui multo citius operantur.'

80 Diego Valadés, *Rhetorica christiana ad concionandi et orandi usum accommodata, utriusque facultatis exemplis suo loco consertis, quae quidem ex Indorum maxime deprompta sunt historiis unde praeter doctrinam, summa quoque delectatio comparabitur* (Perugia: Pietro Giacomo Petrucci 1579). I must thank Adriano Prosperi for having brought this work to my attention. See Adriano Prosperi, 'Intorno a un catechismo figurato del tardo '500,' *Quaderni di Palazzo Te* 2 (1985): 45–53; René Taylor, *El arte de la memoria en el nuevo mundo* (Madrid: Swan 1987); Pauline Moffit Watts, 'Hieroglyphs of conversion: Alien discourses in Diego Valadés's "Rhetorica christiana,"' *Memorie domenicane* 22 (1991): 405–433; Mario Sartor, *Ars dicendi et excudendi: Diego Valadés incisore messicano in Italia* (Padua: Cleup 1992); *Un francescano tra gli Indios. Diego Valadés e la 'rhetorica christiana,'* ed. C. Finzi and A. Morganti (Rimini: Il Cerchio 1995).

81 Jonathan D. Spence, *The Memory Palace of Matteo Ricci* (New York: Viking /
   Penguin 1983).

82 See Mark Munzel and Birgit Scharlau, *Qellqay: Mündliche Kultur und
   Schriftetradition bei Indianern Lateinamerikas* (Frankfurt and New York:
   Campus Verlag 1986); Serge Gruzinski, *La guerre des images de Christophe
   Colomb à 'Blade Runner' (1492–2019)* (Paris: Fayard 1990).

83 Gabriele Paleotti, *Discorso intorno alle imagini sacre e profane*, in *Trattati
   d'arte del Cinquecento fra Manierismo e Controriforma*, ed. P. Barocchi (Bari:
   Laterza 1961), II, 222.

84 On portraiture, see Enrico Castelnuovo, 'Il significato del ritratto pittorico
   nella società,' *Storia d'Italia*, volume V: *I documenti* (Torino: Einaudi 1973),
   pp. 1033–1094; *Il ritratto e la memoria: materiali*, 1–3, ed. A. Gentili, P. Morel,
   and C. Cieri Via (Rome: Bulzoni 1989–1994); Annette Drew-Bear, *Painted
   Faces on the Renaissance Stage: The Moral Significance of Face-Painting Conventions* (Lewisburg: Bucknell University Press / London and Toronto:
   Associated University Press 1994). On portraiture as *imago agens*, see
   Robert Williams, 'The Facade of the Palazzo dei "Visacci,"' *I Tatti Studies:
   Essays in the Renaissance* 5 (1993): 209–244, especially pp. 218–219.

85 Pomponio Gaurico, *De sculptura* ed. A. Chastel and R. Klein (Geneva: Droz
   1969), p. 131. See Pliny *Naturalis historia*, 35.2.9–10.

86 Paleotti, *Discorso intorno alle imagini*, pp. 340, 663.

87 'Propterea utilissimum erit dicta scripta gesta, vitamque praedictorum
   hominum apud varios authores videre, maxime apud Diogenem Laertium.
   Cum enim eorum dicta vel facta cognoveris, erit haud difficile de eis
   aliquam figuram, similitudinem vel simulachrum cuiuslibet conveniens
   mente concipere et excogitare.'

88 Francesco Sansovino, *Delle cose notabili della Città di Venetia* [On points of
   interest in the City of Venice] (Venice: Felice Valgrisio 1587), 55–56. The
   first edition of this work was published in 1556 under the pseudonym
   'Anselmo Guisoni.' On Sansovino, and for a complete bibliography, see
   Lina Bolzoni, 'Costruire immagini: L'arte della memoria tra letteratura e
   arti figurative,' *La cultura della memoria*, ed. L. Bolzoni and P. Corsi (Bologna: Il Mulino 1992), pp. 57–99, especially pp. 87–93; Elena Bonora, *Ricerche
   su Francesco Sansovino imprenditore librario e letterato* (Venice: Istituto
   Veneto di Scienze, Lettere ed Arti 1994).

89 Manfredo Tafuri, *Venezia e il Rinascimento* (Torino: Einaudi 1985).

90 I cite from the 1561 edition, which has a slightly different title: *In materia
   dell'arte libri tre ne' quali si contien l'ordine delle cose che si ricercano all'oratore*
   [Three books on the subject of art containing the order of things required

of the orator] (Venice: Sansovino 1561), 32. This passage is identical in the 1546 edition.

91 David R. Coffin, *The Villa d'Este at Tivoli* (Princeton: Princeton University Press 1960). See also James Ackermann, *The Villa: Form and Ideology of Country Houses* (Princeton: Princeton University Press 1990); David R. Coffin, *The Villa in the Life of Renaissance Rome* (Princeton: Princeton University Press 1979).

92 Pirro Ligorio, *Vita di Virbio, detto altrimenti Hippolito figlio di Theseo descritta e disegnata con immitatione dell'antico in sedice historie*, in Coffin, *The Villa d'Este*, 155. Coffin's 'memoria lotale' is likely an error in the transcription of the manuscript.

93 Lodovico Dolce, *Dialogo della pittura intitolato l'Aretino*, in *Trattati d'arte del Cinquecento*, ed. Barocchi, I, 141–206 (the passage cited is on 162–163). The classical source of this anecdote is Suetonius, *Vitae, Divus Iulius*, 7; see also Sallust, *Bellum Jugurthinum*, 4.5–6.

94 On the traditional mnemonic function of artistic images, see Salvatore Settis, 'Iconografia dell'arte italiana, 1110–1500: Una linea,' *Storia dell'arte italiana* (Torino: Einaudi 1979), III, 177–270, especially pp. 181 ff. The case of Ligorio brings up questions regarding the meaning and function of decorative programs in other sixteenth-century villas. See Simona Boscaglia, 'Dal caos al cosmo: il programma decorativo della Corte Cornaro in Padova,' *Comunità* 37 (1983): 379–399. On the establishment of decorative programs as an actual genre in painting, see Eugenio Battisti, *Cicli pittorici: Storie profane* (Milan: Touring Club Italiano 1981); Julian Kliemann, *Gesta dipinte: la grande decorazione nelle dimore italiane dal Quattrocento al Seicento* (Milan: Silvana Editoriale 1993).

95 John D. Lyons, *Exemplum: The Rhetoric of Example in Early Modern France and Italy* (Princeton: Princeton University Press 1989); Timothy Hampton, *Writing from History: The Rhetoric of Exemplarity in Renaissance Literature* (Ithaca, NY: Cornell University Press 1990).

6 The Art of Memory and Collecting

1 On Quicchelberg, see Julius Schlosser, *Die Kunst- und Wunderkammern der Spätrenaissance* (Leipzig: Klinkhardt und Biermann 1908); Elizabeth M. Hajos, 'References to Giulio Camillo in Samuel Quicchelberg's "Inscriptiones vel tituli theatri amplissimi,"' *Bibliothèque d'Humanisme et Renaissance* 25 (1963): 207–211; Patricia Falguières, 'Fondation du Théâtre ou Méthode de l'exposition universelle: Les "Inscriptiones" de Samuel Quicchelberg (1565),' *Les Cahiers du Musée National d'Art Moderne* 40 (1992):

91–115. On sixteenth-century collecting, and for a complete bibliography, see Giuseppe Olmi, *L'inventario del mondo: Catalogazione della natura e luoghi del sapere nella prima età moderna* (Bologna: Il Mulino 1992); *Macrocosmos in Microcosmo. Die Welt in der Stube. Zur Geschichte des Sammelns 1450 bis 1800,* ed. A. Grote (Leske-Budrich: Opladen 1994); Paula Findlen, *Possessing Nature: Museums, Collecting and Scientific Culture in Early Modern Italy* (Berkeley: University of California Press 1994).

2 'Theatri etiam nomen hic assumitur non improprie, sed vere pro structura grandi, vel arcuata, vel ovali, vel ad formam ambulacri ... Monere hic oportet Iulii Camilli museum semicirculo suo, recte quoque theatrum dici potuisse.'

3 *De ratione dicendi (Rhetorica ad Herennium),* trans. Harry Caplan (Cambridge, Mass.: Harvard University Press 1981), p. 205: 'Nunc ad thesaurum inventorum atque omnium partium rhetoricae custodem, memoriam, transeamus.'

4 Quintilian, *Institutio oratoria,* 11.2.1 [*The Institutio Oratoria of Quintilian,* trans. H.E. Butler (Cambridge, Mass.: Harvard University Press 1961), IV, 213]: 'exemplorum, legum, responsorum, dictorum denique factorum quasdam copias, quibus abundare quasque in promptu semper habere debet orator, eadem illa vis praesentat neque immerito thesaurus hic eloquentiae dicitur.'

5 'Venio in campos et lata praetoria memoriae, ubi sunt thesauri innumerabilium imaginum' (10.8.12); 'ecce in memoriae meae campis et antris et cavernis innumerabilibus atque innumerabiliter plenis innumerabilium rerum generibus ... discurro et volito' (10.17.26).

6 'Haec omnia recipit recolenda cum opus est, et retractanda grandis memoriae recessus et nescio qui secreti atque ineffabiles sinus eius' (10.8.13); 'Istae quippe res non intromittuntur ad eam, sed earum solae imagines mira celeritate capiuntur et miris tamquam cellis reponuntur et mirabiliter recordando proferuntur' (10.9.16).

7 Wendelin Schmidt-Dengler, 'Die "aula memoriae" in den Konfessionem des heiligen Augustin,' *Revue des études Augustiniennes* 14 (1968): 69–89; Wolfgang Hübner, 'Die "praetoria memoriae" im zehnten Buch der "Confessiones" Vergilisches bei Augustin,' *Revue des études Augustiniennes* 27 (1981): 245–263; Dominique Doucet, 'L'*ars memoriae* dans les "Confessiones,"' *Revue des études Augustiniennes* 33 (1987): 49–69.

8 Francesco Petrarca, *Familiarium rerum libri,* ed. V. Rossi (Florence: Sansoni 1937), 17.8.3–4, pp. 254–255.

9 *Ars memorativa,* in Roger A. Pack, 'An "Ars memorativa" from the Late Middle Ages,' *Archives d'histoire doctrinale et littéraire du Moyen Age* 46

(1979): 221–281 (the passage cited is on 243): 'pelvis aurea in qua oriuntur et continentur intellectus et voluntas.'

10 For a bibliography on the Stanzino of Francesco I de' Medici, see n. 22 below.

11 Francesco Bonaini, 'Cronaca del Convento di Santa Caterina dell'Ordine dei Predicatori in Pisa,' *Archivio storico italiano* 12 (1854): part 2, pp. 399–593 (the passage cited is on 521): 'Eius memoria et intellectus ... quasi quoddam armarium scripturarum.' On Bartolomeo di San Concordio, see Cesare Segre's entry *Dizionario biografico degli italiani*, VI, 768–770.

12 Dante Alighieri, *Vita nuova*, ed. D. De Robertis (Milan and Naples: Ricciardi 1980), p. 27. Charles S. Singleton's interpretation of this *incipit* remains among the most powerful: *An Essay on the 'Vita Nuova'* (Cambridge, Mass.: Harvard University Press 1949), chapter 2.

13 Harald Weinrich, *Metafora e menzogna: La serenità dell'arte* (Bologna: Il Mulino 1976), pp. 49–53. See also Maria Corti, '"Il libro della memoria" e i libri dello scrittore,' *Percorsi dell'invenzione: il linguaggio poetico e Dante* (Torino: Einaudi 1993), pp. 27–50.

14 Francesco Petrarca, *Rerum memorandarum libri*, ed. G. Billanovich (Florence: Sansoni 1943), II, 43–49.

15 Thomas Lambert Schenckel, *Gazophylacium artis memoriae* (Strasbourg: Antonius Bertramus 1610), 58: 'there are some important men who claim to be able to reconstruct a whole library in their memories (not just the books, but the content of the books); and they show that they are able to transport such a library by sea, over land, effortlessly and at no cost; and they show that they are able to do so much more easily than any other library, which would require great expenditures and would be a nuisance and very difficult to bring with us' [Non desunt viri graves, qui totam bibliothecam (non libros tantum omnes, sed contenta librorum omnium) in memoria posse construi affirment, quam per mare, per terras, nullo negotio, nullo sumptu circumferri posse demonstrant; ac facilius id fieri quam aliam bibliothecam erigi, quod sine magnis sumptibus fieri nequit quamque circumferre nobiscum esset molestissimum taediosissimumque].

16 Robert Fludd, *Utriusque cosmi ... historia* (Oppenheim: Hieronimy Galleri 1619), pp. 55 ff.; Frances A. Yates, *The Art of Memory* (London: Routledge and Kegan Paul 1966); Yates, *Theatre of the World* (London: Routledge and Kegan Paul 1969), pp. 136–161; Wilhelm Schmidt-Biggemann, 'Robert Fludd's "Theatrum memoriae,"' in *Ars memorativa: Zur kulturgeschichtlichen Bedeutung der Gedächtniskunst 1400–1750* ed. J.J. Berns and W. Neuber (Tübingen: Max Niemeyer 1993), 154–169.

17 Throughout this work there are expressions that allude to an intersection

of knowledge and memory: 'But since there is no more to say of the air, we will descend into the water, and from birds, *we will become fish* in order to see minutely the water and all its pertinent aspects' (p. 68).

18 Paolo Rossi, *Clavis universalis: Arti della memoria e logica combinatoria da Lullo a Leibniz* (Milan and Naples: Ricciardi 1960); Yates, *The Art of Memory*; Lina Bolzoni, 'Il gioco delle immagini: l'arte della memoria dalle origini al Seicento,' in *La fabbrica del pensiero: Dall'arte della memoria alle neuroscienze* (Milan: Electa 1989), pp. 16–65, English translation, *The Enchanted Loom: Chapters in the History of Neuroscience* (New York: Oxford University Press 1991).

19 See especially Luciano Berti, *Il principe dello Studiolo. Francesco I dei Medici e la fine del Rinascimento fiorentino* (Florence: EDAM 1967); Robert Evans, *Rudolf II and His World: A Study in Intellectual History 1567–1612* (Oxford: Clarendon Press 1973).

20 Gesualdo, *Plutosofia*, folios 55v–56r; *Epigramma in encomium artis memoriae* by Isaac Bruschius Egranus, in Schenckel, *Gazophylacium artis memoriae*, folio A8r; this theme returns repeatedly in the text.

21 Quicchelberg, *Inscriptiones vel tituli*: 'Musea, vel theatra, vel promptuaria varie instruxerunt' (folio 30v); 'cogito sequentibus annis plurimos reges, principes ac optimates in fondandis sapientiae theatris ac promptuariis incitare' (folio 16r).

22 For a bibliography on the Stanzino, see Lina Bolzoni, *Il teatro della memoria: studi su Giulio Camillo* (Padua: Liviana 1984), p. 54, n. 3. See also Andreas Grote, 'A System for the Wonders of Creation,' *Materialen aus dem Institut fur Museumskunde. Staatliche Museen Preussischer Kulturbesitz* (Berlin) 7 (1983): 33–63.

23 See Karl Frey, *Der literarische Nachlass Giorgio Vasari* (Munich: 1930, reprint, Hildesheim: Olms 1982); the first redaction of the *invention* is on II, 886–888; the second redaction is on II, 888–891; the passage cited is on II, 886–887. The cited passages are from the 1982 edition. An important document was published by Michael Rinehart: 'A Document for the Studiolo of Francesco I,' *Art the Ape of Nature: Studies in Honour of H.W. Janson* (New York: Abrams 1981), 275–289. On Borghini's method of composing an *invention*, see Rick A. Scorza, 'V. Borghini and "invenzione": the Florentine "Apparato" of 1565,' *Journal of the Warburg and Courtauld Institutes* 41 (1981): 57–75.

24 Arthur O. Lovejoy, *The Great Chain of Being* (New York: Harper and Row 1965).

25 In Borghini's *invention*, the interest in alchemy is linked to the melancholy temperament. Vulcan, he writes, is to be placed in correspondence with

melancholy: 'it is easy to judge how well this fits, since fantasies regarding fire and retorts and foundaries are commonly found in melancholy persons, as Vulcan pretended to be' (II, 891). Francesco I's interests in alchemy have been widely documented. In one painting in the Stanzino, by Giovanni Stradano, he appears among those occupied in alchemical works.

26 Citolini is clearly thinking of the role played by the great collections in the public image of the collector. On this theme, see Paula Findlen, 'The Economy of Scientific Exchange in Early Modern Italy,' *Patronage and Institutions: Science, Technology and Medicine at the European Court, 1500–1750*, ed. B.T. Moran (Rochester, NY: Woodbridge, Boydell 1991), pp. 5–24.

27 'Cubiculis bene formatis, oportet unicuique materiae suam domum seu castrum attribuere: Ut domum grammaticae, domum rhetoricae, dialecticae, etc ... domum unam Bibliis ... domum vocabulis, domum sententiis sacris, domum profanis, domum concionibus, domum festis, domum controversiis, et ut uno verbo dicam una quaeque materia certis suis castris et domibus erit tradenda eo modo quo in civitate bene constituta fit. Si quis enim libros, pannum, vinum, carnes etc. vellet emere et vendere, dirigeret se ad illas domos in quibus haec talia vel emuntur vel venduntur.'

28 See, for example, the woodcut attributed to Vogtherr (1548), in Raimond Van Marle, *Iconographie de l'art prophane au Moyen Age et à la Renaissance* (New York: Hacker Art Books 1971); or the fortress of grammar, one of the images of the card game with which grammar was taught, in Mathias Ringmann (Philesius Vogesigena), *Grammatica figurata. Octo partes orationis secundum Donati editionem et regulam Remigii ita imaginibus expressae ut pueri iucundo chartarum ludo faciliora Grammaticae praeludia discere et exercere queant*, Gualtherus Lud., Saint Dié, 1509, folio 7r (see also Massimiliano Rossi's entry *La fabbrica del pensiero*, 31–32, English translation *The Enchanted Loom*.

29 Lina Bolzoni, 'Le città utopiche del Cinquecento italiano: Giochi di spazio e di saperi,' *L'asino d'oro* 4, no. 7 (1993): 64–81.

30 Paula Findlen, 'The Museum: Its Classical Etymology and Renaissance Genealogy,' *Journal of the History of Collections* 1, no. 1 (1989): 59–78.

31 'Cera vel huiusmodi imagines confingere, quam plurimi multum prodesse memoriae experti sunt.'

32 Samuel Quicchelberg, *Inscriptiones vel tituli*, folio E3v: 'quales solent inter se reginae ac principes, ad peregrinas vestes exterarum nationum pulchre examinandas, aliae aliis transmittere, cum quibus quandoque ipsi gentium mores occurrunt observandi, dum in iis pupis exprimitur: Quis habitus domi forisque, quis nuptiali aut lugubri tempore, praesertim nobilissimis

adhibeatur.' This passage from Quicchelberg and other sources give us some idea of the complex role played by dolls. At the end of the fourteenth century, for example, French dolls were sent to the English court to show the new directions in fashion; see Henry-René D'Allemagne, *Histoire des jouets* (Paris: Hachette 1902), p. 24. In fifteenth-century Florence, in homes of both the upper and the middle classes, dolls representing the Christ child or a saint were common, and they could also be dressed. Klapisch-Zuber has formulated the hypothesis that adults used them, not only for meditation and instruction, but also as models that, when viewed by pregnant women, could influence the foetus; see Christine Klapisch-Zuber, 'Holy Dolls: Play and Piety in Quattrocento Florence,' *Women, Family, and Ritual in Renaissance Italy*, ed. L. Cochrane (Chicago: University of Chicago Press 1985), pp. 310–329. Even here we are faced with a sort of materialization of internal images, of those *phantasmata* upon which the potent forces of imagination and memory work (see chapter 4). On dolls in general, see Jurij M. Lotman, 'Le bambole nel sistema della cultura,' *Testo e contesto* (Bari: Laterza 1984), pp. 175 ff.

33 Quicchelberg, *Inscriptiones vel tituli*, folio 21r: 'Accidit et vestitum domesticum, apud principum filias sibi usitatum in memoriam quandam minutis formulis asservari, cuius generis quidem cum exili et plurima argentea suppellectile, habebantur apud Dominae Annae Ducissae Bavariae et Alberti sui charissimi coniugis filias, Mariam et Mariam Maximilianam, aliquot centurias et maiore adhuc numero, apud neptes ducissae matris ... quae domesticorum officiorum et actionum tanto ordine distinguuntur, ut quisque singula inspiciens, omnia regiae cuiusdam conclavia, et pompas aulicosque mores ad unguem tenere videatur.'

34 This component of the art of memory is studied by Ioan Couliano *Eros et magie à la Renaissance (1484)* (Paris: Flammarion 1984), in English, Ioan P. Culianu, *Eros and Magic in the Renaissance* (Chicago: University of Chicago Press 1987).

35 On this theme, see Pierre-Antoine Fabre, *Ignace de Loyola: Le lieu de l'image* (Paris: Vrin 1992).

36 On the language of mysticism, and for a complete bibliography, see *Scrittrici mistiche italiane*, ed. G. Pozzi and C. Leonardi (Genoa: Marietti 1988); on mysticism in the sixteenth and seventeenth centuries, see Michel De Certeau, *La fable mystique, XVIe–XVIIe siècle* (Paris: Gallimard 1982); Mino Bergamo, *La scienza dei santi: Studi sul misticismo secentesco* (Florence: Sansoni 1984).

37 Teresa of Avila, *The Interior Castle*, trans. K. Kavanaugh and O. Rodriguez (New York: Paulist Press 1979), pp. 128–130. See also Giovanni Della Croce

and Teresa of Avila, *Estasi e passione di Dio. Verso il centro dell'anima: Le sorgenti della mistica cristiana*, ed. E. Ancilli (Rome: Newton Compton 1981), p. 119. For the original text, see Teresa of Avila [Santa Teresa], *Las Moradas* ed. T. Navarro Tomas (Madrid: Espa-Calpe 1968), 'Moradas Sextas,' chapter 4, pp. 150–151.

38 This is part of an ancient phase of Jewish mysticism based on the vision of the Throne of Glory, the Merkabah – the description of the ascension of the soul as a journey through palaces, each more splendid than the last. See Gershom Scholem, *Die judische Mystik in ihren Hauptstroemungen* (Zurich: Rhein Verlag 1957); 'Merkabah Mysticism' [entry], *Encyclopedia Judaica* (New York: Macmillan 1971), XI, 1386–1387.

39 See *Enciclopedismo in Roma barocca: Athanasius Kircher e il Museo del Collegio Romano tra Wunderkammer e museo scientifico*, ed. M. Casciato, M.G. Ianniello, and M. Vitale (Venice: Marsilio 1986).

40 Giovanni Ciampoli, *Prose* (Rome: Manelfo Manelfi 1649), discorso 13, cap. 6 and cap. 7, pp. 347–348. See Ezio Raimondi, 'Il teatro delle meraviglie,' in *Letteratura barocca: studi sul Seicento italiano* (Florence: Olschki 1961), pp. 327–356.

Index